Regional Orders at Century's Dawn

PRINCETON STUDIES IN

INTERNATIONAL HISTORY AND POLITICS

Series Editors
Jack L. Snyder and Richard H. Ullman

Recent titles:

Regional Orders at Century's Dawn

GLOBAL AND DOMESTIC INFLUENCES

ON GRAND STRATEGY

ETEL SOLINGEN

PRINCETON UNIVERSITY PRESS

PRINCETON, NEW JERSEY

Library of Congress Cataloging-in-Publication Data
Solingen, Etel, 1952–
Regional orders at century's dawn : global and domestic influences on
grand strategy / Etel Solingen.
p. cm. — (Princeton studies in international history and politics)
Includes bibliographical references and index.
ISBN 0-691-05879-2 (alk. paper). — ISBN 0-691-05880-6 (pbk. : alk. paper)
1. International relations. I. Title. II. Series.
JZ1305.S68   1998
327.1′01—dc21   98-5128   CIP

This book has been composed in Times Roman

Princeton University Press books are printed on acid-free paper
and meet the guidelines for permanence and durability of the
Committee on Production Guidelines for Book Longevity of the
Council on Library Resources

http://pup.princeton.edu

Printed in the United States of America

1 2 3 4 5 6 7 8 9 10

To the Children of All Regions,

Unwilling Witnesses

of Deadly Coalitional Choices

CONTENTS

A B B R E V I A T I O N S

ABACC	Agência Brasileiro-Argentina de Contabilidade e Controle de Materiais Nucleares
ACIEL	Asociación Coordinadora de Instituciones Empresarias Libres (Argentina)
ASEAN	Association of Southeast Asian Nations
BJP	Bharatiya Janata party (India)
CGE	Confederación General Económica (Argentina)
CGT	Confederación General del Trabajo (Argentina)
DFLP	Democratic Front for the Liberation of Palestine
DGFM	National Directory of Military Industries
ECLA	(United Nations) Economic Commission for Latin America
EPB	Economic Planning Board (South Korea)
EO	export-oriented
EU	European Union
FKI	Federation of Korean Industries (South Korea)
GATT	General Agreement on Tariffs and Trade
GCC	Gulf Cooperation Council
GDP	gross domestic product
GNP	gross national product
IISS	International Institute for Strategic Studies
IMF	International Monetary Fund
IS	import substitution
ISI	import-substitution industrialization
MERCOSUR	Mercado Común del Sur (Common Market of the South) (MERCOSUL in Portuguese)
NGO	nongovernmental organization
OAS	Organization of American States
OECD	Organization for Economic Cooperation and Development
OPEC	Organization of Petroleum Exporting Countries
PA	Palestinian Authority
PFLP	Popular Front for the Liberation of Palestine
PLO	Palestine Liberation Organization
ROK	Republic of Korea
SRA	Sociedad Rural Argentina
UAE	United Arab Emirates
UIA	Unión Industrial Argentina
WTO	World Trade Organization

PREFACE

REGIONAL ORDERS are made of multiple details and changing contingencies, of security dilemmas and economic interdependence, of relations between democracies and autocracies, of war and peace. How do we organize such complexity? In early 1996 two scientists "discovered" a previously unknown muscle in the human head. When asked how was it possible not to have known of the muscle throughout centuries of medical science, the scientists replied that the enforced method of anatomical dissection precluded "seeing" that muscle altogether. Students had been drilled in conventional forms of dissection, leaving the medical community blind to new discoveries: dissecting the conventional way, you get what you know. The search for slicing regional orders in ways that get us beyond what we now know is no easy challenge. At the very least, understanding the impact of domestic coalitions—an old fixture of political life—can help sharpen the scalpel.

In the course of writing this book coalitions have besieged me in more ways than one might imagine, splitting and rejoining, winning and losing, cooperating and warring, and generally meandering around their grand strategies. Yet the very dynamics that make coalitions so elusive also offer an invaluable analytical advantage, as when they alleviate some of the pitfalls of counterfactual analysis. The May 1996 elections in Israel and the new coalition they brought to power did just that. Although generally behaving as anticipated by its coalitional makeup, this quasi-experimental windfall was a small reward relative to the painful course the Middle East peace process had taken. In other cases, factual analysis itself was especially difficult, as when coalitional information on North Korea trickled through sparse channels. Following North Korea's daily *Nodong Sinmun* was not merely soporific but as predictable as deciphering the Iraqi press. That democracies are allies of coalitional analysis is uncontestable, whatever else their international behavior is found to be.

Another unassailable fact is that I could have not completed this book without the support and encouragement of many. A faculty fellowship from the University of California's Institute on Global Conflict and Cooperation (IGCC) was instrumental in the critical initial phase. I am particularly grateful to IGCC Director Susan Shirk and to the IGCC staff as a whole, who kindly included me in their valuable regional security workshops (Track Two). A MacArthur Foundation Fellowship on Peace and International Cooperation allowed me to delve into other regions and to complete the first draft. I am indebted to both institutions for granting me my first extended leave, but no less for providing fellows with intellectual support and gracious encouragement. The University of California-Irvine's Global Peace and Conflict Studies provided partial support for research related to Chapter Six.

I am particularly grateful to Jack Snyder, Stephan Haggard, and Joel Migdal for their comments on earlier versions of the entire manuscript. I would also like to acknowledge Vinod Aggarwal, Stephen Brams, Benjamin J. Cohen, Harry Eckstein, Richard Eichenberg, Albert Fishlow, Jeff Frieden, Peter Gourevitch, Robert R. Kaufman, David Lake, Zeev Maoz, and Steve Weber for commenting on selected chapters. Without the generous remarks of experts in different regions it would have been far harder to understand unique dynamics and odd contingencies that have overturned the general expectations of stylized models. These include Jawad Anani, Bassam Awadallah, Fawaz Gerges, Sung Chull Kim, Chung-in Moon, Manuel Pastor, David Pion-Berlin, Shimon Peres, Ahmed Qurie (Abu ʿAla), Ira Sharkansky, and Abdullah Toukan. I also benefited from the critical comments of faculty and graduate students at seminars at Stanford (Center for International Security and Arms Control), the University of California at Berkeley (International Relations), Hebrew University of Jerusalem, Leonard Davis, Institute of International Relations, and the University of Washington, Seattle.

The earliest version of the general coalitional argument was written in 1992 and applied to explaining nuclear policy outcomes (published in *International Security*, Fall 1994). Further elaboration resulted in an extension of the dependent variable into a broader set of international behaviors, conflictive and cooperative. I benefited from useful comments and suggestions at a May 1994 workshop on regional relations at Laguna Beach, sponsored by IGCC. This version also spelled out the essential differences between the coalitional perspective I proposed—hinging on economic liberalization—and the democratic peace hypothesis. It also cautioned about ideal types, hybrid cases, and unintended outcomes of coalitional behavior. This piece was published in the *Journal of Theoretical Politics* in January 1996. An extension of the argument with a particular focus on the types of regional orders likely to obtain from alternative coalitional balances throughout a region appeared in a volume edited by David Lake and Patrick Morgan, *Regional Orders: Building Security in a New World*, University Park: Pennsylvania State University Press, 1997: 68–100. The last section of Chapter Six, on democratization in the Middle East, builds on a brief overview that appeared in the *Journal of Democracy* 7, 3 (July 1996). My thanks to the *Journal of Theoretical Politics*, the *Journal of Democracy*, and Pennsylvania State University Press for permission to reprint portions of the original material.

The manuscript—largely in its present form—was submitted to Princeton University Press in 1996. The literature on globalization and its impact seems to have exploded since, and will undoubtedly allow a better specification of coalitional arguments and regional orders in the future. Meanwhile, the 1997 East Asian financial debacle exposed some of the vulnerabilities of an internationalist grand strategy depicted in Chapter Two, and will undoubtedly provide new clues regarding dynamic coalitional rearrangements and their regional impacts. I am especially grateful to Malcolm Litchfield for steering the publication process with wit, efficiency, encouragement, and understanding. The task of copyediting fell on Margaret Case who deserves very special thanks. I am also indebted to Diana Sahhar, the dream librarian, and to Cheryl Larsson, who masterfully converted raw drafts into real figures. Fanny Shenhavi was my right hand—and brain—on field-research matters pertaining to the Middle East. My family was always the pillar. Aaron taught me of highly predictable coalitional arrangements (in proteins and DNA), and Gabrielle of the less predictable but enduring ones. In dedicating this book to the young I include them both. Finally, my husband Simon inspired me to connect the slicing procedure with the potential treatment, a task I merely begin at the end of the concluding chapter.

I dedicate the Middle East chapter to my teacher and friend Yehoshafat Harkabi (Fati), who, like Eckart Kehr, warned against the folly of war without getting to see a more peaceful side of the abyss, and without savoring the full measure of his intellectual influence in the crafting of peace.

PART ONE

The Theory

CHAPTER ONE

Introduction

EXPLAINING REGIONAL ORDERS

This book examines the grand strategy of two ideal-typical coalitions. The two coalitions form in response to the requirements of an integrating global political economy. Internationalist coalitions favor economic liberalization and, where they are strong at home and in their region, they often create cooperative regional orders.[1] Statist-nationalist and confessional coalitions often oppose economic liberalization and are prone to create and reproduce zones of war and militarized disputes, particularly where they prevail throughout a region.[2] Each coalition thus pursues different grand strategies at home and vis-à-vis the global political economy, which shape their regional policies as well. The coalitions' relative domestic and regional strength affects the nature of regional security and economic orders.

Regional orders reflect the fundamental ways in which ruling coalitions manage their regional affairs in political, economic, and strategic terms. Such orders run the gamut from highly conflictive to highly cooperative, and are often expressed across issue areas. "Zones of stable peace" reflect the highest cooperative levels, both in intensity and extension across economic, security, and other domains. Although this characterization evokes the concept of a "democratic peace," democracy is neither necessary nor sufficient for such regional orders to come about. Both ASEAN and the Southern Cone of Latin America approach this ideal type in the 1990s.[3] "War zones" exhibit high levels of violence and protracted conflict, such as the Iran-Iraq war in the 1980s or the Arab-Israeli conflict for many decades. In between lies a wide array of regional orders in

[1] Economic liberalization entails a set of domestic policies geared to open the economy to global markets, capital, investments, and technology. An integrating global political economy involves not merely global markets but also international institutions operating in economic, security, and other political realms.

[2] Nationalism generally refers to the granting of prime loyalty to one's own national (civic nationalism) or ethnic (ethnonationalism) group. For alternative definitions, see Brown (1993, 1996). Confessional allegiances or religious ties give rise to "religious nationalism" (Juergensmeyer 1993) and, in their extreme manifestations, to the notion of "fundamentalism." I use the terms "radical confessional" and "fundamentalist" interchangeably, wherever they apply empirically, that is, nearly worldwide. The generic applicability of the concept "fundamentalism" invalidates the critique of this term as ethnocentric. Finally, religious and secular nationalism are species of the same genus— as Juergensmeyer argues—but also potential political rivals.

[3] The Southern Cone comprises Chile, Argentina, Brazil, Uruguay, Paraguay, and Bolivia, a geographical area captured in the late 1990s by the economic entity MERCOSUR. ASEAN includes Thailand, Singapore, Indonesia, Malaysia, Philippines, Brunei, and Vietnam. In 1997 ASEAN will incorporate Myanmar and Laos.

which conflictive and cooperative patterns are enmeshed, and in which the direction of change is far more unpredictable. The coalitional approach developed in this book helps identify the main sources of change as well as their implications for regional orders. Indeed, coalitions provide a means for coming to terms with the otherwise very elusive concept of regions, by subsuming a region's boundaries to the coalitions' respective grand strategies.[4] The scope of a region is thus in the eyes of coalitional beholders, and therefore subject to continuous redefinition. The existence of more or less cooperative regional orders in security and economics does not imply a trend toward "regionalism," a concept that is often used to denote gravitation toward free-trade areas and away from global integration. Indeed, a leading asumption in this book is that the circumstances—political, economic, strategic—that lead to more cooperative regional orders also tend to reinforce further global integration. Put differently, an integrating global political economy can act as the engine of cooperative regional orders, contingent on the nature and strength of prevailing domestic coalitions in a given region.

The focus on economic liberalization as the key fault line in the analysis of coalitions provides a powerful conceptual lever, capturing the main themes of the global world-time at the end of the century. The two coalitional ideal types encapsulate the contrapuntal tension between: an internationalizing global economic system and protectionist challengers, a more institutionalized global political order and the lingering resistance to it, a pluralist (multicultural) political approach to human diversity and its exclusivist radical-confessional counterpart, and regionally differentiated as against globally homogeneous solutions to the opportunities and predicaments of the late twentieth century. Put simply, coalitions formulate alternative grand strategies against the background of a highly integrated global economy (with unprecedented capital mobility), a rapidly integrating multilateral institutional foundation in world politics, a growing web of regional interactions and institutions, and a revival of nationalist and confessional allegiances, dormant throughout the Cold War era. These four features of the late twentieth-century world-time largely define the contemporary research program in international relations. Of particular interest here is identifying how coalitions respond to these features in advancing their grand strategy, and how their behavior influences the nature of regions. Understanding regional orders is compelling, given the rising importance of regions as analytically distinguishable international structures and the fact that interstate wars are overwhelmingly fought among proximate states.[5] The coalitional approach elaborated here thus requires a conceptual blending between the extensive literature, mostly in comparative politics, on the impact of economic liberalization

---

[4] On problems in the conceptualization of "regions," see Buzan (1991b) and Lake (1997). Earlier studies of regions include Russett (1967), Nye (1968), and Thompson (1973).

[5] Bremer (1992); Gleditsch (1995). For historical and analytical studies of the rise of regionalism, see De Melo and Panagariya (1993); Fawcett and Hurrell (1995); Haggard (1995b); Stallings (1995); Gamble and Payne (1996); and Mansfield and Milner (1997). Most of this literature is overwhelmingly concerned with explaining regional trade arrangements.

and the no less extensive literature on domestic, regional, and global dimensions of security policy.

THE MENU: INTERNATIONAL RELATIONS THEORY AT THE END OF THE TWENTIETH CENTURY

Cold War considerations have dominated the study of regional orders for decades. This dominance numbed an analytical sensitivity to explanations based on domestic politics, turning them into "hard cases" for understanding regional policies and outcomes. Although the superpower rivalry indeed framed the scope of action of regional actors quite forcefully, diminished attention to how domestic politics translated Cold War effects in shaping regional policies had its costs. At the end of the century it is even harder to ignore the domestic prism: conflicts are now regionalized, while debates over security have become internalized, severing regional relations from the old inexorable logic of superpower competition.[6] The waning of external political and economic rents underwritten by the former superpowers imposes the need to identify the new domestic distribution of costs and benefits from alternative regional policies. The domesticization and politicization of regional policy, in turn, have made the relevant themes and actors more transparent, offering a better opportunity to study the domestic conditions that shape regional orders.

Not only do new realities compel a turn toward an improved understanding of the domestic impact of international processes and of their consequences for regional orders; the limitations and failures of the classical conceptual kit in international relations theory suggest the utility of alternative analytical paths, as well. Structural realism (called neorealism henceforth) has been a dominant intellectual influence. Centered on considerations of relative power and polarity, neorealism is hard pressed to explain single-handedly the myriad forms of state behavior and regional outcomes, let alone their evolution and change. Consider the following observations taken from important regions throughout the world. First, both declining powers (such as Argentina and Egypt) and rising hegemons (such as South Korea and Israel) have chosen to cooperate with their rivals as a solution to their perceived security dilemmas.[7] Second, regional challengers have either sought to balance against hegemons (Pakistan vis-à-vis India, Iraq and Syria vis-à-vis Israel, Argentina vis-à-vis Brazil for decades), or to bandwagon (Egypt, Jordan, and the PLO, Argentina in the 1990s), rendering power distribution ill-suited to map any general pattern. Third, cooperation has emerged in the least expected multilateral settings (such as the Middle East in

---

[6] On the changed nature of global security externalities from regional conflicts at the end of the century, see Solingen (1997a).

[7] The term "hegemon" here is only used to address neorealist arguments and does not impute hegemonic designs on the part of states whose power has grown considerably relative to that of their rivals, as measured by GNP differentials and military power. The locus classicus of neorealist arguments is Waltz (1979).

the early 1990s), where neorealism would suggest cooperation is most disadvantaged, and has floundered in more bipolar ones (such as South Asia)—and all this, without any dramatic changes in structural power![8] Fourth, state power considerations could not anticipate the emergence of a highly cooperative cluster of states in East and Southeast Asia, where ethnic and territorial issues have far from disappeared. Finally, the sight of a strong regional power (Israel under a Labor-led coalition) mobilizing economic and political support for its frail "adversary" (the Palestinian Authority), must simply boggle the neorealist mind. No balancing-against-third-parties subterfuges can be summoned here. Palestine constitutes the one political entity with the most direct competing territorial claim vis-à-vis Israel, as the Likud-led coalition has consistently emphasized.[9] Clearly, all these anomalies strengthen what is now a stronger disciplinary consensus than ever before on the sobering limitations of neorealist accounts for predicting the behavior of states and, hence, the shape and evolution of regional orders.

The liberal tradition in international relations has deep intellectual roots and enjoys a reinvigorated status toward the end of the twentieth century. This is, however, an ecclectic school that does not posit a single underlying logic explaining conflict and cooperation. Even within the liberal tradition there have been extensive debates over the relationship between economic interdependence and cooperation. After all, cooperation has emerged in the least economically interdependent region—the Middle East—and has collapsed in highly interdependent ones—such as the former Yugoslavia. Moreover, interdependence followed rather than spearheaded cooperation in East and Southeast Asia and the Southern Cone. In one of its newest reincarnations, liberalism has paid greater attention to the independent effect of institutions on cooperation, but is still struggling to define the conditions under which—and how much—institutions matter.[10] Institutional density can perhaps explain cooperation among European Union members, but not among ASEAN states or the Asia-Pacific more generally, or in the Arab-Israeli context, where an institutional tapestry began emerging *as a result* of increased cooperation. Cooperation can thus proceed in the absence of institutionalization in some regions, whereas dense institutionalization does not guarantee deep levels of cooperation (as in Latin America and inter-Arab relations for many decades). A domestic version of neoliberal institutionalism traces conflict and cooperation to democratic institutions. Democratic states are expected to create areas free of violent conflict among themselves. However, several logical and methodological difficulties (discussed in

---

[8] Even neorealist experts differ on whether or not South Asia is a largely bipolar system, or ought to be conceptualized as including China as well. In any case, the region is far less multipolar than the Middle East.

[9] For a systematic critique of the inability of neorealism to explain security outcomes in the Middle East, see Solingen (1994a and 1994b).

[10] On the most recent neorealist and neoliberal institutionalist thinking, see Baldwin (1993). For a critique of the causal logic and empirical fitness of liberal institutionalism, see Mearsheimer (1994/95) and for a riposte, see Keohane and Martin (1995).

Chapter Four) relegate the democratic variable to marginality in explaining regional relations until recently, particularly where stable democratic dyads have been virtually absent (that is, in most of the industrializing world).

Neither are cognitive approaches free of limitations in explaining regional conflict, cooperation, and change itself, without resorting to explanations suffering from omitted variable bias and/or endogeneity.[11] For how did the radical shift from intractable conflict to cooperation in the Middle East come about in the 1990s? Why were old beliefs suddenly revised? Why did revisions take place selectively, with some groups accepting them and others rejecting them? Why did cooperative frames of mind emerge in the 1990s, but not earlier, if not as a result of changes in domestic coalitional balances aggregating redefined material and ideal expectations? Why did cooperation make remarkable strides in the Middle East and not in South Asia? If ideas served as rationalizations for other policy objectives, then they were merely consequences, not sources, of conflictive or cooperative behavior. The anticipation of expected costs and benefits associated with a particular policy may indeed generate a new ideational context, although new ideas can certainly take root independently of such anticipation. The constructivist research agenda includes the development of new tools to explain changes in that context (Katzenstein 1996). Argentine President Carlos Menem's domestic and external revolution and its regional consequences resulted from his accurate interpretation of the country's new ideational and material context. The preceding decades were charged with many cooperative ideas—much as in inter-Arab relations for decades—that yielded very limited concrete results. MERCOSUR (the Southern Cone common market) and regional denuclearization in the Southern Cone in the early 1990s surely required a different ingredient, since a constant (cooperative ideas) produced different outcomes over time. In short, how did the region move "from dichos to hechos" (from talk to action)?

World systems theory (Wallerstein 1979) had the advantage of paying serious attention to the development of a global capitalist system, but could not specify the conditions under which core, semiperipheral, or peripheral states might find regional cooperation or conflict more attractive in pursuing the best possible position in the international division of labor. In fact, capitalist penetration—the presumed underlying source of conflict—appears to be positively correlated with cooperation! As peripheral states became more integrated into the global capitalist system since the 1960s, the more integrated states also became less involved, on average, in regional conflict. The major East and Southeast Asian wars unfolded prior to the birth of the most globally integrated economic "tigers," which have managed to avoid armed conflict. Similarly, a deeper cooperative relationship among Southern Cone Latin American countries followed the unprecedented internationalizing efforts by their respective ruling coalitions. And the most conflict-prone regions of the world—the Middle East and South Asia—were also for many years the most resistant to basing industrialization

---

[11] King, Keohane, and Verba (1994: 191).

on the logic of global markets. Incipient steps toward internationalization in many regions were accompanied by significant, if uneven, steps toward regional cooperation.

Purely systemic (deterministic) approaches are not merely deficient in shedding light on the nature of regional conflict and cooperation. They are also found wanting as conceptual guides for broader systemic changes such as the end of the Cold War and the subsequent behavior of great powers vis-à-vis, for instance, the Gulf War and the Yugoslav debacle.[12] Systemic perspectives claimed the ability to identify symptoms largely compatible with their assumptions, but few patients would still pledge absolute faith in their prognosis or suggested treatment. The increased attention to domestic politics, which some scholars studying foreign policy behavior had never abandoned, was a natural response to these failures.

COALITIONS AND GRAND STRATEGY

Coalitions are omnipresent in politics; single actors can rarely specify an outcome and bind all other actors to it. Coalitional analysis offers an analytical pivot that allows the simultaneous consideration of international and domestic, political and economic aspects of a grand strategy. Such a pivot enables the amalgamation of outside-in—Gourevitch's (1986) second image reversed—and inside-out effects. Thus, beyond dissecting the impact of international considerations on domestic politics, it helps us move toward a theory of how such considerations are converted, via domestic processes, into foreign economic and security policy.[13] Grand strategy throughout this book not only defines a country's relation to global power and economic structures but also the internal extraction and allocation of resources among groups and institutions.[14] The grand strategy of political coalitions thus transcends the disciplinary divide between "industrialization" strategies (often the subject matter of comparative political economy) and security strategies (a subfield of international relations). Political entrepreneurs tailoring alternative coalitions develop an integrated strategy of political survival, addressing development and security as one, and

---

[12] Mueller (1995), Lebow and Risse-Kappen (1995), Katzenstein (1996), but also Wohlforth (1994/95).

[13] Pioneering efforts in this direction include Kahler's (1984) study of decolonization and party politics. Putnam (1988) and Evans, Jacobson, and Putnam (1993) internalized domestic and external factors in the anticipation of foreign policy outputs, generally compartmentalizing issue areas (where the domestic political economy explains foreign economic policy, the domestic institutional infrastructure relevant to security explains responses to international power shifts, and so on). A recent volume by Keohane and Milner (1996) retains mostly the outside-in effort to understand the impact of internationalization on domestic politics.

[14] On grand strategy as an economic, political, and military means-ends chain designed to achieve security, see Posen (1984), Kennedy (1991), and Rosecrance and Stein (1993). For a compatible view of the synergies between domestic, regional, and global dimensions of security, see Kolodziej and Harkavy (1982) and Ayoob (1995).

considering the synergies among external (regional and global) and domestic opportunities and constraints. Grand strategies vary not only in substance but also in the degree to which they are embedded in more or less clearly defined blueprints and political platforms or, instead, are more loosely articulated throughout a wide range of domestic and foreign policies. Quite often, grand strategies unfold in tentative, reactive, and piecemeal steps, in tune with coalitional logrolling, and often in response to unintended and unexpected consequences of previous policies or coalitional entanglements.

Coalitional analyses of grand strategy have thus far been largely limited to the great powers.[15] However, there may be far less conceptual discontinuity between the behavior of system makers—great powers—and other states than is often recognized; even mini-states define grand strategies. This possibility bodes well for the development of a truly international theory of international relations. Snyder's (1991) essential coalitional logic serves as a useful starting point for understanding any state's choices, cooperative and otherwise. Coalitions are "policy networks" spanning state and private political actors. Since state autonomy is both a matter of degree and subject to empirical analysis, focusing on coalitions helps avoid sterile debates between purely statist notions of a completely autonomous state and purely societal-reductionist conceptions of states as instruments of social, particularly economic, forces.[16] A coalitional approach assumes that state agencies and societal actors can undertake "joint projects," and is thus compatible with studies of industrialization strategies by Gerschenkron (1962), Hirschman (1958), and Amsden (1989). This point highlights the importance of understanding the domestic institutional foundation against which coalitions operate, a foundation that helps coalitions prevail at some points and not others (Gourevitch 1986). Institutions—political parties, a balkanized state, democracy, authoritarianism, a powerful military-industrial complex—are a prism filtering the impact of internationalization, at times making its consequences more transparent, at others less so. Thus, incipient democratization and electoral trial runs provided new opportunities for statist-nationalist and confessional coalitions in the Middle East, opportunities that were often removed once they threatened adversarial ruling coalitions. A fragmented party system and proportional representation in Israel has precluded for decades the emergence of a "conquering" coalition. A similar institutional profile in Brazil by the 1990s has burdened presidents in their attempt to logroll coalitions in a

---

[15] Snyder (1991) resorted to the impact of industrialization, cartelization, logrolling, and mythmaking to provide a logic for imperial (over)expansion. Rosecrance and Stein (1993) examined an array of domestic influences on great powers' grand strategy, including interest groups, social ideas, the character of constitutions, and economic constraints. Coalitional analyses exclusively concerned with foreign economic policy, such as Gourevitch (1986) and Rogowski (1989), generally do not explain grand strategy in the sense defined above. Noncoalitional analysis, mostly classical realist or neorealist, has largely dominated the study of grand strategy.

[16] Caporaso and Levine (1992). On different state forms, underpinned by different "historic blocs" or configurations of state-society complexes, see Cox (1987). On historic blocs, see Gramsci (1988: 200–9). On coalitions as "policy networks" linking state and society, see Katzenstein (1989). On states' *embeddedness* (connections to civil society), and *embedded autonomy*, see Evans (1995).

way that their Argentine counterparts could avoid. Elsewhere (as in some former Soviet states) the weakness of political institutions has induced an unstable alternation of precarious coalitions. Clearly, there is considerable variation in the impact of institutions on the aggregation of coalitional preferences as well as on coalitional durability and wherewithal. Political entrepreneurs, in or out of power, play a central role in brokering coalitions, at times relying on extant institutions, at others creating new ones. Once a certain coalition prevails politically, as a function of its size, cohesiveness, and effectiveness, its grand strategy becomes raison d'état. Governmental policy must now reflect the essential contours of that strategy, although the institutional context can impose limits on its implementation and even doom its viability altogether.

Yet other advantages of a coalitional perspective include the ability to: 1. transcend the concept of a unified state with monolithic interests (different state agencies join different coalitions at different times); 2. specify the origin, ordering, and intensity of preferences of relevant actors; and 3. define a set of more restrictive conditions under which democracy matters in the framing of a grand strategy. Once relevant coalitions are identified, we are on firmer conceptual ground in analyzing sensitivity to gaps in gains, definitions of balanced exchanges, receptivity to transparency, the rate at which the future is discounted, and the value of side payments from alternative options. Responses to global and regional constraints and opportunities emerge out of the preferences of different coalitions, each of which conveniently spins constraints and opportunities according to its grand strategy. Coalitions, however, come in many forms and are organized along various issues, leading to a potentially unmanageable conceptual menu. The advantages of a coalitional perspective can thus be reaped more fully by relying on a critical coalitional axis as a lever to gain understanding of a wide variety of cases.

The process of economic liberalization provides such a lever, as it helps identify an overarching axis of political mobilization, one that frequently engulfs social, economic, and ethnic cleavages. The distributional consequences of economic liberalization and integration into global markets and institutions forges this key axis of coalitional politics everywhere, where proponents and foes of integrative policies amalgamate around two basic blocs with contrasting grand strategies. Coalitions more strongly committed to integrative policies (internationalist) are more likely to converge with similar neighboring coalitions in creating cooperative—more peaceful—regional orders. Conversely, coalitions aggregating statist-nationalist interests—often allied with confessional movements—create far less cooperative regions, particularly where they overwhelm their internationalist rivals at home and in the region.[17] This hypothesis departs

---

[17] Chapter Two explains the affinity of interests between statist-nationalist and confessional groups, often leading to "grand coalitions" united by their opposition to different aspects of an internationalist grand strategy. Coalitional theorists often interpret such affinities or convergence in terms of degrees of "ideological distance" (Ames 1987) but common threats can coalesce otherwise ideologically distant partners. Lamborn (1991: 55) argues that the analysis of strategic choice requires "a lens that looks systematically for coalitions of factions that have not only different initial

from traditional arguments about the effects of interdependence among regional partners on cooperative behavior vis-à-vis each other. Rather, it builds on certain assumptions about the way in which political coalitions, in safeguarding their domestic interests and viability, define their association with the regional and international political economy as a whole. As Gourevitch (1978) argued, the kinds of ties binding different coalitional actors (institutions, economic sectors, confessional groups, bureaucracies, political parties) to the global political economy influence their conceptions of interests, and these are expressed domestically as well as regionally. Actors join forces in coalitions when their interests converge and tradeoffs are attractive, in order to safeguard those interests against alternative coalitions. The coalitional cleavage around economic liberalization is not the only political cleavage, but is certainly a dominant one virtually everywhere, and tends to attract other cleavages around its fundamental fault lines.

The grand strategies of different coalitions transcend the domestic-international divide. Cooperative regional orders hold different payoffs for different coalitions. They are expected to have positive political effects, domestically and globally, for internationalist coalitions and negative ones for their rivals. On the one hand, cooperation enables the pursuit of economic reform by increasing predictability and transparency and by improving reputation and investment prospects, as the international community connects internationalist coalitions to rationalization and regional stability. On the other hand, a prospective cooperative order often endangers statist-nationalist and confessional coalitions, because such an order undermines the viability of state agencies and enterprises associated with military functions and production, threatens with extinction the state's ability to disburse unlimited resources among statist-nationalist and confessional rent seekers, and deprives populist leaders (secular and confessional) of a rich fountain of myths. Internationalist coalitions embrace regional and domestic policies that may be politically risky in the short term but potentially rewarding in the long haul. Statist-nationalist coalitions often rely on regional and domestic strategies with short-term political payoffs that are fundamentally counterproductive in the long run.[18]

These are the general political contours shaping coalitional grand strategies. The extent to which strategies can be upheld consistently and unhindered is a function of two main variables:

1. *The domestic coalitional balance of power* is defined by the political strength of respective coalitions vis-à-vis their domestic competitors, reflected by how broad, cohesive, and effective their relative basis of political support is. A ruling coalition that is sizable in resources, attracts key actors, is largely consensual in its macropolitical objectives, and is effectively organized can implement its grand strategy with less difficulty than a less well-endowed one. An

---

policy preferences, but also varying reactions to the interplay of the political and policy risks they confront when participating in policy decisions requiring resource-dependent statecraft."

[18] Lamborn (1991) outlines the domestic politics of strategic choice, paying particular attention to the time horizons and orientations toward risk of different political coalitions.

oppositional coalition with high resource levels can pose a more formidable barrier to the ruling coalition's implementation of its grand strategy, forcing it to water down its preferences in a way that a weaker opposition cannot.

2. *The regional coalitional balance of power* is defined by the identity, relative strength, and interactive dynamics among coalitions ruling neighboring states. The scope and nature of regional conflict and cooperation is largely encoded in the degree of coalitional homogeneity at the regional level. Thus, higher and extensive levels of cooperation can be expected when internationalist coalitions prevail throughout a given region than when statist-nationalist or competing internationalist and statist-nationalist neighbors face one another. A regional equilibrium among internationationalist and statist-nationalist coalitions often exhibits more controlled conflict than statist-nationalist "war zones": neither extensive bloodshed nor intensive cooperation.

Clearly, the domestic coalitional balance of power influences the aggregate regional coalitional balance of power. The more internationalist coalitions prevail throughout different domestic contexts, the more likely it is that the regional coalitional balance of power will favor internationalist coalitions. Conversely, the more dominant statist-nationalist-confessional coalitions are in their respective domestic contexts, the more likely it is that the regional coalitional balance of power will gravitate toward such coalitions. A more dynamic approach must also take into account the impact of regional coalitional balances on domestic ones, a task I undertake in Chapter Three.

In sum, the coalitional approach suggested here involves a two-step analysis: it first builds on "second-image reversed" (outside-in) effects to identify domestic coalitional cleavages, and next takes stock of the internal political and institutional framework that converts these effects into a grand strategy of local, regional, and global reach (inside-out). The world-time under which these effects take place produces a different set of actors and different proclivities among them than might have been expected from existing coalitional frameworks, prominently that of Snyder.[19] Thus, the military and foreign ministries can find themselves as frequently logrolled into internationalist as into statist-nationalist coalitions, whereas business interests join one or the other in response to their calculus of global as against domestic interests. For the most part, the global political economy of the late twentieth century has placed big business exactly opposite the militarist, imperial, and autarkic coalitions that underwrote overexpansion in the great power cases examined by Snyder. Few doubt that global world-time matters. A coalitional perspective provides a way

[19] The nineteenth-century world-time was carefully outlined by Polanyi (1944), who centered it around self-regulating markets which, in turn led to their extension into the international economic domain (via the gold standard) and political sphere (a liberal state at home and an international balance of power). This expansion of the global economy was oriented toward production for domestic markets; states played major roles in it and the background was one of autarchic spheres of influence within economic blocs and great-power rivalries (Mittelman 1996). In time, the expansion triggered a reaction, and the eventual breakdown led to World War II. On the key institutional features of the late twentieth-century global economy, see Ruggie (1995).

of exploring when, how much, and why. Chapter Two examines in greater detail how the interlocked international political, economic, and security structures privilege directly one coalition over the other but, at the same time, unleash unintended consequences that threaten their presumed beneficiaries. Although predicting coalitional realignments or which coalition will seize power, at what point, and for how long is well beyond the scope of this book, this overview makes clear that further work in this area may yield an important contribution to the understanding of regional orders. The unfolding institutionalization of both democracy and markets beyond the Organization for Economic Cooperation and Development (OECD) community makes it far harder to formalize coalitional futures than might be the case within that community. Finally, Chapter Three explores both the impact of regional coalitional balances on domestic coalitional dynamics and the expected responses of alternative coalitions to regional threats and opportunities posed by different coalitional balances.

THE RESEARCH DESIGN

Part I lays out the theoretical framework while illustrating conceptual and definitional issues with examples drawn from virtually every region of the world. The empirical material included in the next three chapters, therefore, adds up to a very large number of observations for both the independent and dependent variables. Beyond this comprehensive overview of cases on which the theoretical framework is based, Chapters Five through Seven provide a more in-depth analysis of coalitions in three different regions: the Middle East, the Southern Cone of Latin America, and the Korean peninsula.[20] The longitudinal analyses include mainly Brazil and Argentina, South and North Korea, Israel, the PLO/ Palestinian Authority, Egypt, Syria, Iran, Iraq, and Jordan, with less inclusive treatments of Lebanon, Chile, Taiwan, Saudi Arabia, the Gulf sheikhdoms, Morocco, Tunisia, and ASEAN states. The wide-ranging empirical contexts chosen to explore the book's hypotheses maximize the potential for generalizable findings. Each state is the subject of a dynamic analysis of successive coalitions of varying political strength over the course of nearly five decades. This succession, in turn, yields a large number of dyadic and regional outcomes over time, reflecting a wide range of conflictive and cooperative behavior. The empirical cases also examine some of the implications of this book's theoretical approach, as stated at the end of Chapters Three and Four. The methodological windfalls from looking closely at numerous cases (providing broad variation in both the dependent and independent variables) also impose clear limitations on the thickness of detail in tracing processes.[21]

---

[20] A fourth region subjected to a coalitional analysis—South Asia—is discussed only briefly in the next two chapters, for reasons of space. For a fuller empirical study, see Solingen (1997b).

[21] On process tracing, see George and McKeown (1985). On understanding history by developing

Taken together, the three regions studied here (four if we include a parallel application to South Asia) offer the opportunity to hold important variables constant so that the impact of economic liberalization and resulting coalitions can be ascertained with greater confidence.[22] First, at least three regions—the Middle East, South Asia, and the Korean peninsula—share similarly high levels of what neorealists describe as anarchic, self-help historical contexts. In principle, this choice makes neorealism a leading theoretical contender, turning these regions into observations "least likely" (Eckstein 1975) to support coalitional dynamics as an alternative hypothesis. Indeed, it could be argued that the enduring rivalries and potential nuclearization of all four regions (including the Southern Cone) privilege neorealist expectations. Second, this particular choice of regions also allows us to control for the potential impact of regional institutionalization on cooperation. All three regions—the Middle East (mainly in the Arab-Israeli and Arab-Iranian contexts), South Asia, and the Korean peninsula—were poorly endowed with an institutional infrastructure that might facilitate cooperation. Third, the dynamic and cross-spatial analysis of these four regions enables us to examine the impact of coalitions and economic liberalization on state behavior and regional outcomes, while holding the democratic (or undemocratic) nature of states constant.

The Southern Cone—examined in Chapter Five—is classically depicted as an exceptionally peaceful region (if one discounts a deplorable record in internal warfare and politicide). Neoliberal institutionalist theories could argue that this region's dense institutional infrastructure explains the absence of war. However, the absence of war preceded that infrastructure and, moreover, such density never resulted in a genuinely cooperative regional order but rather one without effective economic integration and without effective denuclearization. An integrative and denuclearized cooperative order emerged only in the early 1990s, and clearly followed revolutionary coalitional shifts, not the opportunities offered by existing institutions. Neither neorealist accounts, which cannot explain change or cooperation, nor the democratic peace theory provides a persuasive explanation for the evolution of regional relations here. Both authoritarian and largely unstable and ephemeral democratic regimes avoided war and both exhibited a comparable spectrum of conflictive and cooperative behavior. Coalitional analysis cannot claim conceptual exclusivity in explaining the absence of intraregional war—a phenomenon that spans more than a century—but is central to understanding an historical thawing that replaced a century of cohabitation and restrained competition with unprecedented cooperation in the 1990s.

The Middle East—examined in Chapter Six—provides a particularly hard case (indeed a "crucial case study" in Eckstein's terms) for testing the propositions advanced in this book for several reasons: first, economic liberalization is

---

a sense of process, see Trachtenberg (1991). Chapters Five through Seven are condensed versions of more detailed original empirical studies.

[22] On "most similar systems" designs, see Przeworski and Teune (1970) and Meckstroth (1975).

far less developed there than in virtually any other region; second, its political carriers are, therefore, weaker than in most other regions; third, the shadow of an immediate past of noncooperative regional behavior is quite strong; and fourth, the institutional structures, regional and domestic, that might have facilitated regional cooperation were absent. In fact, building on extant international relations theory, cooperation in the Middle East was underdetermined, and it should come as no surprise that none of the major theoretical streams anticipated the momentous cooperative undertakings of the early 1990s. Instead, the domestic coalitional interplay between internationalizing and statist-nationalist and confessional groups suggested, all throughout the preceding decade, that the regional order was pregnant with cooperative breakthroughs.

The Korean peninsula—examined in Chapter Seven—provides a uniquely useful case because it involves one of the earliest exemplars of an internationalist coalition. South Korea, in fact, heralded the emergence of a new grand strategy in world politics—akin to that of a "trading state"—a strategy President Park had labeled "the compass of peace."[23] The avoidance of violent conflict in the Korean peninsula since the 1950s had far more to do with maximizing international economic and political access and domestic support than is usually recognized. The tendency simplistically to reduce the explanation of South Korea's regional behavior to responsiveness to US wishes and protection obscures the understanding of varying coalitional receptivities to hegemonic demands in South and North Korea and elsewhere. Neither a neorealist perspective nor an absent regional institutional and democratic infrastructure can explain the evolution of inter-Korean relations. A coalitional analysis illuminates historical shifts away from war since the 1960s, the modus vivendi of the 1970s and 1980s, and the changing content and timing of the rivals' nuclear policies. Similarly, neither institutionalist nor democratic peace perspectives can claim any bearing on the emergence of cooperative strategies in Taiwan, among ASEAN countries, or in East Asia at large, whereas coalitional trajectories offer a systematic account of the evolution of such stategies.

This overview suggests two additional methodological advantages. First, there is very little overlap in competing explanations of conflict and cooperation in these regions.[24] No rival hypothesis—neorealist, neoliberal institutionalist, cognitive, or world-systemic—performs consistently well across these divergent cases, or is able to explain regional conflict and cooperation through its core variables. Were a coalitional perspective to be found more promising in performing that task, our faith in pursuing this analytical tack further would be strengthened. Second, these regions are, for the most part, not among the easiest cases for supporting the theory. The choice of ASEAN for an in-depth analysis would have provided an easier case for confirming some of the propositions I advance regarding strong internationalist coalitions and a highly cooperative

---

[23] On trading states, see Rosecrance (1986). On the "compass of peace," see Park Chung Hee (1971: 138).

[24] Caporaso (1995: 458).

cluster. Such analysis would have amounted to a "plausibility probe" (Eckstein 1975), potentially a less rigorous test of the argument than the riskier cases chosen. The East Asian chapter thus examines the Korean peninsula in detail and ASEAN far less thoroughly.

Finally, the case studies examine the impact of coalitional competition throughout the last four decades. The 1950s and 1960s were characterized by an incipient and tentative opening to the global economy by very few states, with production being organized mostly within national boundaries. In the 1960s a transition toward greater integration in the global economy began, cul-minating—by the 1980s and early 1990s—in a strong wave of economic liber-alization. The institutional foundations of a global political economy grew progressively stronger, while rigid Cold War structures declined progressively from the 1950s onward until their collapse in 1989.[25] Ethno-confessional alle-giances that had remained lethargic throughout the Cold War era underwent a revival with its demise. Changes in grand strategy and regional orders across different regions are thus analyzed against a common, unfolding, global back-ground or world-time.

A TOUR OF THIS BOOK

Chapter Two outlines a framework for understanding regional orders, building on second-image-reversed (outside-in) effects to identify key coalitional cleav-ages. Two ideal-typical coalitions emerge out of immersing these effects into the specific context of economic liberalization. I describe these coalitions' con-stituent elements and grand strategies, spelling out the synergistic logic of do-mestic and external aspects of those strategies, or the inside-out effects. I spec-ify measures of coalitional strength to facilitate empirical comparisons and end with an outline of evolving global influences on the domestic coalitional inter-play.

Chapter Three specifies a more complete framework for understanding re-gional orders by incorporating interactive effects among coalitions across a re-gion. Thus, it explores the grand strategies of weak and strong versions of alternative coalitions throughout a range of situations where they face each other in a region. These combinations yield three general variants of regional orders: first, zones of stable peace, where strong internationalist clusters prevail; second, war zones and militarized disputes, where statist-nationalist coalitions prevail; and third, zones of contained conflict, where we might expect regional equilibria among internationalist and statist-nationalist coalitions.

Chapter Four examines the implications of a coalitional approach for the democratic peace research program. I first outline the theoretical claims of this

---

[25] Many address the post-1989 period as the "new world order." Cox (1986: 249) uses the con-cept "world order" to denote "particular patterns of power relationships which have endured in time," and which can be contrasted in terms of their principal characteristics. World orders suc-cessively "define the problematic of war or peace for the ensemble of states" (p. 220).

program and the logical and empirical problems it posits for understanding regional orders beyond the classical "zone of peace" that provided the most support for its tenets: the advanced industrialized world in the post-1945 era. I then reconstruct the origins of alternative coalitions schematically as they relate to sequences in political and economic liberalization. The remainder of the chapter spells out the implications of such sequences for the democratic peace research program and for the coalitional analysis advanced in this book. Central to this synthesis is the concern with transitional aspects of economic liberalization and democratization, their interactive effects, and their joint impact on conflict and cooperation.

The chapters in Part Two adopt a common structure to examine three regions in light of the main argument. For the identification of ruling coalitions, their grand strategy, and the mobilizational tactics of political entrepreneurs I relied on a variety of sources, including: personal interviews with high-level civilian and military officials, business leaders, diplomats, economic bureaucrats, officials in chambers of commerce, peak associations, labor, and political parties; public statements, press accounts, memoirs, party platforms, parliamentary debates, legislative proceedings; and an extensive literature in comparative political economy disssecting the coalitional profiles and policies (domestic, regional, international) of the countries studied here.[26] Part Three summarizes the conceptual and methodological advantages—as well as the limitations—of the coalitional approach, its applicability to other regions, and its implications for leading approaches in international relations and for pressing policy-related considerations at century's dawn.

[26] Fortunately, in addition to all other sources, many leading political entrepreneurs studied here left memoirs and written political platforms—in some cases in the form of comprehensive volumes, in other cases as more succinct statements or media interviews—including those of Egypt's presidents Gamal Abdel Nasser and Anwar Sadat, Israel's prime ministers David Ben-Gurion, Menachem Begin, Yitzhak Rabin, Shimon Peres, and Benjamin Netanyahu, Jordan's King Hussein and Crown Prince Hassan Bin Talal, Palestinian president Yasir Arafat, Iraq's president Saddam Hussein, South Korea's presidents Syngman Rhee, Park Chung Hee, Chun Doo Hwan, and Kim Young Sam, North Korea's president Kim Il Sung, Brazil's presidents Fernando Collor, José Sarney, and Fernando H. Cardoso, Argentina's presidents Juan Perón, Raúl Alfonsín, and Carlos Menem, Chile's president Augusto Pinochet, and Singapore's president Lee Kuan Yew. Similarly, many of the political strategists and technocrats on which these entrepreneurs relied have left useful paper trails for the analysis of grand strategies, notably Hasnein Haikal, Domingo Cavallo, Michael Bruno, Abdullah Toukan, and Yossi Beilin.

CHAPTER TWO

Internationalization and Political Coalitions

THE THEORETICAL FRAMEWORK outlined in this book builds on the underlying assumption that the kinds of ties binding different domestic political actors to global processes affect the way in which these actors identify their preferences, whether material or ideal.[1] Domestic considerations are, as is often recognized, most influential in the definition of preferences. Quite often, however, the connections between global and domestic processes are inextricable, as in the case of economic liberalization. Safeguarding a certain preference or value requires the formulation of policies that often span the domestic, regional, and global spheres. Political actors—institutions, interest associations, state agencies, political parties, religious groups, social movements—aggregate those preferences and cloak them in ideological cloth. Political entrepreneurs, individually or through institutions under their control, rely on their actual or potential organizational capacities and popularity in order to broker coalitions among relevant actors. They do so by logrolling, that is, exchanging the mutual rights of partners to seek their most valued preference, using both material and cultural ingredients to define a political strategy.[2] Politics is about brewing the right mix of ingredients, selling it, adapting it along the way, and disposing of the mix altogether if and when necessary; all these entail the ability to interpret the mobilizing capacity of prevailing norms, powerful identity concepts, and historical myths.[3] Entrepreneurs are likely to craft coalitions through which they can maximize their own power and control over coalitional resources. Logrolled coalitions (within which votes are traded across issues) compete against other coalitions.

Actors—individual and collective—vary in the currency (the yardstick for measuring power resources) they bring to bear on prospective coalitions: the military can wield its ability to coerce; capitalists their potential to invest, employ, and exit; labor its option to strike; independent central banks their capacity to maintain macroeconomic stability; threatened state bureaucracies their opportunities to foil the implementation of reform; "symbolic analysts" their

---

[1] Gourevitch (1978, 1986). See Gramsci's (1988: 200) conception of historical blocs, where "material forces are the content and ideologies are the form, though this distinction between form and content has purely indicative value, since the material forces would be inconceivable historically without form and the ideologies would be individual fancies without the material forces."

[2] On logrolling, see Riker and Brams (1973), Mueller (1989), and Snyder (1991).

[3] On the political process as concerned with managing interpretations and creating visions, see March and Olsen (1989: 51). Public statements, private conversations, and memoirs are good sources for understanding the mobilizational strategies of political entrepreneurs. On ideology as the instrument injecting collective purpose and realms of agreement into coalitions, see Gourevitch (1986: 233–34).

technical skill to convert policy into outcomes; and religious fundamentalists their willingness for self-sacrifice in violent havoc.[4] Political entrepreneurs use available rules and structures to translate interests and values into bargaining resources at particular sites, from legislative chambers to bureaucratic corridors, military headquarters, single-party command centers, corporate suites, the ballot box, the *diwan*, the battlefield, and the peace demonstration. Out of these bargains emerge grand strategies designed to pursue the most valued preferences of coalitional partners.

On the basis of these fundamental assumptions, this chapter advances the following general argument:

1. The distributional consequences of internationalization and economic liberalization create two ideal-type political coalitions in each country, one supporting it (internationalist coalitions), the other opposing it (statist-nationalist-confessional coalitions).[5]

2. The political entrepreneurs organizing these two types of coalition endorse contrasting preferences and observable instruments (such as a fiscal or tariff target, a foreign investment blueprint, a budget rule, borrowing ceilings, or the rejection of a given international regime) that advance material and ideal preferences.

3. These preferences are aggregated into a "grand political-economic strategy" (grand strategy, in short, henceforth).[6] Grand strategies reveal a coalition's definition of the state's relation to the global political economy, to the internal extraction and allocation of resources among groups and institutions, and to the regional strategic context. Grand strategies can be explicitly stated—as in a party platform, a coup's pronouncement, a political pamphlet—but more often than not they are implicitly embedded in a wide range of policy positions regarding domestic and global matters.

4. Once a certain coalition prevails politically—as a function of its size, cohesiveness, and effectiveness, and of the institutional context in which it operates—its grand strategy becomes raison d'état. Governmental policy must now reflect the essential contours of that strategy, although the institutional context can hinder and even derail its implementation. Grand strategies identify potential threats to the coalition's survival at home, in the region, and throughout the world, and devise political, economic, and military means to counter such threats.[7]

5. The grand strategy of internationalist coalitions includes the pursuit of economic reform at home, the decimation of political opposition, and the maintainance of secure

---

[4] On political currency, sites, and size of coalitions, see Kenworthy (1970), Kelley (1970), and Ames (1987). "Symbolic analysts" include public and private managerial, technical, scientific, educational, information, and service-oriented elites who benefit from an integrated global economy (Reich 1991).

[5] Kaufman (1989), Nelson (1989), Haggard and Kaufman (1992, 1995). I discuss the historical origins and evolution of each coalition type in Chapter Four, in the context of sequences of political and economic liberalization.

[6] The term has an aura of order and coherence that is not borne out by its empirical referents, which can be quite messy and with fuzzy boundaries. Its conceptual utility remains, however. In some cases a series of improvised responses builds up into a more or less consistent grand strategic path whereas in others this does not happen.

[7] These functions of grand strategy are identified in Posen (1984), who connects them to the survival of the state, rather than of political coalitions.

access to foreign markets, capital, investments, and technology. A cooperative (non-violent) regional neighborhood serves all three interrelated aspects of this strategy well. Regional stability—not regional economic integration—is the main conceptual link between the regional and global dimensions of an internationalist grand strategy.

6. In contrast, the grand strategy of statist-nationalist-confessional coalitions seeks to preserve allocations to statist and military-industrial complexes, to resist external pressures for liberalization, and to weaken political adversaries who advocate economic reform and internationalization. A regional context of insecurity and competition is a compelling requirement for sustaining this grand strategy, as is the fueling of national and religious myths that help justify the strategy.

7. The symmetrical attempt to weaken the adversarial coalition politically is an important component of the grand strategies of internationalist and nationalist-confessional coalitions.[8] Ruling coalitions are constrained by their relative strength vis-à-vis their domestic challengers in their ability to implement their respective grand strategies.

8. International political and economic structures and institutions purposefully—but also unintendedly—influence the domestic coalitional interplay, at times strengthening internationalist coalitions, at others empowering their rivals.

9. The outcome of a ruling coalition's policies affects its own standing vis-à-vis the adversarial coalition, the region, and the global political economy. In this process grand strategies may be reinforced, diluted, or replaced altogether.

This basic understanding of the relationship between the global political economy, its coalitional effects, and grand strategy is outlined in Figure 1.

The essential logic behind the constitution of contending coalitions was encapsulated in Polanyi's (1944) formulation of a dialectic "double movement"—global market expansion and the political response to it—but requires adjustments to the late twentieth-century world-time specified in Chapter One. Polanyi's framework outlined quite specifically both the global economic and political-strategic context of what he labeled "the hundred years' peace." This is an inexorably changing context not only across centuries and within them, but—as the 1989 revolution suggests—within decades as well. The identification of coalitions in the remainder of this chapter takes account of the coalitions' integrated interpretation of this economic—both market and institutional—and political-strategic context, not just of price convergence but of normative and institutional convergence as well.[9] Yet the task of specifying further the precise links between this evolving context and domestic coalitional configurations remains, as will be clear at the end of this chapter. In the next section I identify natural partners of internationalist and statist-nationalist-confessional coalitions, as a consequence of their expected gains and losses—both

[8] On regime survival as the main priority of ruling coalitions in the industrializing world, see Rothstein (1977) and Kolodziej and Harkavy (1982).

[9] The landmark study in this area is Gourevitch (1986), which delineated the need to map production profiles (actors' positions vis-à-vis the global economy, and obtaining preferences), aggregating associations, mediating institutions and rules, refracting ideologies, and international military and economic structures. See also Kindleberger (1951).

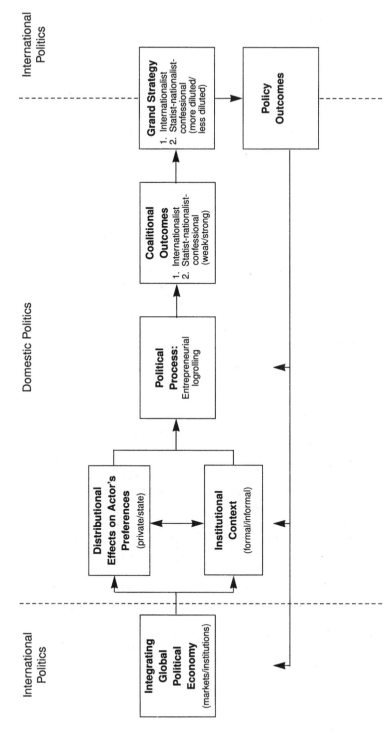

Figure 1. The global political economy, coalitional effects, and grand strategy

material and ideal—from internationalization. I also outline the coalitions' respective patterns of political aggregation, articulation, and logrolling, leaving to Chapter Four the task of clarifying the relationship between democracy and coalitional type. Coalitional partners can include political parties, state agencies, the military as an institution, peak organizations, labor confederations, and confessional movements. Next I specify the elements of each coalition's grand strategy and their logical connections, and end with an overview of the impact of global political and economic processes and institutions on the relative strength and survivability of coalitions.

INTERNATIONALIST COALITIONS

Preferences, Composition, and Patterns of Aggregation and Logrolling

Coalitions can be characterized through their component members who, under a given institutional context, endorse observable policies. The task of identifying coalitional partners must be guided by the understanding that internationalization poses threats not merely to material interests but also to cultures, identities, and values, and to the interests of political entrepreneurs endangered by both types of threats. Thus, coalitions are not merely about alternative positions vis-à-vis economic liberalization and price convergence but also about alternative integrated interpretations of the political-economic and strategic context as it affects domestic coalitional balances.[10] Nevertheless, we may begin the analysis of coalitional responses to internationalization through an understanding of "qui bono" (who gains) and who loses from economic liberalization. Internationalization involves a series of steps geared to impose a market rationale on economic activities. Privatization, the contraction of state entrepreneurship, and openness to global markets, capital, investments, and technology are its central features. External liberalization affects individuals and groups in different sectors through changes in employment status, labor incomes, and returns on assets, through changes in the prices of goods and services consumed, and through the provision of public services.[11]

The most common approach to mapping the distributional impact of liberalization relies on the cleavage between tradable (internationally competitive) and nontradable (noncompetitive) sectors, averring that "laborers, managers, and investors in the protected industry stand to lose, at least temporarily, from the removal of a protective wall in a sector."[12] Whereas owners of noncompetitive

---

[10] Disentangling material from ideal preferences is sometimes a sterile pursuit, as is the case with "quality of life" criteria frequently invoked to praise or condemn the impact of internationalization. Islamist assassinations of tourists have both an ideal content—rejection of foreign ways—and the acknowledged objective of depriving ruling political rivals of material sources of income. On material (class) interests as socially constructed, see Polanyi (1944: 46, 153–55).

[11] Nelson (1992). See also Keohane and Milner (1996).

[12] Bruno (1988: 230). See also Baldwin (1988) and Frieden and Rogowski (1996), who discuss the complementarity of sectoral and factoral (land, labor, capital) analysis. On fixed asset holders

sector-specific assets have incentives to pressure governments to retain protective walls, export-intensive ones benefit from opening up the economy. Related approaches emphasize the preference of large banking and industrial complexes—particularly those already involved in foreign trade, investment, lending, and licensing—to increased openness.[13] Generally speaking, the higher the adjustment costs for competing in the global economy, the greater the incentives to demand protection. Liberalization also benefits the labor force and "symbolic analysts" employed in competitive industries or firms, the latter's suppliers, and consumers of imported products. The preferences of internationalist coalitions transcends the domestic-international divide. The external orientation of overseas investors, competitive producers, and consumers of imported products is translated into a preference for deflationary, internationalist, or "monetarist" policies at home.[14] Export-intensive sectors and liquid-asset holders are more receptive to structural adjustment policies, and opposed to external confrontations with the international financial and investing community.[15]

Beyond these general expectations, however, identifying preferences for or against liberalization might be less straightforward than suggested by the export-oriented / import-competing cleavage. Firms with a more diversified portfolio of activities face a more complex set of incentives, regarding different aspects of the liberalization package, such as stabilization and trade policy.[16] Moreover, quite often the volatile conditions produced by liberalization induce high uncertainty among wide segments of the population, across all sectoral, class, institutional, and occupational categories. This is particularly the case during the initial stages and when the commitment to reforms (and therefore their very credibility) is hard to predict. Only after traversing "the valley of transition," in Przeworski's (1991) inspiring formulation, may a wider political basis in support of liberalization develop. Until then, beneficiaries of economic reform, although likely to organize politically, can face significant resistance from those who stand to gain from the status quo.[17] Economic crises have been identified as an important condition—although neither necessary nor suffi-

---

(such as small import-substituting manufacturers and firms tied to state-owned enterprises) and their opposition to devaluation and liberalizing reforms, see Frieden (1991b).

[13] Milner (1988a and 1988b).

[14] Frieden (1995: 292). On the characterization of these coalitions as "internationalist," see Kaufman (1986) and Stallings (1992).

[15] Structural adjustment is "a set of measures designed to make the economy competitive" (Przeworski 1991: 144). Such measures often include, in different sequences and combinations, currency devaluation, de-indexing of wages, reductions in deficit, consumer subsidies and tariffs, and price deregulation (Nelson 1989; Kaufman 1989). On the bankers' alliance, and their populist nemesis, see Maxfield (1990). On liquid asset holders that profit from devaluation and financial deregulation, see Frieden (1991b).

[16] Stabilization efforts aim at restoring macroeconomic balance through short-term measures to slow down inflation and reduce balance-of-payments and government deficits (Przeworski 1991: 144). They involve reducing aggregate demand through fiscal and monetary measures often accompanied by devaluation, and require shorter time horizons than structural efforts (Nelson 1990: 3–4).

[17] Haggard and Kaufman (1992, 1995).

cient—coalescing and accelerating the political push for economic reform, particularly where the opposition to reform is weakened.[18] Crisis conditions often impose short time-horizons since, as Hirschman (1945: 27) suggested, "harassed statesmen generally have a short-run view."

Clearly, exploring the distributional consequences of internationalization is only a first step. The institutional context in which coalitions operate plays an important role in defining a coalition's political wherewithal, as we shall see below, and the very fate of liberalization. In particular, political entrepreneurs in control of a "dirigiste" developmental state (Johnson 1982) can plan the direction, rate, and extent of economic liberalization in its domestic and external aspects, in accordance with the interests and values of the coalition they have put together. Thus, liberalization from above—as in the classical cases of South Korea and Taiwan—relies on a powerful state, that is, on a strong bureaucratic apparatus imposing central priorities on private actors, and setting the tone and pace of reform. This model can be largely exclusionary in political terms, particularly toward labor, but it is not the narrow preserve of authoritarian regimes, as the Eshkol-Sapir period in Israel and the experiences of many a democratic reformer in the 1990s suggest. Initial support for reform is rarely overwhelming, but as the integrative strategy toward the global economy unfolds, its beneficiaries are expected to grow economically and politically stronger. During more advanced stages of liberalization new political groups may burst the exclusionary mold, a process I discuss in greater detail in Chapter Four. Institutional capacity may be at most necessary (although some cases challenge even this premise) but is certainly not sufficient for the implementation of economic reform, particularly in the absence of political will. Independent central banks can play a key role in steering the conditions favored by internationalist actors.[19]

Liberalization from below is less frequent and can take two main forms. In some cases it can rely on a powerful state for implementation. For instance, according to Migdal (1988), powerful societal actors in some Arab countries pushed for economic reform in alliance with state institutions. Certain state agencies are frequently allies of economic liberalization (often ministries of finance, independent central banks, managers of export-processing zones), whereas other agencies oppose it (industry and trade ministries, military-industrial sectors).[20] In other cases, pressures for economic liberalization from below find organized reformist political groups facing sclerotic state agencies resistant to change, as in Itamar Franco's Brazil and Leonid Kravchuk's Ukraine. In all cases, the ability of big business, both local and foreign-owned, and overseas investors to influence domestic investment patterns and to move capital abroad often gives them an important voice in shaping domestic and external adjustment policies. Political entrepreneurs logrolling an internationalist coalition frequently rely on a core of politically savvy "technopols," characterized by their

---

[18] Nelson (1990); Williamson (1994).

[19] Garret and Lange (1996: 66–68).

[20] On the strengthening of central banks in the 1980s and 1990s and their role in economic reform, see Maxfield (1997).

ability to advance their economic strategy within the bureaucracy.[21] They may also coopt organized labor through a political pact that provides it with safety nets, or with longer-term improvements in exchange for short-term restraints.[22] During periods of high uncertainty the rhetoric of political entrepreneurs can be most powerful in inducing different constituencies to embrace or oppose reform on the basis of its putative impact on their specific material and ideal interests.[23] Indeed, there are times when it may be more cost-effective—from a research standpoint—to study the mobilizational rhetoric used by political entrepreneurs to logroll coalitions than to identify the actual distributional impact of economic liberalization.

As is clear by now, the economic agenda of internationalist coalitions should not be equated with "laissez-faire" policies across the board and does not exclude selective protectionism, continued regulation, and industrial policy in support of specific industries or firms.[24] Liberalization is neither linear nor coherent, and different sectors can be affected in different sequences. This selectivity and gradualism suggest that the adjective "liberalizing" is more appropriate than "liberal" in characterizing these coalitions. The more extensive the range of economic activities targeted for liberalization, the more liberalizing the agenda can be said to be. Absolute liberalization—complete trade openness— can be conceptualized but has little empirical content, with few exceptions. Conversely, the fewer the sectors targeted for economic liberalization—including none at all—the closer we get to a statist, nationalizing (nonliberalizing) agenda. In different combinations and sequences, liberalizing agendas include export drives, opening the domestic market to foreign goods and investment, reducing state entrepreneurial activities, and eventually deregulating financial flows.[25]

What is most central to the economic program of internationalist coalitions is the primacy accorded to macroeconomic stability and to the discipline induced by international competition.[26] Macroeconomic stability reduces uncertainty, en-

---

[21] The term "technopol" was coined by Richard Feinberg and Jorge Domínguez (Domínguez 1997).

[22] Nelson (1992); Haggard and Webb (1994).

[23] On economic uncertainty and gullibility to political persuasion, see Bates and Krueger (1993a: 456–57).

[24] Rodrick (1994: 66) defines protectionism as a mean effective rate of protection greater than 30 percent. Beyond debates over such thresholds, empirical observations where average tariffs drop from 100 percent to 11–12 percent—as in Latin America in the 1990s—offer less controversial measures of a growing openness to trade.

[25] Bruno (1988: 224). Concrete steps—such as removal of quantitative restrictions on imports, the elimination of tariffs, and the unification of import tariffs and export subsidies—are more reliable indicators of a liberalizing agenda than statements of intention, although I use both indicators in the empirical chapters. Financial liberalization—reducing governmental control over the allocation of credit—includes freeing interest rates, removing subsidies and barriers to entry, and privatizing the banks. On the sources, pace, and scope of financial liberalization, see Haggard, Lee, and Maxfield (1993). For an optimum sequencing of financial liberalization, involving balancing the budget, a valid tax system, and bank reform, see McKinnon (1993).

[26] The primacy of macroeconomic stability is reflected in the low tolerance for inflation among

courages savings, and enhances the rate of investment, including foreign investment. Where such programs prevail politically and are effectively executed, the rates of protection decline markedly, and foreign trade and private economic activity increasingly account for growing shares of the GDP. Actual policy success, however, is not a wholly reliable indicator of a coalition's commitment to reform, although success helps strengthen the coalition's political commitment to liberalization. Openness to foreign investment, for instance, is a prerequisite but not a guarantee that such investment will materialize. Success is the daughter of a more complex set of factors, including regional stability, as I discuss below.[27] The degree of trade openness, therefore, is a potential symptom, not a reliable measure of the presence of an internationalist coalition. Korea's trade openness was very low in the early 1960s (below 15 percent) when President Park launched an internationalist strategy. Trade openness doubled by 1967 and reached nearly 72 percent by 1990, as the strategy was firmly in place. High levels of trade openness do indicate a high probability that sustained liberalizing policies have been implemented.

Finally, internationalization—and the coalitions likely to form in response to it—are not merely about trade orientation but also about a fundamental approach to an array of regimes, institutions, and values within which international trade is nested. The remainder of this chapter takes account of these broader sources of coalitional mobilization and of their impact on regional policies.

The Grand Strategy of Internationalist Coalitions

The interests and economic agenda of internationalist coalitions as identified above are served by certain regional policies better than others. From the perspective of these coalitions, cooperative regional postures are often most efficient for both their domestic political and their global implications. Such postures, in general terms, are expected to have three consequences: freeing up resources to carry out reform at home, weakening groups and institutions opposed to reform, and securing access to foreign markets, capital, investments, and technology.

Freeing up Resources to Carry out Reform at Home. Conflict-prone postures require the need to back them up with the internal mobilization of resources for potential military conflict. Such mobilization often contributes to the ailments afflicting these countries' domestic political economy (from the standpoint of internationalist coalitions): the expansion of state power, the maintenance of

---

East Asian liberalizers relative to that, for instance, of Southern Cone countries (up to the 1990s). High inflation induces capital flight and lowers incentives to foreign investors. At relatively modest levels (no higher than 10–15 percent annual) inflation has been shown to avoid many of its adverse effects (Wolf 1981: 86).

[27] On the preliminary status of aggregate knowledge about the determinants, optimal trajectory, and correlates of success of economic reform, see Bates and Krueger (1993a: 1–26, 444–72).

unproductive and inflation-inducing military investments, the protection of state-owned enterprises under a mantle of "national security" considerations, and the perpetuation of rent-seeking patterns.[28] In principle, therefore, internationalist coalitions resist this syndrome, in an attempt to avoid inflated military budgets that increase governmental and payments deficits, raise the cost of capital, curtail savings and productive investment, deplete foreign exchange coffers, induce overvalued exchange rates, currency instability and unpredictability, and distort the human power base.[29] The increasing high-technology content of modern weapons multiplies these effects, rendering the trade-offs imposed by military investments more evident than ever before. In sum, in light of the high opportunity costs of military expenditures, internationalist coalitions are often less predisposed to extract and mobilize societal resources for external conflict, because such extraction threatens the important macroeconomic objectives they endorse.[30]

This is not to say that internationalist coalitions do not invest in weapons at all, but that when they do so, two conditions are likely to hold. First, their levels of military expenditures do not fundamentally endanger their internationalist strategy, or shatter the fiscal discipline essential to their political-economic agenda. This approach to military expenditures is underpinned by a primary concern with sustained economic growth, and is thus compatible with both the capital formation model and the export-led growth model of the impact of military expenditures on economic performance.[31] The capital formation model stresses private investment as the key determinant of economic growth. The export-led growth model argues that military expenditures tend to deprive

[28] Notice that no general "guns-versus-butter" theory of military expenditures is postulated here (empirical evidence suggests these overall tradeoffs vary across states, time, and macroeconomic conditions). Rather, I approach military expenditures in this context from the perspective of an internationalist coalition's core political interests. For a thorough examination of the net consequences of military expenditures in Third World countries, see Ball (1988) and Chan and Mintz (1992). On how predatory taxation—very often adopted for defense purposes—reduces profit margins and discourages private investment, see Feigenbaum and Henig (1994). On the positive relationship between public sector size and military expenditures, see West (1992: 135–37). Rent seeking (Krueger 1974) refers to "unproductive profit-seeking activities" (Bhagwati 1988: 103) by groups lobbying for "rents" or transfers of wealth through the aegis of the state.

[29] On the opportunity costs of military debt incurred as a result of arms imports, see Brzoska (1992). For evidence that countries with a military-industrial complex are more subject to pressures for increased defense expenditures, often financed through external debt, see West (1992: 138–39) and Looney (1989). On the functional needs of military organizations to control resources, to be autonomous from civilian control, and to enhance the social prestige of officers as explaining the armed forces' preferences, see Posen (1984).

[30] Lamborn (1991) focused on the political costs of extracting resources for maintaining a powerful military, and on how domestic constraints on the extraction of resources lead to a restrained foreign policy. The experiences of Japan and Germany relative to the former USSR and the US during the Cold War yielded some general lessons for political entrepreneurs throughout the industrializing world about the relationships between military expenditures, a bloated state, and economic decline. On why the congruence of economic growth and war production in the US in World War II was exceptional, see Kaysen (1993).

[31] Chan (1992a: 4–6). On the macroeconomic dimensions of arms reductions, see Adams (1992).

the most dynamic sectors—those involved in exports—from important resources and skills. The consequent decline in international competitiveness thus leads to a weaker currency, structural unemployment, chronic trade deficits, and a less attractive environment for international investments—all outcomes that are anathema to internationalist coalitions. Where military expenditures are kept at a level that averts such outcomes, hard political choices between guns and butter can be deferred.

Second, military investments are incurred as an insurance policy, particularly against statist-nationalist adversaries in the region or against generalized uncertainty of the kind unleashed, for instance, by the end of the Cold War. Broader foreign policy patterns reflect this defensive posture, as well. The essential ingredient of an internationalist grand strategy is economic access, not military prowess. Yet politically successful internationalist coalitions are able to persuade their domestic and foreign audiences alike that they can provide defense, growth, and welfare at the same time, as the 1996 reelection of Taiwan's President Lee Teng-hui suggests.[32]

These two conditions are key to understanding the role of military expenditures in states ruled by internationalist coalitions, a point frequently muted (and most often missed) by aggregate accounts of military investments. Although subject to constant threats to its survival from North Korea, South Korea has devoted, for the past three decades, between 4 and 6 percent of its GDP to the military sector.[33] The GDP grew at a rate of 10 percent on average between 1965 and 1989 (lower in 1973–1984, at 7.2 percent), but the ratio of military expenditures to GDP remained largely constant, reflecting declining military investments relative to GDP. During the period of consolidation of its export-led strategy (1962–1972), expenditures for economic development were higher than for defense. By 1990 South Korea's military expenditures were 3.8 percent of its GDP, a figure comparable to Argentina's that same year, in a region characterized by the lowest threat perceptions worldwide. Taiwan allocated nearly 8 percent of its GDP to defense on average between 1961 and 1987, with declining percentages by the 1970s as the integrative model of industrialization took root.[34] The military expenditures of South Korea and Taiwan were far lower than those of other states in high-conflict regions like the Middle East, where military expenditures amounted to between 8 and 17 percent of GDP in the 1970s and 1980s. Military expenditures of statist-nationalist coalitions in the Middle East were particularly high, reaching up to 20 percent of GDP in

---

[32] For the view that the relationship between military expenditures, growth, and welfare is contingent on a primarily political process of satisficing—and not the product of an objective assessment of cost effectiveness—see Bobrow (1992).

[33] ACDA (1990); Moon and Hyun (1992); UNDP (1994: 170). A 4 percent average before 1975 increased to 6 percent since 1975, when US military grants declined drastically (Ball 1988: 54).

[34] Chan (1992b: 167); UNDP (1994: 170). Chapter Seven clarifies the point that although US military aid to South Korea and Taiwan facilitated relatively lower military expenditures initially, such levels persisted after US aid had subsided, and were ingrained in the internationalist strategy both states embraced.

Syria and Iraq, or three and four times higher than the world's average.[35] For further contrast, military expenditures in internationalizing East Asia were 4 percent of GDP in 1990–1991 (and even less if China is excluded) and 2.8 percent of GDP in Southeast Asia. Moreover, despite references to military acquisitions in Asia-Pacific as the prelude for armed conflict, as of 1997 there has been neither an arms race nor an offensive build-up in that region that threatened neighboring countries.[36]

Weakening Groups and Institutions Opposed to Reform. The taming and resolution of regional conflicts often has a detrimental impact on three main actors opposed to economic reform (and, therefore, actors that are natural challengers of internationalist coalitions): first, the military, which is weakened both institutionally (by its contraction in size and mission) and personally (when top and middle echelons undergo radical trimmings in material advantages and prerogatives);[37] second, the network of public and private enterprises thriving on the production and distribution of military and ancillary—largely protected—goods; and third, advocates of civic nationalist and / or confessional causes that prosper domestically, in political and economic terms, from regional conflict and competition with neighboring states. I explore the makeup and objectives of these constituencies below.[38] Thus, these three actors often oppose regional cooperation and economic reform because they jointly threaten their survival. The material interests of statist groups are safeguarded at the price of fiscally expansionary policies that engender inflationary spirals and currency weakness and instability. Statist-nationalist, ethnic, and confessional movements also connect internationalization with global (Western) institutions whose policy prescriptions they loathe because they often undermine these movements' own domestic viability. These international institutions provide statist-nationalist coalitions with a convenient ideological lightning rod for mobilizing domestic support against internationalist coalitions, both at home and in neighboring states ruled by internationalist coalitions.

Securing Access to Foreign Markets, Capital, Investments, and Technology. Cooperative regional orders have positive global externalities for internationalist coalitions: they minimize risk considerations and enable foreign investment, they decrease the likelihood of sanctions and penalties from international pri-

---

[35] The average ratio of military expenditures over GDP for developing countries in the 1970s and 1980s was between 4 and 6 percent (West 1992: 25, 31).

[36] Ball (1993/94); Buzan and Segal (1994); Mack and Kerr (1994: 131).

[37] On the military's tendency to inflate both budgets and threats, see Snyder (1991) and Van Evera (1993).

[38] On the affinity between economic nationalism and a "national security" ideology, and on statist and protectionist coalitions as more likely to embrace a more belligerent stand abroad, see Gilpin (1987). Hamiltonian policies are a classical referent for a model rooted in economic nationalism (industrial policy, infant-industry protection through tariffs and subsidies, self-reliance via a diversified national economy), statism (national interest, power, extractive role via taxes, strong executive), and a military-industrial complex (Hamilton 1817).

vate and public actors, and they reinforce the coalition's ties to economic institutions (such as the IMF, World Bank, and private banks) to which they endear themselves through their reform programs.[39] Intransigent and uncertainty-inducing regional policies, instead, raise the propensity for conflict and the risks for foreign investors, may trigger denial of bilateral or multilateral aid (as with the US refusal to provide loan guarantees to Israel's Likud-led coalition), denial of technology, and the like.[40]

The preceding points make it clear that an internationalist grand strategy is far broader than economic reform and involves a definition of the coalition's regional and global relations. Cooperative regional arrangements are not just the product of concessions to external pressures. Internationalist coalitions do not merely trade the right to pursue the national interest regionally (whatever that means) for the right to enrich themselves, as their domestic adversaries often argue (in Egypt, Jordan, and Argentina, for example). Indeed, internationalist coalitions may aim at shrinking the size of the state but, when successful, end up strengthening the leaner state's institutional capacity for societal extraction, and by extension, for mobilizing resources for war.[41] Internationalist coalitions coalesce a range of domestic actors that perceive the downgrading of militarized conflicts and the upgrading of regional cooperation as valuable because these help advance the agenda of liberalizing the economy, rein in adversarial political forces at home, and secure international economic, financial, and political benefits—such as debt relief, export markets, technology transfer, food imports, aid, and investments—that can be used to maintain or broaden domestic political support, and to strengthen the institutional framework underpinning economic liberalization at home and abroad. Where most of the positive externalities from regional cooperation are captured by a few groups with intense internationalist preferences and equally intense political access, these privileged groups are particularly active in advancing the internationalist agenda.[42]

The empirical analysis in Part Two of this book provides examples of a wide variety of internationalist coalitions, spanning cases in which liberalization is most advanced to those in which the process is in its infancy. South Korea and

[39] Cooperation—as openness to foreign investment—is a precondition, not a guarantee of foreign investment (or it may be called a necessary but insufficient condition). On the relationship between security threats and business risks, see Rosecrance and Schott (1997). From the standpoint of the global political economy and its beneficiaries, the positive global externalities from regional cooperation include cheaper oil (Lake 1997). On expectations that the peace process and sustained growth will raise Israel's Standard & Poor credit rankings, see *Ha'aretz* (Tel Aviv) 7 December, 1995: 3.

[40] A European Council official told Israeli correspondents: "Your region is not interesting for European investors because it entails political risks. Thailand and eastern European countries seem far more attractive" (quoted in Kemp 1994: 400).

[41] On how neoliberal reforms have explicitly aimed at strengthening the state by establishing a broader tax base, more effective tax collection, and reorienting public spending priorities toward investment and the provision of basic services, see Haggard and Kaufman (1995: 313).

[42] On the distributional effects of externalities on regional cooperation, see Lake (1997).

Taiwan were pioneers in shedding the inward-looking policies characteristic of the early 1950s as their primary strategies of industrialization. Their initial shift to an export-promoting strategy came about essentially through a substantial reduction of overvaluation and shifting incentives toward exports (by making the average effective exchange rate on exports greater than the average effective exchange rate on imports, or EESx > EERm).[43] In time they became paradigmatic cases of an integrative model of export-driven industrialization, guided by a state-based coalition with growing support over time from budding societal actors.[44] This active state nourished a private sector able to compete internationally, and displaced private initiative to a far lesser extent than import-substituting states of the Latin American, South Asian, and Middle East varieties. State enterprises accounted for 10 to 15 percent of total industrial employment and 25 percent of industrial output in South Korea, even during a brief statist-nationalist interlude in the 1970s. Corresponding figures for the average Middle East state were 50 percent of total industrial employment and 75 percent of industrial output.

In both South Korea and Taiwan, substantial threats to the states' physical existence required highly developed military-industrial sectors but, as argued, these were not allowed to harm the integrity of the political-economic strategy. Bureaucrats, cajoling the military and industrial conglomerates (*chaebols*) in South Korea, and Taiwan's Kuomintang (KMT) apparatus, nurtured a strategy that—despite some protected niches and considerable state entrepreneurship—leaned on foreign markets, capital, technology, and investments.[45] The maintenance of such a strategy and of economic stability required downgrading regional conflict and efforts to enhance cooperation. In effect, once they embarked on this strategy in earnest, the ruling coalitions of South Korea and Taiwan arguably pursued, for the most part, the least confrontational postures possible under a highly adversarial regional context.[46] Both went so far as to renounce openly a potentially expensive nuclear competition, at least since the 1970s. They thus joined the nonproliferation regime effectively (rather than merely in form, like Iraq), despite their inherent ability to match or overwhelm (in the case of South Korea) their rivals in a nuclear race. As will be clear in Chapter Three, the nature of cooperation is contextual, and heavily influenced by the depth of security dilemmas and the shadow of past militarized encounters. The relatively restrained behavior of South Korea and Taiwan must be assessed in this light.

---

[43] Bhagwati (1988: 94); Williamson (1990).

[44] Gereffi and Wyman (1990); Haggard and Kaufman (1992).

[45] Taiwan's foreign trade amounted to about 85 percent of its GNP in 1985 (Chan 1988). On how Taiwan's export drive, fiscal conservatism, and high rate of savings relative to consumption have enabled it to contain inflation despite a heavy defense burden, see Chan (1992b).

[46] On the KMT's overriding concern with economic stability, on Taiwan's shift from rabid militarism in the early years to "an evermore absorbing interest in economic growth," and on the decline of the military institution in Taiwan's political economy, see Amsden (1985). On the minor and indirect role of Taiwan's defense burden on its GNP growth, export expansion, and improving income equality, and on Taiwan's reluctance to finance indigenous arms industries, see Chan (1988).

Other regions reveal cases of internationalist coalitions that are far more embattled politically and much less advanced in the implementation of their agenda, as in the Middle East and South Asia. As relative newcomers to an internationalist grand strategy, Latin America's Southern Cone coalitions have made important strides in implementing the domestic, regional, and global requirements of that strategy. Liberalizing entrepreneurs everywhere rely on the mythical effects of markets and of a leaner (and presumably more effective) state in order to broaden their constituency. They also exaggerate the "peace dividends" expected from downsizing military-industrial complexes at home and from new regional ventures in economics and security, which are depicted as important for downsizing neighboring military-industrial complexes. At times other myths are poured into an internationalist agenda, as with "Asian values" outweighing Western-style democracy or human rights, but the myth remains an instrument by which entrepreneurs forge conformity with the domestic, regional, and global requirements of their essentially internationalist grand strategy.

STATIST-NATIONALIST-CONFESSIONAL COALITIONS

Preferences, Composition, and Patterns of Aggregation and Logrolling

Statist-nationalist-confessional coalitions encompass an ecclectic group that colludes in challenging different aspects of internationalist agendas. This joint challenge generally constitutes the most valued preference of each partner but can otherwise submerge profoundly different objectives, from rejection of a specific economic threat to rebuff of a security regime or a liberal norm separating state and church. Not all potential partners to such coalitions, as outlined below, are present everywhere, and the relative strength of each partner varies across states and regions.[47] These coalitions have an inherent affinity with import-substituting models of industrialization and classical populist programs involving a strong, active government that controlls prices, increases nominal wages, overvalues the currency to raise wages and profits in nontraded-goods sectors, protects state enterprises, allocates credit at low interest rates, and dispenses rents to private industry by discriminating against imports that compete with domestic products (through tariffs, import controls, and multiple exchange rate systems).[48] Kaufman and Stallings (1991: 16) define populism in the Latin

---

[47] I use the label "statist-nationalist" throughout, as a shortcut to characterize these coalitions generically, whether or not they have a confessional component, although occasionally I rely on the full "statist-nationalist-confessional" identification. On the global identity crisis at the end of the twentieth century, fueling ethnic and confessional revivalism, see Huntington (1996).

[48] On the relationship between populism and statism, see Castro and Ronci (1991: 157). Populism is distributive but not necessarily redistributive; the politically powerful benefit, not the very poor. It is generally biased toward an increase in urban middle-class income at the expense of rural producers, exporters, and foreign capital (Cardoso and Helwege 1991: 46). Adjustment measures directed at reducing state controls of prices, wages, and trade and at reorienting services and subsidies

American twentieth-century context as a set of economic policies designed to achieve specific political goals, such as, first, mobilizing support within organized labor and lower-middle-class groups, as well as from inward-looking industries, and second, politically isolating the rural oligarchy, foreign enterprises, and large-scale domestic industrial elites. Import-substitution industrialization, they argue, "provided the intellectual justification for policies that, if carried to extremes, resulted in populism" (p. 21). Economic nationalists found easy refuge in policies that stressed domestic production of goods for strategic reasons. In their extreme form, outright economic autarky and self-sufficiency—even under conditions of very small national markets—have been the cornerstone of inward-looking coalitions such as the "hermit kingdom" of North Korea.[49]

I identified earlier some constituencies likely to resist economic liberalization, such as import-competing firms with close ties to the state ("hothouse" industries), industrial bankers tied to protected industries, and sectors vulnerable to wide changes in international market conditions, all of which employ urban unskilled, formal sector blue-collar and white-collar workers. In addition, state bureaucracies, particularly those connected to planning, industrial policy, capital controls, and import licensing, are also threatened, as are state-owned enterprises and banks, politicians who fear the dismantling of such enterprises and the consequent erosion of their basis of political patronage, and the underemployed intelligentsia and symbolic analysts associated with all these groups.[50] Some of these opponents of liberalization stand to lose irreversibly whereas others bear transitional hardships with the potential—but no guarantees—for longer-term gains. Stabilization packages are far more likely to elicit mass protest than are structural programs, which prompt reactions from specific groups.[51] State entrepreneurship exists virtually everywhere, particularly in the industrializing world. However, whereas statist coalitions make it the pivotal engine in the economy, internationalist coalitions use state entrepreneurship to facilitate private-sector activity as well. The first replaces the market, the second promotes it.

Arms-importing and arms-producing military establishments are often adversely affected by adjustment programs, as is the military as an institution frequently addicted to heavy budgetary transfers supporting the lifestyles of senior officers.[52] There is generally a proliferation of military and security agen-

---

do not necessarily threaten the very poor and indeed may help them (Nelson 1992: 232). On populism and naive (mostly counterproductive) inflationary behavior, see Hirschman (1985: 67–68).

[49] North Korea's foreign trade by 1994 amounted to only 13 percent of its GNP (Pollack 1994a: A3) and was significantly lower in earlier periods.

[50] Kaufman (1989); Kallab and Feinberg (1989); Nelson (1992); Suleiman and Waterbury (1990: 15–19). Certain private economic groups may support privatization in principle but profit no less (and perhaps at lower risks) from expanded state economic activities and resources. On "hothouse" industries unable to compete internationally while enjoying advantages at home, see Sullivan (1994: 147). For a profile of industries that tend to seek protection, see Marks and McArthur (1993).

[51] Nelson (1990: 359).

[52] Sadowski (1993). Personnel costs account for between 50 and 70 percent of military expendi-

cies with overlapping jurisdictions competing for budgets. External threats are used to legitimize their existence, yet domestic repression and the ruling coalition's survival are their most common missions, as in Iraq and Syria.[53] Military-industrial complexes are also beneficiaries of indirect rents, through state subsidies of important inputs, including raw materials and energy, as in the Russian Republic. Such complexes (and rents) are often justified on the basis of their positive impact, or spin-offs, on the development of a modern economic infrastructure.[54] In some cases the military formally endorses broad liberal doctrines of economic organization (as did sections of the Argentine Navy for many years), while exerting pressure for de facto protectionist, mercantilist, and nationalizing policies within the military-industrial complex. For all these reasons, important sectors within the military have opposed economic liberalization, at least initially, in many cases, including Argentina, Brazil, Uruguay, and Egypt, as well as Turkey and Thailand.[55]

In Chile and South Korea, on the other hand, the leading political entrepreneurs (generals in both cases) coalesced their respective armed forces behind a strategy of integration into the global economy. In Algeria and Turkey, the military transformed itself from custodian of the post-independence statist-nationalist project to the main line of defense against recent confessional onslaughts on incipient liberalization. The interests of military factions differ, however, and understanding their respective positions regarding liberalization requires further empirical investigation. As Díaz Alejandro (1983:45) concluded prophetically in his study of international openness, "the nature and laws of motion of the collection of men in uniform are the darkest black boxes in Latin American social science, but one may conclude that the attitude of the armed forces toward economic openness has been neither unambiguous nor steady." Whatever its contextual proclivity, the military has generally exerted "veto player" (Tsebelis 1995) prerogatives throughout the industrializing world. Finally, highly fragmented armed forces have led to factions supporting different coalitional arrangements. Under such conditions, political entrepreneurs within or outside the armed forces (like presidents Park and Menem, respectively) have sometimes been able to impose a leading grand strategy over military factions, adding an intramilitary logrolling task to the more general effort to craft a viable coalition.

Overall, as many empirical examples in Part Two suggest, the possibility that military institutions are far more likely to join statist-nationalist than internationalizing coalitions turns dependencia-style arguments about a basic alliance between global capitalism and local military establishments on their heads. The

---

tures in most Third World countries (Ball 1988).

[53] Migdal (1988: 211–12). On how the level of military spending in most of these countries is determined more by economic constraints than by external "threat" factors, see Looney (1989).

[54] This approach to military investments is compatible with the "modernization model" associated with the work of Benoit (Chan 1992a: 3).

[55] On Turkey and Thailand, see Haggard and Webb (1994). On Argentina and Brazil, see Solingen (1996b). On Chile and South Korea, see Haggard and Kaufman (1995: 43).

domestic allies of global capitalism can be the military's most powerful political adversaries. In broad terms, the fact that the recent explosion of economic liberalization (and the rise of its political bearers) was associated with a dramatic collapse in budgetary allocations to the military—and in the latter's political leverage—deals a serious blow to dependency-deterministic theories of military institutions in the industrializing world.

Given their makeup and interests, inward-looking statist-nationalist coalitions reject fiscal orthodoxy and stabilization plans, particularly as imposed by the IMF and other financial institutions, and favor a more expansionary fiscal and monetary course.[56] Where they have been in power, their rule has often been characterized by persistently high budget deficits, inflation, excessive borrowing, and overvalued exchange rates. The military, state enterprises, and their protected suppliers and clients have captured a lion's share of rationed foreign exchange. The latter's scarcity induced further controls on imports, capital flows, and even foreign travel, to the detriment of export industries and other sectors that benefit from liberalization.[57]

As pointed out earlier regarding the composition of internationalist coalitions, the volatility and uncertainty accompanying market reform leaves wide segments of society behind the "veil of ignorance," that is, unable to figure out where and how they will come out at the end of the reform process. These groups become highly vulnerable to the presumed protective mantle of nationalist, statist, populist, and confessional ideologies.[58] This is no less true for students and intellectuals than it is for blue-collar workers or peasants, as is evident, for instance, in the Middle East and South Asia. Unemployed and underemployed scientists, scholars, and teachers regard statism as their last refuge, whereas their peers in transnationally integrated private firms have far fewer reservations over the dislocations engendered by economic liberalization. Statist-nationalist and confessional ideologies offer some protection from the material and spiritual onslaught resulting from marketization and internationalization.

Statist-nationalist coalitions cast the benefits from protection, statism, and a military-industrial complex as reaching relatively wide segments of the population, but such benefits are in fact captured largely by public bureaucracies, inefficient producers, and the high brass.[59] The onset of economic liberalization gradually concentrates such benefits more and more. That is, the degree of concentration of benefits is positively related with the degree of liberalization

---

[56] On the preference for inflationary, weak-currency, nationalist, or "fiscalist" policies by uncompetitive, domestically bound, and nontradable producers, see Frieden (1995: 293).

[57] Summers and Thomas (1995).

[58] On how a stable political economy rarely breeds populism, whereas political and economic instability—and discontent—begets it, see Castro and Ronci (1991).

[59] Expansionary policies may prevent unemployment in the short run, but often produce high inflation that undermines employment in the longer run (Alesina 1994). On how widespread trade restrictions increase rather than decrease income inequality, see Rodrick (1994: 66). On how public expenditures are used opportunistically to please the military, see Ames (1987).

under way, although benefits are not captured primarily by diffuse interests even prior to liberalization. The economic costs of statism, militarization, and protection for diffuse interests are low relative to the enormous benefits that all three policies yield to the respective beneficiaries. The incentives for political mobilization—given their concentrated interests—are quite high for the beneficiaries of these policies. Their ability to prevail politically is enhanced by their control of important state institutions and symbols. Meanwhile, high inflation worsens income distribution, punishing labor and the middle class the most, while allowing those better positioned to play the financial markets and to be rescued from the negative impact of inflation.[60]

Civic nationalist and majority ethnonationalist and confessional movements are not merely natural partners in the logrolling of these coalitions but are important keys to mass political mobilization.[61] These movements appeal to communal, "organic" values that are often threatened by the crude impersonality of market forces and their guiding principle of efficiency. Statist "*Völkisch* populism laden with racism and nationalism*" (Gourevitch 1986: 27) is clearly not a new socio-political phenomenon under the twentieth-century sun. In fact, inward-looking bourgeoisies share some commonalities, such as uncritical nationalism and idealization of cultural values (*Innerlichkeit*), with the nineteenth-century German bourgeoisie.[62] Particularly during the early stages of marketization, widening social disparities puncture the mantle of solidarity encouraged by ties of nationality, ethnicity, religion, or language. Generalized uncertainty and insecurity prevail at that point.[63] Nationalist and confessional responses to marketization have appropriated long-standing critiques of capitalism as wasteful and corrupting. Leaders of such movements often point to the beneficiaries of economic liberalization as exemplars of venal and unethical lifestyles, quite accurately in some cases, but this phenomenon is no less evident among political entrepreneurs in the nationalist and confessional camps.[64]

Marketization and internationalization are not the only sources of nationalist and confessional mobilization but are certainly powerful ones, as Gellner (1983) suggests, particularly in the hands of skillful political leaders able to

---

[60] Cardoso, Barros, and Urani (1995).

[61] On the historical connection between the rise of nationalism, massive increases in armed forces and taxation, and the growth and centralization of nation-states, see Tilly (1994). On how nationalism and religious fundamentalism converge in the Middle East, see Leca (1994).

[62] See Johnson (1993: 220) and Craig, preface to Kehr (1977: xi). Attacks by populist-nationalists on "internationalists" as agents of central and private banks—laced with religious overtones—are not historically limited to the fascism and Nazism of earlier decades, or to the industrializing world. In the US in the 1990s, Patrick Buchanan, Pat Robertson, and Louis Farrakhan have embraced conspiratorial and allegedly racist theories of international banking, as well (Rich 1995).

[63] On reliance on ethnic ties as a logical means to overcome security dilemmas, see Posen (1993).

[64] A more or less generalized instance of the latter is provided in the rackets run by Islamic agencies in Iran, where the official Islamic neighborhood committees extract payments in exchange for withholding inspections designed to monitor the upholding of religious standards in private activities (Sanger 1995). In the words of former Iranian Prime Minister Mehdi Bazargan, "the scale of corruption is breathtaking" (ibid.).

identify an effective antidote to unwanted and painful change. Expanding global trade exerts pressure toward convergence not just in prices but also in norms and social institutions. Rodrik (1997) points to the arbitraging effects of open trade, which induce stress on long-standing social contracts and norms. Lingering national and confessional memories and myths, particularly where they become threatened by this arbitraging effect, acquire a heightened mobilizing potential.[65] As Cox (1986: 219) argued, collective images of social orders—of the legitimacy of certain power relations, the meaning of justice—are not reducible to material capabilities. Yet economic, technological, institutional, and military configurations tend to encourage certain collective images. Thus the differentiation between "primordialist" and "modernist" approaches drawn by Smith (1986) is useful for a preliminary conceptualization of nationalism, but empirical research often reveals a more integrated operation of so-called irrational and utilitarian (or instrumental) factors. Memories of things past are very important in the political construction of ethnic and religious identity.

Economic liberalization has a global referent. Thus, statist-nationalist and confessional entrepreneurs and movements thrive on popular resentment over what they regard as externally imposed adjustment policies, over reliance on foreign investment, and over the "Western" principles and norms embodied in most international regimes. In extreme cases, as with right or left revolutionaries and religious fundamentalists, the choices are presented more starkly, favoring a sharp delinking from the global political economy that helps establish their power and bring about a radical transformation in the domestic economy and polity.[66] A confessional solvent can be poured successfully into an objective context of crisis and deprivation. Highly organized confessional groups step in to provide a safety net against the compounded explosive impact of a stale populist model and incipient liberalization. Ethno-confessional entrepreneurs excel at mobilizing social movements through welfare associations, schools, and professional networks, as throughout the Islamic world. Turkey's Nekmetin Erbakan relied on democratic procedures and a deep rift among liberalizers to turn his Welfare party's 21.38 percent majority (1995 elections) into his springboard to power. The weakness of his political opponents—Erbakan declared—was their "strongly capitalistic economic program, which helps a very small elite and leaves the rest of our people in misery," their lack of identity and "sick" imitation of the West, and their secularism.[67] Erbakan's campaign speeches further reveal his political strategy: "We will set up an Islamic United Nations, an Islamic NATO, and an Islamic version of the European Union. We will create an Islamic currency." In the context of the rise of confessionalism in Middle East politics, Erbakan has been considered a moderate, not a fundamentalist.

---

[65] On the special role of myths in nationalism, see Hosking and Schopflin (1997). For a specification of the conditions under which these memories and myths have a greater or lesser potential to exacerbate conflict, see Van Evera (1994).

[66] Díaz Alejandro (1983: 48).

[67] All citations in this paragraph are from "Islamic Leader Is First Non-Secular Turk Premier in 75 years," *New York Times*, 29 June 1996: 5.

At times the coalition's material pillar against internationalization and liberalization is stronger, as where state enterprises and import-substituting interests are powerful. At other times, the confessional component becomes a driving force.[68] Very frequently entrepreneurs rely on logrolling across both groups to reinforce their joint appeal, which strengthens their ability to reach new groups who feel uncertain about their own post-liberalization fate. The paradox of weakened statist-nationalist parties (such as Egypt's Socialist Labor party) or weakened Marxist parties (such as the Palestinian movement's PFLP and DFLP) that ally themselves with the Muslim Brotherhood and Hamas quickly dissolves when we bear in mind their calculus of potential advantages from jointly challenging internationalizing coalitions in a marriage of convenience. A natural consequence of logrolling—allowing each partner in the coalition to get what it wants most—can, however, infuse statist-nationalist-confessional coalitions with stress. Certain protectionist, nationalist, and military segments are forced to swallow their more secular outlook, while confessional groups must compromise some religious injunctions (such as *zakat*, Islam's taxes on wealth and income, or *riba*, interest), where these threaten their partners' interests.[69] Islamic movements want to capture the state to exploit its educational and indoctrinating capacity, in addition to its material resources. Despite a presumed fundamental doctrinal affinity between Islam and small private entrepreneurship, the record of Islamist regimes so far suggests that, once in power, they do not dismantle the state economically while building its potential for indoctrination: they use the state's economic power to service indoctrination. Not all confessional movements that oppose internationalization embrace militarized strategies. Some are largely political movements (Algeria's Islamic Salvation Front), as opposed to primarily military organizations (Algeria's Armed Islamic Group), although it is not always easy to disentangle their intricate patterns of reciprocal support. As Salamé (1993) and Razi (1990) have argued, in practice moderates and militants alike have played a political game that mutually bolsters their bargaining power.

In some cases confessionally based political movements become allies of internationalist coalitions. This is mostly the case where such movements benefit from international openness and are potential targets of hegemonic ethnic or religious movements, as has traditionally been the case with Lebanese and Egyptian Christians, Alawite Turks, and, to some extent, Rwandan Tutsis and Iraqi Kurds. Moreover, coalitions can embrace economic liberalization without abandoning their political reliance on a confessional mantle of legitimacy, as in Pakistan, Saudi Arabia, the Gulf Cooperation Council, Malaysia, and Indonesia. However, in these cases Islamic content is pursued insofar as it does not impinge on internationalist political-economic strategies, the reverse of which is

---

[68] For an analysis of the political consequences of privatization that is sensitive to broad distributional consequences across class, occupation, and racial categories, see Feigenbaum and Henig (1994).

[69] See, for instance, Kuran (1993, 1995). On the tension between ideological purity and the desire to exercise power in predicting coalitional formation, see Leiserson (1970).

true (so far and for the most part) for the self-proclaimed "true" Islamic republics in existence—Iran and Sudan—and for the overwhelming majority of fundamentalist Islamist challengers. The Saudi ruling coalition (that is, the extensive royal family) is known more for its commitment to the accummulation and consumption of wealth than for its devotion to ascetic Islamic lifestyles.[70] It has thus relied on an internationalist strategy that advances its most valued preference, subordinating other political instruments to that goal. Similarly, internationalizing coalitions in Pakistan have gone along with the selective application of the *sharia* (Islamic law) insofar as this would not upset the benefits of economic reform and international exchange. Thus, the Saudi and Pakistani coalitions differ from radical confessionalism in that they have subordinated the pursuit of Islamist values to their primary (internationalist) political-economic strategy, whether for instrumental or genuine reasons.[71] Despite heavy weapons acquisitions, their regional policies are essentially more a matter of insurance than of offense, particularly as they face aggressive statist-nationalist and confessional adversaries in the region. The Saudi military often finds ample justification for its appetite for arms in the need to counter the radical coalitions that rule neighboring Iraq and Iran. Pakistan is alleged to pursue a nuclear deterrent, nurtured by its own lingering statist-nationalist coalition. At the same time, while facing a nuclear-capable India, incipient liberalizers in Pakistan have advocated a nuclear-weapons-free zone in South Asia, and even expressed some interest in joining the Nonproliferation Treaty unilaterally (without India doing so), only to be subdued by their resilient statist-nationalist-confessional opposition.[72]

The fit between statism and protectionism on the one hand and nationalism, militarism, and confessionalism on the other is fairly powerful but not perfect. Political entrepreneurs may cater to a nationalist-confessional and an economically liberalizing constituency at the same time, as Israel's Prime Minister Benjamin Netanyahu did during the electoral campaign of May 1996. However, the inherent tension between the two strategies came into relief with the significant flow of internationalist constituencies away from Netanyahu's Likud-led coalition. Moreover, statist-nationalist and confessional parties within this coalition have—as of 1997—overwhelmed a feeble liberalizing fringe (Finance Minister Dan Meridor's resignation is but one symptom of their victory). Reliance on the populist, developing-town, nationalist, and confessional vote has progressively

[70] At the same time, the regime's distributive efforts may have foiled the decades-long prediction—so far falsified—of its imminent demise. Where the benefits are relatively more widely distributed there is less need to rely on external scapegoating. Despite their earlier short-sighted financing of a variety of infamous radical groups, Saudi policy in the region has been generally more restrained than that of other Islamist and secular nationalist regimes.

[71] Nawaz Sharif, a representative of Pakistani industrial interests backed by pragmatic Islamist groups, lamented the political energy invested in domestic debates over Islamization "while the world is marching fast to meet the challenges [of] the twenty-first century" (Mayer 1993: 131). Some Islamist groups do not see any inherent tension between international economic exchange and technological modernization on the one hand and Islamist principles on the other.

[72] *Eye on Supply*, Monterey Institute of International Studies No. 6 (Spring 1992: 11).

submerged liberalizing elements within Likud. Each of these constituencies is inherently rent-seeking, demanding subsidies along socio-economic or religious lines, cheap housing, imperial infrastructural projects, and new settlements in the West Bank and Gaza, all of which can translate into a reality that transcends electoral promises of growth, stabilization and adjustment. Simply put, liberalization is not Netanyahu's most valued preference, and other aspects of an internationalist agenda (such as regional concessions and harmonizing policies vis-à-vis international institutions) are anathema to most of his coalitional partners. Internationalist constituencies in Israel are massively entrenched in Labor's political camp. As will be evident from a variety of cases—from Latin America to Serbia, Israel, and South Asia—one finance minister with internationalist tendencies does not make an internationalist agenda. The implausibility of internationalizing reforms under statist-nationalist leadership is also evident from the case of Syria, where some liberalizing goals have been forfeited when the core objectives of the military-industrial complex were at stake. President Asad thus proclaimed his commitment to "a stubborn pursuit of the national struggle against Israel even at the expense of economic development."[73] Syria also highlights the interesting case of a minority confessional group (Alawites) using Arab nationalism, statism, and populism to deflect a reality of effective dominance over a Sunni majority.

As the last point suggests, the notion of logrolling as exchanging the mutual rights of partners to seek their most valued preference is essential to understanding why the components of a statist-nationalist-populist and sometimes confessional coalition gravitate toward each other. Some aspect of an internationalist agenda—but not necessarily all—fundamentally threatens their political well-being, propelling them into a coalition with otherwise strange bedfellows. The consortium of old-styled statist-nationalist parties in the Arab world with Islamist parties and movements is but one example. The cooperation of fascists and communists in President Tudjman's nationalist Croatian Democratic Union is another. The convergence between Israel's confessional-populist Shas and other Likud coalitional constituents—despite Shas's earlier "conciliatory" positions on regional matters—is a third. Although identifying most valued preferences is rarely an easy feat, this overview suggests that neither is it always elusive, even when such preferences shift over time. Clearly, politician Yaacov Deri estimated correctly that failing to endorse a Hebron agreement with the Palestinian Authority would not break his political hold on Shas.[74]

Finally, this overview highlights the strong personalistic component in the logrolling of statist-nationalist constituent parties / movements and coalitions (both for civic nationalist and confessional variants), even in formally demo-

---

[73] Hinnebusch (1993: 189).

[74] Deri allegedly threatened Prime Minister Netanyahu to withhold support from the key Hebron agreement if a political ally of Deri wasn't selected to be attorney general, expecting that ally to void pending legal procedures against Deri. Shas supporters poured into the streets endorsing Deri's leadership. In the end Deri did not have to oppose the Hebron agreement, but he estimated correctly that he could afford to do so.

cratic contexts.[75] Personalities play an important role in internationalist contexts as well, particularly in the launching of reforms and initial logrolling of support for them. However, once the grand strategy becomes politically entrenched, the centrality of the organizing entrepreneur to the strategy's survival recedes far more frequently in an internationalist context than in a statist-nationalist one.

The Grand Strategy of Statist-Nationalist and Confessional Coalitions

The preferences, composition, organization, and logrolling patterns of statist-nationalist and confessional coalitions make them prone to embrace certain regional policies that advance their grand strategy. Actors aggregated in these coalitions perceive regional cooperative outcomes as weakening them politically and economically, for many of the same reasons that internationalist coalitions expect such outcomes to benefit them. From the vantage point of statist-nationalist and confessional coalitions, prospective peace settlements, cooperative regional contexts, and arms control agreements are generally detrimental to their interests for the following reasons: They legitimize downsized allocations to the military and weapons-producing enterprises; they deprive the coalitions of mythmaking, a major source of political capital; and they weaken the coalitions' ability to justify societal extraction to benefit an array of statist and confessional interests.

Downsizing Allocations to the Military and Weapons-Producing Enterprises. A cooperative regional context weakens the justification for the extraction of societal resources for military purposes. Yet the military regards its institutional mission of confronting external threats as unchanged, and resists having to carry out that mission with fewer resources.[76] Moreover, where external threats are downplayed, it is less justifiable to maintain export-oriented military-industrial complexes as it was, for example, during the Cold War, because the commercial justification for such complexes has withered away as well. Militarization is not subsidiary to larger political-economic objectives but built into the grand strategy of statist-nationalist-confessional coalitions, for which military prowess constitutes a core basis of legitimacy, as in Iraq and North Korea. This is not to say that the military is invariably interested in actualizing its war-fighting potential. Indeed it sometimes seeks to avoid military showdowns that might endanger its leadership or its integrity. But the military as an institution is interested in maintaining (at a minimum) and broadening (where possible) its own share of budgetary resources in order to guarantee its wealth, autonomy, and prestige.[77] As a brigadier in command of Brazil's Aerospace Technical Center explained: "We wished [tensions with Argentina] had continued, because we

---

[75] On the historical affinity between populism, a personalistic, paternalistic, and often charismatic leadership, and mobilization from the top down, see Drake (1991: 36) and Castro and Ronci (1991: 152). On the centrality of "visionary" leaders to economic reform, see Williamson (1994).

[76] At the same time, nationalist coalitions are often reluctant to mobilize resources abroad, and new global realities—political and economic—preclude that option in any event.

[77] Van Evera (1993). On the relationship between the military's offensive doctrines and the production of arms races (that is, the expansion of resources for the military-industrial complex), see Posen (1984).

would have received a higher allocation for our work [on military nuclear technologies]."[78] Finally, external threats are efficient not only for increasing access to material resources but also for amalgamating the armed forces internally, particularly in cases where dangerous cleavages along political, economic, confessional, or hierarchical issues have permeated the military.

Academic and policy analysts have often misread programs aimed at developing weapons of mass destruction in the industrializing world, by considering them as rationally estimated efforts to pursue cost-effective security objectives (as in "more bang for the buck"). In reality, such programs have often become budgetary black holes employing several times the required number of scientists, technologists, and bureaucrats. Nuclear programs in particular have been ideal technological allies of statist-nationalist coalitions for various reasons: they enable the construction of a dense scientific, technological, industrial, and bureaucratic complex, which often dwarfs other statist endeavors;[79] this complex is often beyond the formal budgetary oversight; and the actual or imaginary output of this large-scale provider of rents itself becomes a powerful source of myths. It is not entirely unexpected, therefore, that inward-looking nationalist regimes have historically exaggerated regional threats as a pretext for not joining or complying with the global nonproliferation regime, or with any regional alternative to it.[80]

Devalued Role of Mythmaking. Mythmaking—a major source of political capital—entails the ability to mobilize militant religious, ethnic, or cultural groups against an actual or imagined regional adversary (Snyder 1991). Myths may have some connection to reality, but the connection is often flimsy.[81] Self-reliance is a central myth of inward-looking coalitions, either in their secular form (as in North Korea's *juche* and India's *swadeshi*) or their confessional form. Statist-nationalist and confessional coalitions are prone to rely on legitimating symbols, such as sovereignty, geographical and territorial integrity, self-reliance, and confessional unity and purity.[82] Reliance on con-

[78] Interview with *Veja*, quoted in Joint Publications Research Service, *Latin America* (Springfield, Va.: National Technical Information Service), 22 March 1993: 20.

[79] On the high levels of nuclear industrial investments in Argentina and Brazil, see Solingen (1996b). A nuclear weapons program alone (separate from nuclear industrial investments) in India was expected to require three-fourths of the entire outlay of the proposed Fourth Five-Year Plan (Reiss 1988: 213). For a perspective that helps debunk the conventional wisdom that nuclear weapons are universally cheap, see Miller (1993).

[80] This is different from arguing that nuclear programs in every region have similar origins, although an amazing number do. On the relationship between coalition-type and nuclear postures, see Solingen (1994b).

[81] The Muslim-led coalition labeled Bosnia a "millenial state" when in fact, since its conquest by the Turks in 1462, Bosnia has been ruled by the Ottoman and Austro-Hungarian empires, a royalist Yugoslav government, a puppet pro-Nazi regime, and communist Yugoslavia (Cohen 1994). The Bosnian Serb leaders promoted the image of a Bosnia that has always been Serbian, when in fact the fourteenth-century Dusan Serbian empire included little of today's Bosnia, and certainly not Sarajevo. On chauvinist mythmaking as a hallmark of nationalism, see Van Evera (1994).

[82] On nationalists' affinity with the acquisition of neighboring land through military means, and

spiratorial theories goes hand in hand with the need to protect these symbols. Moreover, these coalitions are more likely to come to power by revolutionary means than are their internationalist counterparts. The postrevolutionary regime often relies on a mobilizing ideology to stabilize its rule and establish its legitimacy. Myths of external threats are central to this legitimation. The use of myths for domestic consumption generates *real* external threats, and at times aggression, even if the revolutionary regime had no actual intention of launching a war.[83]

Eroding Statist-Nationalist and Confessional Privileges. A cooperative regional context with a devalued role for myths also undermines the entitlements of statist-nationalist and confessional interests. For instance, Iraqi and Iranian state exterprises (including Islamist "welfare" patronages), not merely military agencies, have derived significant advantages from external conflicts and heightened mythmaking.[84] Similarly, "national security" myths have proven to be quite effective as a means to justify the protection of state-owned enterprises. As Porter (1994: 13) argues, no theory explains bureaucratic growth as consistently as war and military rivalry. This point evokes Tilly's (1985) notion of external threats as a racket, where statist-nationalist and confessional coalitions fabricate such threats and then extract resources (yielding both tribute and rents) to neutralize the presumed menace.

Where most of the negative domestic externalities from liberalization and regional cooperation are captured by politically strong statist-nationalist and confessional entrepreneurs and constituencies with intense preferences, they resist the internationalist agenda most forcefully, and sometimes quite effectively.[85] Given their constituent basis of domestic political support, inward-looking coalitions, unlike their internationalist adversaries, are also more resilient to coercive international intervention in the management of regional conflict, and even appear to excel in converting such external interventions into domestic political profit. Hence statist-nationalist-confessional coalitions have defied political and economic sanctions from great powers and international institutions, from Iraq and Iran to Serbia, Libya, and North Korea. In all these cases, powerful import-substituting economic interests prospered from international closure, and despite potential bottlenecks in the supply of inputs, the military and its productive complex were largely protected from the effects of sanctions. Moreover, sanctions strengthened a variety of state agencies and industries in charge of

---

on trading states' emphasis on global resources, capital, technology, and markets, rather than territories and population, see Rosecrance (1986).

[83] On the external behavior of revolutionary regimes and the heightened probability of war, see Walt (1996).

[84] On how external threats offer the opportunity to expand state activities, revenues, and rents, see Tilly (1985), Rasler and Thompson (1989), and Lake (1992).

[85] On how concentrated losses often yield a particularly strong political opposition to liberalization, see Haggard and Kaufman (1992).

productive and distributive functions.[86] These effects, however, are relatively short-lived and, over the long haul, can severely threaten the survival of these coalitions (although one wonders how long the haul can be, given the experiences of Kim Il Sung, Muʿammar Ghadafi, Hafiz al-Assad, and Saddam Hussein—not to mention Fidel Castro).

In all these cases, political longevity has everything to do with a ruthless grip on power. Yet the self-defeating (strategically suboptimal) outcome of these policies, reflected in politically weakened and delegitimized regimes, becomes evident. The defiant behavior of extremist statist-nationalist coalitions can be interpreted in five ways. 1. These coalitions may fail to act strategically because their immediate survival imposes a short-term horizon and excessive rent seeking (Argentina's Leopoldo Galtieri, Serbia's Slobodan Milosevic, Azerbaijan's Abulfaz Elchibey).[87] 2. They may act strategically in the belief that their "standing up to the world" will secure future political benefits (Iraq's Saddam Hussein, Egypt's Nasser, Argentina's Perón). 3. They may be impermeable to learning (Libya's Muʿammar Ghadafi). 4. They may have no other choice, given their political makeup, than to play this all-out, risky (sometimes suicidal) strategy. 5. They may fail to estimate accurately the negative consequences of vote trading, as with Snyder's (1991) agents of imperial overexpansion. These mutually compatible possibilities provide a rationale for the higher risk-accepting propensity of statist-nationalist and confessional coalitions, relative to internationalist ones, a characteristic that permeates their domestic, regional, and global policies. Finally, where war is proximate to the revolutionary takeover, statist-nationalist rule often becomes more nationalistic, radical, and centralizing, as with Kim Il Sung, Nasser, Assad, the Ayatollah Khomeini, and Castro.[88]

The empirical cases in Part Two highlight the wide variety of statist-nationalist coalitions, from their most extreme to their more moderate versions, with or without confessional elements. In the Middle East, populist-confessional challengers (fundamentalists, in their most radical variants) offer themselves as an alternative to an array of internationalizing coalitions (royalist with a pragmatic Islamic bent as well as secular).[89] Their political platform advances a political

---

[86] Rowe (1993) explains this logic. Sanctions raise the domestic price of the sanctioned import. The affected government steps in to organize trade in that sector as a monopsonist, helping it capture some of the economic rents generated by the sanctions. Rationed goods become a political resource in the hands of the sanctioned government. Beneficiaries of sanctions—import-competing producers—now become more concentrated and can exert greater political influence.

[87] On the affinity of populism and short-term horizons, see Castro and Ronci (1991). On cartelized systems, immobile interests (assets), and short time horizons, see Snyder (1991: 49).

[88] On the impact of war on the extremism and coercion of revolution, see Gurr (1988) and Goldstone (1996/97).

[89] I follow As'ad AbuKhalil (1994: 677) here in using "Islamic fundamentalism" to refer to "all those movements and groups that aspire to the complete application of Islamic laws, as interpreted by leaders of the movements, in society and the body politic." The generic applicability of the concept of fundamentalism invalidates the critique of this term—by apologists of Islamic fundamentalism—as ethnocentric. In the Middle East, Islamic and Jewish fundamentalists are equally characterized by an effort to build theocratic states, whether they accept democracy as the appropriate means or not.

economy rooted in what they regard as Islamic principles, and involves a rejection of international economic regimes and their perceived associated scourges, such as inequalities, corruption, unemployment, and enslaving indebtedness. In their proposed new socio-political order there is little room for regional reconciliation with "apostate" Arab regimes, let alone with Israel. Both Iran and Sudan, as well as many Islamist challengers that constitute the largest political opposition throughout the region, have legitimized the use of violent means to undermine the viability of domestic and regional internationalizing adversaries.[90]

Statist-nationalist and confessional coalitions in South Asia have also aggregated political actors opposing economic reform and international regimes, as well as those upholding combative postures vis-à-vis their stated regional rival. This is evident in the platforms of Pakistan's radical Islamic party Jama'at-i-Islam and of India's fundamentalist Hindu Bharatiya Janata Party (BJP), although the BJP has used confessional issues more instrumentally. The instrumental use of confessional themes is also characteristic of Israel's Likud coalition, which shares its tent with Jewish fundamentalist groups, in spite of a fairly secular history.[91] As argued earlier (and more extensively in Chapter Six), Likud represented free enterprise liberalism in earlier times but has played a progressively populist, nationalist, and confessional card in the last two decades. Politically captive to these constituencies (particularly West Bank settlers, religious parties, developing-town and protectionist interests) and to some groups resisting the contraction of the military-industrial complex, Likud's Netanyahu and his political allies prevailed by a small margin in 1996 elections, largely by challenging Labor-Meretz peace initiatives toward the Palestinians and Syria.

In the Southern Cone the dominance of statist nationalism for decades precluded effective denuclearization and genuinely integrative regional economic frameworks. Of all the statist-nationalist coalitions that dominated this region in the postwar era—from Perón onward—Argentina's were the least stable, continuously challenged by either competing statist-nationalist factions (military or otherwise) or liberalizing factions, or both. The "outbidding" among statist-nationalist variants is key to explaining the extreme nature of Argentina's grand strategy in its internal, regional, and international dimensions, as well as the strategy's corollaries: military crises and mobilizations (the Beagle conflict), a war with Great Britain (over the Malvinas / Falklands), and a bid for nuclear supremacy (vis-à-vis Brazil).

We can now sum up the relationship between coalitional type and grand strategy (see Table 1).

1. Internationalist and statist-nationalist coalitions differ in their preferences for domestic and international resource extraction and allocation, in the nature of state-society compacts they advance, in their patterns of aggregation, articulation, and log-

---

[90] Haeri (1991); Sisk (1992). On the material and ideal basis of Islamist responses to globalization (in their view, synonymous with Westernization), see Pasha and Samatar (1996).

[91] On the anti-Western element among some religious fundamentalist groups in Israel, see Greenberg (1994).

rolling of coalitional interests, in their time horizons, in their orientations toward risk-accepting regional and international behavior, and in the role of personalistic elements.

2. Statist-nationalist coalitions are oriented toward either what Barnett (1992) labels an "accommodationist" strategy of mobilization of societal resources for security objectives (that is, a strategy that maintains the basic compact between a robust entrepreneurial "state" and societal interests) or toward a centralizing restructural strategy (increasing state control over the economy and society). Internationalist coalitions, instead, aim at restructuring state-society relations by divesting state participation in productive activities while investing "virtual states" with the task of developing a human and physical infrastructure aimed at expanding material wealth in an internationalized economy.[92]

3. Successfully implemented and sustained internationalist grand strategies lead to leaner states with meaner capabilities, as the state can convert high levels of accumulated foreign exchange into military assets and maximize its access to outside inputs.[93] Moreover, such states can rely on a wealthier tax base, should a deepened extraction of resources be required. Conversely, statist-nationalist strategies sap private and public resources in the long run, and are unable to uphold a high level of either military expenditures or societal extraction. Internationalist coalitions may invest in military capabilities but prevent such investments from overwhelming domestic reform, regional stability, or global access. Statist-nationalist coalitions create and maintain a *Werhwirtschaft* (war economy) that functions as their core political pivot.

4. Regional cooperative policies hold different payoffs for each of these coalitions. Cooperation is expected to have positive effects at home and abroad for internationalist coalitions, because a cooperative regional order enables the pursuit of economic reform while spelling transparency, predictability, a good reputation, and the blessing of the international community. A cooperative regional order weakens statist-nationalist and confessional coalitions because it undermines the viability of state agencies and enterprises associated with military functions and production, threatens with extinction the state's ability—heretofore justified in "state-building" and national security terms—to disburse resources among rent-seeking groups, and deprives populist entrepreneurs of a rich fountain of myths. External conflict is the sinew connecting different partners to statist, nationalist, and confessional coalitions.

5. Internationalist coalitions embrace domestic, regional, and global policies that may be politically risky in the short term (as in Israel's Labor-Meretz defeat in 1996) but potentially rewarding over the long haul (as suggested by Argentina's Menem reelection in 1995). Statist-nationalist-confessional coalitions rely on domestic, regional, and global strategies with short-term political payoffs that are fundamentally counterproductive in the long run, as with Egypt's Nasser. Coalitional durability in either case, of course, is not merely a reflection of policy success but also of the existence of democratic institutions, whose absence can make the long run longer.

---

[92] On the virtual state that stimulates and coordinates foreign direct investment under conditions of mobile factors of production, see Rosecrance (1996).

[93] Liberalization does not necessarily shrink the size of the state but invariably changes its nature to accommodate hard budgets, consistent fiscal policy, and shifts in public spending away from the productive sector and into social services and infrastructure (World Bank 1996, chapter 7).

TABLE 1
Selected Characteristics of Competing Grand Strategies

Selected Characteristics of Grand Strategy	Statist-Nationalist-Confessional Coalitions	Internationalist Coalitions
State-society compact	maintenance/expansion of an entrepreneurial "robust state"	divesting state control, ushering of "virtual state"
Ratio of resource extraction to military allocations	high (*werhwirschaft* as core basis of legitimacy)	low (subordinated to liberalizing economic requirements)
Short-term risks and advantages	risks: war	risks: vulnerability to international markets; economic crisis ("valley of transition"); and diminished military capabilities
	advantages: high political mobilization potential	advantages: high economic mobilization potential (particularly of international resources)
Long-term risks and advantages	risks: economic collapse and sapped military strength	risks: international political vulnerability
	advantages: higher (but not unlimited) resilience to international pressures	advantages: deepening of resource extraction and military capabilities
Implications for regional cooperation	cooperation threatens: 1. viability of statist, inward-looking, military, and ethno-confessional enterprises and bureaucracies; 2. their associated myths, and hence: 3. the very lifeline of the coalition	cooperation enables: 1. economic reform at home; 2. the flow of international resources, and hence: 3. strengthening of the coalition's political lifeline
Role of ethno-confessional card	logrolled to *buttress* the coalition's rejection of an internationalizing strategy	logrolled to *tame* ethno-confessionalism while subordinating it to an internationalist strategy
Role of entrepreneurial personalism	central to both logrolling and long-term survival of the coalition's grand strategy	less central to the long-term survival of a liberalizing grand strategy

Both coalitional strategies have coexisted with democratic and authoritarian institutions. Global market and institutional structures—discussed at the end of this chapter—affect that durability as well, through a mix of threats and opportunities.

These are the general political contours shaping the grand strategies and regional policies of internationalist and statist-nationalist-confessional coalitions. As contours, they portray more about the ideal type than about the real ones, which often approximate hybrids. Indeed the empirical analysis in Part Two, like some of the examples above, suggests that many coalitions pursue hybrid strategies, although often with a predominant emphasis. The "purity" of the strategies and the extent to which they can be followed unhindered is contingent on the relative political strength of the respective coalitions, to which I turn now.

COALITIONAL STRENGTH AND THE PURSUIT OF GRAND STRATEGY

There is no deterministic relationship between the character (composition, goals, and objectives) of a coalition and policy outputs, let alone outcomes. Coalitional policy preferences (aspirations) are important, but the actual constraints and incentives they face matter a great deal, shaping the probability that coalitional makeup and performance will match. The ability of either coalition type to implement its preferred strategy in both its domestic and external aspects is contingent on its cohesiveness and on the amount of political resources it has amassed relative to its opposition, including the resources to buy off groups otherwise inimical to the ruling coalition's preferred policy.

A coalition's internal cohesiveness is given by the degree of macropolitical consensus reigning in its midst. Macropolitical consensus is the expression of widely shared preferences over macropolitical goals among major actors.[94] Macropolitical goals are those at the apex of the coalition's hierarchy of goals and means. They may involve the pursuit of export-led growth and macroeconomic stability, or of a more egalitarian income distribution, or of a confessionally based new economic order. Such goals can be deduced from an analysis of policy options most likely to advance their agenda. For instance, insofar as a political entrepreneur puts together a coalition representing politically powerful import-substituting producers and a dominant labor union aggregating mostly nontradable sectors, policy demands are likely to converge against reform.[95] The intensity of preferences and organizational skills of coalitional partners affects the likely conversion of demands into policy. Thus, the institutional arrangements mediating between the preferences of socio-economic and political actors (such as the military) encode a large part of the story regarding how convergent and cohesive a coalition is likely to be. Macropolitical goals are

[94] Solingen (1996b).

[95] On the organization of labor market institutions and their orientation toward internationalization, see Garrett and Lange (1996: 57–60). On asset specificity, industrial concentration, and the intensity of preferences, see Frieden (1991b).

often captured in declaratory policy and informal statements by coalitional partners and political entrepreneurs, as well as in party platforms and legislative
debates. High levels of macropolitical consensus lower the costs of logrolling,
produce internally consistent strategies, and strengthen coalitional stability.

The strength of coalitions and their representative entrepreneurs is also affected by their ability and commitment—as a result of historical trajectories,
for instance—to broaden their basis of support. Coalitional resources can thus
be applied to compensate groups and institutions that either have a built-in
preference for the alternative grand strategy, or are unable to assess the longer-
term impact of reform. Inherited conditions such as economic collapse, fragile
political institutions, and defeat in war tend to constrain the availability of com-
pensating resources, as in many a Middle East state. Coalitions that are cohesive and resourceful end up broadening their electoral appeal, legislative votes,
and approval rates. In addition to these "positive" measures of coalitional
strength, "negative" measures are equally important in estimating coalitional
strength. These include, for instance, the incidence and scope of challenges to
the coalition in the form of no-confidence votes, mass protests, threats of a
military coup, capital flight, terrorist bombs, labor strikes, and a general unrelenting political mobilization against it. Together, positive and negative measures of coalitional strength provide a foundation against which one can estimate a coalition's ability to implement its grand strategy in a more or less
coherent and expedient fashion. The weaker the ruling coalition is vis-à-vis its
opposition, the less coherent and expedient that implementation can be expected to be. An opposition that is largely consensual in its macropolitical objectives, has considerable command over resources, and is effectively organized
can pose a formidable barrier to the implementation of grand strategies. A divided and loosely organized opposition, on the other hand, allows a ruling coalition greater latitude, without forcing it to water down its preferences.[96]

From our overview so far it is clear that there is considerable variation in the
way in which the preferences of different coalitions are aggregated throughout
the world and that institutions play a major role in shaping coalitional arrangements. Democratic institutions, for instance, can strengthen diffuse interests at
the expense of concentrated ones, a subject I discuss in Chapter Four. In some
cases institutions benefit internationalist coalitions, in others their opponents.
Proportional representation can make it more difficult for an internationalist
coalition in which each constituent group holds a veto power to apply economic
stabilization measures, as the case of Brazil suggests.[97] Political parties, trade
unions, and ethnic and confessional movements can help make the consequences of economic liberalization more transparent than they would otherwise
be. They may also play on uncertainties about distributional outcomes—of material and ideal values—to buttress policies they prefer. Institutional resources
are thus very important in shaping the political field on which coalitions vie for

---

[96] On watering down preferences in foreign policy, see Hagan (1993).
[97] Alesina (1994: 53).

political power. Whether political parties or their equivalent aggregate interests over broad sectoral categories or represent specific classes has consequences for the policies pursued and the political outcomes obtained.[98] Whether organized labor is excluded, repressed, replaced by other sources of mass support, or drawn into coalitions can seal the fate of reform.

States with different organizational capacities can embrace different mixes of market-conforming and interventionist strategies. The degree of lateral and vertical autonomy (from other state agencies and from the executive) and of insulation from societal political forces often allows state agencies to implement economic reform. However, lateral autonomy has also perpetuated extensive rent seeking by the military-industrial complex and associated state and private enterprises. Institutions that are highly autonomous and amass considerable political power can throw their weight in support of statist or internationalist entrepreneurs, either consistently or intermittently.[99] Although certain state bureaucracies are sometimes associated with either an internationalist project (often central banks) or a statist-nationalist one (often commerce ministries), the coalitional proclivities of state agencies are a matter of empirical investigation. Israel's Foreign Ministry had become embedded in Labor's internationalist strategy by the mid-1990s, and consequently its bureaucracy and mandate expanded dramatically in tandem with broadened diplomatic and economic relations. Egypt's Foreign Ministry, on the other hand, is still perceived as bearing the lingering imprint of a more statist-nationalist era. In the end, political entrepreneurs rely on the available institutional infrastructure (parties, bureaucracies and electoral systems) or attempt to fashion new ones to build political support for either program or a hybrid of both.

Ruling coalitions thus enjoy varying degrees of political stability and longevity which, in turn, affect the conduct of grand strategy. A conquering internationalist coalition in Argentina in the early 1990s was able under President Carlos S. Menem to revolutionize the country's decades-old grand strategy, in its internal and external dimensions alike. Similar coalitions emerged in different East Asian countries, although not overnight and rarely under democratic sponsorship. Weaker coalitions in Egypt since the 1970s and India since the early 1990s have pursued less coherent and expedient strategies, binding their preferred policies to their immediate political survival in the face of powerful statist-nationalist, military, and confessional opponents. These and other examples throughout Part Two suggest that the weaker the political foundations of

---

[98] Haggard (1995a). For instance, populist parties within relatively polarized party systems in Latin America mobilized urban labor movements that resisted anti-inflationary stabilization efforts. The weak representation of rural interests in political parties mutes their effective political support for adjustment efforts (Nelson 1990: 355).

[99] This point of course, begs the question of how such institutions acquire power in the first place, a theme I address in Solingen (1996b). On the role of such institutions in economic reform in eight different political-economic contexts, see Haggard and Webb (1994). On the organizational capacities of the state in the context of economic reform, see Migdal (1988) and Evans (1995). Migdal also discusses how political leaders coopt state agencies through "big shuffles."

internationalist coalitions, first, the greater the pressures are to dilute their reform program (as Benazir Bhutto's Pakistan and India before Rao), and second, the more compelled they are to gravitate toward the themes, myths, and interests of political challengers to avoid their own collapse, (as in the strengthening of Islamic *sharia* in Saudi Arabia and Pakistan and in the opposition to "destatizaçào" under Fernando Collor de Mello in Brazil).[100] As a result, they find themselves less able to downplay regional security threats, and their capacity to forgo the support of statist elements in the military-industrial complex is lowered. Thus, although scapegoating the external enemy, often the neighbor, is generally the tool of statist-nationalist and confessional coalitions, insecure internationalizing coalitions may use that instrument as well.

The high incidence of weak internationalist coalitions evident from the empirical cases in Part Two begs the question of why internationalist coalitions are prone to political weakness. Clearly, economic reform unleashes in many cases a painful process, Przeworski's "valley of transition." However, inflationary cycles and widespread scarcities are part of antireform contexts as well, building a potential political base for favoring change. Moreover, the valleys of economic reform have been far deeper in some cases than in others, and not always as a function of pre-existing endowments such as capital, education, and infrastructure. A most important source of weakness of internationalist coalitions may be their failure to distribute the spoils of reform more equitably, or their tendency to pursue their short-sighted, instead of enlightened, self-interest.[101] This phenomenon is widespread, with Egypt providing a classical case, given the longevity of the process (since the mid-1970s), its tentative nature, and its meager successes. Accounts of market reform in Russia and Eastern Europe are rich in details of income concentration and widespread impoverishment, reminiscent of the experience of some industrializing countries. International conditionality requirements have in some cases reinforced the natural tendency of these coalitions to focus on the unfettered pursuit of wealth while paying little attention to the risky political consequences of concentrated benefits.[102] Stabilization programs often lead to recessions together with reduced public subsidies and investments in infrastructure, whereas trade liberalization exacerbates unemployment. Food riots in Egypt, Sudan, Algeria, and Morocco followed the reduction of staple subsidies, as was the case with the conservative 1991 Russian coup. In many cases a popular shift to statist-nationalism and fundamentalism followed. Shock-style therapy without safety nets and social insurance thus ends up weakening, not strengthening, the power of agencies in charge of economic reform

---

[100] In Van Evera's (1994: 30–31) formulation, "the temptation for elites to engage in mythmaking is . . . inversely proportional to their political legitimacy."

[101] On the impact of adjustment programs on the (overwhelmingly rural) very poor, and on the relatively better-off urban popular working class, see Nelson (1992).

[102] Conditionality refers to the terms that recipients of external financing agree to fulfill in exchange (as a condition) for such aid. The terms include specific economic policy changes such as revised fiscal and budgetay targets. On liberalization and the sharp increase in poverty in Russia and Eastern Europe, see World Bank (1996: 65–84).

and their societal allies.[103] Domestic forces and institutions offering alternative, if unreal, solutions to the predicaments of economic transition, reap the political benefits.

The net result of the political dynamics of nondistributive internationalist coalitions can be summed up in a paradox: such coalitions—prodded by international economic institutions—may plant the seeds of their own destruction when they pursue myopic self-interests. Regional cooperation can—and has—become a collateral casualty, as internationalist coalitions fight for survival by moving toward more symbolic, nationalist, or ethnic-confessional instruments to build political support. In the Middle East, all three ruling coalitions with incipient internationalist tendencies where antiregime Islamic forces did rather well electorally (Jordan, Yemen, and Algeria) ended up supporting Saddam Hussein during the Gulf War.[104] Similar dangers of gravitating toward less cooperative regional policies may loom on the horizon in Egypt, India, and Pakistan. Notably, where integration into the world economy evolved in tandem with a more egalitarian income distribution, as in Taiwan and South Korea, internationalist coalitions were able gradually to muster enough political support to render their grand strategy—at home, in the region, in the world—least reversible.[105] There was less regional adventurism and saber rattling once internationalist stategies were in place. South Korea's cautious response to the vagaries of the North (including nuclear threats) in the 1970s and 1980s, and Taiwan's cool restraint vis-à-vis militarized Chinese offensive threats in 1996 are symptomatic of relatively strong internationalist coalitions.[106]

Statist-nationalist-confessional coalitions also vary in their political strength. At the height of their political dominance, they are able to implement their strategy at home and abroad almost unchallenged, as with Perón's Argentina, Nasser's Egypt, and the Ayatollahs' Iran in the period immediately following their respective revolutions. Support whittles down once the strategy falters for a combination of internal and external reasons, compelling them to revive or renew the strategy, precisely when the resource base to maintain it is all but consumed. The weaker the political base of statist-nationalist and confessional

---

[103] Surveys reveal, for instance, that in Poland parliament and the government enjoyed greatest citizen confidence *before* the reforms; the army, the police, and the Church, *after*, at least for a while. On this and other negative effects of neoliberal economic reform on democratic institutions, and on the flimsy knowledge on which the neoliberal program of international economic agencies relies, see Przeworski (1992).

[104] Ibrahim (1994: 80).

[105] On equitable land distribution, equitable wages and salaries distribution, and East Asian growth, see Amsden (1991). On South Korea's remarkable performance in percentage of school-aged population in school, literacy rate, physicians per head of population, infant mortality rates, per capita calorie and protein intake, and percentage of women among university students, relative to other industrializing countries, see UNDP (1995). In Latin America, income inequality is two and a half times as great as in East Asian countries (Kaufman and Stallings 1991: 19–20). See also World Bank (1994).

[106] This characterization relates to the period of advanced liberalization. During earlier phases (1950s) there was neither liberalization nor moderate regional postures, as described in Chapter Seven.

coalitions, the stronger the pressures for economic liberalization, and the more intractable the choice between overplaying external threats effectively and using scarce resources to coopt wavering groups at home. As a result, the coalition's capacity to infuse the military-industrial complex with economic rents is lowered. These conditions limit the wherewithal of statist-nationalist-confessional coalitions to implement their grand macropolitical designs; even Perón and Iranian and Sudanese leaders begrudgingly and quietly occasionally followed IMF policies.

The sources of weakness of these coalitions are embedded in the very nature of the political strategy they pursue: populist, self-reliant, statist, and military-intensive. Even with the fortuitous blessing of a rich endowment (oil, for instance) the bonanza that permits both guns and butter eventually withers away. Redistribution can be effective in coalescing political power, as in Iraq, but is thwarted in the end by other, higher-ranking objectives, such as gargantuan investments in a scientific-military-industrial machine with little social overhead value. The Iraqi nuclear program by itself is estimated to have absorbed $15 billion in the 1980s, whereas arms imports reached $32 billion between 1982 and 1986 (against a total GDP of $47 billion in 1985). The Iraqi military and its associated weapons programs are estimated to have absorbed $85 billion between 1980 and 1988.[107] As a result, income disparities and creeping poverty levels became as evident here as in myopic internationalist contexts. Over time, nationalist and confessional purity become devalued political instruments, as was apparent in Iran and Iraq by the mid-1990s. The compounded effect of a defiant foreign policy, subsequent sanctions, deprivation, and external hostility in time dilutes the rally-round-the-flag effect, exacerbating the coalition's domestic weakness.

Overall, the terms of the bargain struck by partners in a coalition of statist, populist, nationalist, and confessional forces may lead to the "paradox of vote trading," in which logrolling leaves the partners worse off than they would have been without trading votes, as some Likud politicians found out merely a year after the inception of the Netanyahu coalition.[108] Partners to such coalitions in the Middle East—from former Marxists to humanist and moderate Islamist groups—occasionally ponder such unintended effects, particularly when widespread violence ceases to recognize the political boundaries of coalitional camps, as in Algeria since 1991. At the regional level, the coalition logrolled by Saddam Hussein—including the then-PLO and radical Islamist factions from throughout the Arab world—experienced dramatic losses from their joint venture in the Gulf crisis. The ensuing decline in the power of statist-nationalist and confessional coalitions throughtout the region infused new life into nascent internationalist platforms.

There are instances of stalemate, when the competition between internationalist and statist-nationalist coalitions fails to yield a clear victor. Three main

---

[107] International Institute for Strategic Studies (1995: 265).
[108] On the paradox of vote trading, see Riker and Brams (1973).

scenarios obtain from such domestic coalitional equipoise. Under the first scenario, the rough balance of political forces leads to a highly unstable succession of alternative coalitions, none of which can hold on to power for any significant time. Postwar Argentina with its stop-go cycles for over four decades, until the early 1990s, is a paradigmatic case. Under the second scenario, the two coalitions find enough room to rule as a condominium, often by dividing up the state and policy areas into coalitional fiefdoms. This can happen under democratic rule (as with Israel's government of national unity, 1984–1990) or under authoritarian sponsorship (as with Iran's Ruhaniyat and the opposing Ruhaniyoun in the last decade, and in North Korea more recently). Neither of the first two scenarios holds much promise for the ability to implement a coherent grand strategy in its domestic, regional, and international aspects.

Under the third scenario, contending coalitions find no grounds for mixed-motive games that enable at least limited cooperation. The security dilemma is now internalized into the domestic politics of states. Such zero-sum conditions seemed to prevail in some African states in which violent competition—civil war—has led to the absence of a central government backed by any type of coalition. Somalia, Rwanda, and the period of war between Ethiopia's Mengistu Haile Mariam's regime and the EPRDF-Eritrean People's Liberation Army, provide gruesome examples of this scenario. A domestic power vacuum, in turn, precipitates regional conflict when neighboring ruling coalitions scramble to minimize the potential negative consequences on their own rule. Thus, the absence of a ruling coalition, or intractable domestic coalitional strife, is a warning signaling the presence of preconditions for regional conflict. At the same time such cases may offer, as in Cambodia, an opportunity for the regional and international community to develop, mostly through political and economic inducements, a coalition promoting broad-based reform and cooperative regional policies. Such intervention is an extreme instance of the influence of the global context on domestic coalitional power struggles, the concluding theme in this chapter.

THE GLOBAL CONTEXT: IMPACT ON THE DOMESTIC COALITIONAL INTERPLAY

As is evident from our discussion of the makeup and orientation of internationalist and statist-nationalist coalitions, their competition at home is not carried out in a global vacuum. Far from it; domestic politics are never removed from systemic incentives, and do respond to global constraints.[109] Virtually every potential partner to a coalition anticipates, with different degrees of accuracy, the way in which external structures and institutions may aid or thwart the

[109] On the constraints posed, and the opportunities offered, by international economic structures, see Lake (1988). On how world order bears directly on national coalitions (historic blocs), see Cox (1986). On how the institutional setting can favor the emergence of some coalitions over others, see Snyder (1993a). On world historical timing and the emergence of strong states, see Migdal (1988: 271–74).

policies they advance at home. In the words of a prolific social scientist turned president of Brazil, Fernando H. Cardoso (1995: 5): "The exercise of politics in the modern world requires that we dovetail domestic and international considerations." In this section I explore the impact of a nested international political, economic, and security structure on coalitional dynamics. Predicting which coalitions are likely to seize power at certain points and for how long is beyond the thrust of this book. Rather, this overview suggests the general direction and evolution of global influences on the emergence and durability of coalitions.

International economic, security, and normative structures and institutions purposefully, but also unintendedly, influence the domestic coalitional interplay, at times strengthening internationalist coalitions, at others empowering their rivals. Different international regimes (an institutional cluster around a given issue area) privilege the interests of one coalition over another. Accordingly, statist-nationalist coalitions sought a global regime more compatible with their domestic agendas in the 1970s. This New International Economic Order (NIEO) favored authoritative statist mechanisms over market-oriented ones, and was as much conceived to gain leverage over rival coalitions at home as it was to maximize collective gains vis-à-vis the industrialized world.[110] The former Soviet Union provided powerful practical and ideological support for the statist, import-substituting paradigm and for wars of "national" liberation in the industrializing world, particularly in the early Cold War era. The United Nations General Assembly and other UN agencies beyond the control of Western powers provided a convenient site for the coordination, elaboration, and diffusion of statist-nationalist platforms, in their domestic, regional, and international dimensions. The superpowers' competition for dominance in different regions privileged—indeed gave life to—many a military-industrial complex, even where regional threats and the reach of the adversarial superpower were remote. The collapse of statist-nationalist regimes of various characteristics, most prominently in the former Soviet Union and in Eastern Europe, dealt a heavy blow to their collective ability to advance compatible international institutions and regimes.

International economic structures and regimes at the end of the twentieth century favor internationalist coalitions worldwide, to an extent never evident before. By providing credit and defining the terms of trade and investment, public and private international institutions are central to the political longevity of these coalitions. The World Bank and the International Monetary Fund (IMF) have become ever more powerful in shaping the economic orders of industrializing states, particularly following the debt crisis of 1982.[111] Externally induced structural adjustment policies have frequently strengthened institutions in

---

[110] For a similar interpretation of the NIEO, see Levy and Barnett (1992). For a realist interpretation of the NIEO, see Krasner (1985) and for a critique, Rothstein (1988). On how international institutions in the 1940s and 1950s, in both the economic and security realms, foiled alternatives to import substitution and rigorous exchange controls, see Díaz Alejandro (1983: 35).

[111] On the decisive impact of IMF pressures for stabilization and World Bank pressures for structural adjustment, see Nelson (1990) and Stallings (1992).

charge of reform (particularly finance ministries, central banks, export-promotion bureaus, and export-processing zones), at least initially. Several rounds of trade liberalization through the General Agreement on Tariffs and Trade (GATT) resulted in a progressively more open trading system, leading in 1995 to the creation of the World Trade Organization (WTO).[112] WTO membership consolidates access to international markets while binding members to domestic economic reform. New institutional layers such as the Group of Seven leading industrialized states (G–7) included in its agenda the need for a "currency early warning system" to prevent crises—such as Mexico's 1995 "Tequilazo"—that threatened embattled internationalist coalitions. The formal pronouncement of the G–7 in 1997 specifically stated: "Our goal is to realize the full benefits of globalization for all while meeting the challenges it presents."[113] The G–7 has grown to define these challenges in ways that transcend macroeconomic coordination by focusing on the embedded nature of economic, social, and security regimes. War-prone and terrorism-prone statist-nationalist and confessional coalitions have become frequent targets of opprobrium, although members of the G–7 differ in their approach to this issue, with the US advancing containment and others engagement.

The new structures of international production (multinational administrative hierarchies) and financial intermediation (obsolescent capital controls) have made it easier for "internationalist" firms and financial investors to pursue strategies of evasion and exit, helping these firms prevail over state agencies seeking capital controls or stiffer capital taxation. The ability of such firms, both local and foreign-owned, to influence domestic investment patterns and to transfer capital abroad thus increases their political weight in shaping adjustment policies.[114] These same international structures have posed formidable challenges for statist-nationalist coalitions: dwindling external financing has disabled populist strategies and preferential credit programs; foreign direct investment has altered domestic coalitional balances by injecting jobs and technology at some points and not others; the critical role played by a dynamic technological edge in the global economy has favored symbolic analysts most enmeshed in international markets—via networks and "strategic alliances"—at the expense of those in state bureaucracies and domestically oriented firms; educational institutions and other international training agencies in industrialized countries have reinforced the ranks of internationalist state and private

---

[112] On the balance of discrimination and liberalization in the trade regime since the 1980s, and on the broadening of antiprotectionist coalitions, see Oye (1992). On the preliminary achievements and outstanding challenges of the WTO, see Schott (1996).

[113] Tyler Marshall and Carol J. Williams, "Global Leaders Adopt Regimen for Healthy Economies," *New York Times*, 22 June 1997: A1. On the evolution and challenges facing the G–7 at century's end, see Whyman (1995).

[114] Goodman and Pauly (1995); Kaufman and Stallings (1991). On how increased international capital mobility tends to influence domestic political coalitions, via its impact on exchange rates, see Frieden (1991a). On these and other effects of emerging global production, trade, and financial structures and institutions, see Stallings (1995) and Ruggie (1995).

technocrats, experts, and symbolic analysts whose skills are essential to the implementation of economic reform.[115]

International economic structures and regimes have also undermined the viability of military-industrial complexes and military establishments, frequent partners in statist-nationalist challenges to economic liberalization. Structural adjustment efforts often threaten these complexes, as does the very demand for greater budgetary accountability and transparency in intergovernmental relations. Whatever disagreements on guns-versus-butter tradeoffs there may be in the scholarly community, it is clear to the relevant political actors that economic stagnation exacerbates such tradeoffs.[116] The tradeoff is most salient for developing countries facing severe financial constraints. International investors understand such tradeoffs well, and the World Bank has began addressing, more directly than ever, the size and transparency of military budgets.[117] The fact that the interlocutors of these international institutions are mostly central banks and finance ministries and not military agencies is a double-edged sword. On the one hand it can undermine the domestic legitimacy of such agencies, who are accused of taking their cues from foreign institutions. On the other hand it can be used to shift the blame for downsizing "national" symbols such as the military sector to external actors, while highlighting the positive economic, social, and political outcomes of that process.

The international economic environment, which is otherwise generally favorable to internationalist coalitions at the end of the century, can also lead to unintended consequences and severe crises, most recently of the kind endured by Mexico in 1995 and by the Southeast Asian states in 1997. Structural adjustment, stabilization programs, and economic liberalization more generally involve a painful transition for relatively large sections of society who bear the burden of recessions, unemployment, and reduced public subsidies and investments in infrastructure. As argued earlier in our discussion of coalitional strength, international conditionality requirements reinforce the tendency of internationalist coalitions to pay insufficient attention to the highly concentrated benefits of liberalization during its initial stages, and to the risky political consequences of such inattention.[118] In so doing, conditionality requirements often end up weakening the political agents of internationalist coalitions and their societal allies, as well as eroding democracy itself (as I discuss in Chapter Four). Regional cooperation can become a collateral casualty, as internationalist coalitions fight for survival by embracing more symbolic, nationalist, or confessional instruments to increase political support. To some extent, conditionality

---

[115] On the international socialization of these agents, see Kahler (1992). On the training activities of the World Bank Economic Development Institute, see World Bank (1996: 139).

[116] Chan (1992b: 165); Frederiksen and Looney (1983); Chan and Mintz (1992).

[117] World Bank (1993b: 14); Preston (1991: 5).

[118] On the economic impact of conditionality as questionable, with modest effects on the balance of payments, negligible effects on the rate of inflation, and uncertain effects on growth, see Taylor (1987) and Kahler (1992: 95). On detrimental distributional effects of conditionality, see also Nelson (1992).

requirements imposed by international donors on the new Palestinian Authority (PA) have hurt it, insofar as its inability to meet such requirements has slowed down critical financial aid. In the longer term, donors have argued, early conditionality might help the PA avoid statist habits and rent-seeking patterns. The state-in-the-making would thus be internationalist at birth. However, the trickle of international aid and constraints in attracting investments have resulted in growing pressures from statist-nationalist and confessional constituencies on the Palestinian leadership.

The survival of internationalist coalitions requires that the benefits from economic liberalization be broadened to include more than the concentrated interests that often sustain these coalitions initially. Providing resources, compensatory payments, export incentives, targeted (rather than general) subsidies, and training geared to improve relevant skills can temper domestic opposition to liberalization.[119] Indeed, data on the OECD (Organization for Economic Cooperation and Development) community itself reveals a remarkably positive correlation between openness to trade and the amount of spending on social programs (Rodrik 1997: 25–26). Resources for upgrading social insurance mechanisms can be marshaled (at least partially) from funds freed by the contraction of military budgets, a policy that increases support for reform within civil society while extinguishing a historical source of political power in the hands of military establishments. Furthermore, a shift in the style of foreign institutional intervention to one of effective consultation over domestic political needs, and toward increasing the active participation of industrializing states in the decision-making process within international institutions, can deflate nationalist resentment.[120] The other side of this coin, of course, is the power of internationalist coalitions to use the threat from statist-nationalists and radical confessional movements to extract concessions from their international partners and to alleviate the conditions for continued credit and investment. This "reverse conditionality" can be an effective bargaining strategy of struggling internationalist coalitions, a strategy for which Egypt is said to have written the manual while Russia's Yeltsin may have improved on it.

Protected markets in the industrialized world are another global challenge for internationalist coalitions.[121] Whereas the prospects of trade concessions and access to favored wealthy states' markets strengthen the appeal of liberalizers, protectionist policies (tariffs or quotas) undermine such appeal, as South Korea's President Park learned in the early 1970s. To a large extent, therefore, internationalist coalitions find themselves at the mercy of a global process of economic liberalization that is not entirely irrevocable, but rather intermittently

---

[119] On compensatory payments that do not exacerbate fiscal pressures, see Nelson (1989 and 1992), and Haggard and Webb (1994). See Rodrik (1997) on the range of social insurance mechanisms across Western Europe and North America, East Asia, and the industrializing world at large.

[120] Kahler (1992).

[121] On how external economic threats can undermine the influence of weakly institutionalized liberal coalitions, see Snyder (1989).

threatened by the possibility of cyclical "shifting involvements."[122] Where global processes contribute to unsuccessful stabilization and to uncontrollable external balances, economic reform at home is more likely to flounder, and their political agents with it. The resurgence of neomercantilistic tendencies could thus undermine what Cox (1986: 234–35) labels the "transnational managerial class" of multinational executives and finance ministry officials, as well as internationally oriented labor and symbolic analysts. These potential developments notwithstanding, appropriate external support for internationalist coalitions does improve these coalitions' political credibility and overall performance. Such support has become ever more critical with respect to financial crises fueled by currency speculation.

In the realm of security, the dominance of industrialized liberal democracies, and the US in particular, within international power structures and security regimes is virtually unchallenged. Moreover, even though power hierarchies generally breed resentment, the overwhelming majority of states in the international system at century's end share in the fundamental principles upheld by these international regimes. The most powerful states can operate through international institutions that invest their own preferences with greater universality and legitimacy.[123] These principles include progressive disarmament, nuclear nonproliferation, antiterrorism, banning nuclear testing and prohibiting the production, trade, and use of chemical and bacteriological weapons. The domestic agendas of internationalist coalitions are not threatened but helped by these international regimes, for the reasons specified earlier in this chapter. At times Western countries in conjunction with international institutions representing the rest of the world provide concrete military, moral, and political support for internationalist coalitions under assault by their rivals at home or in the region. Such support can range from sending military forces and equipment to the Persian Gulf to showing a massive international presence at the funeral of Israel's late Prime Minister Yitzhak Rabin, to mobilizing a "summit of peacemakers" against terrorist challengers of the Middle East peace process. Clearly, where the stakes of war and potential losses are higher, international intervention tends to be more dramatic. Such intervention poses yet another challenge to military establishments. Claiming a monopoly over the development and use of military power on their national territory, the armed forces often regard international institutions (peacekeeping, export-control regimes, on-site inspection mechanisms) as inherent competitors with an agenda of puncturing national sovereignty. Expanding international institutional prerogatives have helped cre-

---

[122] On "shifting involvements," see Hirschman (1982).

[123] On the strength of multilateralism, see Ruggie (1993). Cox (1986) explains this legitimacy as the product of Gramscian hegemony, where the powerful are willing to make concessions to secure the acquiescence of the weak in their leadership. According to Buzan (1991a), great powers have established at the dawn of the twenty-first century a multipolar, ideologically cohesive security community of capitalist states that lays the ground for an international society with common goals and values.

ate constituencies in civil societies throughout the world that support these international allies as preferred guarantors of their physical protection over their own national military.

Despite a mutually supportive international environment among liberalizers (a global alliance?), the fact that international regimes strengthen the influence of the most powerful states that created them is not lost on constituencies in industrializing states. Even internationalist coalitions in these states raise issues of international equity and hegemonic prerogatives. The potential erosion in the legitimacy of these regimes can be prevented by implementing fully the most powerful states' own part of the bargain, such as the reduction and eventual elimination of their nuclear arsenals according to Article VI of the Nonproliferation Treaty. Toward the second half of the 1990s even in the United States there has been a growing acceptability of "zero-option" nuclear futures by former military and security analysts, notably former Defense Secretary Robert McNamara. The conclusion of a Comprehensive Test Ban Treaty in 1996 and of a Chemical Weapons Convention in 1997 further strengthen the legitimacy of a multilateral order, while sealing off yet another domain for statist-military-technological constituencies throughout the world.

As this overview suggests, international economic and security regimes influence the domestic balance of power between coalitions, and, as second order effects described in Chapter Three, can help shape regional orders. This analysis helps specify the ways in which international regimes and institutions make a difference—at times more than others—a subject of much debate in the international relations literature. The extent to which they do weigh heavily is largely contingent on the nature and strength of domestic coalitions. In choosing a grand strategy, coalitions face choices regarding external allies and the extent to which they are willing to risk conflicts with international economic, political, or military actors. Internationalist coalitions are generally more sensitive to international injunctions and requirements than their statist-nationalist counterparts, because many such requirements reinforce a liberalizing domestic agenda. This is different from arguing that international institutions determine the fate of economic reform, domestic political change, or regional orders. The domestic coalitional balance is not merely derivative of global forces. Evidence from systematic studies points to the inability of external actors to tip the political scale in favor of reform when the domestic institutional and coalitional environment is unfavorable.[124] After all, international pressures for trade liberalization and macroeconomic adjustment did not bear fruit for many years among inward-looking states such as Argentina and India. Syngman Rhee resisted macroeconomic reform in the late 1940s and 1950s, even when South Korea was under virtual US occupation, and Park introduced his "deepening" program despite US and World Bank opposition. Saddam Hussein's military-industrial complex continued its activities in nonconventional weapons production for

---

[124] Nelson (1990), Kahler (1992), Haggard and Webb (1994: 5), Haggard and Kaufman (1995), and partially dissenting, Stallings (1992).

years, notwithstanding the most stringent United Nations regime for on-site inspections in history. Policies result from changing dynamics between what Gourevitch (1986: 217) labeled "the force of epochs" (world-time) and "the force of national trajectories." Notwithstanding the differental domestic conversion of global influences it is important to recognize how free capital mobility has deepened the international impact on coalitional balances in an unprecedented way, as it can reward or punish coalitional policies and behavior—at home, in the region, and vis-à-vis the world—virtually overnight.

Before concluding this chapter, it is worth reaffirming that: the domestic impact of economic liberalization and international institutions is far more complex and unpredictable than stipulated by any single theory; the coalitional cleavage around economic liberalization is not the only political cleavage but is certainly a common and prominent one; this cleavage tends to attract other cleavages that often cluster along its fundamental fault lines; the distance between ideal and empirical coalitional types can be wide, as expected in social science abstractions, while hybrid forms abound. A final point deserves careful consideration. As argued, strong versions of each coalition are expected to be in better position to implement their grand strategies—other things being equal—than are their weaker counterparts. A critical component of the "other things" now becomes more evident: the identity of the actors that these coalitions face in their regional neighborhood. The risk inherent in a given regional policy cannot be assessed without reference to this interactive component. The nature of ruling coalitions in neighboring states, and of their own domestic challengers, thus acts as an important intervening variable in explaining regional orders, defining the ability of contending coalitions to implement both the domestic and regional pillars of their grand strategy. It is to this requirement to endogenize the regional context in order to understand a coalition's behavior and its regional implications that I now turn.

CHAPTER THREE

Coalitions, Strategic Interaction, and Regional Outcomes

THE REGIONAL BEHAVIOR of domestic political coalitions (in and out of power) is highly responsive to the identity and strength of the actors it faces throughout the region. Put differently, the nature of a ruling coalition in country A creates regional externalities or spill-overs, captured by the ruling coalition (and its opposition) in country B, as well as in other neighboring countries. In effect, in supporting one coalition or another, the coalitional preferences of the domestic public in country A have strategic implications. In some cases actors are more conscious of such implications than in others, but a general increase in that awareness seems evident at the end of the twentieth century.[1] Clearly, the interactive regional context influences the electoral appeal, behavior, and policies of coalitions, in both their domestic and external expressions. This chapter spells out the ways in which the identity and political strength of coalitions in neighboring states influence a coalition's behavior and policies in a particular state: the ontogeny of a domestic coalition is intimately linked to its related regional phylogeny. In general terms, the scope and nature of regional conflict and cooperation is encoded in the degree of coalitional homogeneity / heterogeneity at the regional level. Thus, higher and extensive levels of cooperation can be expected where internationalist coalitions prevail throughout a given region than where statist-nationalist, or competing internationalist and statist-nationalist neighbors, face one another.

Cooperation implies active attempts to adjust policies to meet the demands of others under conditions of discord or potential discord. Such attempts involve the willingness to forsake, in repeated instances, the unilateral pursuit of one's own interests and to undertake commitments on a basis of diffuse reciprocity.[2] These commitments can run the gamut of substantive issue areas. Very often, security and economic cooperation hang together, not merely because of econ-

---

[1] Chapter Six documents, for instance, how Israel's high-tech entrepreneurs voted massively for the Labor-Meretz coalition in 1992 and 1996, with an eye on the domestic, regional, and global windfalls from prospective regional cooperation. See also Kemp (1994), Arian and Shamir (1995), Elazar and Sandler (1995). The regional externalities of President Menem's program were far more relevant to the electoral calculus of those who voted him into power in 1995 than they were in 1989.

[2] Keohane (1986). In the security realm, behavior oriented to initiate, maintain, and/or exacerbate armed conflict—such as a direct attack or blockade, threats to use force or invade a territory, mobilizations and swaggering near the borders—is considered to be conflictive. Behavior oriented to resolve disputes and to avoid armed confrontations is considered cooperative. Issues of perceptions and thresholds are incorporated, as will be clear throughout this chapter, in the analysis of coalitional type.

omies of scope but because of the complementary role they play in the grand strategy (domestic, regional, and global) of different coalitions.[3] The broader the scope of issues, the more *extensive* the cooperative framework. The deeper the level of commitments, the most *intensive* cooperation can be said to be. Highly extensive and intensive cooperative relations yield a pattern akin to a pluralistic security community.[4] The willingness to undertake commitments based on diffuse reciprocity and routinely to forsake the pursuit of self-interest declines as we move toward the other end of the spectrum. This decreasing disposition often transcends most issue areas and, in its extreme case, is evidenced in the open articulation of the war option as inevitable and even desirable. Although fundamental patterns of cooperation and war-proneness may be easily identifiable in some cases, the meaning of behavior cannot be separated from the security context in which it takes place. The shadow of the past filters the interpretation of a given behavior, rendering the definition of purely "objective" categories equivocal and vague. Knowledge about the depth and longevity of regional security dilemmas is essential for interpreting cooperation in different regional milieus. The mere existence of a direct dialogue entailed meager cooperative achievements in the Southern Cone for decades whereas such dialogue implied a revolution in cooperation in the Korean peninsula, China-Taiwan, and Arab-Israeli contexts. Initial security conditions do matter, and coalitions differ across regions in terms of their starting points for the construction of regional orders.

To explore the interactive dynamics among coalitions throughout a region, Figure 2 provides a schematic plotting of all the possible coalitional combinations for the simplified case of a dyad, states A and B. The schema takes note of our discussion in Chapter Two of the centrality of a coalition's political strength at home, by differentiating between weak and strong coalitions in both states A and B. As argued, positive and negative measures of a coalition's strength—relative to its domestic challengers—provide us with important information regarding the likelihood that such a coalition can implement its grand strategy in a more or less coherent and expedient fashion. The other side of this coin is, of course, that an opposition that is sizable in resources, largely consensual in its macropolitical objectives, and effectively organized is likely to pose a more formidable barrier to the implementation of a ruling coalition's grand strategy. In general, weaker ruling coalitions tend to have shorter time horizons than stronger ones.[5]

Both state A and state B may be ruled by a weak or strong, internationalist or statist-nationalist coalition, defining four basic possibilities for each state. In a

---

[3] On the complementarity of economic and security policies, see Gowa and Mansfield (1993). On how economies of scope lower the transaction costs involved in negotiating, monitoring, and enforcing agreements, see Lake (1997).

[4] The term "pluralistic security communities" was first used by Deutsch (1957) to point to sustained and widespread institutional practices that build dependable expectations of peaceful change.

[5] On how insecurity of rule and intense political competition lead to high future discount rates, see Levi (1988: 13).

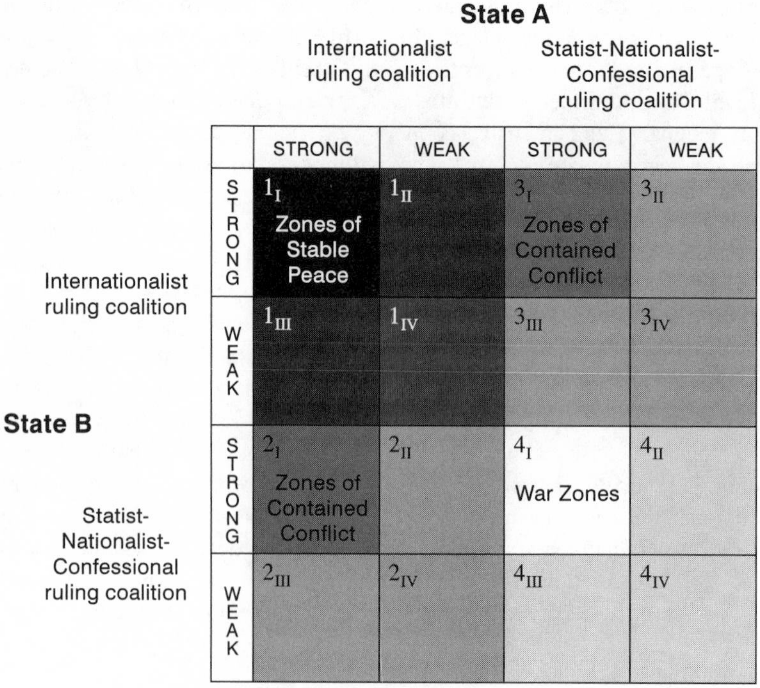

State A

		Internationalist ruling coalition		Statist-Nationalist-Confessional ruling coalition	
		STRONG	WEAK	STRONG	WEAK
Internationalist ruling coalition	S T R O N G	1_I Zones of Stable Peace	1_{II}	3_I Zones of Contained Conflict	3_{II}
	W E A K	1_{III}	1_{IV}	3_{III}	3_{IV}
Statist-Nationalist-Confessional ruling coalition	S T R O N G	2_I Zones of Contained Conflict	2_{II}	4_I War Zones	4_{II}
	W E A K	2_{III}	2_{IV}	4_{III}	4_{IV}

(left side labels: "Internationalist ruling coalition" and "State B / Statist-Nationalist-Confessional ruling coalition")

Figure 2. Coalitional combinations and regional orders

dyadic situation, this matrix yields twelve possible coalitional combinations (notice that cells 2 and 3 involve analytically indistinguishable combinations, with only the identity of the coalitions reversed). The darker the shaded areas in Figure 2, the more cooperative the bilateral relationship is expected to be. Cooperation declines as we move to mixed cells 2 and 3—where internationalist and statist-nationalist coalitions face each other—and declines even more in the lighter-shaded areas depicting relations between statist-nationalist dyads. The remainder of this chapter explains why this pattern obtains.

ZONES OF STABLE PEACE: CONVERGING GRAND STRATEGIES IN STRONG INTERNATIONALIST ORDERS

Cell 1 captures the situation in which both A and B are ruled by internationalist coalitions. Despite variations among the four quadrants in cell 1, this is generally the most extensive and intensive cooperative relationship of all those depicted in Figure 2. Quadrant 1_I reflects zones of stable peace, whereas quadrants 1_{II} and 1_{III} portray less stable but largely cooperative relations. The synergies between economic and security cooperation become evident when the domestic implications of regional policies are taken into account.

In the realm of security, relations between internationalist coalitions are characterized by the following features.

First, as argued in Chapter Two, domestic considerations of political survival drive economic rationalization—and military downsizing—as much as external factors. There is therefore a virtual built-in guarantee that fellow internationalist coalitions—everything else being equal—will be reluctant to defect through militarized strategies. This is not to say that internationalist dyads never have long-standing disputes, territorial, confessional, and otherwise. However, the primacy of their grand strategies tames such disputes, rendering reliance on militarized means highly unlikely. For internationalist dyads and clusters de-escalation is dominant in managing their disputes. The potential for armed conflict and extensive military build-ups threaten the economic and political fundamentals—fiscal conservatism; macroeconomic, political, and regional stability; access to capital, technology, and markets—that the program of internationalist coalitions requires.[6] These programs function, in essence, as tacit self-binding commitments that do not always require formal alliances. These symmetric conditions not only alleviate what might otherwise become situations of prisoner's dilemma (as in most arms races), but also help internationalist coalitions defend their own platform—of economic reform, a contained or shrinking military complex, and cooperative regional postures—from attacks by domestic challengers. The domestic programs of internationalist coalitions, in sum, create positive security externalities in the region. According to Jusuf Wanandi, one of Indonesia's leading strategic analysts: "If each [ASEAN] member nation can accomplish an overall national development and overcome internal threats, regional resilience can result, much in the same way as a chain derives its overall strength from the strength of its constituent parts."[7] This statement lays out the logic of regional requirements for the domestic fulfillment of a liberalizing agenda.

Second, the mutually reinforcing domestic and interactive regional inducements to allay conflict reduce the transaction costs in relations between internationalist coalitions. Agreements on issues under dispute are easier to reach, and there is less need to monitor or punish compliance or improve information. This transparency is highest when internationalist grand strategies are more fully in place and their political agents more strongly entrenched—conditions that are of, course, interrelated. Thus, internationalist coalitions beget the conditions for self-sustained, rather than externally imposed, regional cooperation, as in the Southern Cone in the 1990s. Even where international actors (powerful states or international institutions) do play a facilitating role in conflict management or conflict resolution—as in the Middle East—the engine of regional cooperation

---

[6] To reiterate a point from Chapter Two, these coalitions are not blind to potential regional threats to their own survival, and do acquire weapons to protect themselves, but restrain their defense expenditures so as not to endanger their grand strategy. Such expenditures are often compatible with the world's average (about 4.5 percent of GDP in the 1970s and 1980s), even in high-conflict regions, in contrast to the expenditures of statist-nationalist coalitions, which are three and four times higher.

[7] Quoted in Mack and Kerr (1994: 135).

is progressively more internal if and when internationalist coalitions grow stronger. Conversely, their political deterioration requires more active international intervention on their behalf. The historical breakthrough between the PLO and Israel's Labor-Meretz coalition in 1993, known as Oslo I, bypassed the formal process of negotiations in Washington, D.C., under (mainly) US sponsorship. Similarly, the Jordan-Israeli rapprochement of July 1994 and the subsequent peace treaty revealed a strong internal and regional logic reflected to some extent in the public meetings held by King Hussein and late Prime Minister Rabin at their mutual border, even prior to the White House lawn routine. The US played an important role as moderator and guarantor in most Middle East peace negotiations, but more so as internationalist coalitions came under strain or in relations between mixed dyads, as in Syrian-Israeli interactions even under Labor-Meretz or Jordanian-Israeli interactions under Netanyahu.[8] Strong internationalist coalitions have not found a place in the Middle East thus far.

In the realm of economic cooperation, where internationalist coalitions take a firmer hold throughout a region than in the budding case of the Middle East—as with the paradigmatic European Union (EU), or in the still-evolving cases of ASEAN, the Southern Cone's MERCOSUR, and the Gulf Cooperation Council (GCC)—their domestic political-economic strategies are often transferred to the regional institutional arena.[9] New regional cooperative and integrative regimes emerge that serve the purposes of strengthening the liberalizing model at home while disabling its opposition, and lubricating external ties to the global political economy. Establishing markets requires harmonization of product standards and legal and administrative infrastructures, which, in turn, deepens the institutional links among internationalist coalitions, as well as their mutual interdependence. These coalitions embrace trade-creating schemes that emphasize positive regional and global externalities, largely compatible with "open regionalism."[10] The progressive expansion of bilateral and regional trade benefits the domestic economies directly and strengthens the flow of outside investment, creating pressures for further—more generalized—liberalization.

Although an absolute increase in regional trade and investment often results

---

[8] Following the most dangerous episode in the implementation of the Gaza-Jericho agreement between Israel and the PLO/PA (riots in the Erez checkpoint on July 17, 1994), Israel's Deputy Foreign Minister Yossi Beilin declared in response to Arafat's call for international observers: "It's about time that Arafat understood we have to solve our problems by ourselves" (Clyde Haberman, "Arab Police Clash with Israeli Army during Gaza Riot," *New York Times* 18 July 1994: A1, 4).

[9] On how regional groups like ASEAN and the GCC operate with an eye on domestic challenges to their regimes, see Acharya (1992). Malaysia's foreign minister argued: "The concept of free enterprise . . . is the philosophical basis of ASEAN" (quoted in Acharya: 152). MERCOSUR includes Argentina, Brazil, Uruguay, Paraguay, and Chile.

[10] Trade-creating schemes are those in which trade replaces home production or results from increased consumption. Trade-diverting schemes replace trade with third parties by trade between partners to the scheme (Cable and Henderson 1994, Bhagwati 1993). Viner (1950) is the locus classicus.

from the interaction among ruling internationalist partners, regional economic integration is not always required for cooperative relations to be maintained. For instance, when competitive—rather than complementary—economies are involved, the drive for integration is initially weaker, as with GCC.[11] Extensive intraregional economic exchanges are not a necessary condition for embarking on a cooperative regional order. The Egyptian-Israeli peace exemplifies why, even in the absence of dramatic economic benefits from bilateral economic interactions, internationalist coalitions find it in their interest to maintain cooperative relations. The underlying logic of economic liberalization is global; regional arrangements may become stepping-stones subordinated to that logic. Put differently, nation-to-system interdependence is the engine of regional cooperative arrangements, in both economics and security.[12] This is quite different from arguing—as in classical interdependence theory—that the expectations of bilateral economic gains fuels broad-based cooperation between or among regional partners. Yet, where the international credibility of the liberalizing agenda throughout the region is questionable—as was the case in the Southern Cone and continues to be in the Middle East—formal regional arrangements in the direction of freer trade can, of course, signal a more believable commitment to extraregional investors. ASEAN and the early liberalizers in South Korea and Taiwan embraced a global focus at the outset. In fact, ASEAN's intraregional trade as a percentage of total trade declined in the 1980s.

So far I have discussed cell 1 in a general way although, as is clear from the examples, the variance between interactions among strong and weak internationalist partners—across cell 1 quadrants—is significant. The most extensive and intensive levels of cooperation within cell 1 can be expected when both A and B are ruled by strong internationalist coalitions (quadrant 1_I). The regional orders created by such coalitions—often enjoying relatively long time-horizons—have elements of what Keohane (1984) defines as "harmony," alluding to situations in which policies are pursued to advance a unilateral self-interest, thus facilitating the attainment of similar goals by the other side, and without a constant need to adapt policies to take into consideration the other side's interest. However, even these orders require cooperation, or adjusting one's policies to facilitate the goals of others or to reduce the negative consequences of one's policies on others. To some extent, cooperation in strong internationalist contexts assumes the form of an assurance game, where the benefits from joint cooperation are higher than those from unilateral defection, and where assurance comes from the domestic incentives of internationalist coalitions. The compatibility of their domestic agendas minimizes "the balance of threat": internationalist partners perceive their own political resources to grow in tandem

[11] GCC established a free trade area in 1983, but its implementation has been slow and intermittent. Imports from other GCC states account for very small fractions of their respective total imports.

[12] On the importance of extraregional trade for each of the emerging trading blocs, see Lawrence (1995: 411–12).

with those of their internationalist neighbors.[13] The level of cooperation in quadrant 1_I is high enough to ensure stable zones of peace, as within the European Union. Even in North America, where peaceful relations among the US, Canada, and Mexico have been a constant for much of this century, the deepest levels of cooperation were not forged until the strongest version of an internationalist coalition in Mexico's history came to power, that of former President Salinas de Gortari.

Levels of cooperation decrease somewhat where a weak internationalist coalition faces a strong internationalist neighbor (quadrants 1_{II} and 1_{III}). In the Southern Cone, a weak internationalist coalition in Brazil under pressure from statist-nationalist challengers was more tentative about the bilateral cooperative process launched in 1991—in economics and security—than its counterpart in Argentina. The ascension of Itamar Franco to the presidency of Brazil in 1992, his wooing of a statist-nationalist constituency and of the military, his attacks on international institutions and their domestic "allies," and some retractive statements on Brazil's sovereignty in nuclear matters, all temporarily tamed but did not eliminate, the drive toward a new regional order. The stronger Argentine neoliberal coalition at the time under President Menem continued to push its program forcefully, through privatization, low inflation, downsized military expenditures, and balanced budgets, complete with a commitment to unilateral accession to the Nonproliferation Treaty (not conditioned on Brazil's moves), a step Argentina had resisted for decades. Some of this dynamic was also evident in Egyptian-Israeli relations during 1993–1995, at the height of the internationalist interlude in Israel. Egypt's cooperative approach to the peace process at the time—in both their bilateral and multilateral venues—was far more tentative than Jordan's, for King Hussein had managed to deflect the opposition to economic liberalization and regional accommodation more successfully than had his Egyptian counterpart during that period.

Under the circumstances prevailing in quadrants 1_{II} and 1_{III} the relatively stronger internationalist coalition (in A for instance) faces a dilemma: if it maintains its liberalizing program, it helps its weak internationalist neighbor (in B) uphold cooperative postures. However, at the same time, it risks raising domestic doubts—fueled by a lingering if weakened statist-nationalist opposition—about giving in to an unstable partner. The weak internationalist coalition in B is, of course, at the mercy of a stronger statist-nationalist opposition at home. This opposition, in turn, exploits the asymmetry (between a strong liberalizer in A and a weak liberalizer at home) by accusing the weak liberalizers in power of yielding to the regional "adversary's" hegemony. President Yasir Arafat has endured this delicate position heroically since the inception of the Palestinian Authority, even when Labor-Meretz held a stronger political base. The asymmetry under these conditions can become unstable, as the weakness of the weak liberalizer in B spreads to the hitherto stronger liberalizer in A. This is

---

[13] On balancing against threats that stem both from offensive capabilities and perceived intentions, see Walt (1987).

largely a result of the stronger opposition in B begetting a stronger opposition in A, a situation that led to the progressive weakening of Labor-Meretz in Israel and its eventual replacement in power by its statist-nationalist-confessional rival in 1996. High and consistent levels of asymmetry are thus not very conducive to maintaining concessions that might broaden the scope of diffuse reciprocity.

Cooperation is even more tentative and unstable—within the largely cooperative cell 1—when two rather weak internationalist coalitions face each other (quadrant 1_{IV}). This is so because, despite risking accusations of sellout, a weak internationalist coalition in B finds it easier to survive politically while pursuing compromising regional policies in situations where A is steered by a strong internationalist coalition, as when Brazil under President Franco faced Menem's Argentina. As argued earlier, A's pursuit of state-shrinking policies, lower military budgets, and easier access to international markets, capital, and technology, makes it easier for B's weak internationalist coalition to justify its cooperative posture vis-à-vis A when facing its domestic opponents. Instead, where B's weak internationalist coalition faces a similarly weak one in A, it is likely to encounter greater domestic resistance to accept the risks of downsizing military endowments and engaging in diffuse reciprocity. Time horizons are shorter here. The accusations of statist-nationalist challengers resonate far more effectively when they can point to the frailty of reform and to the strength of their statist-nationalist-confessional counterparts in the neighboring state.

This effect is particularly evident in the difficulties that incipient internationalist Indian and Pakistani coalitions have encountered since 1991. Their respective political fragility in both countries has made it harder for each to transcend old patterns of domestic and regional enmity. In a sense, the domestic weakness of such dyads raises issues of more discounted future payoffs and involuntary defection. Under such conditions, the benefits of an alleviated security dilemma are more likely to be dissipated than in the case of strong internationalist interlocutors. However, even where they face serious challenges at home, weak internationalist coalitions are on far stronger ground to cooperate when they face an internationalist interlocutor than when they do not. The most cooperative Arab dyads—relative to others in the region—historically fall under this category, including Egypt and Jordan (1980s), Egypt and Tunisia (1970s–1990s), and Egypt and Saudi-Arabia (particularly since the 1980s). However, as these cases suggest, the bilateral relations between weak internationalist coalitions—as those between mixed dyads—cannot be taken out of a broader regional context where statist-nationalist-confessional coalitions dominate. Such context affects the ability of an internationalist dyad or cluster to transcend militarization and compels it to balance coalitional adversaries in the region, frustrating many components of its grand strategy.

To a significant extent the multilateral Middle East peace process of the early 1990s was the product of incipient quadrant 1_{IV} conditions. Variants of nascent internationalist coalitions were beginning to emerge throughout the region, from the financial, tourist-based, commercial-agriculture, and *munfatihun* economies in Egypt and Jordan to the oil-exporting industries in the Gulf and the Arabian

70

peninsula, and the high-tech export-oriented sectors in Israel. Egypt had pioneered a regional rapprochement since the mid-1970s, when Sadat embarked on an effort to replace Nasser's import-substitution strategy with a policy of liberalization (*infitah*), accumulation, and growth.[14] Liberalizing agendas had overtaken even important factions of the Palestine Liberation Organization (PLO) once the convulsive energy of the late 1980s *intifada* (uprising) had spent itself out. At the time of the 1991 Madrid Conference most participants were under extremely fragile and highly diluted versions of internationalist coalitions shackled by strong statist-nationalist and confessional opponents. Core participants such as Israel and Syria—who attended Madrid largely under forceful United States prodding—were dominated by statist-nationalist-confessional coalitions under strain. The immediate results of the conference were limited. As incipient PLO liberalizers grew stronger and attracted unprecedented international support, they also articulated unprecedented cooperative principles by 1993. Meanwhile, in the 1992 Israeli elections Labor-Meretz had won a mandate for socio-economic renewal at home and a territorial compromise with the Palestinians. This convergence led to the historical Oslo agreements in September 1993. A stronger set of liberalizers regionwide was able to transform the multilateral working groups born in Madrid in 1991 into more viable cooperative undertakings after 1993.

These internationalist coalitions throughout the region laid out the foundations of a brand new regional order, both at the bilateral level (Palestinian-Israeli and Jordanian-Israeli) and in multilateral negotiations over economic, security, environmental, water, and refugee issues. Superseding decades of regional and global power balancing, these coalitions planted the seeds of what might, in time, come to be multilateral collective security arrangements.[15] Each, however, continued to be threatened by the specter of intransigent and violent statist-nationalist-confessional oppositions. As of 1996 the short time horizons of these weak coalitions had become a major barrier to deepening cooperation, and their contagious domestic fragility eventually stalled both bilateral and multilateral cooperation, particularly following the ascent of a radical nationalist-confessional coalition in Israel. The incipient cooperation among liberalizers had created a new balance of power in the region, between the partners to the peace process on the one hand, and statist-nationalist-confessional coalitions—mainly Iran, Iraq, the Palestinian Islamic Resistance, and Sudan—who chose to remain outside the process, on the other. That cooperative frameworks can have

---

[14] In this process Egypt reduced its military expenditures from 52.4 percent of its GNP in 1975 to 13 percent in 1979, while foreign exchange from tourism, workers' remittances, and canal revenues (activities made possible by peace with Israel) grew from $700 million in 1974 to about $9 billion in 1981 (Karawan 1993: 17). On *munfatihun* economies (those attempting to increase "openness" to the global economy), see Waterbury (1983) and Barkey (1992).

[15] On the incipient multilateral institutions springing out of the peace process, see Sayigh (1995) and Solingen (1995). For a definition of the Wilsonian concept of collective security as the rejection of alliances, the commitment of all members to resist any attack against another member, the "all for one, one for all" rule, see Betts (1993: 268).

negative security externalities for third parties is not startling. Neither is it un-expected—given the coalitional logic outlined so far—that the new regional coalitional balance was largely shattered after 1996 in tandem with the new domestic coalitional balance in Israel.

WAR ZONES: BALANCING POWER AND MYTHS IN STATIST-NATIONALIST ORDERS

What forms do regional orders take when statist-nationalist-confessional coali-tions face each other in a region, as in cell 4? In principle, where they confront a coalitional clone supported by similar political and economic interests across the border, one might expect cooperation—even attempts at political and eco-nomic integration—to be more likely. The history of statist-nationalist (mostly military) Arab regimes during the 1960s and 1970s provides many examples of this scenario, as with the Ba'thist coalitions in Syria and Iraq. Yet, as we know, the duration of cooperative schemes among Nasser's Egypt, Gadhafi's Libya, Hussein's Iraq, and Asad's Syria was invariably brief, even when their respec-tive coalitions were quite strong.[16] This is not entirely unexpected, if we bear in mind that statist-nationalist coalitions thrive on regional competition. Integra-tive efforts have the potential of forcing many of these coalitions' natural politi-cal constituencies to go out of business. Collective security arrangements or integrative schemes weaken these regimes' rationale for maintaining high levels of unilateral military preparedeness. At best, the presence of internationalist coalitions in the region might justify the maintenance of a common military effort, but such effort implies a division of labor among would-be statist-nation-alist allies that could undercut the individual military-industrial constituencies of each statist-nationalist ally. These constituencies are often very large, de-manding between 15 and 25 percent of GDP or over three times the world's average. Even levels of cooperation lower than integrative schemes have the potential of alienating confessional (and territorially irredentist) groups whose aspirations often refuel hitherto dormant territorial disputes. Eastern and Central Europe are an abundant source of examples for this, as are South Asia and the Middle East. As a consequence, statist-nationalist-confessional coalitions facing each other in a region are prone to embrace hypernationalist (or hyperconfes-sional) postures designed to accentuate rather than blur their differences.[17]

Given the constituent elements or political pillars of statist-nationalist-confes-sional coalitions, their domestic program itself (emphasizing extensive state en-trepreneurship and militarization, economic closure, and national or confes-sional purity) often has negative security externalities throughout the region.[18]

---

[16] On the failure of alliance formation among these similar regimes in the Middle East, see Walt (1987).

[17] On hypernationalism as involving a belief in the inferiority of other national groups, in their threatening nature, and in the need to suppress them, see Mearsheimer (1993) and Van Evera (1993).

[18] On how states characterized by small export sectors are more prone to choose war, see Domke

Differentiation along national or confessional lines and insistence on territorial aspirations are as defining characteristics of statist-nationalist and confessional coalitions and are integral parts of their survival strategy. Sovereignty over disputed territories acquires a centrality and zero-sum quality that differentiates statist-nationalist interactions from all others. Sovereignty over Shatt al Arab, for instance was far less subject to negotiation for the Iranian-Iraqi statist-nationalist and confessional dyad than was the case with the West Bank and Gaza for Israel's Labor-Meretz and the Palestinian Authority, despite the greater centrality—indeed the existential quality of these territories for both Palestine and Israel. Notably, intractable approaches to territoriality are defining features of this last pair's respective domestic opposition, Likud, Hamas, and their allies. This comparison highlights the contrast between cells 4 and 1. In cell 4, relatively smaller security threats—an area separating two territorially massive rivals such as Iran and Iraq—could produce a war zone of vast proportions. In cell 1 a dramatic reciprocal vulnerability, overlapping claims over essentially the same territory, and a deep historical security dilemma do not preclude dialogue and compromise.

The centrality of national symbols, territoriality, and self-reliance among statist-nationalist dyads tends to foil attempts at pan- or trans-regional movements, even among otherwise "natural" allies such as Nasserite and Ba'th-ruled regimes, Kampuchea and Vietnam, or the Islamic republics of Iran and Sudan. Weaker statist-nationalist coalitions can be expected to be more tempted than stronger ones to rely on integrative efforts—particularly with a strong statist-nationalist partner that shares its political platform—in order to strenghten their own delicate position at home. Yet such efforts involve the risk of being absorbed by the stronger partner and, consequently, of impairing the weak coalition's position even further, as Ba'thist officers quickly realized after the aborted United Arab Republic with Egypt. Military alliances between or among statist-nationalist coalitions are thus ephemeral. The presence of neighboring statist-nationalist coalitions heightens the "balance of threat" for these coalitions no less—and in some cases even more—than the presence of internationalist coalitions in the region. In sharp contrast to internationalist clusters, a heightened balance of threat at its borders offers a statist-nationalist coalition opportunities to thrive politically and advance its grand strategy. The rhetoric of these coalitions is imbued with a contradictory assertion that their adversaries posit awesome security threats but are essentially inert "paper tigers."[19]

Thus, in the realm of security, statist-nationalist coalitions further their parochial interests by creating a climate of risk, instability, conflict, and competition. At the same time, they are not invariably interested in actualizing their war-fighting potential, that is, in resorting to war. Yet the logic of their political-economic strategy (particularly extensive militarization) and their risky postur-

---

(1988). On how the emphasis on "groupness" (of ethnic, religious, cultural, and linguistic collectivities) is inherently threatening and constitutive of security dilemmas, see Posen (1993: 30).

[19] Snyder (1991). The behavior of these coalitions is compatible with Walt's (1987) view that states sharing certain ideologies are more likely to compete than to form durable alliances.

ing often lead—or make them stumble—into armed conflict.[20] At times, even while trying to avoid showdowns that might endanger their leadership or physical integrity, war becomes an unintended consequence, as Iran discovered in 1980. The individual proneness to brinkmanship in a regional context dominated by balance-of-threat considerations explains the high incidence of militarized conflict, war zones, and regional overexpansion in such regions, evident in Kim Il Sung's attack and ejection from South Korea, Nasser's encroachment in Yemen, Begin's encroachment in Lebanon, Galtieri's Malvinas / Falklands debacle, and Saddam Hussein's fiascos in Iran and Kuwait.[21] The idea of multilateral conflict management (or of forsaking the unilateral pursuit of their own interests) is oxymoronic for regimes thriving on myths of self-reliance, military prowess, sovereignty, and national or confessional purity. Saddam Hussein could thus submit to his own domestic public that the most compelling response to the putative aggressive intentions of Shi'ite Islamic Iran was to counterbalance its ruling coalition first, and defeat it next.

As if all these conditions were not enough to exacerbate conflict, another characteristic of statist-nationalist-confessional coalitions identified in Chapter Two is expected to intensify the hostility typical in such dyads. These coalitions are often held together by a strong leader, sometimes worshiped as a virtual deity, adding a personalistic adversarial touch—and an important source of myths—to this relationship.[22] The personalistic element tends to fuel—rather than repress—the slippery slope into war zones. This personalistic element, as argued, is not unique to statist-nationalist-confessional coalitions (or to nondemocratic contexts), but its incidence is higher and its role more integral to the strategy than is the case for internationalist coalitions. Even where authoritarian leaders spearhead an internationalist strategy, once the strategy is in place it transcends the original leadership, as in South Korea, Taiwan, and Chile. Instead, the actual or prospective death of a statist-nationalist-confessional leader often creates disarray and opens the question of the survival of the coalition, as in North Korea, Iraq, Sudan, Libya, and Argentina at the time of Perón. This uncertainty renders personalistic transitions within statist-nationalist-confessional regimes particularly vulnerable to the temptation to lash out in external aggression as a means to rescue the coalition from the loss of a coalescing leader. Diversionary wars as a first resort are risky but nonetheless a viable instrument in the grand strategic kit of these coalitions.

The scope of regional devastation in war zones resulting from encounters between statist-nationalist coalitions is widespread and, in the aftermath of

---

[20] On war as the "waste by-product" of the military's pursuit of growth, wealth, and prestige, see Van Evera (1984), Posen (1984), and Snyder (1991). On how international disputes accompanied by armed races are much more likely to induce wars than those in which armed races are absent, see Chan (1992a).

[21] Overexpansion can be estimated a priori by considering the heightened security and economic costs associated with expansion relative to the security and economic benefits (Snyder 1991: 60).

[22] Weber (1978) identified this extreme form of patrimonialism as "sultanism," a highly nepotistic regime in which the public sphere overlaps with the sultan's private domain.

much bloodshed and destruction, their political exit is far from assured. Indeed, wars can further strengthen the political pillars of statist-nationalism. Particularly where democratic institutions are absent, these coalitions manage to retain a strong hold on remaining political, economic, and organizational assets. Put differently, there is no simple transitivity between the folly of war and the folly of political defeat. As Salamé (1994: 17) argued, military defeats have arguably strengthened rather than weakened dictatorships in the Arab world, which have been overwhelmingly statist-nationalist. The popularity of challenging an adversary compensated for the opprobrium of defeat. This phenomenon helps explain why such coalitions are less likely to shy away from war. Democratization, of course, forces greater accountability for regional adventurism but tends to face special challenges under regimes ruled by statist-nationalist and confessional coalitions, a subject I discuss in Chapter Four. Finally, the relatively higher affinity of statist-nationalist coalitions with regional policies that are risky and potentially devastating is evident in their consistent pursuit of weapons of mass destruction. Indeed, such coalitions have stood at the vanguard of nuclearizing regions, with expensive nuclear programs playing a central role in the call for "redeeming" solutions to regional threats (threats that in some cases, like South Asia, were perhaps more real than in others, like the Southern Cone).

Historical examples of strong statist-nationalist coalitions include those headed by Pakistan's Zulfiqar Bhutto, Iran's ayatollahs, Egypt's Gamal Abdel Nasser, Libya's Mu'ammar Gadhafi, North Korea's Kim Il Sung, Iraq's Saddam Hussein, Argentina's Juan D. Perón, and Brazil's Getúlio Vargas. With few exceptions, these coalitions helped create some of the most conflict-prone regions. Particularly bloody were encounters between strong statist-nationalist rivals (quadrant 4_I) such as South and North Korea (1950s), Kampuchea and Vietnam (1978–1979), India and Pakistan (1948, 1960s), Iran and Iraq (1980s), Israel and Egypt, Syria, and Iraq (1950s–1960s). The Serbian-Croatian-Bosnian debacle of the 1990s falls largely under this category as well. Territorial issues—highly malleable material in the construction of myths—are almost invariably central to these disputes.

Pairs of weak statist-nationalist coalitions (quadrant 4_{IV}) and mixes of weak and strong statist-nationalist coalitions (quadrants 4_{II} and 4_{III}) are similarly prone to slide into militarized confrontations, such as those between Indonesia and Malaysia (1960s), Somalia and Ethiopia (1977–1978), Israel and Syrian-occupied Lebanon (1982), and South and North Yemen (1979, 1994). In all three cases (of quadrants 4_{II}, 4_{III}, and 4_{IV}) a weak statist-nationalist coalition is particularly constrained domestically, and can hardly afford to engage in "appeasement" exercises vis-à-vis its equally weak statist-nationalist neighbors. Domestically embattled coalitions are more concerned with short-term survival than with potential benefits in an uncertain future; this is not merely the case for coalitions constrained by democratic electoral cycles but also for those led by authoritarian entrepreneurs challenged by competitors, particularly by competitors logrolling even more extremist statist-nationalist-confessional partners, frequently fellow military officers. In sum, weak versions of statist-nationalist co-alitions are likely to be more affected by the competitive outbidding effect identified in Chapter Two, which tends to radicalize the rhetoric and actions of competing factions.

In the realm of economic arrangements, statist-nationalist coalitions face conflicting incentives. On the one hand, satisfying the domestic economic constituencies that sustain them may involve a measure of regional economic cooperation, for instance where such cooperation broadens the protected market for import-substituting firms. This pattern of preferential trading blocs largely characterized many of the efforts at regional integration in Latin America, including LAFTA (Latin American Free Trade Association), CACM (Central American Common Market), and the Andean group.[23] ECLA (the UN Economic Commission for Latin America) provided the regional institutional foundation of this model, one that resisted integration into the global economic system because of its alleged exploitative stance in relation to the in-dustrializing world.[24] Intrabloc trade among COMECON (Council for Mutual Economic Assistance) partners and regional schemes in Africa and Asia also exemplified efforts at import-substitution writ large. Quite often, economic cooperation between these coalitions resulted in trade-diverting schemes, with negative externalities for third actors in the region and beyond.

On the other hand, private and state monopolies threatened with competition from regional counterparts resist lowering trade barriers. Where such monopolies play a critical role in sustaining statist-nationalist coalitions, they strive to maintain a regional system of competing rather than complementary economies. As a fundamental pillar of such coalitions, protected sectors that balk at cooperative undertakings which are likely to threaten their niches generally prevail under these conditions.[25] In the Middle East at the end of the twentieth century, some statist-nationalist-confessional coalitions propose a political economy they regard as rooted in Islamic principles, largely rejecting many of the tenets of international economic regimes.[26] These coalitions have only attained full power in Iran and Sudan, and have proven willing to drown

---

[23] Notably, even in the relatively benign Latin American system, conflict and wars in the last fifty years or so often involved inward-looking, nationalist rivals, with territorial issues looming large in their regional postures. As Mares argues (1997), it would be inappropriate to define that system as a security community throughout those years of import-substituting industrialization and powerful military institutional presence. Mares also discusses the lingering effects of the principle of "sovereignty"—which has historically played into the hands of statist-nationalist-military coalitions—in slowing down progress toward a security community in Latin America.

[24] As I discuss in Chapter Five, this was not the kind of regional framework favored by Chile's strong liberalizing coalition since 1973, which pushed for changes in the direction of eliminating common external tariffs and lowering effective protection.

[25] On how liberalizing forces—rather than protectionist ones—are propelling regional trade blocs, and on how these arrangements are building blocks toward global openness, see Lawrence (1995). On the liberalizing effects of preferential agreements, particularly when domestic biases toward closure are significant, see Oye (1993).

[26] Sahliyeh (1990); Esposito (1991); Kuran (1993).

the benefits from regional economic exchange in a politically more rewarding sea of confessional radicalism, at least initially.

A statist-nationalist coalition in control of a large regional power can avail itself of the imperial commercial strategy so aptly described by Hirschman (1945). It thus seeks to import goods for which there are no substitutes at home (or only poor and expensive ones) and goods required for its war machine, relying on the supply effect of foreign trade. At the same time it uses foreign trade to increase its regional power and influence, inducing maximum dependence by its neighbors through various means: exporting industrial goods in which it has a monopolistic position; diverting its trade to weaker trade partners (particularly poor and small ones) for whom the utility of trade is higher; increasing the others' adjustment difficulties of discontinuing trade; actively deindustrializing weaker potential competitors in its export markets; creating "exclusive complementarities" (products with little demand elsewhere) within the targeted trading partners; and purchasing some of their products at uncompetitive and stable prices to drive them out of alternative markets. A statist-nationalist regional power can also rely on exports of an abundant commodity such as oil to reinforce bilateralism, dependence, and domination. Nazi Germany in the late 1930s and early 1940s provides the textbook case of an imperial strategy, but less successful statist-nationalist hegemons have tried their hand at it as well, as Iraq has occasionally done with Jordan.[27] An imperial commercial strategy allows the large regional power to maximize economic profit, military power, and regional influence, all of which sustain and reproduce its ruling statist-nationalist coalition. Meanwhile, although the strategy may weaken neighboring states as a whole, it also strengthens statist-nationalist partners who benefit economically (as monopolies and monopsonies) and politically from the coercive trade practices of their powerful neighbor. Statist-nationalist coalitions thus put their commercial regional strategies to work by seeking subservient political accessories across the border. This pattern of attempted regional influence is not very different from that of internationalist coalitions, even though the structure of regional trade policies is. Hirschman (1945: 29) depicted these efforts at transnational political activation of "vested interests" well when he argued that: "In the social pattern of each country there exist certain powerful groups the support of which is particularly valuable to a *foreign* [italics in the original] country in its power policy; the foreign country will therefore try to establish commercial relations especially with these groups, in order that their voices will be raised in its favor."

In 1996 statist-nationalist and confessional forces in Israel and South Asia have ridden the crest of a political backlash against internationalization. In Israel, the opposition to the Labor-Meretz coalition's efforts at internationalization and a regional peace settlement gravitates toward Likud and its associated

---

[27] Economic sanctions on Iraq in the 1990s reversed somewhat Jordan's dependence on its neighbor's economy via "transit trade" effects, which are otherwise presumed to benefit the imperial commercial strategy of a regional hegemon (Hirschman 1945: 33–35).

parties on the religious and secular nationalist extremes, which returned to power in 1996. This opposition sustained significant political losses with the achievements of the Labor-Meretz government and the regional breakthroughs with the PLO in 1993 and Jordan in 1994. However, the political knockout of this camp was declared prematurely, and its appeal was revived primarily by bloody radical Islamic attacks on Israeli civilians as well as by the political reorganization of a populist-confessional camp resisting liberalization (the doubling of Shas seats in the 1996 Knesset was a symptom of the latter). Statist-nationalist-confessional coalitions in Israel and Palestine feed on each other's success, as is evident from the growing political difficulties facing the Palestinian Authority (PA). This relationship exemplifies the dynamics of regional diffusion of statist-nationalist-confessionalism and a heightened likelihood of military confrontation. At time T the radical statist-nationalist opposition to the PA shifts the coalitional balance in Israel toward its own statist-nationalist-confessional camp. It does so by engaging in terrorist activities against Israeli citizens and undermining the PA at home. At time $T+1$, the political reinvigoration of statist-nationalist-confessionalism in Israel gives new life to its Palestinian counterpart, no longer marginalized by the peace process and by prospects of a regional economic revolution. Indeed, the opposition to the PA has consistently foiled such prospects by inducing political and economic insecurity and by triggering—via terror—Israeli closure of the territories, which deprives Palestinians of their daily livelihood from work in Israel. Not unexpectedly, even Labor-Meretz succumbed to the flawed logic of territorial closure in response to a massive assault by nationalist-confessional opponents. The fury of that assault gave life to extremist corollaries, including the assassination of Israel's Prime Minister Yitzhak Rabin in November 1995. At time $T+2$ the bilateral and multilateral peace processes have reached their deepest valley, reversing many of the achievements of the liberalizing episode of 1993–1995. As of 1997, many fear the region has shifted toward Cell 4.

In South Asia, the platform of India's fundamentalist Hindu Bharatiya Janata party (BJP) proposed a two-pronged approach to the solution of India's predicaments: banning foreign loans, investments, and imports on the one hand, and deploying nuclear weapons on the other.[28] This coalition draws support from import-competing industries (food-processing, automobile, banking, and communications), from a large and influential sector of Brahmins, from a broad base of public-sector employees, and from some rural sectors opposed to economic reform, internal or external. In the 1996 general elections BJP won a plurality of votes in a highly fragmented contest, but proved unable to organize a viable coalition and was forced to surrender power merely two weeks after being entrusted with that task. Pakistan's radical Islamic party Jama'at-i-Islam is somewhat of a mirror image of Hindu fundamentalism, although the BJP

---

[28] *New York Times* 24 January 1993. The BJP leader endorsed a nuclear deterrent, but there is no party consensus on the nuclear issue. On supporters and detractors of economic liberalization in India, see Kohli (1990).

uses confessional issues more instrumentally (as does Israel's Likud). Jama'at has challenged the Western-style modernization policies of former Prime Minister Nawaz Sharif and of Prime Minister Benazir Bhutto, and exploits primordial confessional passions to advocate combative policies vis-à-vis India. The coalitional dynamics here, as in the Middle East, portrays weak liberalizing coalitions intermittently challenged—and sometimes replaced—by statist-confessional rivals, a cycle that has precluded the achievement of any significant cooperative breakthrough in South Asia. Indeed South Asia has lagged behind the Middle East in the early 1990s, despite arguably better initial conditions and a more manageable number of states required to converge on cooperation.

The statist-nationalist-confessional backlash in these two regions raises the issue of transitivity between positions advanced by statist-nationalist and confessional coalitions while in the opposition and their actual policies once they are in power. In general, the reigning assumption holds that the process of shifting from opposition to government has a moderating effect. Two factors call into question such an expectation for most of these cases: the political logic that sustains these coalitions, and the historical legacy and contemporary empirical record of statist-nationalist and confessional coalitions in power. The empirical chapters dissect the political logic and empirical record of such coalitions in greater detail.

In sum, statist-nationalist-confessional regional orders strengthen the internal consistency of the grand strategies that create them. External threats (in the form of neighboring statist-nationalist and confessional coalitions) give coherence to a program of domestic militarization, the expansion of state influence and intervention, and the use of myths. Instead, the presence of internationalist coalitions in the region challenge the collective consistency of statist-nationalist grand strategies in ways I explore next.

The Paradox of Contained Conflict: Grand-Strategic Equilibria among Strong Mixed Dyads

Cells 2 and 3 depict mixed dyads, where alternative coalitions—internationalist and statist-nationalist—face each other. I first consider the general case for all four generic variants of mixed dyads (eight, if we reverse the identities). These conditions lead a statist-nationalist-confessional coalition in B to use the internationalist coalition ruling neighboring A as a lightning rod for both regional tensions and for its own domestic difficulties. Statist-nationalist entrepreneurs in B thus depict A's efforts to liberalize its domestic economy only through its negative fallouts, portray A's overtures to liberalize regional trade as hegemonic designs, and interpret A's greater affinity with international regimes and institutions as a complete surrender to dictates of foreign powers executing their imperial will in the region. The portrayal of internationalist coalitions often includes the labels "lackeys," "flunkeys," "paper tigers," and "puppets"—notably in the Middle East—or *sadaejuui* (puppets) in the Korean context.

In essence, the ruling coalition in A provides yet another arena for carrying on B's domestic battle against its own internationalist opposition. This phenomenon is evident, for instance, in the Middle East, where secular nationalist and radical-confessional challengers in Iran, Iraq, Sudan, and Libya offer themselves as an alternative to an array of internationalizing coalitions (some royalist, most with a pragmatic Islamic bent). These statist-nationalist coalitions exploit the existence of internationalizing rivals in neighboring states to kindle domestic support for their own programs. By rejecting "apostasy" (in religious or economic terms), "moral decadence," and "cosmopolitan" values, they expect to reinvigorate their own agenda. Their internationalizing rivals, under such conditions, are more constrained domestically in their ability to pursue cooperative regional postures. Moreover, the task of military contraction becomes more difficult where an adversarial statist-nationalist-confessional coalition promotes regional threats and instability. The basis for a stable cooperative framework is missing, in varying degrees, throughout cells 2 and 3. Within a "mixed" region, alternative coalitions create negative externalities for, or impose costs on, their neighboring adversarial coalitions. This is mostly so when the neighbor's model can be credited with transparent political achievements (as in South Korea's "miracle"), or when, in the absence of such achievements, the neighbors' defiant regional postures place serious barriers on the implementation of domestic goals. Finally, mixed dyads are not likely to develop extensive trade relations, given the inherent economic closure and adversarial ideology of statist-nationalist regimes and the primarily global orientation of internationalist ones. This does not preclude instances of unilateral or mutual dependence on markets and raw materials, where the benefits of trade are carefully channeled to the respective coalitional beneficiaries, statist or internationalist.

Where strong adversarial coalitions (one internationalist, the other statist-nationalist) rule in A and B (quadrants 2_I and 3_I), cooperation is undermined by the fact that both sides are compelled to reaffirm the political-economic strategy that sustains and legitimizes them, while keeping the adversary at bay. Yet despite this intense ideological competition, the coalitions' respective strength allows them to achieve a certain modus vivendi, a "live-and-let-live" framework, an ersatz cooperation, less tainted by short-term considerations of political survival than among their weaker counterparts. Despite the strength of the statist-nationalist coalition, imperial commercial schemes are out of the question under the circumstances of a strong, successful internationalist neighbor with access to the rest of the world. To be sure, strong mixed dyads are not friendly—hardly the stuff that evolves into security communities. Although wars remain a definite possibility, the preliminary empirical evidence in Part Two supports the expectations that quadrants 2_I and 3_I do not elicit as many examples of extensive bloodshed as quadrants in cell 4. A methodological difficulty arising in these quadrants is the overall scarcity of strong internationalist coalitions ruling industrializing states, at least until very recently. This scarcity limits the number of mixed dyads involving a strong internationalist and a strong statist-nationalist coalition. An examination of a few actual cases, however, is illustrative of the dynamics of strong adversarial co-alitions.

I discussed South Korea in Chapter Two as evolving from a statist-nationalist phase in the 1950s under Syngman Rhee into a pioneering internationalist case by the 1960s. North Korea, instead, has provided one of the most durable in-stances of a statist-nationalist coalition in power, largely held together by the near-mythical figure of Kim Il Sung. The Korean War—launched by the North—unfolded against the background of parallel efforts at statist-nationalist and, in the case of the North, revolutionary consolidation, much as expected from the profile of such coalitions, particularly in the aftermath of a revolution. By the late 1960s, both the export-led model in South Korea and the statist inward-looking strategy of the North (*juche*) were solidly in place. Since that time the political rivalry between the two was expressed in a regional context of tension and mistrust but not armed conflict. Indeed, the absence of war might be considered particularly remarkable given that the postwar armistice of 1953 was never replaced by any formal instrument indicating the cessation of a state of war (official talks to that effect would not start until mid-1997, a develop-ment compatible with the coalitional dynamics explored in Chapter Seven). Yet an unprecedented dialogue between these fierce opponents was under way by the 1970s, even as radical statist-nationalist factions in the North persisted with aggressive acts against the South's leadership, including the assassination of President Park's wife, of South Korean cabinet ministers, and of civilians.

This incremental cooperative pattern, embraced by the South in spite of its greater economic power vis-à-vis the North, was a natural extension of its grand political-economic strategy premised on domestic and regional stability and peaceful change, all of which were key to the survival of an internationalist project. These conditions help explain the absence of a major war between the strong versions of an adversarial dyad since the Korean War, even in a regional context of intermittent threats and high ideological polarity. The unfriendly but war-free modus vivendi of these two decades, however, was altered by changes in North Korea that eroded the statist-nationalist grip on power by the early 1990s. This was no longer a strong adversarial dyad, but one involving a strong internationalist coalition in the South facing a coalitional struggle in the North. The new coalitional structure developed into a different regional dynamic, most efficiently discussed in the context of the next pattern.

A weak statist-nationalist coalition confronting a strong internationalist coun-terpart (quadrants 2_{III} and 3_{III}) faces a hard dilemma: On the one hand, it can pursue a cooperative regional policy with its internationalist neighbor at the risk of finding itself weakened even further domestically, because such policy alien-ates its natural constituencies. On the other hand, it can pursue an aggressive regional policy that tends to the political needs of those natural constituencies but that also involves two main risks. First, such a policy provides political ammunition to internationalist challengers at home, who can accuse the ruling coalition of fabricating security threats where there are none, and second, an aggressive regional policy forces the adversary's internationalist coalition to deepen its own military preparedness. The strength of the neighboring internationalist coalition is likely to derive from a successfully implemented grand strategy that has now begun to yield substantial resources, both to maintain the strategy in place and to buttress military capabilities if required. As a result, the weak statist-nationalist coalition misses the opportunity of a regional modus vivendi, and instead finds itself weakened further externally—as it confronts an even stronger internationalist neighbor—and internally. A strong internationalist coalition in the neighboring state offers cooperative opportunities, having a built-in proclivity to lower conflict, downsize the state and the military-industrial complex, and to upsize its international status as a stable and reliable target of investments.

In essence, a weak statist-nationalist coalition is caught in a double whammy when it faces both a budding internationalist coalition at home and a strong internationalist neighbor at its borders, a situation that heightens the potential for a concerted political challenge by both. With the growing strength of internationalist constituencies in the early 1990s, Syria's President Assad faced this dilemma at the height of the internationalist convergence in Arab-Israeli relations (1993–1995). With an even more tentative internationalist camp, North Korea's statist-nationalist coalition has been confronted with a comparable dilemma. Reliable information on the unfolding tug-of-war between the two coalitions—their exact composition and relative strength—is extremely scarce. However, few observers doubt the actual existence of political competition between supporters of the statist-nationalist ancien regime and those endorsing an internationalizing shift that would transform and save the regime at the same time, as in China. The relations between North and South Korea in the 1990s have borne the imprint of this coalitional struggle in the North, where incipient North Korean liberalizers pursue cooperative approaches only to be undone by their statist-nationalist opponents at home. Given the personalistic nature of the North Korean regime, the political entrepreneurship of Kim Jong Il (Kim Il Sung's son) may well hold the key to the evolving coalitional balance. In the meantime, the internationalist neighbor—now arguably stronger by virtue of having invested its internationalist strategy with democratic legitimacy—was able to duck the provocations of statist-nationalists in the North, including (presumably nuclear) threats to engulf Seoul "in a sea of fire." Despite lingering statist-nationalist protests in the South enhanced by the economic crisis, stresses in the internationalist strategy, and the consequences of the grand strategy's conversion from an authoritarian to a democratic mode, the vast constituencies supportive of the internationalist strategy endorse the "soft-landing" approach to the North's predicament, in order to secure a peaceful—and economically less exacting—transition in the peninsula. South Korean conglomerates increasingly interested in shifting their labor-intensive operations to the North are a pillar of the South's strategy in the 1990s.

A situation in which a strong statist-nationalist coalition faces a weak internationalist neighbor (quadrants 2_{II} and 4_{III}) overturns the previous double-whammy scenario, allowing the statist-nationalist coalition to ride roughshod over the weak internationalist opposition at home and a similarly weak neighbor. These conditions are likely to whet the appetite of this hegemonic statist-nationalist coalition for physical aggression and imperial commercial practices, everything else being equal. Cashing in on its own solid domestic political support and the neighboring coalition's absence thereof, the strong statist-nationalist coalition faces the optimal conditions for implementing its grand strategy, including the preferred regional policies of its core constituents. It is better able than in most other circumstances to extract vast resources from society and to convert them into a powerful military machine. This machine, in turn, is enabled (and emboldened) to extract vast resources from the neighborhood as well, through threats and imperial fiat. The weak internationalist coalition across the border is now afflicted with the double-whammy syndrome of a politically strong statist-nationalist challenger at home and in the region. It is highly constrained in implementing its domestic reform program, in translating economic efficiency and growth into an effective military deterrent, and in retaining internationalist postures that lubricate foreign trade and investment. It is thus pressured to turn to the themes of its own opposition so as to advance its short-term survival, and to embrace policies that run counter to its long-term interests at home and abroad. At the same time, unless it is prepared to yield to the demands of its strong statist-nationalist neighbor, this coalition becomes an easy target of external attack, turning quadrants 2_{II} and 3_{III} into the ones with perhaps highest potential for militarized hostilities in cells 2 and 3.

Some of the dynamics of quadrants 2_{II} and 3_{III} were evident in Syrian-Lebanese (1970s), Libyan-Moroccan (1980s), and Algerian-Moroccan (1960s) relations. Similarly, the rise of Nasser drew rivals from the House of Saud in Saudi Arabia and the Hashemites in Jordan and Iraq to coalesce under the "King's Alliance," to stem potential Nasserite inroads in their own yard.[29] However, closer to the textbook case—as outlined in Chapter Six—are Iraqi-Kuwaiti relations. Iraq has been a nearly prototypical statist-nationalist, highly militarized regime, held together tightly by Saddam Hussein's strong leadership. Saddam's forces swallowed Kuwait whole in August 1990, in an attempt to apply Kuwaiti oil assets toward maintaining and expanding its statist and militarized grand strategy, one that devoted $85 billion between 1980 and 1988 to military and weapons programs. Facing a weak internationalist opposition at home and a rather weak (and wealthy) internationalizing neighbor in Kuwait whetted Saddam's appetite for bellicose and risky adventurism. Alas, this "mother of all statisms"—Iraq—proved the "mother of all battles"—the Gulf War—to be yet another instance in a long list of unproductive brinkmanship by statist-nationalist leaders, from the Korean War to the Six-Day War and the Malvinas / Falklands, among others. Kuwaiti rulers were able to rely on powerful international allies with a particularly strong interest in the preservation (and deepening) of internationalizing forces in the Arabian Peninsula and the Gulf. As argued at the end of Chapter Two, the international context is not precisely

---

[29] Walt (1985).

neutral to domestic and regional coalitional balances and in this case it pulled together its military might to reverse Saddam's designs.

The final scenario of mixed dyads pits a weak ruling statist-nationalist coalition against a weak ruling internationalist neighbor (quadrants 3_{IV} or 2_{IV}). The weak statist-nationalist coalition in A, for instance, faces a more or less formidable opponent at home, ready to challenge any deepening of resource extraction and the continued expansion of state controls and activities, including those related to the military-industrial sector. The conditions to promote both the domestic and regional interests of this ruling coalition are largely curtailed. The weak internationalist coalition in B, in turn, is fettered domestically by a relatively strong statist-nationalist front that resists liberalization and warns against the perils of cooperating with a competing statist-nationalist neighbor. This situation seems to have been at play in the interaction between Jordan and Israel during the 1991–1992 hiatus between the aftermath of the Gulf War and the electoral defeat of Likud in 1992. A nascent, still-feeble internationalist coalition in Jordan—emboldened by the defeat of statist-nationalist supporters of Saddam Hussein—faced a weakened statist-nationalist adversary in Israel under Prime Minister Shamir, fiercely opposed to compromise with the PLO. This environment of weak adversarial coalitions with short time horizons created little incentive for reciprocal concessions and devalued the expected future benefits of cooperation. Instead, the internationalizing shift in Israel in 1992 bolstered its Jordanian equivalent and paved the way for the historical mutual recognition and diplomatic normalization between Israel and Jordan in 1994. Elsewhere, a weak statist-nationalist coalition in the Ukraine headed by Leonid Kravchuk and a weak internationalist coalition in the early days of Yeltsin's presidency were unable to reach an accommodation such as the one arrived at in 1995, in a much-improved political context for internationalizing agendas.

From Dyads to Regional Dynamics

Figure 2 depicts a simplified regional system, mapping the interaction between the ruling coalitions of two states. In many cases this bilateral interaction is critical in determining a region's level of conflict or cooperation.[30] This is the case, for instance, in the Southern Cone of Latin America, where the Argentine-Brazilian relationship has largely defined the nature and scope of regional rivalry and cooperation, even if other bilateral interactions between these two and others in the region (notably Chile) are not necessarily derivative from the main dyad. Other regions, such as the Middle East, involve a more complex situation, in which a larger number of states helps define the obtaining regional order. Figure 2 retains its utility in accounting for such situations, as many of the examples reviewed suggest.

One can think of A as "the regional environment" facing coalition B, or as an

---

[30] On why the most efficient group of contributors to the management of regional relations is often smaller than the group of potential contributors, see Lake (1997).

aggregate measure of the relative strength of internationalist versus statist-nationalist coalitions. An internationalist regional environment is one in which a more or less homogeneous group of internationalist coalitions holds power, whereas the reverse is true for a statist-nationalist (including confessional, where relevant) regional environment. Converging internationalist grand strategies are collectively stable, creating an environment least propitious for statist-nationalist strategies.[31] The more internationalizing the regional environment, the higher the region's reliance on concerts (at a minimum), collective security, and multilateralism. Concerts convey situations in which partners do not perceive immediate threats from each other, do not consider aggressive steps toward each other, accept the status quo in matters pertaining to their territorial sovereignty, and assist any member subject to such threats or agression.[32] A concert arrangement at the regional level enables the simultaneous implementation of the domestic components of these coalitions' grand strategies, setting in motion a cooperative ratchet. An internationalist regional order, in economic terms, makes statism and a populist-expansionary and military-oriented policy in a given member of that region particularly hard to pursue, as the ruling coalitions of Vietnam and Myanmar could attest, following the consolidation of such an order around ASEAN. The collective achievements of an internationalist model in the region threatens a statist-nationalist coalition's political hold, particularly through demonstration effects, effects that are well understood in North Korea, as well. The East Asian financial crisis of 1997 reveals one of the specific vulnerabilities of internationalist strategies as depicted in Table 1 (Chapter Two). However, some interpret the crisis as the result of deficiencies in the "economic fundamentals" of the internationalist model—widespread corruption, distorted financial markets—that might have been avoided had the model been operating in full. The likelihood that responses to the crisis will largely follow internationalist prescriptions suggests that collective regional strategies of cooperation may be maintained.

For their part, dominant liberalizers act to broaden the sphere of regional stability by coopting and transforming residual statist-nationalists in the region where possible, and without endangering the collective stability of their own grand strategy. Where cooptation and "soft-landing" strategies are not viable, or where internationalist coalitions are not strong enough at home and throughout the region, they cooperate among themselves to protect their own domestic wherewithal against assaults—direct or indirect—from neighboring statist-nationalist-confessional rivals. Thus, GCC (Gulf Cooperation Council, comprising Saudi Arabia, Bahrain, Qatar, Oman, the UAE, and Kuwait) excluded at the outset (1981) the strong statist-nationalist and confessional regimes in Iran and

---

[31] On collective stability as a measure of a strategy's robustness against invasion by other strategies, see Axelrod (1984).

[32] Job (1997); Jervis (1982). A less benign definition of concerts emphasizes their enforcement through strong power collusion and their conditional postponement—not suspension—of balance of power mechanisms (Betts 1993). On concerts and collective security, see Kupchan and Kupchan (1991). On multilateralism as an analytical category, see Ruggie (1993).

Iraq. Similarly, ASEAN (Association of Southeast Asian Nations) initially ostracized Vietnam, Kampuchea, and Laos. After years of deriding ASEAN as the "puppet of the Western imperialists," and while moving toward economic liberalization (and a concomitant downsizing of its military), Vietnam acceded to ASEAN's Treaty on Amity and Cooperation in 1992.

Overall, the association between internationalist coalitions and reciprocal cooperation appears, prima facie, to challenge Maoz and Russett's (1992: 257) finding that rapidly growing states are more likely to fight each other than would be expected by chance alone. However, such tendency during the 1946–1986 period was mostly evident among non-OECD states, many of whom were ruled by statist-nationalist coalitions, particularly in the earlier decades. In the early postwar period, some inward-looking statist-nationalist coalitions both spawned considerable economic growth and waged wars against each other. Even weak (let alone strong) internationalist coalitions were quite rare beyond OECD states at the time, as I discuss in Chapter Four. Once internationalist coalitions took root in some industrializing states (South Korea, Singapore, Hong Kong, Taiwan, Thailand, Malaysia, Indonesia, Chile, Brazil, and Argentina, Israel), they unleashed both unprecedented rates of growth and cooperative ventures. Where these coalitions were strongest and dominant in a region, armed conflict was generally avoided, even in regions with a long history of wars and rivalries. ASEAN has a record of defusing internal disputes, and its members have managed to conduct an effective diplomacy on regional matters, notably in the case of Kampuchea.[33] The finding of an inverse relationship between trade openness and international conflict provides some indirect support for the expected behavior of internationalist coalitions.[34] Ruling internationalist coalitions carefully underplay nationalism and ethno-confessionalism, for these forces have the potential of shattering the internationalist model both at home and in the region.

A regional environment dominated by statist-nationalist ruling coalitions multiplies the inherently conflictive logic identified above for statist-nationalist dyads. This is a multipolar balance-of-threat system par excellence that strengthens the logic of expanding state prerogatives, deepening military-bound resource extraction, and developing baroque weapons. Willy-nilly, this logic lowers the barriers against military conflict and places statist-nationalist-confessional coalitions in a position of having to consider war options even more frequently than they would otherwise prefer. Converging statist-nationalist grand strategies are collectively rather stable—feeding on each other's existence—creating an environment of war zones most immune to internationalist strategies, at least in the short term. Statist-nationalist war zones prevailed in most of the Middle East following independence, and continue to dominate those subregions within the Middle East that have remained largely resistant to

---

[33] On the weakness of populist challenges in East and Southeast Asian countries in the 1980s, see Haggard (1995a: 455). On ASEAN institutional deepening into security issues, see Shirk (1997) and Richardson (1994/95: 37).

[34] Gasiorowski (1986); Domke (1988); Oneal and Russett (1997).

internationalizing shifts (the Iran-Iraq-Syria tripod in particular). As I discuss in Chapter Six, weak internationalist coalitions, such as Lebanon's in the 1970s and Jordan's intermittently for decades, found it hard to survive in a regional environment dominated by strong statist-nationalist coalitions. In such an environment, they either adapted, by embracing the themes of their own opposition (as in Jordan), or died (as in Lebanon). War zones were also dominant in Indochina throughout the 1950s and 1970s, and the Korean peninsula in the 1950s. A mutating global context—with the effects depicted in Chapter Two—eventually can undermine the immunity to change of statist-nationalist war zones, as do demonstration effects from other regions. Ultimately, however, the domestic political and institutional prism determines such shifts and their durability.

In regions where alternative coalitions vie for the legitimacy of their respective models we might expect less cooperation and a higher incidence of balance-of-threat mechanisms than where ruling internationalist coalitions share a common agenda, but perhaps lower levels of military confrontation (both in incidence and scope) than in statist-nationalist war zones. The Middle East of the 1990s as a whole seems to exhibit this tendency. The cooperative impasse within the Arab Maghreb Union (Algeria, Libya, Mauritania, Morocco, and Tunisia) and the Arab Cooperation Council (Egypt, Jordan, North Yemen, and Iraq) can be similarly traced to competing ruling coalitions in the region, where liberalizers face heavy domestic and regional challenges from statist-nationalist-confessional challengers. As argued in Chapter Two, there are instances in which the competition between the two ideal-type coalitions within a single state fails to yield a clear victor, one that can hold on to power effectively for any significant time. Conditions of rough domestic parity between competing coalitions generally yield the most erratic pattern of regional behavior, exemplified by North Korea in the late 1980s and early 1990s and Algeria's in the 1990s. Policies are ridden with unwieldy inconsistencies over time and across issue areas. Under such conditions, a highly homogeneous cluster of neighboring coalitions can play a central role in swaying the domestic impasse in one direction or another, depending on whether the cluster is internationalist or statist-nationalist. Conversely, a regional coalitional balance may be expected to exacerbate domestic coalitional competition.

Finally, for every combination in a region, the relationship between external policy risk and internal political risk varies. Lamborn (1991: 56) defines such a relationship as positively interdependent (that is, policy failure damages the coalition politically, or policy success builds the coalition up) or negatively interdependent (that is, a low policy risk involves a high political risk, or a high policy risk is associated with a low political risk). Policy and political risks can be positively (or inversely) interdependent in the short run and inversely (or positively) interdependent in the long run. In statist-nationalist orders, first: Co-operative regional policies are politically risky in the short run (for all the reasons specified in Chapter Two); and second: aggressive regional postures are quite risky in the short and longer term (they can slide into wars), but such policy risks are less positively interdependent with political risk than in alternative orders, particulary in nondemocratic contexts. In mixed orders, cooperative regional policies are less risky where strong coalitional variants enjoy considerable domestic strength. In internationalist orders, cooperative postures carry positively interdependent (low) policy and political risks.

BROADER THEORETICAL IMPLICATIONS

Before turning to the impact of the democracy variable on coalitional interactions, it is time to take stock of several implications of interactive regional effects on coalitional dynamics and regional orders. The empirical studies in Part Two will return not only to the main theoretical argument outlined in Chapter Two but also to the implications of strategic interaction among coalitions in a region. These implications include the following.

1. Domestic ethno-confessional diversity per se is not an efficient indicator of a state's proneness to conflictive or cooperative behavior vis-à-vis its neighbors. The coalitional pattern available to ethno-confessional actors at home, the relative political strength of the coalition they join, and the identity and strength of the coalitional cluster they face at the border provide a more proximate indication of their potential behavior. Thus a region ridden with domestic and regional ethno-confessional cleavages—ASEAN for instance—can exhibit high levels of cooperation in the presence of a cluster of strong internationalist coalitions.

2. The degree of regional homogeneity / heterogeneity of political regimes per se does not provide enough information regarding the likelihood of conflict and cooperation, as some theories have suggested. Knowledge about the identity and strength of the regional coalitional cluster is essential: highly homogeneous internationalist clusters exhibit higher levels of extensive and intensive cooperation; highly homogeneous statist-nationalist clusters exhibit higher levels of military conflict; and heterogeneous clusters span a wide range of conflictive-cooperative behavior that generally eschews high values at either end. Driven by different approaches to the global political economy, coalitional clusters create regional "identities" and shared expectations about conflict and cooperation. Paradoxically, Asia's Asianization is the result of the globalization of its economy, and internationalist strategies have done more to build a MERCOSUR community than decades of regional "self-reliance" discourse.[35]

3. Internationalist clusters are more likely than statist-nationalist-confessional or mixed clusters to rely on broader definitions of security (including economic) than on military confidence-building measures and arms control. This expectation derives from the logic of self-binding commitments that internationalist agendas engender, particularly the unilateral interest in avoiding unwanted levels of militarization that threaten core macroeconomic objectives. This logic also explains why codification (treaties) and high institutionalization are not always necessary, and in effect can lag behind praxis, as with ASEAN's Regional Forum, created in 1994. In contrast to internationalist clusters, the highly mixed groups of states that converged around CSCE

---

[35] Funabashi (1993).

(Conference on Security and Cooperation in Europe) emphasized security confidence-building measures and codified CSCE guidelines prior to their implementation.[36]

4. Military expenditures as a percentage of GDP (or of central government budgets) are likely to be higher overall among statist-nationalist and confessional or mixed clusters than among internationalist ones. An internationalist coalition in the midst of a statist-nationalist regional environment is likely to spend more on defense (as a percentage of GDP) than it would otherwise. The military expenditures of statist-nationalist clusters in the Middle East reached sometimes 20 percent of GDP (and over 40 percent of central budgets). The mixed Northeast Asia system spends 600 percent more in defense than ASEAN countries do, although liberalizers in South Korea had maintained military expenditures comparable to the average in the industrializing world, in a region ridden with security dilemmas.[37]

5. Internationalist clusters, particularly where coalitions are robust domestically, are expected to be more prone to denuclearize their region—eschewing nuclear weapons—than their statist-nationalist-confessional and mixed counterparts. Preliminary support for this expectation is evident in the fact that, of all states (beyond the original five nuclear powers) considering a nuclear option in the last three decades, not one embraced a nuclear weapons-free zone under a statist-nationalist coalition. Furthermore, only internationalist coalitions undertook effective commitments and implementation of denuclearization.[38]

6. A solitary internationalist coalition sorrounded by statist-nationalist-confessional neighbors is likely to have enormous difficulties in implementing its grand strategy, in both its domestic and regional aspects. To avoid being exploited, such a coalition is forced to expand its military infrastructure and to deny its rivals the advantages of cooperation. This recalls Axelrod's (1984) principle that only a minimal number of cooperative (nice) strategies can overcome an environment of "meanies." Below that threshold, internationalist coalitions may be more prone to mirror statist-nationalist-confessional strategies. Precluded from embracing the preferred strategies of its core constituents, the duration of internationalist islands in statist-nationalist seas is likely to be short. As with most other propositions here, this one only points to a general tendency, which makes deviant cases such as Costa Rica particularly attractive for understanding the survival of such coalitions in the midst of militarized statist-nationalist neighbors.

7. A solitary statist-nationalist coalition sorrounded by internationalist neighbors will find it progressively more difficult to maintain its traditional domestic base of support or to use external threats to prop it up. The reigning grand strategy in the region—economic liberalization, growth, and cooperative relations—is likely to doom

---

[36] This does not mean that internationalist coalitions never opt for security confidence-building measures or institutionalization (the European Union has) but that neither is required for cooperation to come about. When defense has the advantage (offense is too costly, in our framework: costly for the coalition) arms control are less necessary and unilateral defensive policies obtain (Glaser 1994/95; Jervis 1982).

[37] International Institute for Strategic Studies (1992); ACDA (1990); World Bank (1996).

[38] Solingen (1994b).

the legitimacy of the statist-nationalist agenda, as ASEAN neighbors such as Vietnam belatedly discovered.

8. A statist-nationalist regional cluster is rather stable collectively, creating an environment quite resistant to internationalist grand strategies in the short term, but not completely immune in the longer haul to mutating—globalizing—international pressures and their regional corollaries. A predominantly internationalist regional environment is collectively stable as well, creating an environment quite resistant to statist-nationalist strategies but not completely immune to the unintended effects of globalizing pressures—such as currency crises—or to potential international mutations in a protectionist direction. Despite this chapter's attention to regional interactive effects, such effects constitute only one input into the domestic strength of a given coalition. At the same time, independent and parallel domestic dynamics in different states can add up to changes in the existing coalitional center of gravity in a region.

9. A coalitional analysis thus highlights how numbers may affect cooperation, a concern raised in game-theoretic and collective-action approaches that regard large numbers as encumbering cooperation. Low numbers of internationalist coalitions in a region make cooperation difficult, but not low numbers of statist-nationalist confessional coalitions. High numbers of internationalist coalitions in a region do not preclude—indeed they bolster—cooperation, whereas high numbers of their coalitional opponents burden it. Numbers only matter once we have a proper understanding of coalitional identities and dynamics.

The basic hypotheses outlined in Chapter Two and the additional implications listed in this concluding section can be falsified by evidence of internationalist or statist-nationalist and mixed clusters that behave differently from the way they were expected to. A particularly strong challenge could come in the form of a strong cluster of internationalist coalitions that exhibits a highly conflictive and militarized pattern of interaction, particularly if few statist-nationalist-confessional rivals remain in that region. Another strong challenge to this chapter's propositions would be rendered by observations of an extensive, intensive, and highly stable cooperative pattern of regional relations between / among statist-nationalist-confessional coalitions. Before submitting these propositions to empirical analysis we must examine the extent to which they may be affected by a variable formally omitted thus far from our discussion: the democratic / non-democratic context within which coalitions operate.

Economic Liberalization, Coalitions, and the Democratic Peace

THE PRECEDING CHAPTERS outlined the hypothesized relations between the political implications of internationalization, economic liberalization, and the probability of regional cooperation or, more specifically, between coalitional types and regional behavior and outcomes. A major outstanding task is to clarify the possible connections between three variables: economic liberalization, democracy, and regional outcomes. A number of methodological and conceptual issues compel a discussion of democracy in the context of the general argument advanced so far. First, the democratic peace hypothesis has now become a leading contender in explaining the absence of war. Indeed the hypothesis has been granted a status of lawlike generalization (Levy 1988) that forces a serious consideration of its applicability to regional orders, irrespective of any other considerations. Moreover, the possibility that the relationship between economic liberalization and regional orders might be an artifact of the democratic peace effect needs to be considered. In order to disentangle all these presumed interactions we must first clarify the following causal relations:

1. The independent effects of economic liberalization on conflict and cooperation.
2. The independent effects of democracy on conflict and cooperation.
3. The logical and empirical connections between economic liberalization and political liberalization (democratization).[1]
4. The joint impact of economic liberalization and democratization on regional conflict and cooperation.

The independent effects of economic liberalization on regional orders—via the coalitional struggle—have been my focus heretofore. Both the conceptualization of such effects and the empirical examples make it clear that both internationalist and statist-nationalist coalitions can be either democratic or nondemocratic, and that their expected regional behavior has been postulated—and expected to vary—while controlling for the democracy variable. This chapter is devoted to the other three sets of relations. The next section reviews the literature on the democratic peace, its applicability to the industrializing world, and its implications for an ancillary connection: that between democratization (in

---

[1] I have thus far used the term "liberalization" only in reference to the economic sphere. I prefer to rely on the term "democratization" in this chapter—where processes involving political liberalization are involved—only to avoid unnecessary confusion between political and economic liberalization. This is not always possible, however, particularly when citing relevant literature that invokes the term "political liberalization."

contrast to democracy) and regional conflict and cooperation. I then examine the interactions between economic liberalization and democratization, a core endeavor in the field of comparative politics. The last section explores the implications of all these interactions for understanding regional conflict and cooperation.

THE LOGIC OF THE DEMOCRATIC PEACE

A rich literature has emerged in the last decade dealing with alternative hypotheses designed to explain first, why democratic states are not likely to wage wars among themselves, and second, why they are as likely as nondemocratic states to engage nondemocratic partners in armed conflict. I first disaggregate these somewhat complementary hypotheses (most of which combine institutional, perceptual, and normative considerations) and extend them to the analysis of cooperation, rather than the mere avoidance of war. I then explore why the logical underpinnings of this hypothesis might be only partially applicable beyond the empirical domain (largely the industrialized world) that upheld the renaissance of this line of theorizing.

Definitional issues have haunted the democratic peace research program, but have not shattered its fundamental thrust.[2] For our purposes here, Robert Dahl's analysis of "polyarchy" provides a basic, comprehensive, working definition for a most contested term. While relying on this definition, I retain the concept "democracy" (instead of polyarchy). I also generally avoid the usage of "liberal" states as an equivalent of "democratic" states to preclude any confusion between economic and political liberalism (except in the section that follows, when citing literature that often conflates those terms). Dahl (1989: 221) describes seven institutions of polyarchy: 1. elected officials, 2. free and fair elections, 3. inclusive suffrage, 4. right to run for office, 5. freedom of expression, 6. alternative information protected by law, and 7. associational autonomy. These institutional characteristics of democracy are universal (even if the strength and mix is not) and cannot be modified by relativist and exceptionalist concepts derived from different religious, cultural, or other doctrinal sources. In the remainder of this chapter the terms "nondemocratic" and "authoritarian" indicate a state that has not yet attained such characteristics, even if it is undergoing some of the transitional phases of democratization.

The bulk of the democratic peace literature is devoted to establishing—and understanding—the absence of war among democratic dyads and clusters. In what follows I attempt to extend the propositions accounting for this outcome to hypothesize first, why democratic dyads and clusters might be also more prone to *cooperate*, and not merely refrain from warring; and second, why democracies behave differently vis-à-vis nondemocracies. I do so to maintain a certain symmetry in my treatment of economic liberalization and democratiza-

---

[2] See, for instance, Ray (1993).

tion as sources of regional order. While discussing the impact of coalitions as an independent variable I examined a broad range of outcomes, from most conflictive to deeply cooperative. I now extend the democratic peace mode of theorizing to a similarly broader behavioral domain, even if these relations have never been postulated formally by the democratic peace research program. On what basis, then, can we link the democratic or nondemocratic nature of a regime to war-likeliness or cooperation?[3] The following list of hypotheses is suggestive of such linkages but there is very little agreement on the relative merits of different hypotheses.

Domestic Legitimacy and Accountability. According to this proposition, rooted in a Kantian conception of citizens' consent, the legitimacy granted by the domestic public of one liberal democracy to the elected representatives of another has a moderating effect leading away from violent solutions.[4] Although disagreements and even conflict may remain, democracies are likely to shy away from armed conflict and to search for cooperative solutions in their dealings with fellow democracies.[5] Instead, the abhorrence of authoritarianism and its lack of popular accountability presumably lowers the barriers in democracies to resorting to more violent means in handling their conflict with nondemocratic adversaries. The ability to cooperate is arguably greatly handicapped for a mixed (democratic / nondemocratic) dyad, for both normative and instrumental reasons. First, cooperation requires trust, and democracies find it harder to trust commitments by adversarial leaders who lack legitimacy at home.[6] Second, not only do nondemocratic leaders lack accountability but their lack of legitimacy arguably renders their hold on power more precarious, shortening the shadow of the future and impairing cooperation.

Institutional Checks and Balances. A second proposition holds that free speech, electoral cycles, and the public policy process act as restraints on the ability of democratic leaders to pursue extreme policies vis-à-vis fellow democracies.[7] According to Kant, the public hesitates to initiate wars because of the heavy costs that it might have to bear.[8] Thus, the greater the input of civil society, the lower a democratic state's reliance on war is presumed to be, when managing conflict with other democracies. Conversely, the more concentrated the monopoly of political power, or the more praetorian the domestic structures, the higher the probability that extreme, violent solutions might be embraced.[9] An adversary's authoritarianism and praetorianism can arguably cancel the moderating effects of institutional checks and balances among those democ-

---

[3] For a preliminary attempt to examine both the conflictive and cooperative implications of the democratic peace hypothesis, see Solingen (1996a).

[4] Doyle (1983, 1986); Van Evera (1991).

[5] Maoz and Abdolali (1989).

[6] Doyle (1983); Owen (1994: 103).

[7] Bueno de Mesquita and Lalman (1992); Ember, Ember, and Russett (1992).

[8] Doyle (1986: 1,160).

[9] On praetorianism and external conflict, see Snyder (1993a).

racies facing security threats from nondemocratic opponents. This proposition is more useful in explaining why democratic dyads avoid armed conflict than in indicating that checks and balances necessarily buttress cooperation between them.

Domestic Transparency, Communication, and the Costs of Regime-Creation. Democracies are information-rich societies assumed to maximize transparency. The expectation that mutual information about the internal evaluations of a policy, or of the intensity of the preferences, will be available to a democratic dyad should thus improve their chances for arriving at cooperative arrangements, beyond the mere absence of war.[10] Maximizing information is of particular importance in the creation of security regimes, where the risks of error and deception can be catastrophic.[11] Transparency presumably allows a democratic dyad to embrace concessions at a much lower risk of the other side defecting, because of the public nature of the process involved in reversing policies. Thus, states sharing an open political system can develop high levels of mutual formal and informal communication which, in turn, lower the cost of reaching agreements and joining regimes.[12] Openness allows the transgovernmental networks of democratic dyads to share information on their respective domestic conditions, thus facilitating transnational logrolling of support for such regimes. Conversely, asymmetric levels of transparency arguably lower democracies' incentives to cooperate, because they find it harder to foresee potential assaults—by nondemocratic would-be partners—on the stipulations of cooperative arrangements. Mixed or nondemocratic dyads thus might be expected to engage in more contained communication patterns, which deprive them of the positive externalities of communication for cooperation. In such cases, the attempt to protect the autonomy of decision making from outside interference raises the costs of cooperating, which now include prior efforts at improving mutual communication.

Democratic Process, Credibility, and Ratification. Some studies suggest that democracies are respectful of the rule of law and appear to undertake more credible and durable commitments.[13] This tendency, it may be argued, strengthens their reputation as predictable partners—of fellow democracies—who may be more accepting of cooperative agreements and regimes binding their behavior. This credibility can help democratic dyads rely on diffuse reciprocity, where the benefits from cooperation can be distributed over extended periods of time, rather than on a quid-pro-quo basis. Stable democracies are likely to bind successive governments to international agreements, whereas nondemocratic regimes can be replaced by challengers capable of reshuffling international commitments to maintain legitimacy at home. In fact, nondemocratic rulers may

---

[10] Keohane (1984); Bueno de Mesquita and Lalman (1992); Starr (1992).
[11] Jervis (1986).
[12] Keohane (1984: 95–97); Fearon (1994).
[13] Doyle (1983); Siverson and Emmons (1991); Gaubatz (1996).

enter an agreement and soon after defect, without any serious domestic constraints. This is evident, for instance, from Saddam Hussein's consistent violations of Iraq's international commitments. A democratic dyad would thus arguably operate under conditions of strong mutual credibility, whereas problems of uncertainty over ratification, compliance, and implementation could be more severe in asymmetric or nondemocratic dyads. Such uncertainty may be more pronounced where nondemocratic interlocutors do not follow easily tractable procedures or where their rulers are too weak domestically to implement reciprocity.[14] No effective security regime can come about under conditions of severe uncertainty and low credibility. Despite the inherent logic in this reasoning, the expectation that nondemocratic regimes would be less transparent and credible in their commitments and less reliable on ratification is often postulated but very seldom explained or tested.[15]

Sensitivity to the Human and Material Costs of War. Citizens of liberal democracies are assumed to be particularly wary of wars because these often exact heavy losses in life and property.[16] This general aversion to losses, particularly if it is shared by democratic adversaries, induces caution in the management of conflict among them. Conversely, the sensitivity to loss changes when democracies face a nondemocratic adversary suspected of seeking total—rather than limited—objectives. According to this logic, democracies assume a lower sensitivity to losses among nondemocratic regimes, where a few leaders can risk a lot in material and human terms, without the need for consent or accountability, to secure their aims. Thus the need to resist aggression is assumed to be particularly compelling for democracies in this predicament, and the opportunities for cooperation far fewer. Another way of formulating this proposition is to say that democratic dyads, even under conditions of conflict, avoid wars because of reciprocally high levels of aversion to loss. Conversely, cooperation between mixed (or nondemocratic) dyads is arguably hindered because initial asymmetries in sensitivity to loss lead to a greater need to rely on deterrence, in order to offset a lower authoritarian sensitivity to losses.

These five propositions summarize some basic conceptual links between democracy and the likelihood of conflict and cooperation that might be extrapolated from the literature on the democratic peace. Efforts to reconceptualize regional relations in the post–Cold War era on the basis of the democratic peace research program must specify which underlying logic is expected to be at work in explaining regional orders. This is particularly the case in light of the wide variation in democratic forms, both between established and new de-

---

[14] Oye (1986). Israel's Netanyahu wields this argument frequently to explain reluctance to cooperate with the PA, although it is hard to disentangle this motive from ulterior coalitional considerations, as will be clear in Chapter Six.

[15] Indeed, trade-dependent autocracies might be assumed to require the rather stable rule of law and fair enforcement of contracts and property rights (Esty et al. 1997: 18).

[16] Schumpeter (1955); Doyle (1986).

mocracies, as well as among an array of emerging democratic states. There is an understandable intellectual excitement offered by the possibility that the global reach of democratization might solve not only the internal security dilemma of citizens throughout the industrializing world but also the classical interstate security dilemmas afflicting most of these regions. Alas, this prognosis may be premature.

Empirically, an overview of the industrializing world in the last decade of the century suggests that regional cooperation has generally not been the result of a meeting of democratic minds. The most cooperative dyads and clusters analyzed in Part Two include a significant number of nondemocratic states, as in ASEAN and GCC. In the Middle East, which lags behind most of the industrializing world in democratization, an ecclectic mix of more or less authoritarian states and a long-standing democracy have jointly spearheaded an unprecedented peace process.[17] This pattern does not violate the democratic peace tenets because democracy is considered to be a sufficient but not a necessary condition for cooperation. However, the rumblings of confessional politics in the Middle East have led to suggestions that a more democratic Middle East (that is, one with presumably effective democratic dyads) might result in a higher rather than lower probability of war. The assumption is that if radical Islamic forces prevail electorally in the Arab world and maintain democratic institutions, a greater symmetry in regime type between Israel and its neighbors and among those neighbors as well might arguably exacerbate (rather than mitigate) regional conflict. This possibility could be traumatic not only for the region but for the democratic peace hypothesis as well.[18] The hypothesis might conceivably be saved by arguing that Islamic democracies are distorted versions of the real thing, which raises definitional and contextual issues, and perhaps problems of ethnocentricity. However, as stipulated above, certain institutional characteristics of democracy are universal and cannot be tinkered with by relativisms of any kind. Hence, genuine Islamic democracies are thus far counterfactuals or hypothetical, and one can only explore the implications of a reality of slow democratization, a category that has received far less attention in democratic peace theorizing.[19]

---

[17] Israel within the 1967 borders has been a democracy since its creation in 1948. Perhaps the least democratic state in this group is Syria (Iraq and Iran, sharing this end of the spectrum, are not part of the peace process at all). Jordan, Egypt, Palestine, and Lebanon are undergoing democratization at different rates and with different degrees of success. Other Arab participants / observers in the multilateral peace negotiations, such as Algeria, Yemen, Saudi Arabia, and the Gulf states are similarly groping with pressures to democratize. References to democratization and peace in the Middle East build on Solingen (1996c). Chapter Six includes a more detailed analysis of economic liberalization, democratization, and regional conflict and cooperation in that region.

[18] Preliminary Evidence from Iran, Sudan, and other radical Islamic challengers throughout the region suggests that Islamist regimes (whether assuming power democratically or not) are more likely to resist peace with Israel than the regimes they challenge. This assumption is unrelated to debates over Islamic threats to the West, over the likelihood of a unified Islamic world, or over the inherent (in)compatibility between democracy and Islam (see Chapter Six).

[19] See the pioneering article by Mansfield and Snyder (1995).

Not only has democracy been marginal as the engine of cooperation in the industrializing world but where democratic dyads have faced each other in certain regions they have yielded less cooperation than might be expected from the propositions above. Thus, in sharp contrast with the high levels of cooperation among mixed (democratic-nondemocratic) ASEAN countries and the cooperative breakthroughs in the Middle East, two democracies in South Asia have been unable to transcend their historical feud. The dispute in Kashmir has characteristics of a war by proxy, with ominous potential. It is quite suggestive that at the twentieth century's end the Indo-Pakistani conflict ranks highest in its potential for a nuclear conflict.[20] In the Southern Cone sometimes facile connections are drawn between the existence of democracy and the unprecedented cooperation between Argentina and Brazil in the 1990s. In reality, the absence of war in that region for over a century has coexisted with the extensive absence of democracy. Morever, the relationship between democracy and conflictive or cooperative behavior has a very mixed historical record here, as will be clear from Chapter Five. On the one hand, regional cooperation was arguably quite high under common authoritarian (military) rule because of a convergence of interests among these regimes to suppress subversion at home, a pattern reminiscent of ASEAN and GCC (as well as of the nineteenth-century European concert). In effect, it was the dictatorships of generals Jorge R. Videla in Argentina and João Figueiredo in Brazil that took the first steps toward nuclear cooperation in the late 1970s and early 1980s even if these never implied regional denuclearization. On the other hand, the democratic regimes that assumed power in the 1980s did not effectively deepen cooperation in either economics or security. Only the internationalist coalitions of the 1990s reversed decades of competition, alienation, and refusal to abide fully by the nonproliferation regime.

In adjacent South America two democracies—Peru and Ecuador—became involved in military hostilities in 1981, 1984, and 1995.[21] Statistical conventions of the democratic peace hypothesis conveniently helped dispose of this case, as fewer than one thousand battlefield deaths are not considered war events in these data sets. However, these violent encounters between democracies in a region with few militarized disputes for over a century cannot be dismissed as easily, even if they only amount to legitimate anomalies of an otherwise robust hypothesis connecting democracy to peace. Indeed, in the continent with the fewest wars—South America—another potential recent anomaly can be added to the list of exceptions. Two democracies—Colombia and Venezuela—mobilized border troops in 1995, avoiding all-out war (and a place in the leading data sets) but not a militarized dispute with a dozen casualties, over a thousand

---

[20] This was the assessment of former US Director of Central Intelligence James Woolsey (*New York Times* 22 February 1994: A15), among many others.

[21] Mares (1997) reports 200 battlefield deaths in the Peruvian-Ecuadorian war in 1981. The three South American wars in this century include the Chaco War between Bolivia and Paraguay (1932–1935), the war between Peru and Ecuador (1939–1941), and the war between Argentina and Great Britain (1982).

forceful expulsions of foreign nationals, and over five thousand soldiers mobilized on each side of the border.[22] These militarized—if low-level—disputes acquire significant prominence, given the small absolute number of militarized interstate disputes worldwide since 1989.[23]

The experience of all these regions suggests, at the very least, that some caution is in order when applying democratic peace theorizing to the industrializing world.[24] Beyond ongoing debates over statistical inference and the significance of a few anomalies, the attempt to extend the hypothesis may be problematic on conceptual grounds. Such effort amounts, after all, to an extrapolation of the democratic peace relationship beyond the geographical and temporal domain that provided most support for the hypothesis, that is, beyond the industrialized world's "zone of peace" since 1945.[25] The democratic predisposition to avoid wars and build cooperative regimes is firmly rooted in the universe of economically advanced democracies, where democratic stability is far more abundant than in other regions.[26] There have been very few democratic dyads or clusters throughout the industrializing world with a history of stable democratic regimes. Moreover, the concern with democratic continuity has been central to virtually every ruling coalition there. This dearth of enduring democratic regimes—the building blocks of the democratic peace—is clearly reflected in databases on which the democratic peace was tested.[27] The conditions for the operation of any of the five hypotheses linking peace to democratic structures, processes, and norms have been arguably rare beyond the OECD community until the recent wave of democratization. These conditions presuppose, in Doyle's (1983: 213) terms, "*constitutionally secure* liberal states" (my emphasis). Democratic continuity implies secure tenure and transitions. The

---

[22] James Brooke, "Nationalist Fever Helps Heat up Another Latin Border," *New York Times* 18 March 1995: 5.

[23] Militarized interstate disputes did not reach a total of six (1989–1995), according to the Stockholm International Peace Research Institute (1996).

[24] Incidentally, neither does the record provide support for an alternative—symmetric—hypothesis of "authoritarian peace." The list of wars between nondemocratic dyads in most regions is a hefty one, with Vietnam and Cambodia in the 1970s, the Koreas in the 1950s, and Iran and Iraq in the 1980s providing only some of the most gruesome examples.

[25] For a critique of the presumed robustness of the democratic peace evidence, even within this set, see Spiro (1994). For a critique of the weak theoretical foundations of the democratic peace, see Owen (1994). For skepticism in extrapolating the democratic peace to the Third World, see Rothstein (1992).

[26] Maoz and Russett (1992: 245) argue that "states which can be perceived as *stable democracies* [my emphasis] are less likely to be involved in disputes with other democracies." Most and Starr (1989) argue that *democratic continuity* and the entrenchment of democratic norms played a role in the democratic peace of the postwar era. Doyle (1983: 213) interprets the anomaly of the Peruvian-Ecuadorian war as a function of its occurrence "before the pacifying effects of liberalism could become deeply engrained."

[27] According to Maoz's coding of regime type (Russett 1993: 94–98), Turkey and Cyprus should have been included as a democratic dyad which, alas, went to war that year. Weede's (1992) study finds only twenty full democracies in the 1962–1980 period, with only Costa Rica and Israel representing the industrializing world.

task of explaining lags—or the required lead time for democratic institutions to breed stable cooperation—remains.

A related problem points to the need to examine whether the presumptions of the five hypotheses apply also to the process of democratization, rather than merely to the final product (a democratic state). In effect, this is a more virulent form of the instability affliction. Not only did we lack stable democratic interlocutors (dyads, clusters) throughout much of the industrializing world until very recently, but most of our potential observations were—and still are—traversing different phases of the journey toward democracy. As such, these transitional democracies may be subject to political pressures affecting their conduct of external affairs that are different in nature from those pressures familiar to stable democracies. Identifying such pressures, and their implications for regional conflict and cooperation, is an important item that Mansfield and Snyder (1995) helped introduce in the agenda of the democratic peace research program.

Summing up this overview of the democratic peace hypothesis in the industrializing world, clearly democracy has proven to be an unnecessary condition for the avoidance of war and for the achievement of cooperation. Indeed, it has perhaps been even an insufficient condition for the avoidance of militarized disputes and certainly insufficient for the emergence of genuine regional cooperation. As argued, only the sufficiency clause and war / militarized conflict outcomes posit difficulties for the democratic peace hypothesis. Moreover, the distinct possibility that democracy might bear a generally positive relationship to cooperation remains, even if that relationship is found to be less strong than some studies imply, particularly in transitional contexts. Given the centrality of economic reforms to the pace, stability, and longevity of democratic transitions, a review of the interaction between political and economic liberalization is in order.[28]

UNTANGLING THE GLOBAL GLASNOST-PERESTROIKA: SEQUENCES AND INTERACTIONS

It is not the objective of this section to summarize the literature on the mutual interaction between the introduction of democracy and the introduction of markets, a subject that can fill the walls of a political science library. A more modest effort involves taking stock of whatever emerging consensus on transitions there might be in this field of inquiry, a field boosted by the recent transformation of the industrializing world (including the former planned economies of Eastern Europe). In particular, what do we know about temporal sequences regarding the onset of political and economic liberalization and about these twin projects' interactive effects once both have been launched?

---

[28] Rummel (1983) considers the impact of "economic freedom" among various correlates of propensity for violence, suggesting that the more freedom (not merely economic), the lower that propensity. However, the need to disentangle the political and economic dimensions of freedom and to consider the regional interactive context—absent in Rummel—is clear from the discussion that follows. Weede (1995) proposes a link between free trade, democracy, and peace.

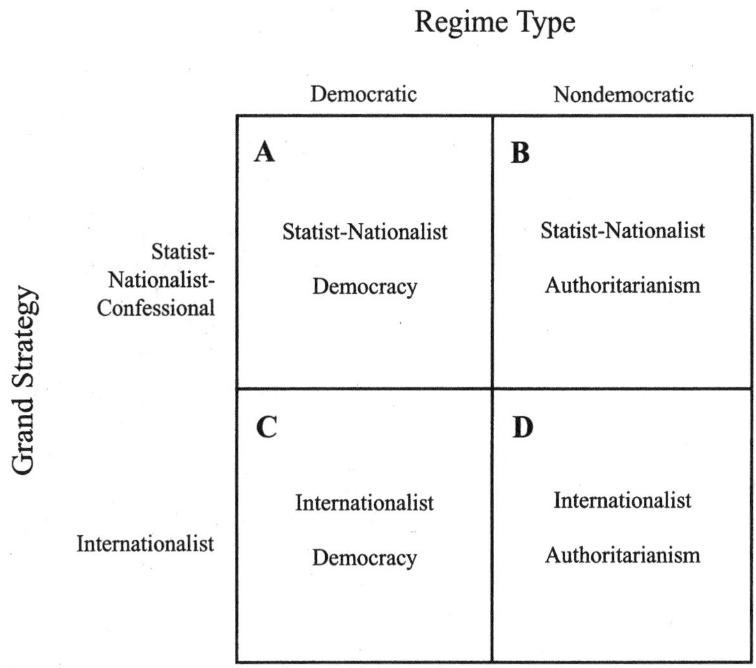

Regime Type

Figure 3. Grand strategies and democratic transitions

Figure 3 portrays four possible ideal-type combinations. The horizontal axis discriminates between democratic and nondemocratic regimes. The vertical axis summarizes the prevailing coalitional grand strategies, as outlined in Chapter Two. As argued, economic liberalization is neither linear nor coherent, different sectors can be affected in different sequences, "dirigiste" states can selectively orchestrate these sequences, and all dimensions of an internationalist grand strategy may take a long time to develop. The export-oriented (EO) strategies of South Korea and Taiwan, for instance, were not a product of laissez-faire approaches but of an industrial policy aimed at integration into global markets. In that sense, the two are early precursors of internationalist coalitions attentive to the primacy of macroeconomic stability and the discipline induced by international competition. The inward-looking import-substituting (IS) models of industrialization involved a strong, active state oriented to domestic markets, controlling prices, increasing nominal wages, overvaluing the currency to raise wages and profits in nontraded-goods sectors, and protecting state enterprises.[29] This was a favorite strategy of statist-nationalist and populist coalitions that steered most of the industrializing world during the postwar era.

The combination of grand strategies and regime type (democratic / nondemocratic) yields four schematic blueprints. Type A denotes a democratic state ruled by a coalition committed to an inward-looking statist-nationalism: Israel

---

[29] The classical statement of this model is in Hirschman (1958).

and India provide the classical historical examples. Type B points to a non-democratic state ruled by a coalition similarly committed to inward-looking statist-nationalism and import-substitution (IS): examples abound, but post-1958 Iraq can be cited as near-typical. Type C indicates the case of a ruling coalition steering a democratic state through an internationalist strategy: the dearth of historical examples here is suggestive, with Costa Rica partially approximating this pattern after 1966. With the onset of democracy and economic liberalization in the last decade, this cell becomes crowded. Type D represents a nondemocratic state captured by a coalition committed to EO industrialization: Taiwan and South Korea stand out in this category. It should be noted that the internationalist row (across the democracy variable) was practically empty until the 1960s.

For the most part, with most the industrializing world and former market economies in mind, the old order, throughout the Cold War era, was richly endowed with Type B statist, protectionist, and nondemocratic states, in different degrees and combinations. On economic grounds—building on the lessons of external shocks from the 1930s—ruling coalitions favored statism and widespread trade restrictions as a means to industrialize and to foster infant industries.[30] National economic planning by increasingly powerful civilian and military technocrats was also politically appealing because it could counter the negative effects of external shocks on a wide range of vulnerable domestic groups. According to Kaufman and Stallings (1991: 21), IS provided the intellectual justification for policies that, when carried to extremes, resulted in populism. Populism provided "a coherent political response to the dislocations caused by the increasing tempo of industrialization, social differentiation, and urbanization."[31] Populism cut across the democratic-nondemocratic divide, and quite often involved politically exclusionary nondemocratic—mostly military—control. The military as an institution was a natural ally of statist projects that placed them at the center of "nation-building" ideologies, as in post-1952 Egypt.[32] The international context reinforced the vast militarization of the industrializing world during the Cold War era. "National-security states" throughout all regions replicated patterns of political-economic organization of great powers, including military-industrial complexes and the domestic repression of dissent (at times even in formally democratic states). This was the product of more than mere emulation: it resulted from rather tight alignments with a superpower that laid its grand-strategic imprint on allies and proxies.

Type A was less prevalent than B, and often haunted by the prospects of becoming Type B overnight (by virtue of a coup d'état), as during the brief democratic interludes in a long authoritarian succession of Argentine military regimes. Exceptionally stable cases of statist-nationalist democracies included

---

[30] Rodrick (1994).

[31] Drake (1991: 36).

[32] As Kaufman (1990a: 115) argues, in Argentina and Brazil "nationalist currents within the armed forces constituted the most important pressure group favoring state-sponsored industrialization."

India and Israel. Following independence, both came under the control of coalitions strongly supportive of an import-substituting (IS) model enveloped in an ideology of self-reliance and domestic redistribution that helped galvanize their nascent democratic states. These cases portray an historical affinity between inward-looking populism, a personalistic, paternalistic, and sometimes charismatic leadership, and democratic mobilization from the top down. Notwithstanding civilian control over the military, even in these cases the armed forces played a central role in statist industrialization and nationalist protectionist state-building.

Type D was largely an innovation of the 1960s, pioneered by what became known as the Asian tigers. These authoritarian—often military-led—coalitions previously committed to inward-looking IS now began steering their states toward an internationalizing and EO strategy (cell D).[33] Many trace the origins of this shift to the 1960s and the crisis of IS, when variously stagnation, slow growth, or the unevenly distributed benefits from growth increased the numbers living under the poverty line, left intractable problems of nation building unresolved, and contributed to foreign aid fatigue.[34] However, responses to these crisis varied. In many cases (as in Latin America, South Asia, and the Middle East) politicians were slow in recognizing the end of the brief period of IS-led economic expansion and continued to spend heavily, leading to inflation, balance-of-payments crises, and further decline.[35] In South Korea and Taiwan— where the political opposition to this shift was far weaker—export-oriented growth strategies were in place by the mid-1960s.[36] Moreover, new groups favorably affected by EO, eventually extending to the middle class and large segments of the working class, progressively joined in a widening coalition. In a classical positive feedback loop, the eventual success of EO industrialization turned this into a truly conquering internationalist coalition. The turn by pioneering EO ruling coalitions toward the global political economy gave rise to the theory of "authoritarian advantage," holding that authoritarian regimes were better equipped to carry out painful reforms, through their ability to repress protest.[37] Some Asian tigers evolved into democracies—as I elaborate below— whereas others did not.

As noted, type C was largely an empty cell for most of the Cold War era. At century's end it had become the most crowded, following massive transitions from cells A, B, and D into C. Our discussion of these different transitions begins with the transformation of statist-nationalist import-substituting democracies into internationalizing export-oriented ones. The development of economically liberalizing coalitions in countries in cell A was slow and piece-

---

[33] Chapter Seven summarizes the vast literature attempting to explain such a shift. See, inter alia, Haggard (1990) and Gereffi and Wyman (1990).

[34] Rothstein (1977, 1988).

[35] Hirschman (1985); Ames (1987: 23).

[36] Haggard (1990); Deyo (1990).

[37] For an early full exposition and critique of the "authoritarian advantage" argument, see Díaz Alejandro (1983).

meal. Once the bottlenecks bred by IS became apparent, selected politicians organized political and economic forces (within and outside the state) that were either disillusioned with the old model or envisaged the prospects of benefiting from an internationalizing shift. The challenge to statist-nationalism came at times from historical opponents of the ruling coalition who, after decades of political oblivion were able to oust their ensconced rivals through electoral means. The challengers rarely held a coherent strategy, as they often represented hastily assembled coalitions with little macropolitical convergence. Prime Minister Morarji Desai's Janata-led replacement of Indira Gandhi's Congress party and Prime Minister Menachem Begin's Likud-led replacement of Labor—both in 1977—brought the post-independence era of relatively coherent statist-nationalist IS to an end.[38] Yet the cleavage over grand strategy cut across both the routed and the challengers. Indeed, strategic shifts also took place within the party hitherto identified with statism, as was the case with Israel's Labor and, to some extent, India's Congress and Mexico's PRI. The intraparty shift was piecemeal and nonlinear, with brief aborted episodes of liberalization, as under Eshkol and Sapir in Israel in the 1960s. Two decades later the former challengers—now led by India's BJP and Israel's Likud—were entangled in coalitional arrangements enmeshed in populism, nationalism, and confessionalism. Conversely, a reorganized Labor-led coalition in Israel instituted the most comprehensive internationalist shift in Israel's history in 1992. Clearly the transition from cell A to cell C reflects a sequence in which democracy preceded economic liberalization and internationalization.

States in cell B, traditionally ruled by a nondemocratic coalition committed to inward-looking IS, evolved in different directions.

First, where the democratic process took hold first, internationalist entrepreneurs and coalitions could use democratic institutions to organize themselves politically, steering their states toward economic liberalization (cell C), albeit not always under the first democratic administration. This sequence is fairly characteristic of Latin America, with the notable exception of Chile.[39] In some cases statist-nationalism, IS, or related hybrids were largely maintained, at least for some time—as in Argentina and Brazil in the 1980s—in the transition from authoritarianism to democracy (from cell B to A). The relative political strength of internationalist challengers was heightened where the magnitude of economic collapse was most dramatic, as in Argentina with its Weimar-level inflation, making it easier to trace the collapse to the old statist-nationalist guard. This two-step sequence (cell B, to A, to C) thus involved democratization first and economic liberalization later.

Second, without a democratic process in place, states in cell B followed two different paths. The first resisted both democratization and economic liberalization and involved no genuine transitions, with an entrenched statist-nationalist

---

[38] On India, see Frankel (1978), Kohli (1988, 1990), and Solingen (1997b). On Israel, see Chapter Six.

[39] On sequences in Latin America, see Haggard (1995b:77).

ruling coalition particularly reluctant to abandon inward-looking policies in a significant sense or authoritarianism itself, as with Iraq's and Syria's Ba'th. As of the mid-1990s, nascent internationalist groups still exhibit a hard time getting stronger—economically and politically—under intractable cell B conditions. The second path, taken by Chile's military regime, replicates the experience of the Asian pioneers in the late 1960s and 1970s, or a sequence of liberalizing the economy without the concomitant introduction of democracy (from cell B to D). A number of Middle Eastern states fall into this category, although reform was far less significant than in Chile; in some cases incipient economic liberalization was quickly followed by, or implemented hand in hand with, incipient democratization, as in Egypt, Morocco, Tunisia, Algeria, and Jordan.[40] Behind this strategy is the "democratic efficiency" theory, avering that authoritarian leaders realize the need to democratize—even if at an exceedingly slow rate—to enable economic reform, without which their grip on power would wither. This theory turns the myth of an "authoritarian advantage" in implementing market reforms on its head, and is supported by empirical evidence from different regions.[41] Counter to the claims of "authoritarian advantage," supporters of the "democratic efficiency" argument advance that features of authoritarian rule—including rent-seeking allies, the military establishment, and the alienation of civil society—in effect hinder economic liberalization.

A final transitional pattern (from cell D to C) encompassed the transformation of early authoritarian economic liberalizers into democratic states, as in South Korea and Taiwan in the late 1980s and early 1990s. A number of Asian states—notably a majority in ASEAN and the People's Republic of China—remain in cell D.[42] These proponents of the "authoritarian advantage" approach openly expose their fundamental adherence to what Hirschman (1991: 7) defines as the "jeopardy" thesis of conservative thought, one that argues that the cost of a proposed reform is too high "as it endangers some previous, precious accomplishment." Democracy has the potential, they argue, of undoing much of the gains from economic reform and of precluding industrializing states from coming to a welcome rest, one based on prosperity if not universal participation.[43] The "democratic advantage" theory counters the "jeopardy" thesis with

[40] Pool (1993) and Clawson (1992). For fuller bibliographic detail, see Chapter Six.

[41] The "authoritarian advantage" hypothesis tends to look only at the success cases, or at authoritarians that succeeded economically. However, as Przeworski et al. (1996) argue, one must compare the average, not the best, practice. For an argument against the myth of an "authoritarian advantage" even in East Asia, see Pei (1994). On the rationale of democratic efficiency, see Remmer (1989), Maravall (1994), Geddes (1994).

[42] Indonesia, Singapore, Malaysia, Brunei, and Vietnam are not democratic as of 1997, nor are ASEAN associate states Myanmar and Laos.

[43] See, for instance, the statement by Malaysia's Prime Minister Datuk Seri Mahathir bin Mohamad: "Should we enforce democracy on people who may not be able to handle it and destroy stability?" (quoted in Maravall 1994: 18). Singapore's Prime Minister Goh Chok Tong explained his regime's prohibition on students' waving of political banners: "If you allow students to do so, then workers will begin to do so over the slightest grievance, and if you have several such demonstrations, right away the impression is created the government is not in control of the situation—

the notion that democratization makes economic reform more palatable because of its legitimacy, informational advantages, and the structure of political incentives. Democracy and economic reform are thus seen as complementary, harmonious, and synergistic, but not by East Asian ruling internationalist coalitions wielding the "Asian" way. The expressed need to justify the unwillingness to move from cell D into C (at home and to the outside world) brings into relief the importance of international context or "world-time" at the end of the twentieth century.

As argued in Chapter Two, the rise, fall, and transformation of domestic political coalitions does not take place in a global vacuum. Different schools of thought in international relations clash in their account of the precise nature and extent of global influences on internal processes. Neorealism defines the shift toward markets and democracy largely as the outcome of the hegemonic triumph of US interests and designs. Thus, with the demise of the alternative model (the former Soviet Union), power asymmetries between the US and its Western allies on the one hand, and industrializing states on the other (that is, between creditors and debtors), arguably have pushed the industrializing world into economic orthodoxy and democratic institutions. Similarly, critical theorists stress both Gramscian hegemony and the ruthless operation of global market forces that impose liberalization on weaker global segments.[44] Neoliberal institutionalists phrase this process as a consequence of the growing importance of international economic and political institutions, such as the World Bank, the IMF, a consolidating international trade regime, and pro-democracy public and private international institutions.[45] Finally, a more voluntaristic approach points to global demonstration or contagion effects, or to the emulation of successful economic and political models.[46]

These different interpretations share the view that first, global forces—particularly the collapse of the international lending boom of the 1970s and the ensuing debt crisis of the early 1980s—were at work in the more or less collective shift toward cell C, and that second, these forces tended, more often than not, to strengthen internationalist coalitions. However, domestic policy failures and internationalizing political entrepreneurship seem to have been the main driving forces behind the reform efforts of the 1980s and 1990s, as the empirical chapters in Part Two suggest.[47] Moreover, in spite of global influences, not all internationalist coalitions have embraced democracy (a significant number has not), and the jury is still out on the question of irreversibility of both markets and democracy. Internationalist coalitions, subjected to the concerted challenge of

---

that the place may become unstable, and that will have an impact on foreign investors" (quoted in William Safire, "Honoring Repression." *New York Times*, 10 July 1995: A13).

[44] Cox (1987).

[45] On how the IMF came to be a powerful source of policy change in industrializing countries, see Nelson (1990) and Stallings (1992).

[46] For a comprehensive overview of the sources of "the third wave" of democratization, see Huntington (1991).

[47] Haggard (1995b: 109).

statist-nationalist and confessional adversaries, are not anywhere near the end of history.

The nature of the sequence and interplay of economic and political reform surveyed in this section affects the relative strength of internationalist and statist-nationalist coalitions, and their consequent ability to implement their respective grand strategies. The next section examines aspects of this interplay bearing on regional conflict and cooperation.

COALITIONS, DEMOCRACY, AND COOPERATION

On the basis of our discussion in the first two sections, we are now in a position to distill some general connections—convergences and divergences—between expectations from the democratic peace hypothesis and from coalitional analysis, and their implications for regional behavior and outcomes. To do so, we take into account the reality of the industrializing world, where democratization as a long and tortuous process is more often the norm than is long-term democratic stability. Democratization is a process that involves the incremental attainment of the characteristics of democracy identified by Dahl. The more elements of this formula that are present in a given polity, and the fuller their operational content, the more advanced that polity can be said to be in the path toward democracy. The democratic nature of some states is more contested than others.

The preliminary nature of evidence regarding recent democratic and market transitions limits our ability to draw any definitive connections between these transitions and their meaning for regional policies. What follows is an attempt to derive tentative hypotheses about such connections, but it is by no means an exhaustive attempt, given the richness of arguments and the scarcity of consensus in the comparative politics literature on transitions.[48]

Transitional Democracies and Populism

According to Kaufman and Stallings (1991: 26–27), transitional democracies are especially susceptible to populist policies because, first, authoritarian regimes (and thus transitional democracies) are most likely to occur in countries with exclusionary or unstable multiparty systems (systems that are often identified with populist tendencies); second, transitional democracies face considerable pent-up economic demand from their constituents; and third, in new democracies—where institutional uncertainties tend to shorten the time horizon of incumbents and their opponents alike—there is a premium for meeting distribu-

---

[48] For a sample of this literature, see Przeworski (1991), Rueschemeyer, Stephens, and Stephens (1992), Bresser Pereira, Maravall, and Przeworski (1993), Shain and Linz (1995), Haggard and Kaufman (1995), and Linz and Stepan (1996).

tive expectations early on while disregarding the longer-term detrimental effects of populist policies (such as high inflation and balance-of-payment crises).[49]

The affinity between populism and transitional democracy suggests that greater opposition to internationalist platforms might be expected among transitional democracies. Instead, both authoritarian regimes and consolidated democracies would be less likely than transitional democracies to experiment with populism; therefore, both might be expected to initiate and implement internationalist strategies with far less resistance. The role of populist pressures (and responses to them) is less clear under a fourth scenario, in which authoritarian regimes undergo democratization without yet reaching Kaufman and Stallings's "transitional democracy" status, as is the case in some Middle Eastern states. However, given the general direction of this process—even in the absence of fully competitive elections—a growing susceptibility to populist demands may be expected, in line with Kaufman and Stallings's general argument.

If these general relationships indeed hold, the implications for the coalitional analysis I have advanced so far, and for the democratic peace hypothesis, are significant. First, both these conceptual strands converge in the case of consolidated democracies with internationalist agendas which, for different reasons (according to each theory), are more likely to pursue cooperative strategies, particularly when facing fellow internationalist democracies across their borders. The zone of peace encompassing the OECD community is the classical case.[50] Second, authoritarian regimes are expected to be less subject to populist pressures than democratizing ones, and might therefore face less resistance to an internationalist grand strategy, if such is the strategy they advance.[51] Under these conditions, internationalist authoritarian regimes may create cooperative regional orders when facing other internationalist regimes in the neighborhood, as in ASEAN. However, where authoritarian regimes are undergoing democratization as well—and hence a higher exposure to populist pressures—these conditions might be less applicable, as in some Middle East and some Eastern

---

[49] Kaufman and Stallings (1991: 16) define populist policies as seeking the political support of organized labor, lower middle-class groups, and domestically oriented business, via the expansion of domestic demand, nominal wage increases and price controls, and exchange-rate control or appreciation in order to lower inflation and to raise wages and profits in nontraded-goods sectors. In their radical incarnations (Juan D. Perón, Salvador Allende, Alan García) populist policies, they argue, have led to economic stagnation, high inflation, capital flight, political polarization and eventual political collapse. Kaufman and Stallings characterize authoritarian regimes as not allowing competitive elections (therefore subsuming what I labeled earlier democratizing regimes). In their study transitional democracies are those that recently changed from authoritarian to democratic but, unlike consolidated democracies, have not yet sustained repeated turnovers of government.

[50] Even here populist movements acquire traits that are questionably democratic, highly nationalistic, and xenophobic, and therefore, short in cooperative regional policies. Patrick Buchanan represents the US version of a wider phenomenon operating in Western Europe and Japan, as well as in the industrializing world.

[51] As argued in Chapter Two, in principle authoritarian regimes do not have an inherent preference for either internationalist or statist-nationalist strategies. Their political makeup, largely shaped by a leading political entrepreneur, determines what their general orientation to grand strategy might be.

European instances. Third, transitional democracies are assumed to be more subject to populist pressures and therefore can be expected to offer less resistance to statist-nationalist grand strategies at best, and to embrace them in their extreme forms at worse. Pakistan in the late 1980s and some former Soviet states provide examples here. However, with increasing democratic turnovers— that is, after "graduating" from the transitional democracy category—Latin America and Eastern Europe come closer to Kaufman and Stallings's "consolidated democracy" status, a condition that, in their view, makes them less vulnerable to populist pressures. This graduation improves the prospects of internationalist grand strategies—at home and in the region—while laying the ground for democratic peace effects as well.

Democratization, Nationalism, and Ethno-Confessional Radicalism

According to Snyder (1993c: 17), the most institutionalized democracies of advanced industrialized states exhibit the lowest levels of nationalist behavior: "mature, representative, party and press institutions have tended to act as a check on the more extreme forms of nationalism." There is evidence that stable and mature democracies are also better able to deal with confessional discord, which can be channeled into established political parties and legal institutions able to adjudicate along more or less neutral (civic)—rather than confessional—lines.[52] Clearly, without discounting the existence of ultranationalist, fundamentalist, and sometimes violent fringes amongst them, mature democracies can generally marginalize such constituencies and are better able to protect their internationalist grand strategies from those influences.

Democratizing regimes, instead, are found to be more subject to nationalist and confessional pressures, a tendency that recent Eastern European and Middle Eastern transitions generally confirm.[53] This expectation is reinforced by the historical affinity between nationalism and the expansion of mass participation in European history, where popular nationalist forces aimed at overturning the rule of aristocratic elites. Democratizing states (including transitional democracies) would thus arguably be more susceptible to political coalitions that deliver statist-nationalist grand strategies and that use the confessional card as often as it is required for such strategies to remain afloat. Given the slippery slope of such strategies, as analyzed in Chapters Two and Three, it should be hardly surprising that democratizing states are also found to be more war-prone than stable regimes, or about 60 percent more likely to go to war than either

---

[52] For empirical evidence on the relative immunity of democratic states to violent ethnic upheaval, see Hill and Rothchild (1993) and Esty et al. (1997).

[53] This section builds on empirical data on democratization, nationalism, and war from Mansfield and Snyder (1995). Notice that their definition of democratizing states includes both: 1. an authoritarian state undergoing political liberalization, or changing into an "anocracy," following Russett (1993), and 2. a "transitional democracy," à la Kaufman and Stallings (1991), or one that has crossed the threshold into democracy without having yet experienced democratic turnovers. For an overview of the generally detrimental impact of ethnic conflict on democratization, see Diamond and Plattner (1994).

mature democracies or stable autocracies.[54] All three protagonists of the Bosnian debacle offer a deplorable example of this tendency.

Finally, Mansfield and Snyder find stable autocracies to be significantly less prone to go to war than regimes undergoing democratization. To be sure, stable authoritarian regimes have been involved in wars but, as can be recalled from our overview in Chapter Three, they may be less prone to war than unstable ones (that is, authoritarian regimes subject to periodic assaults, countercoups, and strong pressures to democratize). Beyond the explanatory potential of regime stability per se, coalitional analysis sensitive to regional interactive effects provides a more robust profile of the likely regional behavior of authoritarian regimes. On the one hand, authoritarian regimes pursuing an internationalist grand strategy and facing internationalist neighbors (democratic or not) are expected to underplay regionally divisive nationalist and ethno-confessional politics, lest these undermine the internationalist project or its authoritarian vehicle, as the Asian cases and even Chile (in the Beagle dispute) suggest. Such regimes may on occasion wield the nationalist card but, for the most part, create regions of far more contained conflict than where authoritarian coalitions held together by statist-nationalist and confessional themes are dominant.[55]

Democratic Transitions and the Military

Several factors characterize the relationship between democratic transitions—before and after reaching full democratic status—and the military. First, the military has often played a central role in the authoritarian regimes that democracies in transition are designed to replace. Political leaders of transitional democracies have thus struck quite elaborate and variable Faustian bargains with the military establishment to seek their nonintervention, if not their commitment to democracy. Only the interim success of such pacts can be assessed, although in some cases the political decline of the military is deemed more permanent than cyclical, as in Latin America.[56] Second, for reasons established in the preceding section, transitional democracies tend to be more subject to nationalist pressures, and the military often embodies—in fact, is often the instrument for—nationalist designs. Transitional democracies might thus successfully disengage the military from political life at one level and engage it at another. Internationalist coalitions may grant some autonomy to the military and encourage their professionalization (including UN peacekeeping missions) in exchange for the military's commitment to their agenda of domestic and regional stability. Statist coalitions often find their embrace with the military to

---

[54] Mansfield and Snyder (1995: 6).

[55] Authoritarian regimes with high levels of confessional differentiation (along ethnic, religious, or linguistic lines) are more commonly associated with the hegemony of one confessional group over the others, sometimes representing a minority (Alawites in Syria), or, more frequently, a majority (Shi'a in Iran) (Diamond and Plattner 1994).

[56] Pion-Berlin (1995).

be far more lethal, its demands occasionally offsetting the political benefits that the armed forces provide to a nationalist agenda, a lesson latter-day Peronists appear to have learned well from decades of Argentine politics.

An examination of the military institution in the context of coalitional battles over economic liberalization provides more useful information on the military's potential role and political wherewithal. The military has been a partner, sometimes a leading one (as in South Korea and Chile), in spearheading internationalist strategies, and a critical component of the "authoritarian advantage" theory. However, the maturation of internationalist strategies has often lead to a weakening of the military, both as an institution and as an industrial complex, as a result of both economic reform and democratizing tendencies among the most advanced economic liberalizers. The military has also played a central role in statist-nationalist coalitions, with which it shares much affinity throughout most regions.[57] After all, the military expenditures of such coalitions have reached in many cases between 15 and 20 percent of GDP (and over 40 percent of the central budget), or three and four times the industrializing world's average. Moreover, military establishments are generally affected adversely by internationalist grand strategies, because domestic economic adjustment and regional cooperation reduce direct budgetary transfers and indirect rents to military and ancillary activities. Both democratizing (but still authoritarian) states and transitional democracies dominated by statist-nationalist coalitions thus offer the military better means to stem the erosion of their political power than do strong internationalist coalitions, at least in the short term. The success of internationalist coalitions in downsizing the military-industrial-complex structurally and politically has logical implications for the survivability of democratic transitions at home, and for the survivability of internationalist coalitions in the neighborhood, through the regional externalities discussed in Chapter Three.

Myopic Economic Liberalization and the Erosion of Democracy

Another interactive effect of political and economic reform worth considering in the context of assessing democratic peace and coalitional interpretations of regional orders relates to the distributional aspects of economic reform. The failure to distribute the spoils of economic reform equitably—and to thwart the risky political consequences of concentrated benefits—endangers both democratization and economic liberalization. First, economic reform, with its negative initial impact on income distribution, economic stability, societal polarization, and crime, is of great consequence for the ability to consolidate democratic institutions. Without dedicated political efforts to generalize the benefits from economic liberalization, the democracy project can fizzle, and that danger

---

[57] On the Latin American military as prone to raise expenditures in search for popularity during the first year after the coup, see Ames (1987: 28). Austerity and orthodoxy are more likely three years following the coup, according to this study.

grows stronger with the passage of time.[58] From a democratic peace hypothesis standpoint, therefore, if myopic economic reform endangers democratic institutions, such reform endangers peace as well. Second, economic reform that is insensitive to distributional considerations endangers internationalist coalitions, whether democratic or not, and their regional policies. Short-sighted reform thus multiplies the barriers for implementing internationalist grand strategies and can be expected to increase the likelihood of military conflict.

Informational Advantages, Mythmaking, Democratization, and Coalitions

Political and economic transitions may be particularly propitious for the propagation of myths, both by ruling coalitions and by their opponents, including myths bearing on the state's relations to the adjacent region and beyond. Institutionalized democracies might be expected to be less susceptible to mythmaking in general, given the ability of a free press and "truth squads" to deflate claims with weak roots in reality and to undermine policies based on flimsy facts.[59] At the other end of the spectrum are authoritarian regimes that rely heavily on myths because they lack legitimacy to maintain control, and can get away with myths unassailed by "truth squads." Lying at different points in this spectrum are regimes undergoing different stages of democratization, and progressively shedding their monopoly over unchallenged mythmaking. To be sure, democracies are not invulnerable to attempts by cartelized interests to cloak their preferred policies in a mantle of national interests or confessional values, whether religious or civilizational.[60] Yet the opposition has a far better chance to voice disagreement than under nondemocratic conditions. Nor are democracies completely free of coalitions of rogue state agencies and cartelized private groups capable of exaggerating myths and even acting on them. The operations of the US National Security Council under Lt. Colonel North, in collaboration with private arms dealers, is but one instance that became public knowledge. Moreover, no democracy is fully immune from rabid nationalist myths capable of overtaking its institutions, as the dawn of Nazi Germany constantly reminds us. Yet, and in spite of these caveats, the informational checks and balances of a stable democracy tip the balance against mythmaking. The assurance game of internationalist clusters—analyzed in Chapter Three—requires perfect information, and democracies are likely to supply more of it than nondemocracies.

---

[58] On how democracy can become a casualty of rigid approaches aiming at economic stability and efficiency, see Bresser Pereira, Maravall, and Przeworski (1994). The dangers of antidemocratic mobilization are higher among middle-income and blue-collar strata than among the poorest sectors (who have fewer political resources and can become targets of poverty-alleviation programs).

[59] Van Evera (1994: 32) defines as "truth squads" institutions like free speech, a strong free press, independent universities, researchers, and historians, which can provide a measure of the myth's validity.

[60] Snyder (1991: 44) defines cartelized systems as dominated by a number of interest groups (cartels), "each with concentrated interests different from those of other such groups." Cartelized systems exclude diffuse groups with diffuse interests, such as taxpayers and consumers.

Chapter Two identified different sets of myths that leaders of internationalist and statist-nationalist coalitions wield to maximize their respective appeal. Self-reliance, for instance, is a central myth of statist-nationalist coalitions, as is sovereignty, geographical and territorial integrity, and in some cases, confessional purity. On the one hand, in the absence of democratic institutions, there are far fewer constraints on such coalitions in the production of myths. Complete control over information and the media allows them to minimize contact with the outside world and with perspectives likely to challenge core myths. Technologies such as faxes and private satellite dishes, however, increasingly threaten such monopolies. Even in democratizing states where democratic practices are weakly institutionalized, booming mass political participation stimulates strategic mythmaking, as Snyder (1991: 320) argues in the context of new Eastern European states. On the other hand, democratically elected statist-nationalist coalitions are subject to greater checks and balances in mythmaking. However, these controls are sometimes diluted by the tendency of statist-nationalist coalitions to exploit their control of—and political support from—the educational, military, and informational apparatus of the state, to advance myths cloaked in national trappings. Symbolic analysts (teachers, scientists, technologists, managers) in import-substituting sectors and employed by the state play a central role in this campaign. Where private informational alternatives, particularly a nonstate press, are weak, internationalist coalitions are disadvantaged in the battle for the minds (and votes), even under democratic conditions.

Internationalist coalitions exaggerate the virtues of economic reform and minimize its costs, particularly the distributional and political inequities likely to ensue in the absence of dedicated political intervention. They also strive to underplay the price tag of an internationalist grand strategy that requires them to forgo the unilateral pursuit of self-interest, sometimes recurrently so. On the one hand, democratic institutions enable the opposition to unveil the myth of unfettered markets as a panacea leading to domestic prosperity and regional peace. On the other hand, without democratic institutions, internationalist coalitions in power have been better able to rely on such myths to force rapid economic reform under enormous political repression and brutal exploitation. In those cases, internationalist coalitions have taken advantage of their monopolistic media outlets to convey mythical accounts of their success, without exposing the domestic distortions and international side-payments compelled by their grand strategy. Where these coalitions imbue a myth with confessional content—such as "Asian values"—the myth becomes an instrument by which liberalizers forge conformity with the domestic, regional, and global requirements of their grand strategy.

Revising Kant's Sequence

Kant's claim that democracy (republicanism) leads to peace involves the following logical reasoning: first, the mere existence of democratic partners en-sures their nonviolent interaction, because of their responsiveness to their respective publics. Second, this pattern of interaction leads to the creation of "pacific unions" held together by common moral values. Third, the pacific unions grow stronger with the consequent expansion of economic cooperation and interdependence. Thus, according to Kant (1784/1991), because democracy endows states with freedom of trade and economic advantages, other states are likely to emulate democratic polities, leading to an expanding "pacific union." Yet the analysis of economic liberalization and democratization suggests that the alternative sequence is far from an anomaly. Economic liberalization (although not necessarily bilateral interdependence) can precede the inception of democratic regimes while engendering cooperation, an outcome that can be ultimately reinforced by stable democratic regimes. Democratic partners are in far better position to create a pacific union once domestic and regional stability, as well as global access, have become their guiding political objective. Either path to pacific unions—democracy first or internationalization first—can be foiled by the presence of powerful statist-nationalist regimes in the region, a warning highly relevant to the Middle East peace process.

Economic Liberalization, Democracy, and Winning Wars

Democracies are more likely to prevail in wars with nondemocratic adversaries.[61] Most empirical cases supporting this finding involve democratic states that are significantly stronger in economic terms (wealthier in overall industrial capital, monetary reserves, and technological competence) than the nondemocratic adversaries over which they prevailed. Most of these stronger democratic states have more often than not been ruled by internationalist coalitions. Hence, it is at least plausible that internationalist coalitions not only maximize cooperative relations with fellow internationalist coalitions but also maximize their chances of success in war (waged mostly against statist-nationalist and confessional coalitions). As we may recall from Chapter Two, internationalist coalitions aim at shrinking the size of the state but, if successful, end up strengthening the leaner state's institutional capacity for societal extraction, and by extension, for mobilizing resources for war. Lake (1992: 24) associates democratic states with decreasing levels of rent, increasing levels of wealth, and consequently greater absolute resources that can be applied to national security. These characteristics are the same as those of strong internationalist states, even undemocratic ones (such as South Korea and Taiwan in the late 1980s), and even where rents remain but are highly contingent on their contribution to the internationalist model. Internationalist democracies may thus have special advantages for prevailing in wars, as a product of the mutually reinforcing effect of their democratic polities and their internationalist grand strategies.

---

[61] Lake (1992).

CONCLUSIONS

Given the scarcity of relevant (neighboring) democratic dyads in the industrializing world until the 1990s and the small number of wars in general, the democratic peace hypothesis does not shed much light on the relationship between democracy and war in this temporal and geographical domain. That wars were mostly fought among nondemocracies in a universe of predominant nondemocracies is not surprising, begging the question of which nondemocracies were more prone to war than others and why. In the post-1990 period the number of democracies have become more significant and interstate wars have been few.[62] Although the Peru-Ecuador anomaly acquires added significance in this new context, it seems too early to draw strong inferences about the democratic peace effect in the 1990s, given the short history of global democratic expansion.

We can now distill the mutual interactions between economic liberalization and democratization, and their more general implications regarding regional orders.

1. The framework developed in this book predicts a generally positive relationship between internationalist coalitions and the propensity to cooperate regionally—particularly with similarly oriented neighbors—and a reverse relationship for statist-nationalist-confessional coalitions, regardless of whether or not they are democratic.

2. Both democratic and authoritarian (including democratizing) regimes have initiated and sustained statist-nationalist and internationalist strategies.[63] Political entrepreneurs put together supportive coalitions for an internationalist or a statist-nationalist agenda, whether through democratic institutions or through more centralized procedures of logrolling. The centralized path can range from what Johnson (1993: 221) labels "soft authoritarianism," where a covert hegemonic alliance rules via a formal system of legality and popular sovereignty, to highly centralized systems.[64] Either agenda—internationalist or statist-nationalist—can be pursued by dictator-entrepreneurs such as Saddam Hussein in Iraq, Hafiz el Assad in Syria, Ferdinand Marcos in the Philippines, Augusto Pinochet in Chile, and General Ne Win in Burma. Regime type does not seem to determine success in implementing economic liberalization, leading to a devaluation of "authoritarian advantage" theories.[65]

---

[62] The proportion of democratic states grew from 25 percent of all states in 1975 to a little over 30 percent in 1995 according to Gaubatz (1996: 140–41) and from 32.4 percent of all states in 1962 to 45.4 percent in 1990 according to Huntington (1991: 26).

[63] Haggard and Kaufman (1994); Haggard and Webb (1994: 6–16).

[64] On economic reform via presidential "decretismo," even under democratic rule, see Bresser Pereira, Maravall, and Przewoski (1993: 208).

[65] Summers and Thomas (1995: 432) found no systematic relationship between political freedom and rates of economic growth. On how the growth performance of dictatorships and democracies, on average, is indistinguishable, see Alesina (1994: 46) and Przeworski, Alvarez, and Cheibub (1996).

3. Democracy has been found to be impregnable where annual per capita income is above $6,000 (Przeworski et al. 1996). At lower income levels, economic growth with a moderate rate of inflation—a key objective of internationalist coalitions—heightens democracy's probability of survival. To the extent that internationalist coalitions can produce those conditions—the $6,000 threshold and growth with moderate inflation—more often than their adversaries, they might be expected to yield enduring democracies as well. To the extent that these coalitions generate growing income inequality they make democracy less survivable (at below income threshold levels).

4. Both ruling internationalist coalitions and statist-nationalist-confessional coalitions can thrive in cartelized systems (Snyder 1991: 31), where power assets (material, organizational, and informational) are concentrated in the hands of parochial groups pursuing their limited interests. To the extent that cartelization is particularly compatible with statist-nationalist rule, democratization faces special challenges there. Both types of coalitions can also benefit from democratization, particularly when they are in the opposition. A process that grants diffuse interests greater political access through the ballot advantages internationalist challengers facing entrenched centralized statist coalitions, a development that also advances regional cooperative efforts. Statist-nationalist-confessional challengers can use democratization to propel them into power (as in Algeria in 1991), with the potential for returning the political system to greater concentration and cartelization. The hypothesized greater accountability for regional adventurism under democratic conditions is thus lost.

5. The confluence of political and economic liberalism may make the relationship between internationalist coalitions and cooperative behavior more robust, but only under certain conditions, and not merely because "all good things go together," as end-of-history optimism implies.[66] On the one hand, democracies are not immune to militant—and even belligerent—statist-nationalist coalitions, particularly under conditions of high uncertainty regarding the outcome of liberalization, trends in the global economy, or regional threats, as the ascent of Turkey's Erbakan and Israel's Netanyahu suggest. Nevertheless the comparative politics literature on recent transitions suggests that fewer democratic states—at least for now—are ruled by coalitions entrenched in statist-nationalist agendas. On the other hand, where internationalist coalitions are politically strong—domestically and throughout a region—and democracy adds to their legitimacy (as in the Southern Cone, South Korea, and Taiwan), the chances for a peaceful order should be enhanced. However, where such coalitions are weak internally and externally (as in South Asia and the Middle East), and subject to frequent electoral challenges, this potential can fall short of realization.

6. The absence of democracy has not precluded internationalist coalitions from implementing their grand strategy at home and regionally. Indeed, such absence made it easier at times to secure the domestic requirements of regional cooperation without major political upheaval (as with some Asian tigers and Middle East states). However, weak internationalist coalitions in nondemocratic contexts can also become the targets of an unpleasant "double whammy": a concerted challenge from an alliance of protectionist and statist interests with prodemocracy groups, as in many a Middle East state.

---

[66] On end-of-history optimism, see Snyder (1993a).

Such a challenge does not bode well for regional cooperation, as we shall see in Chapter Six. Strong nondemocratic internationalist coalitions that expand societal support for their economic program can afford to reinvent themselves through the democratic process (as in South Korea and Taiwan). Other such coalitions (as in the PRC and Singapore) grope with the not-so-theoretical question of how long an economically liberalizing context can remain undemocratic.

7. Political closure and repression, as in Iran and Iraq, can be a major barrier to liberalizing the economy, and consequently, to regional peace. However, authoritarianism can be just as frequently the instrument for economic liberalization, and requires cajoling business leaders into the coalition. Business leaders exhibit a variable approach to democratization across different segments and over time, at times endorsing it and at others opposing it. In principle, inward-looking business leaders are likely to play an important role in demanding democratization from internationalist ruling coalitions, whereas internationalist businesses play that role to challenge their coalitional opponents. At the same time, both segments can act as agents for democracy within their respective coalitions in order to advance certain conditions of political stability.[67]

8. The more conflictive and threatening the regional environment, the easier it is for a coalition to broaden the sphere of the state, and to restrict the sphere of civil society, on the grounds of national security. In that sense, a conflict-prone regional environment strengthens statist-nationalist coalitions and antidemocratic forces at the same time. Arguably acting on this principle, Middle East regimes have historically fueled the Arab-Israeli conflict, as well as conflicts among them, in order to maintain their repressive control of the state and of its productive potential.

9. Both democratic and nondemocratic states have sought nuclear weapons in different regions, and both types have also opted for nuclear-weapons-free-zones (NWFZ). Coalitional analysis provides a better predictor for the nuclear behavior of states. The drive toward NWFZ was most forceful among internationalist clusters, democratic or otherwise.[68] Of all states (beyond the original five) considering a nuclear option in the last three decades, not one endorsed a nuclear-weapons-free zone fully and effectively under a ruling inward-looking, statist-nationalist coalition. Only internationalist coalitions in power undertook effective commitments to denuclearization—from Taiwan to South Korea, Egypt, Spain, South Africa, Brazil, and Argentina—commitments made in tandem with economic liberalization. The stronger the internationalist coalition the swifter the shift toward denuclearization. Weaker internationalist coalitions were more constrained in curbing their nuclear programs, even under democratic regimes, as in Franco's Brazil, India, and Israel.

---

[67] Payne (1994). Private bankers with close access to President Pinochet are reported to have wielded "national costs" to persuade him to comply with a court order to imprison military officers convicted of political murder (Calvin Sims, "Chile's Armed Forces Allow Arrest of Convicted General," *New York Times* 21 June 1995: A7). The bankers were primarily concerned with the disruption of an ongoing internationalization of the Chilean economy that had benefited them the most. Most particularly, the political crisis over the court order came about just as Chile began pressing for its inclusion in NAFTA.

[68] For a fuller overview of the democratic peace, economic liberalization, and nuclear restraint, see Solingen (1994b).

10. This chapter extrapolates a broader set of values for the dependent variable than democratic peace theorizing is generally prepared to support. For the most part, it is the absence of war (and militarized disputes, including threats to use, or actual use of military force) that provides common ground to most studies in this tradition. In that sense, the democratic peace has a more limited scope than coalitional analysis which, as shown in Chapter Three, sustains a wider range of specific cooperative and conflictive behavior.

11. Finally, the democratic peace research program provides a rich array of potential links between democratic polities and the absence of war amongst them, but no single explanation is universally accepted to be at work. Coalitional analysis does offer a more explicit theoretical logic that may help identify the conditions under which the democratic peace is more likely to operate beyond the OECD community.[69]

The time has now come to examine in greater detail what the evidence—from four regions, over twenty states, and numerous instances of coalitional alternations over time—suggests regarding the association between coalitional forms, democratic rule, and regional outcomes.

---

[69] Neither levels or rate of development (Maoz and Russett 1992) nor levels of wealth (Ember, Ember, and Russett 1992) capture the coalitional logic advanced here. Rummel (1983) suggests that "economic freedom" reduces significantly—more than does "political freedom"—the level of violence for a state overall or between particular states. However, he provides a rather static (preindustrial / industrial) and doctrinaire (capitalist / socialist) classification of states, and no concrete theory about how the political dynamics of economic strategies shape interstate conflict and cooperation.

PART TWO

The Empirics

CHAPTER FIVE

The Southern Cone: Argentina and Brazil

THE SOUTHERN CONE, with Argentina and Brazil as its historically dominant dyad, has largely been at peace for most of the twentieth century.[1] However, there have been militarized confrontations among enduring rivals (the Argentine-Chilean Beagle dispute), a war with a major power (Argentina against Great Britain), and a relentless nuclear competition between Argentina and Brazil, with both rejecting the global and regional nonproliferation regime. Moreover, regional economic cooperation was the prevailing rhetoric of the last fifty years but never transcended the level of symbol and discourse. This rather limited record of cooperation, even if it avoided wars, is particularly intriguing in light of the region's dense institutional infrastructure, including the Organization of American States, the Economic Commission for Latin America, the Tlatelolco Treaty, and many others. From a neoliberal institutionalist perspective, one might have expected such density to promote deeper levels of cooperation across issue areas, including effective economic cooperation and denuclearization.

Only in the early 1990s did a brand new regional order emerge in the Southern Cone—complete with unprecedented denuclearization and a common market (MERCOSUR)—an order far closer to a stable zone of peace than had existed anytime before. Why now and not before? What accounts for the significant shift away from the pattern characteristic of the preceding half century? Clearly, no neorealist account that builds on intractable security dilemmas can explain either change from one era to another or the cooperation that such change engendered. Cognitive and institutionalist approaches do not provide a compelling explanation for this evolution either, because much of the ideal, normative, and institutional infrastructure that might have produced such an order in earlier decades did not. The democratic peace theory is largely irrelevant to this region, which has been free of intraregional wars under both democratic and nondemocratic rule. Neither did democratic interludes differ systematically from other periods in the intensity and extent of regional cooperation until the 1990s. Nor does classical liberalism—bilateral or regional economic interaction breeding progressively deeper levels of cooperation—hold up well here. Interdependence followed, rather than led to, growing cooperation in the Southern Cone. The rise of internationalist coalitions implementing an unprecedented revolution at home and an equally unprecedented integration into the global political economy in the 1990s constitute the genesis of this new regional order.

[1] Bolivia and Paraguay fought the Chaco War from 1932 to 1935.

Coalitional analysis is helpful in explaining the old order, as well. I begin with an overview of the domestic coalitions that upheld a statist-nationalist era for decades, and of the resulting pattern of regional interaction. The focus on Argentina and Brazil stems from the centrality of their relationship to the prevailing regional order, but does not necessarily imply that all other relations are merely derivative of this dyad. The domestic coalitional evolution of Chile is also discussed where pertinent. The second section examines the crystallization of internationalist grand strategies in Argentina and Brazil and the nature of the new regional order in the 1990s. I turn next to the applicability of democratic peace considerations to the Southern Cone. The final sections elucidate interactive effects between democracy, economic liberalization, and the new regional order.

Import Substitution, Statism, the Military-Industrial Complex, and Guarded Competition

The Coalitional Profile, 1940s–1980s: Argentina

Between the 1940s and the late 1980s Argentina and Brazil were largely ruled by statist-nationalist coalitions of one sort or another: democratic or authoritarian (mostly military), with varying mixes of import-substituting approaches and with differing versions of an independent position in the global politics of the Cold War era. Argentina's President Juan D. Perón (1946–1955), an outspoken admirer of Mussolini, epitomized the statist-nationalist coalition that vied for control of the state for half a century. Perón became a landmark populist political entrepreneur in the industrializing world, mobilizing statist-nationalist political energies when Nasser was still a young Egyptian conscript.

The political coalition that sustained Perón progressively included nationalist military officers, the working and lower-middle classes represented in the central trade union Confederación General del Trabajo (CGT), small and medium-sized firms involved in import-substitution and aggregated under the Confederación General Económica (CGE), state firms producing infrastructural inputs, white-collar groups, and the state bureaucracy.[2] Perón orchestrated this coalition while crushing an independent labor movement as well as an independent congress and judiciary. He quickly introduced tariffs and credits that favored national over international manufacturing, and attempted to redistribute income through inflation (higher wages, increased social security benefits). His policies aimed at marginalizing the traditionally powerful agro-exporting interests organized in the Sociedad Rural Argentina (SRA) by means of overvalued exchange rates and subsidized interest rates. Argentine beef was to be served primarily on Argentine tables (86 percent of beef production in 1951 was consumed domestically); this was intended particularly to offset declines in real wage rates once

---

[2] Hirschman (1985: 60); Ames (1987: 14); Kaufman (1990a: 121); Sikkink (1991). Milenky (1978) specifically labels this coalition *statist-nationalist*.

the large reserves accumulated during the war years had been spent. Perón also purchased large quantities of weapons for the military, built the Argentine military-industrial complex, and coopted military officers with sinecures, perks, and inflated salaries.

The economic nationalism and protectionism, the xenophobia, and the emulation of authoritarian and aggressive rule were all components of the "integral nationalism" (Goldwert 1972) that had characterized the Argentine army until the last decade of this century, a nationalism with a strong base among inward-looking industrialists and labor.[3] Argentine entrepreneurs were historically divided into two rival camps. On the one hand, an umbrella group—the Asociación Coordinadora de Instituciones Empresarias Libres (ACIEL)—included the largest and most powerful commercial, agricultural, financial, and industrial interests that had dominated Argentina's early internationalist phase (1880s–1920s). Associated in ACIEL were the agro-exporting SRA, the Argentine Chamber of Commerce, and the Unión Industrial Argentina (UIA), aggregating the major transnational corporations and the largest internationally competitive national firms. This camp, often charged with having "hegemonic" aspirations by competing Argentine industrial sectors, had traditionally rejected state entrepreneurship and artificial state protection of uncompetitive firms.[4] On the other hand, the CGE created by Perón in 1952 included more traditional industrial sectors opposed to foreign capital, which favored protection and corporatist arrangements. Integral nationalism was a useful doctrine for maximizing political impact, and the CGE often relied on slogans against *entreguismo* (literally "handing over" the national patrimony, or denationalization) and on calls for domestic control over economic decision making and national sovereignty. These were "patriotic entrepreneurs," who frequently identified with politically appealing notions of military nationalism, statism, and regional power aspirations. The CGE had influential military allies within the state apparatus, and was Perón's ideal industrial partner for a coalition that also included Peronist labor and the military.

Perón's populism made ample use of the cult of personality and mythmaking. To begin with, import substitution in heavy industrial and military industries underpinned the myth of national self-reliance. The external expression of national populism involved challenging free trade and the unpredictability of international markets, and rejecting foreign investment, the IMF, GATT, and the World Bank. Consistent provocations against US policies and demands provided an additional layer of "independence" designed to turn Argentina into the indomitable maverick of the industrializing world. The crowning achievement

---

[3] Rock's (1993) comprehensive study of Argentine nationalism labels it a "fundamentalist movement pledged to violence and dictatorship" (p. xiii). On Perón's "nationalization of the Central Bank," a tool of "private and international banks," see Perón (1950: 221–23).

[4] Smith (1991); Domínguez (1982); Kenworthy (1970). In the 1970s the UIA looked at protectionism more favorably than did ACIEL as a whole, and was prepared to join CGE industrialists in a common front when advantaged by monopolistic positions in the domestic markets. ACIEL was dissolved in 1973.

in this effort in Perón's mind was to be Argentina's mastery of controlled nuclear fusion ahead of the superpowers. Perón—misled by a false claim from
expatriate Austrian physicist Ronald Richter—prematurely announced to the
world in 1953 that Argentina had succeeded in these efforts. The origins of a
well-funded nuclear program in Argentina are thus deeply rooted in the statist-
national populism of the Perón era and in the myth of self-reliance and technological superiority.

These myths were very effective in coalescing domestic support and were
to nurture Argentine nationalism for many decades to come. Eva Perón, the
president's wife, was herself a willing—and central—instrument in a populist
strategy, one that reached mythical proportions during her lifetime and beyond. Her reknowned social projects favoring the *descamisados* (shirtless
ones), the poor, and children, and enfranchising women, while challenging the
economically privileged and their allies in the upper echelons of the Catholic
Church, raised the passion of Argentine masses. If populist politics converted
Evita into a near-saint during her generation, her untimely death at 32 cata-
pulted her memory into history. Thousands of programs, schools, public institutions throughout the country, and even a whole Argentine province (Chaco)
were renamed Evita Perón. Even her corpse has been used into the 1990s by
Perón and his followers in an attempt to maintain her life and deeds as important sources of myths.

Evita's death in 1952 was not the only event that left Juan Perón despondent.
By the early 1950s the exhaustion of accumulated wartime reserves impaired
his import-substitution model and threatened his original coalition. Perón was
forced to launch half-hearted stabilization policies in 1951–1952 to reduce current account deficits and improve the ability to borrow abroad. The military,
with the navy leading the charge, put together the anti-Peronist alliance, which
included agro-exporters and the higher echelons of the Catholic Church, that
brought Perón's downfall in 1955. What followed henceforth until the late
1980s was an unstable succession of military and civilian regimes, notable for
alternating stop-go economic and industrial policy cycles, reflecting the inability of any coalition to prevail politically for a sustained period. Explanations
for the low level of macropolitical consensus that characterized the post-1955
period abound.[5] Agro-exporting sectors, industrial entrepreneurial segments,
and labor consistently challenged state autonomy, precluding the state from
consolidating a stable industrialization strategy. Potential partners to a ruling
coalition saw their interests better served by exercising a veto power and by
providing an erratic, selective support for policies than by effectively throwing
their lot into a stable alliance. The position of industrialists and Pampean producers appeared contradictory and elusive as a firefly: now either or both were
inside the coalition's tent, now they were not. Interpretations of this behavior
include an imputed short-term view of profitability and the deterring effect of a

---

[5] Kaufman (1990a), Hirschman (1981: 192–93), Erro (1993), Manzetti (1993), and a bibliographic survey in Solingen (1996b). On stop-go cycles, see Díaz Alejandro (1970).

tight alliance with either a demanding labor movement or a conflict-ridden and ineffective military institution.

The narrow and ephemeral set of converging objectives among potential partners to a ruling coalition precluded the emergence of a strong and durable macropolitical consensus over industrialization strategies. As a result, Argentine coalitions were highly unstable and their shifting boundaries were hard to identify. O'Donnell (1978) outlined two contending coalitions that vied for power since 1955: 1. the nationalist-populist expansionist coalition of urban wage workers, small national industrialists, and, at times, an "upper bourgeoisie" oriented mostly to domestic markets; and 2. a "devaluation-stabilization" coalition of export-oriented Pampean producers with intermittent support from the "upper bourgeoisie" (mostly under balance-of-payments difficulties). This coalition's exclusion of small-scale producers of standardized products, labor, and political parties for most of this period was designed to strengthen consensus for antipopulist measures. However, these political forces proved to be too powerful to be discounted altogether, as the intermittent assaults by the CGE, the Frondizi period, and the May 1969 mass urban uprising (Cordobazo) revealed. The attempt to genuflect to nonmembers or occasional members of the coalition in exchange for political support weakened the consensus even further, as did tensions within the military stemming from diverging interservice interests.

Argentina's shifts between attempts at macroeconomic balance and inward-looking policies and their reversal for most of the post-1955 era were a symptom of this feeble consensus. Incoherent policy and the resulting turmoil, in turn, reinforced factionalism and dissent. Low consensus also explains an arresting level of cabinet instability and why a succession of economic "czars" failed to imbue state agencies with a coherent program. Between 1941 and 1970 ministers of the economy averaged only 0.88 years (321 days) in power each.[6] Challenges by the National Development Council and state enterprises frequently undermined orthodox policies as soon as they were formulated. Statist-nationalist currents within the military constituted the most important pressure group protecting state entrepreneurship.[7] In 1955 the armed services divided state bureaucratic and industrial assets among themselves, allocating the presidency to the army, the vice presidency to the navy, and the three other places in the junta to the army, navy, and air force, respectively. This structure was to cast its shadow on continued interservice rivalries and to reinforce the fissiparous nature of grand coalitions.

The army assumed control over the National Directory of Military Industries (DGFM) in 1941. By 1945 DGFM already included fourteen state enterprises and twenty thousand employees.[8] The army also controlled state firms in the

---

[6] There were years (1955, 1962, 1963) when three different ministers occupied that position, often to be replaced by their nemesis, in terms of outlook and clientele (Most 1991: 56).

[7] Kaufman (1990a: 115).

[8] Rouquié (1982); Fontana (1987: 33). About 80 percent of DGFM's output in the 1960s went to army-controlled enterprises and private industry. On the army's statism and aversion to privatization, see Mallon and Sourrouille (1975).

steel, pharmaceutical, chemicals, iron ore, timber, and construction sectors, an expansion that reveals the army's growing statist stakes. The army had become the dominant service since 1963, following actual combat between the *azules* and *colorados* factions within the military (roughly divided along service lines and ideological orientation). Formally the air force's niche, the state-run aircraft industry came under DGFM's (army) control as did the navy's shipyards (AFNE) and—intermittently—the ministries of interior and labor. The air force nurtured the Condor II missile, allegedly funded by Iraq and Egypt. The navy controlled the National Atomic Energy Commission's (CNEA) ambitious nuclear program, and had considerable influence over Argentina's Ministry of Foreign Relations, which formulated nuclear policies along CNEA's institutional preferences. The navy's emphasis on "state subsidiarity" implied generous protection of national private firms under the mantle of developing "strategic" sectors with high spillover effects on industrial capabilities and economic development.[9]

In practice, Argentina's president had limited effective control over agencies and programs under the jurisdiction of each service branch. This military-industrial complex was privileged for decades, became a major budgetary drain without ever yielding returns through exports, and led the battle against privatization. This industrial complex was a pivotal component of statist-nationalist coalitions and one fiercely opposed to foreign investment in the myriad sectors under its control. The global strategic environment created by the Cold War and relatively rigid alliances, and the regional corollaries of rabid anticommunism, helped consolidate the institutional and industrial strength of the military as a paramount partner in statist coalitions, with special prerogatives in economic entrepreneurship and domestic repression.

After Perón, General Pedro E. Aramburu sustained deficit-ridden state enterprises, a dramatically expanded state bureaucracy, price controls, import quotas, multiple exchange rates, export taxes, and consumption subsidies. Real blue-collar and white-collar wages in 1957 were the same as in 1954.[10] The agro-exporting SRA and UIA industrial entrepreneurs quickly realized that Aramburu would not unleash a liberalizing revolution. President Arturo Frondizi from Unión Cívica Radical Intransigente (1958–1962) was elected with Peronist support, which he rewarded with a 60 percent wage increase, expanding the government deficit by nearly 5 percent of GDP. Frondizi later accepted IMF and World Bank stabilization plans that forced declines in real wage rates, announced the privatization of a military-controlled conglomerate (DINIE), and sought foreign investments in areas (notably oil) controlled by the military, all of which alienated his statist-nationalist base of support among Peronists and the military. Inflation, balance-of-payments difficulties, and Frondizi's approval of Peronist candidates to salvage populist support accelerated his ouster by the military. His hybrid and unstable grand strategy—in an attempt to build an

---

[9] For an empirical study of these spillover effects and their mythical claims, see Solingen (1996b).

[10] Manzetti (1993: 292).

inclusive grand coalition—could not deliver any of the most valued preferences of cajoled partners. Following the brief tenure of President José Mariá Guido (1962–1963), President Arturo Illía (1963–1966) from the Unión Cívica Radical del Pueblo was elected with 26 percent of the votes. He refused to put together a supportive coalition with other parties, labor, or business despite his congressional minority status, but maintained statist, import-substituting, and populist policies. A new coup ended this democratic interlude, in what had become an endemic economic crisis.

The equipoise between internationalizing and statist forces was evident under the military regime headed by General Juan Carlos Onganía (1966–1970), labeled the "Argentine Revolution."[11] In 1966 Onganía appointed an economic leadership—Jorge N. Salimei as economy minister and Francisco R. Aguilar at the Industry and Commerce Secretariat—representing the small and medium-sized firms of national origin affiliated with the CGE. Among the CGE allies in the bureaucracy was retired army general Juan E. Guglialmelli, the director of a military program—Consejo Nacional de Desarrollo (National Development Council)—entrusted with "homogenizing" state agencies within the broader statist-nationalist thrust, and linking heavy industry with national security and independence from foreign pressures. Discontent among liberalizing groups mounted, and Onganía replaced this economic leadership with Adalberto Krieger Vasena. Vasena attempted—unsuccessfully—a major break with the past to promote modern financial, large-scale industrial exporting sectors. By 1967 Vasena had imposed anti-inflationary measures and encouraged foreign investment, but had also levied export tariffs and taxes on farm-imported products that alienated agro-exporters. By 1968 the coalition had fractured, compelling Onganía once again to turn to statist-corporatist and nationalist allies and to dismiss liberal-minded army, navy, and air force chiefs, notably Julio Alsogaray. The opposition to Onganía's major devaluation and austerity measures erupted with fury in a popular uprising—the 1969 Cordobazo—to which Onganía responded with statist-populist themes. Amid these coalitional swings, budgetary expenditures first declined (1966–1969) and later expanded (1969 onward). Onganía's ouster led to a brief interlude of renewed statist-nationalist corporatism under General Roberto Levingston (1970–1971) and Economy Minister Aldo Ferrer, who granted GCE entrepreneurs their strongest representation within state institutions (including the central bank) since 1955. Under a new "Buy National" law, national state and private firms enjoyed generous subsidies. The rival association UIA fiercely opposed Ferrer's statist-nationalist and inflationary policy of "Argentinization," as did the navy and air force officers who ousted Levingston.

The new army chief General Alejandro Lanusse launched the "Gran Acuerdo Nacional" in 1971, courting the CGE and corporatist arrangements. Within a year the CGE and Peronism were firmly opposed to Lanusse, who scheduled

---

[11] On coalitional cleavages under Onganía, see Smith (1989), Kaufman (1990a: 120), and Ames (1987: 18). Manzetti (1993: 300) argues that UIA and ACIEL were part of the coalition that deposed Frondizi, but their access to Onganía's regime in power was rather limited.

elections for 1973. With a victory of 62 percent of the vote, Juan Perón returned to Argentina after decades of forced exile. He purged the Peronist Left and empowered neofascists and conservative labor activists, while his economy minister, José Gelbard, sought out CGE allies to advance the Plan Trienal. Upon Perón's death in 1974 his third wife and successor, María E. Martínez de Perón (Isabel), allowed increased control by paramilitary groups fighting "Marxist subversives." Violence, political unrest, nationalization of foreign firms and major banks, and protectionism, suppressed foreign investment and the ability to borrow. Arms purchases remained characteristically privileged, doubling by 1973 (from 1971 levels, in constant 1982 dollars) and trebling by 1975.[12] Fiscal deficits, hyperinflation, and an acute balance-of-payments crisis were the defining features of this Justicialista administration, a record that left deep marks on Peronist strategic thinking.

General Jorge R. Videla's 1976 coup and regime lasting until 1981—labeled Proceso de Reorganización Nacional—replaced Isabel Perón's regime with an orthodox agenda under Economy Minister Martínez de Hoz, representing agro-exporting groups. The liberalizing team criticized the Onganía period as statist and protectionist, freed domestic banking and cross-border capital movements, challenged the bloated and inefficient state sector and uncompetitive private industry, and outlawed the CGE and powerful unions. All these, including the military-industrial complex, fought Martínez de Hoz and the central bank through disaffected cabinet ministers.[13] Videla's own faction within the military resisted privatization, particularly in sectors controlled by the military, like the oil monopoly YPF. The navy successfully repelled budgetary threats to its nuclear industry. The effectiveness of this opposition unraveled Videla's liberalizing attempt, which initially had reduced fiscal deficits from 11.7 percent of GDP in 1976 to 6.8 percent in 1978, and brought down inflation from 444 percent in 1976 to 176 percent in 1977, while slashing real wages. The overvaluation of the peso remained after 1976 and export tariffs were reimposed in 1978. The main beneficiaries of expanded foreign borrowing after 1976 were state and military enterprises, large banks, and private firms producing nontraded goods and services and competing with imports. The foreign debt grew from nearly $8 billion in 1976 to $11.7 billion in 1977 and nearly $35.6 billion in 1981. The overall rate of effective protection in the 1970s was 100 percent (and 85 percent in 1979).[14] Videla—responsible for the execution and disappearance of over ten thousand Argentine citizens—was unprepared to accept massive unemployment (which remained under 5 percent) and unable to downsize the state, slash inflation and arms purchases, reverse an overvalued peso, and stem massive capital flight. A reversal of trade and capital-account liberalization followed.

General Roberto Viola's 1981 coup terminated orthodox measures, raised

[12] Scheetz (1992: 188 n.16).

[13] Canitrot (1994); Frieden (1991b: 214–15).

[14] Pion-Berlin (1985); Di Tella and Dornbush (1989: 326–37); Kaufman (1990a: 127–29); Haggard (1995b: 129).

tariff barriers, and eased the flow of credit and subsidies to the private sector, triggering another counter-coup by General Leopoldo Galtieri the same year.[15] Galtieri imposed new export tariffs but reinstated some elements of an orthodox program, triggering a fierce and immediate challenge by the same coalition that had foiled his predecessors Onganía and Videla. The CGT organized a general strike in March 1982 and nationwide demonstrations, the first major popular march since the 1976 coup, which ended with thousands of arrests. Retreating from what he perceived as a certain political dead end, Galtieri organized a new coalition—statist and hypernationalist—that would doom liberalizing efforts: the coalition that endorsed Argentina's invasion of the Malvinas / Falklands in April 1982. Galtieri's gross miscalculations—domestic and international, as analyzed below—led to his replacement by General Reynaldo Bignone. Aware of the military's shattered reputation as failing in political, economic, and military battlegrounds at home and abroad, Bignone was primarily concerned with softening the military's retreat into the barracks while increasing real wages and restructuring private debt, thus accelerating spiraling inflation.[16]

Nearly three decades of intermittent military rule had come to an end. The dominance of statist-nationalist coalitions throughout this period, even if occasionally challenged by short-lived episodes of economic reform or longer episodes of hybrid policies, is rather clear. None of these interludes amounted to the birth of an internationalist grand strategy in all its components, as would take place in the early 1990s. The confessional element that sometimes joins in statist-nationalist coalitions was less evident in Argentina—compared with the Middle East or South Asia—but far from absent. The established hierarchies of the Roman Catholic Church had backed statist-nationalist military regimes, wielding the defense of a "Christian world" as an effective coalitional glue, and endorsing massive killings and disappearances during Argentina's infamous "dirty war."[17] Argentina's opening to the world was never a natural preference of this confessional elite threatened by the material culture of global capitalism and by the potential influx of competing (non-Catholic) Christian denominations.

The era of militarism ended with President Raúl Alfonsín (1983–1989). Not so the era of a coalitional equipoise between internationalizing and statist-nationalist strategies. The new Radical administration was concerned with fostering support for a nascent democracy, not with initiating a coalitional breakthrough. Alfonsín's political center of gravity was among Radical party activists with an agenda that resembled that of their Peronist rivals in many respects, in

---

[15] Frieden (1991b: 206–17); Haggard and Kaufman (1995: 50–65); Kaufman and Stallings (1991: 26).

[16] On this period's essentially populist character, see Kaufman and Stallings (1991: 26).

[17] Moneta (1984: 123); Kenworthy (1970: 128). On the Church complicity, see Calvin Sims, "Argentine Tells of Dumping 'Dirty War' Captives into Sea." *New York Times* 13 March 1995: A1, A5. On the extensive use of Christianity by Argentine hypernationalists, see Rock (1993). Radical Catholic priests who challenged the highest Church hierarchies joined competing statist-nationalist movements, including the Peronist Montoneros (Manzetti 1993: 46).

order to preempt their political challenge. Alfonsín's heterodox policies remained inflationary (inflation increased by 700 percent in 1984 alone), with real wage increases, huge budget deficits, industrial protectionism, and a failure to comply with IMF stabilization targets.[18] Military budgets declined but Alfonsín maintained some military programs, including the medium tank, submarine development, the training jet Pampa, missile-carrying corvettes, and ballistic missiles. In 1985 he launched the Austral Plan, a heterodox program to control inflation while avoiding economic contraction and maintaining international credit. The plan—which sought to maintain both business and popular support—unraveled and with it the Radical administration, which lost the 1989 elections to Peronism. Campaigning largely under the old populist banner, President Carlos S. Menem was to achieve the unachievable in decades of Argentine history: the crystallization of an internationalist grand strategy.

The Coalitional Profile, 1940s–1980s: Brazil

The beginnings of a centralized and interventionist state in Brazil can be traced to the revolution that ended the Old Republic (1930) led by Getúlio Vargas. His Estado Nôvo (New State) fostered nationalism, state enterprise, military participation in industrial development, and populism, a pattern that evokes early Peronism. Soon after World War II a coup removed Vargas and President Eurico G. Dutra (1946–1951) from the Social Democratic party attempted to dismantle some import controls, but an overvalued exchange rate led to a crisis in 1947 and to their reimposition.

The postwar populist era spanned 1952 to 1963, and was steered by a coalition of parties representing the working and lower-middle class. Vargas returned (1951–1954) imbued with economic nationalism, statism, xenophobia, and fiscal expansion, although he initially allowed some foreign investment. A perfunctory stabilization program in 1954 was partly foiled by his opposition to central bank independence. The World Bank refused to finance Vargas's program or that of his successors until 1964. In a farewell letter written before his suicide, Vargas attacked foreign enterprises and upheld statist populism.[19] The old Vargas coalition supported President Juscelino Kubitschek, while antistatists and free traders opposed him. Kubitschek (1956–1961) resisted IMF stabilization programs and was more concerned with building his power base through basic industry, energy infrastructure, and the new city of Brasília than through price stability and balancing payments.[20]

---

[18] Kaufman and Stallings (1991: 26). On Alfonsín's failure to make state reform a central component of his coalitional strategies, see Manzetti (1993: 56–59) and Canitrot (1994). Heterodox policies place greater emphasis on direct administration of price and currency, whereas orthodox policies rely more on conventional fiscal and monetary instruments to manage demand (Kaufman 1990b: 64). For Alfonsín's political platform, see Alfonsín (1983).

[19] Vargas blamed international oil companies that fought his successful creation of Petrobrás (the national oil monopoly) and condemned US pressures against Brazil's attempt to keep coffee prices high (Skidmore 1988; Castro and Ronci 1991: 156).

[20] Kaufman (1990a: 126).

The early 1960s was a turbulent period in Brazil's political history, characterized by particularly low political consensus. The populist alliance collapsed and a severe economic crisis precluded governing without alienating one segment or another of potential coalitions. President Jânio Quadros resigned within seven months of assuming power (1961), in the midst of a deepening economic crisis. His successor João Goulart (1961–1964) inherited recession, hyperinflation, and default on international debt, but maintained Quadros's populist program. Strong class and sectoral tensions led to increased political mobilization and intense polarization. The middle and upper classes feared a "subversive" threat from below, while militant labor leaders supported Goulart.

This volatile crisis ended with the 1964 military coup that inaugurated a fairly consensual strategy—despite some discrepancies within the ruling coalition—that lasted nearly a decade. The strategy, with state entrepreneurship at its heart, aimed at rapid growth emphasizing macroeconomic stability, exports, and continued import-substitution in selected sectors.[21] The state was to maintain and expand control over high-technology infrastructural and intermediate goods characterized by low returns, high risk, and long gestation, which are basic inputs to modern private industry. The state was the engine of growth and the key to the strategy's—and the ruling coalition's—success. Major beneficiaries were to be the mostly public metallurgic sector, chemical and petrochemical industries, paper, and users of intermediate products, but also private mechanical and electrical machinery firms. The military was to control several industrial fiefdoms in tune with the developmentalist strategy propagated by the Escola Superior de Guerra (Higher War College). The main economic bureaucracies and the military intelligence apparatus were the guardians of the model. Private industrialists supported this hybrid strategy as junior partners in what came to be known as the "triple alliance" of state, national private, and multinational capital.[22] Most modern industrial sectors, national finance, and agribusiness supported the model in the expectation that it would leave behind the era of populism and single-minded import substitution. Labor was harshly repressed and would see its wages slip dramatically for the next decade. A strong IMF-backed stabilization program was in place immediately following the coup.

The new strategy led to Brazil's so-called economic "miracle," a 10 percent annual rate of growth (1967–1973). Despite an impressive export performance, the strategy retained an inward-oriented emphasis on consumer durables and capital goods for the domestic market, and high protective tariffs. There was some effort to resolve foreign exchange shortages through minidevaluations and export subsidies, suggesting a drive toward an "export-adequate" rather than

---

[21] On statist—not private—entrepreneurship as the most valued preference of this coalition, see Barros (1978: 132). Only Castello Branco's group was committed to liberalizing the foreign investment regime, but even the 1964–1967 period falls under the hybrid strategy, with the Castelistas unable to implant central bank independence, liberalized exchange rates, or market prices in strategic inputs (Castro and Ronci 1991: 161–62; Sola 1994: 161).

[22] Bresser Pereira (1978); Evans (1979); Collier (1979); Stepan (1988).

"export-led" growth strategy.[23] Industrial sectors controlled by the military multiplied and were paraded as examples of Brazil's *grandeza* (grandeur), although they often amounted to expensive white elephants.[24] Military spending (1965) reversed a long-term decline since the 1940s, and President Médici (1969–1974) gave military spending first or second priority in his budgets, so that it absorbed over 20 percent of central expenditures on average.[25]

The impressive gains for all partners muffled internal dissent within the ruling coalition during this period. However, the economic contraction that followed the 1973 oil crisis undermined the gains for national private firms. The economic crisis of the mid-1970s under President Geisel (1974–1979) sharpened the choice between maintaining macroeconomic stability and strengthening private firms. In a much publicized "manifesto," prominent entrepreneurs—freer to challenge the regime than any other sector—chastised "estatizaçao," the massive growth of state entrepreneurship. More state enterprises had been created between 1970 and 1975 than during the preceding thirty years combined.[26] Investments in military industries continued to grow in the mid-1970s, pushing government deficits from 1.4 percent of GDP (1974) to 13.1 percent (1979). Inflation grew from 15 percent to 40 percent in the same period.

Statism, import substitution, trade protection, and industrial policy remained strategic political pillars throughout the 1970s and 1980s. The 1980s saw a stop-go sequence from austerity to expansion and back to retrenchment. Budgetary deficits and inflation worsened under President Figueiredo (1979–1985), with the military, business groups, and labor opposing austerity measures, which lead to the collapse of an IMF stabilization package. The monetarist president of the central bank was removed (1983). As in Argentina, powerful statist-nationalist currents within the armed forces constituted a most important pressure group protecting state entrepreneurship. Intraservice competition became strongly entrenched by the 1980s, with each service running a separate ministry in control of its own industrial niche. The two decades of military rule in Brazil had dramatically reinforced rather than weakened statist-nationalism and the military-industrial complex.

The reinception of democracy in 1985 brought little added macropolitical consensus regarding a preferred strategy. José Sarney (1985–1990) was no dedicated populist but followed macroeconomic policies—budget deficits and wage increases—in tune with populist sentiment. Sarney's coalition was fractured at the top, with Finance Minister Francisco Dornelles representing the liberalizing camp and Planning Minister João Sayad representing a populist alliance of inward-looking, statist, and labor groups close to the Partido do Movimento Democrático Brasileiro. Sarney replaced Dornelles with Dilson

---

[23] Fishlow's (1985) characterization, quoted in Kaufman (1990a: 129). See also Fishlow (1989), Haggard (1990).

[24] "Pharaonic" projects absorbed $90 billion in foreign curency (Ames 1987; Solingen 1996b).

[25] World Bank (1991); ACDA (1990).

[26] Domínguez (1987: 256). State enterprises grew from 81 in 1959 to 251 in 1980 (Trebat 1983). See also Castro and Ronci (1991: 161–63).

Funaro and discontinued negotiations with the IMF.[27] In early 1986 Sarney unveiled the heterodox Cruzado plan aimed both at controlling inflation without slowing growth and at appeasing the statist-nationalist camp. An ambitious public investment program (Plano do Metas) and the large wage increases built into the Cruzado plan led to its unraveling in less than a year and to debt moratoria twice in 1987. Funaro's replacement, Luiz C. Bresser Pereira, could not block fiscal draining by the military, by subsidized private firms, and by public employees. Defense appropriations were privileged under an explicit directive to the presidential cabinet, which increased the military share of central expenditures relative to the preceding six years of military rule.[28]

The 1988 constitution reflected both the lingering power of the military and the newly gained influence of a statist-populist coalition, in its guarantees of military prerogatives, lifetime employment to state employees, and severe restrictions on foreign capital. Once the Cruzado plan had failed, Congress further undermined liberalizing initiatives. By the late 1980s, drops in real wages, price freezes, and tax reforms alienated Sarney's popular constituencies, forcing him to turn to an IMF-style orthodox stabilization package. The low level of macropolitical consensus was evident in the proliferation of de facto parties and legislative factions in the Chamber of Deputies. This institutional fragmentation, in turn, undermined the consolidation of a stable coalition favoring reform. Hyperinflation took hold (1989–1990), preparing the political ground for the birth of a coalition under President Fernando Collor de Mello, who launched a short-lived liberalizing program, to which I return below.

This overview of coalitional profiles in Argentina and Brazil (1940s–1980s) reveals entrenched statist-nationalist coalitions, mostly military but at times civilian, and a dominant inward-looking strategy favoring protected firms, state enterprise, and the military-industrial complex. Some coalitions included popular sectors but most did not, even where their policies were laced with populist rhetoric (military presidents also resisted large unemployment and privatization to retain power). These features overwhelmed brief episodes of macroeconomic stability, fiscal restraint, and tariff reductions, none of which amounted to a truly internationalist strategy with its full domestic and international requirements, including state and military contraction and effective adherence to global political, strategic, and economic regimes. The military governments identified with "neoliberal" revolutions (1960s–1970s) in fact reversed long-term postwar declines in military expenditures and rarely approached competitive real exchange rates, trade liberalization, low inflation, and low fiscal deficits as pivotal requirements of their political strategies.[29] Brazil's exports as a share of GDP

[27] Sarney (1986); Drake (1991: 38); Fishlow (1992); Haggard and Kaufman (1995: 120). On the heterogeneity of Sarney's government and how policies depended on whether liberals or populists controlled the economic ministries, see Kaufman (1990b: 72–86) and Stallings (1992: 66).

[28] *Latin America Weekly Report* 30 November 1985: 5; Bresser Pereira, Maravall, Przeworski (1993: 49).

[29] Tulchin (1984: 192–93); Ames (1987: 93). On how the large anti-export bias introduced in Argentina's economy by Perón remained a permanent characteristic into the 1980s, see Cavallo (1988).

during the "miracle" years (1967–1973) increased from 5.8 to 8.3 percent, in contrast to Taiwan's doubling of its export shares from 21.3 to 46.7 percent of GDP in the same period. As Díaz Alejandro (1983: 46) argued in his study of international openness, military officers in the Southern Cone were no great enthusiasts of free trade in goods and services, were skeptical of direct foreign investments, and unlikely to accept tariff reductions in sectors dominated by public enterprises under their control. Coalitions that went in with initial political support from liberalizing quarters witnessed their strategy hastily unravel, and became little more than transitory "reformist intermezzos."[30] Truly independent central banks never quite took off throughout those decades. In contrast to South Korea and Taiwan, political entrepreneurs in Argentina and Brazil were far more constrained in altering economic models by powerful beneficiaries of the status quo in state agencies and enterprises and in private industry.

Competitive Patterns in Economics and Security

The Southern Cone has exhibited the puzzling characteristic—relative to other regions—of avoiding wars for most of the twentieth century, if not ancillary afflictions of politicide and large-scale repression. The Chaco War between Paraguay and Bolivia (1932–1935) is the main exception. Yet the relative absence of war did not amount to a peaceful, cooperative region. First, all was not well in Argentine-Brazilian relations, which were characterized by a historical competition over territories, resources, and influence over buffer states that occasionally developed into expressions of obsessive mutual distrust and military competition.[31] The two fought their last war in 1825–1828, but Argentina's alignment with the Axis powers during World War II while Brazilian troops joined the Allies in Europe exacerbated the lingering rivalry. Indeed, Argentina and Brazil became frequent subjects in studies of nuclear proliferation, given their four decades of intensive efforts to develop nuclear programs outside the global nonproliferation regime. By the late 1980s, only a handful among over 170 states refused to join the 1968 Nonproliferation Treaty, and the hand included them both. A second uneasy relationship for many decades involved Argentina and Chile, a military rivalry that propelled them to the brink of war over the Beagle Channel in the late 1970s. A third major conflict in the Southern Cone erupted in fury with Argentina's invasion of the Malvinas / Falklands islands—Malvinas henceforth—leading to a full-scale war with Great Britain in 1982. A coalitional analysis sheds light on the sources of all these instances

[30] Castro and Ronci (1991: 158).

[31] On Itamaraty (Brazil's Foreign Ministry) as the source of Brazil's imperial threats to Agentina, see Perón (1974: 90). Child (1990: 154) characterizes competition with Brazil as a "quasiobsession of Argentine geopolitical thinkers," not matched in intensity on the Brazilian side. An Argentine foreign minister, Carlos Pastor, portrayed Argentine-Brazilian relations as one of "competitive schemes" (quoted in Hilton 1985: 27). On Brazil's perceived threats from an alliance of Spanish-speaking neighbors under Argentine leadership, see Vidigal (1989). See also entire issue of *Política e Estratégia* (São Paulo) 6,2 (April–June 1988).

of violence, near violence, and brinkmanship (conventional and otherwise), as well as on the absence of genuine economic cooperation in the Southern Cone until the 1990s.[32]

Argentina was at the center of these conflicts and nuclear competition, and its special coalitional dynamics and makeup bear heavily on this record, as suggested by the following interconnected points. The first element that sets Argentina apart is the fact that of all the statist-nationalist coalitions that dominated the region in the postwar era, Argentina's were the least stable, continuously challenged by either competing statist-nationalist factions (military or otherwise) or liberalizing factions, or both.[33] The fragility of such coalitions, and the "outbidding" among statist-nationalist variants in particular, explain the extreme nature of Argentina's grand strategy in its internal, regional, and international dimensions. This succession of unstable and short-lived coalitions essentially extended many elements of Perón's strategy for decades after his downfall.

Second, statism was firmly implanted in Argentina early in the postwar era, prior to the rapid expansion of state entrepreneurship in Brazil in the late 1960s. The political basis for statism in Argentina was strong even beyond the military, particularly after the Peronist mobilization of a large working class, a large state bureaucracy, and a politically belligerent group of protected industries (CGE). This camp's receptivity to "organic nationalism" was arguably unparalleled in the region.[34] Even when fiscal populist policies were suspended for some time, populist rhetoric and nationalist themes remained. Selected interludes by fragile internationalist coalitions often collapsed as soon as the liberalizing wave reached the shores of a state bureaucracy or a military enterprise.

Third, and connected to the previous points, the military and its associated complex had penetrated Argentina's political and economic life as none of its neighbors had.[35] The military justified its investments in domestic arms production (as early as the 1940s, preceding most Brazilian activities in this area) as at least partly in response to potential "threats" from Brazil's closer relations with the US. The major impetus to a hitherto nascent military industrial complex came under Perón (1946–1955). After his ouster, the tripartite arrangement that institutionalized coalitional tradeoffs among the three services resulted in permanent industrial fiefdoms and the continuous control of certain ministries. The longevity of the nuclear program—sheltered from cyclical economic chaos for decades—is but one paradigmatic symptom of the military's stranglehold on all coalitions after Perón.

Fourth, Perón's legacy was reflected not only in the domestic political econ-

---

[32] On the compatibility between import-substituting models, populism, and conflict-prone geopolitical thinking in the Southern Cone, see Mármora (1988: 25).

[33] Between 1952 and 1966 alone, Argentina had 7 presidents, 17 foreign ministers, 18 ministers of economics, 16 of the interior, 15 of war, and 15 commanders-in-chief of the army (Kenworthy 1970: 118).

[34] On Argentina's "pathological" nationalism, myths of external conspiracy and of self-achievement, see Escudé (1987) and Rock (1993).

[35] Rouquié (1982).

omy of Argentina. Many of Perón's policies vis-à-vis the outside world persisted for many decades as well, including an emphasis on national sovereignty, territorial integrity, hostility toward the US, economic independence, and nuclear prowess. Beyond the region, Perón's international policies advanced an innovation—"La Tercera Posición" (the Third Position)—that others later refashioned in Green Books (Libya), *juche* (North Korea), and similar "nonaligned" doctrines. For Perón, international economic regimes such as the IMF and GATT, and international institutions such as the UN and the OAS were anathema to a statist-nationalist grand strategy (Perón 1973: 221–23). Even after Perón, Argentina joined only selected regimes while maintaining a rhetoric and policy of defiance.

Fifth, Perón's legacy for Argentina's role in the region implied the fulfillment of Argentina's destiny as a regional power, particularly at Brazil's expense. Military expenditures not only protected the military's material and political base but were usefully wielded as ensuring external protection and independence. How else could such expenditures be justified in a region that had enjoyed a century nearly free of wars? Tilly's notion of military racket schemes has far more resonance here than perhaps in any other region covered in this study. Not unexpectedly, Argentina's military investments intensified mistrust and engendered efforts to balance such investments.

Sixth, Argentina's coalitional makeup and ancillary policies did not provide a friendly political environment for the germination of an alternative—internationalist—grand strategy, one rooted in international political and economic integration, genuine regional cooperation, and an effective contraction of the statist and military complex. Internationalist forces were disadvantaged politically, but remained alive if not always well (a prominent leader, Pedro Aramburu, was assassinated in 1969). This camp had consistently bet on a political alliance with an unlikely partner, the military, within which statism and corporatism generally gained the upper hand. Groups with an internationalist political orientation, anxious to revoke Argentina's nationalist reputation and to support international institutions and emerging global norms and regimes, were rather feebly represented in the Foreign Ministry, which was under heavy statist-nationalist and military influence. In Tulchin's words (1984), Argentina's leaders "never had a global sense of their national interest;" they "aspired to greatness and to influence in world affairs but refused to compete with the other great powers on the usual terms." Had a strong and effective internationalist coalition ever prevailed, Argentina's grand strategy would have perhaps avoided regionally destabilizing policies toward Chile, Brazil, and Great Britain. Instead, statist-nationalist contenders promoted militarization and risk-prone policies, expecting regional "threats" to help maintain their entrenched position at home.

Argentina's hypernationalism was thus a natural result of intense competition *within* the statist-nationalist-military camp, among political entrepreneurs outbidding each other to attract the large populist, bureaucratic, and military-industrial constituencies mobilized under Perón. Attempts to implement orthodox adjustment programs were quickly doomed by these constituencies, forcing a rapid retreat. Onganía, we recall, turned to statist-corporatist and nationalist allies, devalued the currency, taxed traditional exports heavily (antagonizing liberal agro-exporters), and responded to a popular uprising with statist-populist themes. It was under Onganía that the first plans for invading the Malvinas were drafted (circa 1968) and a border dispute with Uruguay escalated into a naval occupation of a contested island in 1969. The Peronist statist-nationalist interlude raised tension vis-à-vis the islands in 1974, and in early 1976 it unleashed a diplomatic crisis by refusing to allow the British Shackleton mission to fly to the islands through Argentina.[36] A conciliatory note by British Foreign Secretary Callaghan was dismissed and the Peronist president proceeded to break off diplomatic relations with Britain and to fire at the British vessel en route to the Malvinas.

Under Videla—responsive to pressures from navy quarters—Argentina occupied a British island in the South Sandwich group and established a military presence on the British dependency of South Thule, both in November 1976. A naval and air contingency plan for the Malvinas' invasion was in place by early 1977. The unraveling of Videla's program and of his liberalizing allies, we recall, was a product of statist-nationalist opposition at large and within the military (including the navy) and from its industrial and arms-purchasing complex. Admiral Emilio Massera's faction—advocating populism at home and nationalism abroad—spearheaded Argentine provocations around the Malvinas. Although Videla had initially attempted to curb the "hawks and the geopoliticians" on border disputes with Chile and Brazil, his opponents in the military—including Massera—succeeded in exacerbating tensions with Chile, unleashing the Beagle crisis.[37] Chilean control over three barren islands in the Beagle Channel—adjudicated in a 1881 treaty and recognized in a 1977 International Court of Justice ruling—curtailed the Argentine military's geopolitical claims in the South Atlantic and Antarctica. Videla was forced to advance a revisionist position designed to restore Argentine control of the islands. Military mobilization in both sides, maneuvers, and incidents on a prewar footing flared in 1978, replacing the Malvinas as the most likely target of war for the Argentine military.[38]

Chile was at this time under the repressive military rule of Augusto Pinochet, who had deposed Salvador Allende in 1973 and initiated economic liberalization praised by international institutions and investors. Countering natural tendencies amid a Chilean military imbued with nationalist doctrines, Pinochet was restrained in his response to the Beagle dispute by the need to maintain his

---

[36] The newspaper *Crónica* advocated an outright invasion in 1974 (Dillon 1989: 10) which, together with other incidents, prompted the British Ambassador in Buenos Aires to warn that "an attack on the islands would meet with a military response." The ambassador characterized the 1976 episode as "rapidly moving toward a head-on collision."

[37] Freedman and Gamba-Stonehouse (1991: 6) describe Argentina as being "on the verge of war with Chile" during the Beagle incident. See also Varas (1985: 55, 100, 104).

[38] Pittman (1981: 167–69). For a legal perspective on respective claims to the Beagle Channel, see Olivera (1978).

strategy on course, and his supportive coalition together. In his own words (Pinochet Ugarte 1991: 167, 172, 178), Chile "should maintain tranquillity and moderation," and "avoid fueling the fire" (*hechar leña al fuego*), because choosing war "would be madness." A risky Chilean response to the risky Argentine challenge could have doomed Pinochet's incipient program, which was barely beginning to yield expected results (a negative growth of 12.9 percent in 1975 became a positive 9.9 percent GDP growth in 1977). Pinochet's liberalizing efforts demanded a measured and reluctant response, endorsed by prominent Chicago School Chilean economists and businessmen in his coalition.[39] The military's rigid hierarchical organization and Pinochet's personalistic control of it—both in sharp contrast to the Argentine case—provided an efficient transmission belt for a coherent institutional strategy.[40]

The military had no deficiency of radical nationalists, yet Pinochet understood that a neofascist corporatist agenda, with statist, xenophobic, redistributive, and anti-internationalist overtones, would not yield any reliable partners for a stable coalition. Instead, liberalizing the economy would not only secure powerful coalitional consociates but had a significant potential—if the pie were to grow as economic orthodox partners predicted—for increasing the military's own institutional resources and political windfalls. Labor was harshly repressed (with unemployment at 20 percent) and shock treatment (1975–1976) replaced a more gradual approach to economic reform that had yielded poor results. Structural adjustment reduced the average fiscal deficit to less than 3 percent of GDP (1974–1983), down from 16 percent of GDP (1971–1973).[41] Chile's maximum tariff plummeted from 750 percent under Allende to 10 percent by 1979. Banks were privatized (1975), all quantitative trade restrictions were eliminated (1975–1979) as were all restrictions on capital outflows by foreign investors (1974), and a unified multiple-exchange-rate system followed a large devaluation. From over 500 state enterprises under Allende, 457 were privatized by 1980.

Chilean military expenditures during the Beagle Channel conflict and in its aftermath reveal more of an insurance policy than an offensive buildup, in line with its status quo position in the conflict. First, military budgets were clearly reactive rather than proactive. Increases followed border tensions with Argentina (1977–1978) and with Peru and Bolivia (1978), as well as Videla's increase in Argentine military expenditures after 1976. Second, being a much smaller country than its neighbors, Chile also had a smaller economy from which to draw military resources, so that a higher military investment relative

---

[39] Muñoz (1984: 165); Selcher (1984a: 105–12); Labán and Larraín (1995). On pressures from economic technocrats to maintain a foreign policy compatible with capitalist modernization, see Agüero (1989: 88) and Silva (1991). On Pinochet's strategy in his own words, see Pinochet Ugarte (1974).

[40] Ames (1987: 237–39); Remmer (1989); Varas (1989). On Pinochet's veto of "patriotic campaigns" over the Beagle and his taming of militaristic responses within the armed forces, see Pinochet Ugarte (1991: 166–72).

[41] Bruno (1988: 229). On financial liberalization, see Haggard and Maxfield (1996: 50–53).

to GDP continued to yield a smaller military budget in absolute terms, dampening the temptation to match neighboring capabilities. Third, rather than being the pivotal budgetary item, military expenditures as a percentage of health and education were much smaller in Chile (95 percent between 1974 and 1989) than they had been in Argentina for nearly four decades (or than they would be under Alfonsín later). Whereas Argentina spent over 34 percent of its budget on the military (1977–1982), its Chilean counterpart earmarked only 16 (and 18 percent for health and education, twice as much as Argentina). Finally, Pinochet reduced military expenditures when stabilization efforts required it (1975–1976, 1981).[42] Indeed, military expenditures as a percentage of GDP remained at about 7 percent after 1973, despite significant GDP increases after 1977. José Piñera, the labor minister who fathered Chile's new social security system, recounts these priorities: "It was wonderful: every time the military asked for more destroyers, I said no—we need the money to pay off social security."[43] Unlike Argentina and Brazil, Chile procured weapons abroad and eschewed the establishment of a statist weapons-producing industry.

On the Argentine side, the background to both the Beagle crisis and the subsequent Malvinas invasion points to a ruling junta—Videla's first and Galtieri's later—bereft of coalitional partners and prone to yield to a statist-nationalist political center of gravity. On the one hand, military rule had devastated organized labor. On the other hand, inconsistent and hybrid economic policies had alienated broad segments of the business community, along the import-substituting and export-oriented divide. Despite motions toward financial and trade liberalization, few would confuse the Videla and Galtieri administrations with an internationalist coalition implementing the panoply of domestic, regional, and international components of an internationalist grand strategy.[44] Proclaimed efforts at economic reform were never matched by effective steps: the fiscal deficit declined initially but returned to the levels of Isabel Perón's chaotic days by 1981, rising to nearly 19 percent in 1983. Moreover, military spending grew after 1976, reaching the highest levels in decades (4.2 percent of GDP), with Videla according it budgetary priority and allowing 5 percent yearly increases (1976–1982), three times greater than in Chile.[45] Argentine generals' fear of alienating their primary base of support explains their feeble and unsustained attempt to dismantle the statist and military-industrial complex. Indeed, this complex offered both Videla and Galtieri a last political refuge, once their programs had run aground and all erstwhile coalitional partners had

---

[42] Scheetz (1992: 184). Additional income for the Chilean military—between 18 and 30 percent of the military's total budget—came from a 1958 law that granted a percentage of taxes levied on copper exports for the use of the armed forces.

[43] *Newsweek* 12 December 1994: 50.

[44] On the basis of World Bank data, *The Economist* (23 September 1989) classified industrializing states into moderately or strongly outward-oriented and moderately or strongly inward-oriented. During both periods (1963–1973 and 1973–1985) Argentina was classified as strongly inward-oriented (Stopford, Strange, and Henley 1991: 11).

[45] Acuña and Smith (1995: 132); Cavallo (1988: 283).

deserted them. Saber rattling against Chile and Great Britain had the potential of uniting political forces otherwise headed for collision, particularly the military and labor. Admiral Massera's faction played a central role in challenging a long-standing status quo on the Malvinas in 1976–1977 and against Chile in 1978. Among other things, the navy was anxious to regain political capital lost to the army since the 1960s.

The Beagle dispute ended with a 1980 Vatican proposal favoring Chile, to the dismay of the Argentine junta, which quickly submitted a counterclaim. In 1980–1981, bank and business failures, devaluations, low growth, and upward shooting foreign debt, inflation, and military budgets were evident signs of the junta's ruinous performance. GDP per capita was now below 1970 levels, while presidential turnover among competing coalitions accelerated (Videla, Viola, and Galtieri in rapid succession). Against this competitive statist-nationalist outbidding at home and waning expectations of a favorable Vatican verdict on the Beagle, Galtieri's cabinet endorsed the Malvinas onslaught (January 1982). Preparations for a large-scale labor demonstration in March were an ominous political sign for Galtieri, who remembered the 1968 Cordobazo and Onganía's subsequent exit. In February 1982 the committee coordinating political parties under authoritarian rule—the Multipartidaria—demanded "the immediate restitution of the Malvinas." This signaled the islands' potential for igniting nationalist support among Peronist labor, state bureaucracies, religious organizations, protected industries, and the armed forces themselves.[46]

Galtieri understood the wide receptivity to a variant of a Sammlungspolitik— a social pact cementing a hypernationalist offensive alliance—that could relieve his own political dilemma.[47] Erstwhile Peronist opponents of the junta now rallied behind it, with Peronist leader Deolindo Bittel embracing Galtieri and the labor CGT pouring into the streets to show their support for the invasion. The invasion also helped Galtieri catalyze the military, forcing it to transcend centrifugal factionalism. He had promised different things to rabid statist-nationalists and lukewarm economic liberals in the military, seeking the navy's (that is, Admiral Anaya's) support for Galtieri's coup against Viola in exchange for Galtieri's support of a military occupation of the Malvinas.[48] Hoping never to confront the inherent tension between the two, Galtieri publicly acknowledged his political plan to convert expected gains from the Malvinas—*to be won without a war*—to advance a subsequent presidential candidacy. Alas, the opportunity was to be less golden than he had estimated and Galtieri ended up sacrificing more than his economic plan. While guessing right on the tactical— "rally-round-the-flag"—effect, Galtieri miscalculated strategically, considering

[46] On the statist-nationalist, protectionist, expansionist, and populist character of the Multipartidaria platform, see Pion-Berlin (1985: 65–66). On the "wild" popularity that a policy restoring the islands enjoyed at the time, see Tulchin (1984: 195).

[47] Lebow (1989: 114); Levy and Vakili (1993: 131). According to Kehr (1977: 38–49), the original German Sammlungspolitik—which benefited industrialists and agrarian interests at the expense of the working class—led to World War I, also a strategic miscalculation of British resolve.

[48] McGuire (1995: 187).

the outcome of the war: he was defeated in battle and booted out of power. The most severe miscalculation of all, he acknowledged, was his expectation that Great Britain would not attempt to regain the islands by force.[49] Notably, among the few who opposed the Argentine invasion at the outset were the "leaders of the financial and entrepreneurial sectors most closely connected with transnational capital, for the obvious reason that the conflict affected their interests" in a negative way.[50] Their views—often articulated by traditional economic-liberal parties—were a faint lament overpowered by massive support for the war.

As in other regions, statist-nationalist reliance on myths of sovereignty, territorial integrity, defiance, and independence as part of a risk-prone strategy to rally domestic support had slid into a real war. Military defeat—as with Nasser's in 1967—helped change the fate of Argentina's statist-nationalist coalition in the long term. Private entrepreneurs who might once have relied on the military to achieve an ever-elusive macroeconomic stability now considered this partnership exhausted for good. The junta had deepened Argentina's classical domestic economic and political instability with a foreign adventurism and unholy international alliances (with Libya, Cuba, and the USSR) that isolated the country as never before. Its own neighbors Chile and Brazil, although formal partners in a regional collective defense mechanism, reportedly colluded with British war efforts.[51] Although Brazil publicly endorsed Argentina's claim to sovereignty over the Malvinas, Brazilian air force officers warmly greeted British planes refueling during the war and condemned Argentina's use of force. This was no sign of a deep cooperative thrust in Southern Cone relations.

Perhaps the most serious challenge to the concept of a peaceful Southern Cone was the nuclear competition between Argentina and Brazil throughout four decades, the history of which is remarkably entangled with the unfolding struggle between dominant statist-nationalist coalitions and their less than formidable liberalizing rivals.[52] Perón spearheaded the call for external (and domestic) attention to Argentina's independent nuclear capabilities in the early 1950s. Brazil's populist Vargas did not dwell long on his response, demanding nuclear technology in exchange for uranium or thorium sales to the United States (1952). Admiral Alvaro Alberto attempted to purchase three ultracentrifuge systems for uranium enrichment—essential to any weapons-related program—from Bonn (1954), an effort foiled by US intervention. Café Filho succeeded Vargas, quickly reversing policies by emphasizing foreign invest-

---

[49] Freedman and Gamba-Stonehouse (1991: 79, 225–26). General Galtieri confessed to Oriana Fallaci: "I'll tell you . . . that though an English reaction was considered a possibility, we did not see it as a probability. Personally, I judged it scarcely possible and totally improbable" (quoted in Lebow 1989: 110).

[50] Moneta (1984: 128–29).

[51] Freedman and Gamba-Stonehouse (1991: 225–29); Gordon (1984: 90); Selcher (1984b: 110). Argentina got the OAS, under Rio Treaty stipulations, to formulate a supportive statement during the Malvinas war, but not one strong enough to back fully the use of military force. Betts (1993: 281) defined the Rio Pact as a "*de jure* overlay of collective security norms on a *de facto unorganized* security system."

[52] Poneman (1984); Solingen (1996b).

ments, dismissing Alberto, and allowing the US a monopoly on uranium research and extraction. Statist-nationalist Kubitschek appointed a parliamentary commission of inquiry in 1956 that denounced "improper" US influences on Café Filho. The commission urged independent nuclear capabilities and the creation of a National Atomic Energy Commission under direct presidential control. Statist-nationalists Quadros and Goulart (1961–1963) reaffirmed an independent nuclear policy in tune with their broader industrial and political priorities.

Meanwhile, in Argentina the military's tripartite division had allowed the navy to shelter the nuclear program for over thirty years of stop-go political-economic cycles. The National Atomic Energy Commission developed a clientelistic network of protected private suppliers, scientists, and technologists around an industrial undertaking that symbolized "organic nationalism" perhaps more than did any other Argentine program. Brief attempts at economic liberalization coincided with moderate efforts to curtail the nuclear program (Frondizi, Videla). These attempts were resisted successfully as part of the overall obstruction of state reform by the military-industrial complex and ancillary industries.

The military regimes in Brazil and Argentina were hardly exponents of an internationalist grand strategy. Despite some steps in that direction, which required stronger economic ties with the Western powers and international institutions, the guardians of statist-nationalist programs prevailed in maintaining a defiant position toward the nonproliferation regime and the US in particular. Brazil signed a comprehensive nuclear industrial agreement of statist-nationalist vintage with West Germany in 1974. Argentina's Atomic Energy Commission steadily developed the full range of fuel-cycle technologies as well, including those with weapons potential. The Nonproliferation Treaty (NPT) was a lightning rod for statist-nationalists in both countries, who pointed to its discriminatory nature to reject it. Statist-nationalist dominance was also evident in their joint resistance to making the Latin American nuclear-weapons-free-zone effective on their territory, according to the 1967 Tlatelolco Treaty. Moreover, some military and allied constituencies in both countries advanced the idea of developing nuclear weapons, openly or secretly. Retired army general Guglialmelli— cited earlier as an ally of economic nationalist and statist groups within ruling circles—advanced the position that Argentina does not know "when it will happen, but we are sure Brazil will build the atomic bomb. . . . If our neighbor gets the bomb, without a counterbalance, our own security will be affected."[53] Nuclear exports to rogue regimes—notably Iran and Iraq—were also part of the statist-nationalist diplomatic kit, both in Argentina and Brazil.

Would-be liberalizers could not ignore the costs of defiant nuclear policies— over which statist-nationalists had a stranglehold—in access to capital, markets,

[53] Quoted in Gordon (1984: 91). See also Guglialmelli (1976). On Brazil's Solimões plan, including presumed nuclear testing sites, publicly acknowledged only in 1990 under liberalizing President Collor de Mello, see James Brooke, "Brazil Uncovers Plan by Military to Build Atom Bomb and Stops It," *New York Times* 9 October 1990: A1, A4.

and technology, resources highly valued by liberalizers. Their formal rejections of imputed intentions to develop nuclear weapons must be read in the context of stemming international sanctions, as were efforts to diffuse bilateral nuclear competition. Thus, Argentina's Videla and Brazil's Figueiredo signed an agreement in 1980 on fuel cycle cooperation, a moderate declaration of intent rather than more substantive commitments. Soon afterward (1983) Argentina announced its development of uranium enrichment technology with weapons potential.

The democratic administrations of Sarney and Alfonsín did not usher in internationalist grand strategies, and accordingly proceeded with joint declarations of peaceful intentions (yearly between 1985–1990) and mutual visits to sensitive facilities, but no real breakthrough in nuclear cooperation, such as a mutual inspections regime or contractual denuclearization through regional or international mechanisms. Alfonsín allowed the Cóndor II missile—arguably the first Argentine weapon of mass destruction—to proceed unabated, maintained Argentina's opposition to the NPT and refusal to ratify Tlatelolco, and maintained its right to peaceful nuclear explosions. Sections of Brazil's military continued their "parallel program" with weapons applications even after attempts to place all nuclear activities under democratic control.[54] Against a perception of a peaceful and cooperative—even democratic!—Southern Cone, there was a reality of two nuclear-capable regional powers that resisted what the overwhelming majority of states in the international system had accepted: full international supervision of their nuclear programs.

Beyond the nuclear realm, the dominance of statist-nationalism for decades also precluded genuinely integrative regional economic frameworks. Argentina, Brazil, and Uruguay, among others, joined the Latin American Free Trade Area (LAFTA, 1960), which aimed at reaching free trade by 1973. However, state bureaucracies and enterprises, and protected industries, were not natural candidates for embracing trade liberalization, particularly when wider markets would benefit multinational corporations. Such an arrangement would have precluded them from capturing custom tariffs and quota rents, which would go to benefit trading partners. Limited cooperative arrangements lingered where broadened protected markets would not damage national monopolies—many controlled by the military—threatened with competition. The United Nations Economic Commission for Latin America (ECLA) provided a vision of wider regional markets to support import-substitution. By the end of the 1960s, LAFTA was a clear failure. A continent-wide institution, SELA (Sistema Económico Latinoamericano), was established in 1975 as a "collective economic security" system. ALADI (Asociación Latinoamericana de Integración, 1980) became yet another link in a long institutional chain that never delivered economic integration. At this time, Brazil attracted an average of 11 percent of Argentine foreign investments (1977–1982) and Argentina an even lower share of Brazil's. By 1981 Brazil exported one-third of 1 percent of its GDP to Argentina and Argentina about half of 1 percent of its GDP to Brazil.

---

[54] Stanley (1992).

The democratic administrations of Alfonsín and Sarney signed protocols (1985–1990) that created working groups to study different sectors. Prominent among these was the 1986 Acta para la Integración Argentino-Brasileña and the 1988 Tratado de Integración, Cooperación y Desarrollo. These were agreements of a limited and cautious nature, as Argentine labor and industrial entrepreneurs opposed a broader agenda, which the failure of the Austral and Cruzado plans in Argentina and Brazil rendered impracticable anyway. It is not that economic cooperation at this point was largely rhetorical and resembled "shallow" as opposed to "deeper" integration.[55] Even progress toward shallow forms was slow and piecemeal, and most protocols were never executed. Firm-level cooperation, joint ventures, and technology transfers were weak. The leap from product-by-product discussions and specific reciprocity to broad tariffs reductions would not come until the 1990s. Whatever regional cooperation in both economics and security had managed to emerge during all these decades, it was frequently watered down to a joint tactical rejection of "hegemonist" US power in the region. Even the nuclear agreements between Videla and Figueiredo and Alfonsín and Sarney were more concerned with notions of "horizontal self-reliance" and rejection of international regimes than with concrete steps toward economic integration and denuclearization and toward a cooperative strategy invested with positive, rather than defensive, long-term objectives.

In 1969 Argentina, Brazil, Paraguay, Uruguay, and Bolivia signed a treaty aimed at the common development of hydroelectric power and water resources. By 1973, mutual recriminations dominated this issue area, particularly Argentina's opposition to the joint Brazilian-Paraguayan Itaipú project (on the upper Paraná River) which was seen as endangering the viability of downstream Argentine projects.[56] Brazil acted unilaterally, refusing to delay the project until negotiations or international adjudication settled the conflict. The democratic Peronist administration in Argentina mobilized nationalist public opinion against Itaipú. After the 1976 coup, the junta joined its counterparts in Brazil and Paraguay in a 1979 agreement that achieved some coordination of the Alto Paraná projects, but not a genuinely integrative infrastructural and transportation framework. In sum, joint energy and infrastructural projects mirrored the fate of security and economic cooperation, all of which stalled until the internationalist revolution of the 1990s.

THE INTERNATIONALIST REVOLUTION: THE BIRTH OF A NEW REGIONAL ORDER

The sources of the internationalist revolution in Argentina and Brazil can be found at virtually all levels: international, regional, and domestic. The joint operation of multilateral economic institutions, US influence, East Asian models, regional pioneers like Chile, and the domestic collapse of heterodox

---

[55] Haggard (1995b); Mármora (1988); Hufbauer and Schott (1994: 226–27); Ferguson (1984).
[56] Llaver (1979); Olmos (1986).

programs had perhaps overdetermined the radical departure from the past, making it hard to assess the relative impact of each. The ascendancy of new political coalitions does not take place in an international vacuum but ultimately feeds on the domestic realignment of political forces and institutions. Political entrepreneurs use new external and internal realities to put together what they see as the politically most promising agenda. Liberalizing politicians at the end of the 1980s could thus portray the legacy of statist-nationalism as one of bankrupt economies and failed polities, transcending some of its earlier contributions. Exposing the old populist rhetoric and the hybrid programs of civilian and military predecessors, these politicians "unmasked" the true beneficiaries of inward-looking models, either before but most often shortly after elections.

An iron triangle—the military and its state enterprises, protected industries, and Peronist labor—had strapped Argentina's political economy, either sequentially or in concert. This pattern led not only to the deindustrialization of Argentina but also to its statist-nationalist emphasis vis-à-vis regional and international relations. The relative political strength of liberalizing challengers like Menem was heightened where the magnitude of economic collapse, particularly relative to the state's economic endowments, was most dramatic. Statism and the military complex fared better in Brazil during the 1970s, despite Brazil's heavy reliance on foreign oil, but also resulted in uneven, unsustained, and income-concentrating growth. The performance of Asian tigers by the late 1980s—growth cum equity—now challenged inward-looking strategies. For the first time in decades a powerful array of societal and institutional forces was ready to back a new strategy.

The unraveling of Alfonsín's policies in the late 1980s had left him isolated even within the Radical party. The 1989 electoral campaign of Peronist Menem relied on classical statist-nationalist populist themes, including a moratorium on the foreign debt, wage increases, and recapturing the Malvinas with "blood and fire."[57] However, Menem had extensive contacts with the agro-exporting and business community as well, suggesting that a key ingredient of what Hirschman has labeled a "reform-mongering" strategy was already in place: duplicity, that is, conveying different and contradictory messages to opposing constituencies.[58] Menem's complete strategic reversal after the elections became evident with the appointment of representatives from agro-exporting and industrial associations (SRA, UIA, Cámara Argentina de Comercio) as well as leaders from the economic liberal Unión de Centro Democrático (founded by Alvaro Alsogaray in 1982) to governmental positions. Menem attracted broad congressional support for the 1989 twin "Reform of the State" and "Economic Emergency" acts, gaining him an 81 percent approval rating. Both measures

---

[57] Acuña (1994: 38–40); Menem won 47 percent of the vote against 37 percent for the Radical candidate Eduardo Angeloz (Manzetti 1993).

[58] Hirschman (1965: 271–97); Kenworthy (1970: 113). Williamson (1994) defines this pattern of reversal in effecting reforms as "voodoo politics." On how "populist" leaders in Argentina learned their lesson from the failed Austral and Primavera plans under Alfonsín, see Fernández (1991: 142–43).

authorized large-scale privatization and the suspension of industrial subsidies and tax breaks, domestic procurements regulations, and public hiring. "To enact these reforms," Eduardo Vaca, president of the Peronist party acknowledged, "we were forced to take a strong change of direction and make alliances with groups that were not characteristic of Peronism, like the industrial and financial sectors."[59]

By late 1989 Menem had gained the support of most top business associations and some factions of labor, and their acquiescence to drastic austerity responses to intractable inflation and ballooning debt. The immediate privatization in 1990–1991 of the national airline Aerolíneas Argentinas, state phone company, several petrochemical firms, and TV channels, among others, signaled his commitment to structural adjustment efforts and to eliminating $7 billion in governmental debt. Menem granted Economy Minister Antonio E. González centralized power (including power over the central bank). To continued inflation, economic volatility, and high unemployment, Menem responded with even more radical orthodoxy. Economy Minister Domingo Cavallo—a business community insider—introduced a Convertibility Plan in 1991, fixing the peso by law at parity with the dollar, requiring the central bank to maintain the existing ratio between reserves and the monetary base, and suspending indexing in wage agreements.[60] A majority of Peronist deputies and economic liberals in Congress supported the "Cavallazo," the first frontal attack on statism in over four decades, aimed at privatization, deregulation, and bureaucratic contraction.

The program reduced inflation from over 5,000 percent in 1989 to 2 percent in 1996. An average growth rate of 8 percent yearly in 1991–1994 replaced a GDP contraction (-0.3 average annual growth between 1980 and 1990). Liberalized foreign investment led to the doubling of direct investments in 1990–1992, while portfolio investments soared. The influx of $25 billion in 1990–1993 propelled Argentina into the top of emerging markets. Trade liberalization brought an average tariff of 37 percent (1982–1988) down to 10 percent in 1991. Argentina's economic openness (imports and exports as a percent of GDP) climbed impressively from 30 percent before the reforms to 54 percent barely two years after their inception. State bureaucracies eliminated 280,000 jobs between 1990 and 1994, and privatizations removed the public burden of most deficit-ridden state enterprises, yielding about $18 billion in revenues. Domestic investment grew from an average of -4.7 percent during the 1980–1990 period to an average of 22 percent in 1990–1994.[61] By 1997, after surviving the serious crisis induced by Mexico's Tequilazo while maintaining strict convertibility rules, Menem's key economic concern was a fiscal deficit of 2 percent of GDP, lower than the European Union's Maastricht target.

---

[59] Calvin Sims, "Peronists Shun Rally Honoring Founder," *New York Times* 18 October 1996: A9.

[60] Cavallo, a Ph.D. in economics from Harvard University, was close to the business community, particularly in Córdoba—his native province—where businessmen placed him at the head of the Mediterranean Foundation, a lobby and think tank that supplied Cavallo with ranking members in his political team (Aftalion 1995).

[61] World Bank (1996): 188–222.

The highly concentrated benefits from privatization went to large *grupos económicos*, foreign investors (mainly Italian, Spanish, Chilean), and some former suppliers of the state. Internationally uncompetitive (particularly CGE-affiliated) firms were decimated. Unemployment reached 16 percent nationwide in 1995, and over 20 percent of the population was now unable to meet its basic needs, as acknowledged by the minister of social action.[62] Argentine provinces, lagging in economic reforms, suffered a particularly severe economic contraction, with local government—in some cases employing 50 percent of the labor force—unable to attract private investment. Unemployment and pay backlogs led to 60 major strikes in sixteen of Argentina's twenty-four provinces in 1995. Menem approved a program to create 750,000 jobs in 1996–1997 and new legislation to reduce employer taxes and stimulate demand for labor. Despite accusations of inefficiency and corruption, price stability and increased economic activity helped maintain broad support for the Peronists, who won an even larger majority in the 1993 congressional elections. Menem himself was reelected in 1995 with nearly 50 percent of the votes, against 29 percent for his main rival José Bordón (Radicals), double the margin he enjoyed six years earlier, prior to his reforms. How had he done it?

Menem extracted executive emergency powers from the congress in 1989, which allowed him to concentrate control over the implementation of reform. Packing the Supreme Court with his own followers eliminated another potential institutional challenge to his program. However, beyond executive centralization a broader political revolution was at work. Peronist Menem had transformed Argentina's political economy by standing Perón's policies on their head. At home he had done so by coopting private capital and labor sectors through political representation, the spoils of privatization, and the political and economic benefits from internationalization. He exploited sharp divisions within labor to split it institutionally between the pro-Menem CGT San-Martín and the oppositional CGT Azopardo, responsive to public-sector and inward-looking Peronist labor. As a political windfall, Menem decimated the opposition within and outside his party and induced deep intraparty schisms among political competitors, including the newest political carrier of liberalization, Unión del Centro Democrático. His policies toward the military bore similar attributes, exacerbating internal cleavages initially and reaping civilian control over a reconstituted military at the end. Menem eroded the military's institutional power in an unprecedented way, moving from Alfonsín's de jure civilian control to a far reaching de jure and de facto control.[63]

Having used ultranationalist junior officers and noncommissioned officer mutineers during his presidential campaign, Menem eventually emasculated the *carapintadas* movement, a failed reincarnation of Peronist populism. Military expenditures reached all-time lows both relative to past military expenditures (1

---

[62] Luigi Manzetti, "Argentina: Trickle Down—And Out." *Hemisfile* 7, 2 (March–April 1996): 1, 12.

[63] Acuña and Smith (1995: 129–32).

percent of GDP in 1992) and relative to health and education (51 percent), the lowest in three decades. The military's total size shrank by 60 percent (from the 1970s) in absolute terms, and by 70 percent relative to population. Human-power in military industries declined by 80 percent, the officer corps was dramatically reduced, compulsory military conscription ended in 1996, and DGFM—the largest drain on the federal budget—was privatized.[64] Finally Menem, in contrast to Alfonsín, scrapped the Cóndor II project, dealing a severe blow to the last program by which the military hoped to redress decades of Argentine failure in arms production. Menem pointed to foreign pressures and tradeoffs in dismantling this program. However, the benefits of increased US support and international recognition in fact complemented his own domestic priority of killing the vestiges of a historically powerful statist rival: the military-industrial complex.

As the Cóndor II episode suggests, the external dimension of Menem's policies reinforced his domestic onslaught on political rivals. His unprecedented embrace of liberal trade rules and of international economic institutions (the IMF and World Bank) dealt a fatal blow to statist, military, and protectionist interests. His equally unprecedented embrace of international political and strategic regimes, shunned by Argentina for decades, overwhelmed the political and institutional bastions of Argentine statist-nationalism, from unreformed Peronist unions to military academies and foreign policy bureaucracies.[65] Argentina's place in the world was no longer defined by the dubious prestige of launching "anticolonial" wars, defying international regimes, and spreading sensitive nuclear capabilities, but by becoming an active supporter of such regimes. It joined the Missile Technology Control Regime, ratified the Non-proliferation Treaty, joined the Wassenaar export control regime, abandoned the Non-Aligned Movement, and sent a naval contingent to the Gulf—through executive fiat—as part of the US-led allied forces against Iraq. In Menem's own words (1993: 107–8), Argentina had been transformed, after decades of "mistrust and erraticism," into a "trustworthy and predictable state" (*país confiable y previsible*)."

Relations with the United States exemplified the reinvention of Peronist foreign policy. Foreign Minister Guido Di Tella defined the United States as a partner in "carnal relations," and laid out the international pillar of Argentina's new grand strategy in simple terms: "We want to belong to the First World."[66] In her motion-picture portrayal of Evita, most likely, Madonna would have not sung from Evita's favored balcony in Buenos Aires under any Argentine administration preceding Menem's (including archrivals of Peronism). Sing she did in early 1996, offending the sensitivities of old-guard Peronists and other now, far more weakened, nationalists. By 1997 Argentina had become a formal US non-

---

[64] DGFM's foreign debt in 1984 was $1.5 billion (Varas 1989: 53). Its cumulative deficit was estimated at over $700 million and its assets at $5.6 billion in 1990 (Manzetti 1993: 197).

[65] Russell (1992). On his international policies as pivotal ("punto de apoyo") for Argentina's takeoff, see Menem (1993).

[66] Manzetti (1993: 70); Aftalion (1995).

NATO ally. In a clear statement of the grand strategy that had led to this break-through, the president of the American Chamber of Commerce in Buenos Aires, Carlos Fedrigotti, explained: "The non-NATO status is like a seal of approval—it reinforces the notion that Argentina is a safe, attractive place to do business" (quoted in Sims 1997: A6). Menem also renewed diplomatic relations with Britain immediately (in February 1990), welcoming its investments and those of the European Union, and formally committing Argentina to protect them. In 1995 Foreign Minister Guido Di Tella confirmed Argentina's informal initiative to pay $800,000 to each Falkland family for transferring the islands to Argentine sovereignty.[67] This was nothing less than a revolutionary approach to Malvinas—a long way from 1982—symptomatic of an internationalist grand strategy aimed at internal and regional stability and global access. By 1997 Britain had extended an invitation to President Menem for an official visit.

In Brazil, political resistance to economic liberalization and to the contraction of the state lasted longer than in Argentina, and can be similarly traced to the entrenched power of state enterprises, related state bureaucracies, private suppliers and beneficiaries, labor unions affiliated with the Central Única dos Trabalhadores (Central Union Confederation), and lingering institutional prerogatives of the military and its associated industrial complex.[68] The 1988 constitution had codified political fragmentation and a certain equipoise between liberalizers and statist-nationalists. The political impasse and the failures of heterodox attempts to stem inflation (which stood at 2,500 percent by 1990), offered insulated bureaucracies the opportunity to impose an orthodox break-through. The opportunity was taken by Fernando Collor de Mello (1990–1992), elected with a slim 53 percent runoff majority against Luis Inácio da Silva (Lula), who was backed by unions and import-substituting sectors, and who had prompted a massive capital flight in 1989.[69] Collor quickly endorsed stabilization and major trade reform (lowering average tariffs to 25 percent and rescinding the Law of Similars), reaping a 90 percent approval rate. He attacked the bureaucracy, referring to highly paid civil servants as "maharajahs," and eliminated budget deficits by the end of 1990. Of twenty-six state enterprises scheduled for privatization, twenty-two were in private hands by 1992. Congress was Collor's foremost institutional opponent, with the military trailing right behind. Collor slashed military budgets from 6 percent in 1989 to 2.2 in 1990, denied salary raises to 320,000 military personnel, and purged officers from important

---

[67] Calvin Sims, "Argentina Plans Bid to Buy Falklands' Allegiance," *New York Times* 8 June 1995: A9.

[68] Sola (1994); Barros (1990); Zagorski (1992).

[69] Lamounier (1994: 78); Sola (1994). Collor was elected with significant support from the unorganized poor but not from trade unions or middle-strata organizations, old beneficiaries of import-substituting strategies. On Collor's grand strategy, see Collor (1991). Notably—from the point of view of the characterization of statist-nationalist coalitions in Chapter Two—many of Lula's supporters were dubbed "Shiites" to denote their zeal against privatization and external liberalization (John Powers, "Fighting for the Soul of Brazil," *Los Angeles Times Magazine* 27 March 1994: 14–20).

bureaucratic positions.[70] His coalition soon came under strain, with rampant corruption aborting not only Collor's presidency but also an internationalist strategy.

Collor's successor Itamar Franco (1992–1995) rallied statist-nationalist and military constituencies while slowing down privatization, exempting the military from budget cuts, and attacking international financial institutions and their domestic "allies."[71] Domestic, regional, and international policies partly reverted to old patterns, although Collor had unleashed the seeds of a new strategy that could not easily be undone. As Franco's finance minister, Fernando H. Cardoso instituted a coherent structural adjustment plan in 1994 that reduced monthly inflation from 50 percent to under 1.5 in four months. The Real plan established fixed exchange rates as a pillar of a stabilization program that succeeded where many had failed. The average tariff declined to 12 percent. The 1994 elections pitted Cardoso (Partido da Social Democracia Brasileira) as the newest leadership of the internationalist camp against Lula (Worker's party) as the newest leadership of a reformed statist-nationalism. An erstwhile forceful critic of anything military, Lula was now wooing military nationalists into his coalition. Cardoso campaigned on a platform stressing anti-inflation, privatization, foreign investments, free trade, and IMF discipline, and was elected with the largest majority of any Brazilian president with backing from all socioeconomic groups.[72]

Cardoso resumed in early 1995 the privatizing and liberalizing agenda stalled under Franco, with an intellectual property rights bill protecting foreign patents and trademarks and a presidential decree allowing foreign capital—unprecedently in Brazil—to purchase failing banks. He also cajoled a reluctant congress into undoing some of the provisions of the 1988 constitution. Less than a year into Cardoso's term Brazil joined the Missile Technology Control Regime, so strongly resisted by the Ministry of Aeronautics. Foreign investments in the first half of 1996 surpassed the combined total of the previous three years. Brazil's average tariff (52 percent in 1990) was 14 percent in 1996. Finance Minister Pedro Malan defined the administration's policy to be "100 percent committed to the privatization program."[73] Although falling somewhat short of the official target, during the first eighteen months in office the government sold thirteen companies (or portions thereof) for $3.8 billion. By 1997 half of the voting shares of the state mining company Vale do Rio Doce were to be in private hands, in the largest privatization ever undertaken in South America

---

[70] James Brooke, "Brazil's President Makes the Military Toe the Line," *New York Times* 9 September 1990: A7.

[71] Joint Publications Research Service, *Latin America* (Springfield, Va.: National Technical Information Service) 29 March 1993: 22.

[72] Diana J. Schemo, "Brazil's Economic Samba," *New York Times Magazine* 7 September 1996: 119.

[73] Paulo Sotero, "Privatization Program Begins to Roll," *Hemisfile* 7,4 (July–August 1996): 3–4. McDonald's announced plans to increase its outlets in Brazil from 200 to 530 and Blockbuster Video to 170 by the end of the century.

(expected to yield $5 billion for Brazil's treasury).[74] Telebrás, Eletrobrás, and Petrobrás the telephone, electricity, and oil and gas state monopolies respectively were next. Cardoso may be credited—either through actions or by creating positive expectations—with bringing Brazil's ranking in a leading index of global competitiveness from 44th place in 1993 to 33rd in 1997.[75] In the cluster labeled "Government" (a composite of national debt, government expenditures, fiscal policies, state efficiency, state involvement, and justice and security) Brazil rose from 34th place in 1994 to 16th in 1997. Foreign direct investments soared from less than $4 billion in 1995 to over $16 billion in 1997.

However, Cardoso faced a political and institutional context different from Menem's. To begin with, his coalition—including most of Brazil's top five hundred executives, rural landowners demanding subsidized credit, public works contractors, and even some state-owned corporations—was riddled with dissent.[76] Moreover, Cardoso confronted a congress—highly fragmented by proportional representation—in which his own party was a minority within the coalition that elected him (the three parties that backed Cardoso's candidacy controlled roughly a third of congressional seats). The largest coalitional partner in the congress was the Partido da Frente Liberal, the most vocal advocate of privatization but not immune to concerns about reducing patronage jobs they had helped create under the statist program of the 1970s. Cardoso thus encountered difficulties in reducing the 1.5 million-strong bureaucracy, shutting down corruption-ridden state banks, lowering fiscal deficits, and eliminating concerns regarding inflation. Institutional constraints and the lingering power of statist-populist challengers could easily be marshaled to explain Cardoso's attention to distributive issues (unemployment in 1997 remained below 6 percent).[77] However, Cardoso's approach here—although attentive to political expediency, given the 1998 elections—reflected his much longer-held concern with equity as an erstwhile prominent theoretician of dependencia theory. The means had now changed, in light of evidence that contradicted the premises of that theory.[78] Hence, Cardoso seized the opportunity to build on the internationalist revolution to address the social agenda, as well. For that purpose, his international approach also stood dependencia arguments on their head. His reformulated view of the North-South cleavage now led him to state that "Contrary to the widespread perception of the 1960s and 1970s, I do not see the interests of the North and South as conflicting or as preventing cooperation. I see rather a commonality of interests based on the values that won the Cold War."

The political-economic strategies—domestic and international—of Argentine

[74] Diana J. Schemo, "Brazil's Nationalism Rises over Proposed Sale of State Mine," *New York Times* 3 May 1997: 4.

[75] International Institute for Management Development (1997).

[76] James Brooke, "Brazil's Big Winner," *New York Times*, 5 October 1994: 1; Barros (1995: 108). On Cardoso's self-defined difficulties with Congress, see Hoge (1995: 74).

[77] *Carta IBGE* 2,32 (February 1997): 4.

[78] Cardoso (1996). Subsequent Cardoso quotes are from Hoge (1995). On Cardoso as a social scientist and "político," see Domínguez (1997).

and Brazilian liberalizers had created the conditions for a new regional institutional framework. Out of their unilateral policies of economic liberalization emerged new regional trade arrangements. Regional economic integration and broad-based regional cooperation were both an expression of grand internationalist strategies and also helped reinforce them domestically. Collor and Menem signed the Buenos Aires Act in 1990, accelerating the timetable for the establishment of a common market by 1994 and instituting automatic tariff‑ reductions across the board. Argentina, Brazil, Uruguay, and‑Paraguay signed the Treaty of Asunción in 1991, creating MERCOSUR (Mercado Común del Sur, or MERCOSUL in Portuguese). The treaty stipulated the free circulation of goods and services within the region by 1995, an automatic schedule for tariff reductions, the institution of a common external tariff, the harmonization of laws and regulations concerning rules of origin and dispute settlement, and the coordination of macroeconomic policies. MERCOSUR was designed to strengthen the internationalist model at home, weakening groups and institutions opposed to reform, and increasing the costs of reversing tacks for potential domestic challengers. Private entrepreneurial associations played a leading role in shaping MERCOSUR, in contrast to all preceding integrative efforts in the region. Brazilian business with investments in Argentina created a new lobby—Grupo Brasil—dedicated to defending MERCOSUR against potectionist attacks. MERCOSUR was also a means of lubricating external ties to the global political economy and of persuading global investors of the credibility of the internationalist shift, at home and in the region.[79] Total foreign direct investment to MERCOSUR grew from $2.5 billion in 1990 to $10.5 billion in 1995, for a total of nearly $31 billion in that period. MERCOSUR signed a framework agreement with the European Union for a common market in 1994 (to become effective by 2001) and signed the Rose Garden (4 + 1) agreement establishing consultations with the US. MERCOSUR became the principal destination for European foreign direct investment flows in the 1990s.[80] In 1996 the World Economic Forum—a Swiss-based organization gathering key international political and economic leaders—held its Second MERCOSUR Economic Summit in Buenos Aires, signaling the increased competitiveness of the region from the perspective of global investors. By the mid-1990s MERCOSUR—still an "imperfect customs union"—had become the fourth largest trading bloc after the EU, NAFTA, and ASEAN. At the first Summit of the Americas in 1994 MERSOCUR members joined the initiative to create a Free Trade Area of the Americas by 2005.

Under Menem and Collor, tariff reduction timetables were not merely met but occasionally implemented ahead of schedule. Franco's responsiveness to statist-nationalist constituencies temporarily tamed, but did not eliminate, the

---

[79] *Integración Latinoamericana* 16,167 (May 1991); Haggard (1995a); James Brooke, "More Open Latin Borders Mirror an Opening of Markets." *New York Times* 4 July 1995: 29. For data on MERCOSUR's intra- and extra-regional trade, see IRELA (1997).

[80] IRELA "European Union-Latin American Economic Relations Statistical Profile," *IRELA Briefing* 15 November 1996: 6.

drive toward a new regional political and economic order. The stronger Argentine coalition under Menem continued to push its program forcefully. MERCOSUR participants approved an unprecedented project ("Hydrovía") to lubricate trade routes. Trade within MERCOSUR rose from $3.5 billion before 1991 to $14 billion in 1994; bilateral trade between Argentina, Brazil, and Chile trebled. Brazil's share of Argentine trade doubled between 1989 and 1993, from 10 to 20 percent of the total. Argentina's share of Brazil's trade trebled between 1989 and 1993, from 3.7 to over 13 percent. By 1996 Brazil absorbed 28 percent of Argentina products, whereas Argentina absorbed 10 percent of Brazil's exports. Chile signed an Acuerdo de Complementación Económica with Argentina in 1991, securing mutual access to mining, energy, ports, highways, and transportation. Chilean investment in Argentina grew from $100 million in 1991 to $2.7 billion in 1994 with MERCOSUR absorbing over 70 percent of Chilean investment outflows.[81] Menem diffused tensions with Chile by subjecting border disputes to OAS arbitration and by reversing old patterns of border relations, now lubricating exchanges rather than limiting them. Chilean-Argentine relations were now defined as "the most cordial political relations this century."[82] MERCOSUR leaders emphasized their goal of nurturing a trade-creating scheme with positive regional and global externalities, as opposed to one threatening nonmembers. Chile and Bolivia formally joined as associate members in 1996. MERCOSUR and Andean Community states launched negotiations in 1996 for a South American Free Trade Area (SAFTA).

Regional integration is a building block and an accessory to the global logic of liberalization. In Cardoso's words, "We see integration schemes as playing an important role in expanding world trade flows even further. They complement rather than substitute for international rules such as those of the World Trade Organization," and "Brazil is a global trader. . . . Maintaining important trade flows with different regions . . . is less risky than relying on a single trading partner. Brazil is . . . interested in strengthening the world system." Félix Peña (1995: 115), Argentina's under-secretary for MERCOSUR, emphasized the latter's double goal of transforming each country and seeking "a competitive insertion in world markets," in the context of "open regionalism." Thus, although the expansion of Southern Cone exports to the United States, Europe, and Asia is the ultimate objective, intraregional trade has come to sustain growth until new international agreements make access to other regions easier. Maintaining an appropriate investment environment throughout the continent as a whole is evident in Menem's own treatise (1996a) on MERCOSUR and in Cardoso's statement, "I will employ diplomacy vigorously and with urgency when necessary. That is why I acted directly to help resolve the recent border conflict between Ecuador and Peru. *Maintaining Latin America as a peace zone gives the continent an enormous advantage*" (my emphasis).

No zone of stable peace is compatible with ambiguous nuclear programs and

---

[81] Naim (1995: 47).

[82] Eduardo Aninat, "Good Neighbors, High Hopes," *Hemisfile* 3,3 (May 1992): 3–4.

imputed intentions to develop nuclear weapons, even if nuclearization has been less a real possibility in the Southern Cone than in the Middle East or South Asia. Moderate nuclear cooperation since the late 1970s never amounted to a real breakthrough. As a former Argentine ambassador associated with the old nuclear policy (Carasales 1995: 42) himself pointed out, the words "inspection," "control," and "safeguarding" were absent even in documents signed by civilian and democratic administrations in the 1980s. Explicit denuclearization came about only as part of the grand internationalist strategies of the early 1990s. Collor and Menem signed a Declaration on the Common Nuclear Policy of Brazil and Argentina (1990) explicitly renouncing nuclear weapons for the first time, and establishing mutual verification and inspection procedures. Declarations accepting an updated version of the Tlatelolco Treaty followed, and a new agreement on the Exclusively Peaceful Use of Nuclear Energy (Guadalajara, 1991) created an agency for accounting and control of nuclear materials (ABACC, Agência Brasileiro-Argentina de Contabilidade e Controle de Materiais Nucleares). ABACC began coordinating mutual on-site inspections and maintaining inventories of nuclear materials. A Quadripartite Agreement (among the International Atomic Energy Agency, ABACC, Argentina, and Brazil) applied full-scope safeguards to all nuclear facilities in both countries, an unprecedented renunciation of what both had defined as sovereign rights for decades. Internationalist leaders Menem, Collor, and Aylwin also signed the Mendoza Accord (1991) among Argentina, Brazil, and Chile banning chemical and biological weapons.

These agreements gained particular reciprocal credibility because of the unilateral policies Menem and Collor pursued at home, bearing down on their similarly entrenched nuclear programs. Both leaders had targeted military enterprises and bureaucracies as part of their privatization and fiscal plans. Collor challenged the military directly by closing down Brazil's presumed nuclear weapons test sites in Cachimbo, by formally exposing the military's secret plan to develop an atom bomb, and by removing military officers from important posts on nuclear issues.[83] Menem ended thirty-five years of unassailed navy control over the nuclear program—a chronic budgetary black hole—and neutralized sensitive nuclear facilities.[84] These unilateral steps taken to advance an internationalist grand strategy at home alleviated the potential prisoner's dilemma considerations otherwise present in agreements (and nonagreements) of this nature. As argued, reassurance comes from the domestic incentives of internationalist coalitions. Argentina also adopted caution and deference with respect to international nuclear export guidelines, joining the Nuclear Suppliers

---

[83] *Joint Publications Research Service* (21 August 1991: 5); Redick (1994); Carasales (1995: 48); Tollefson (1996: 19–20) reports on findings by a Brazilian congressional investigating committee that the Institute of Advanced Studies at the Aerospace Technical Center designed two atomic bomb devices (203 kilotons and 12 kilotons, respectively).

[84] On the politics of denuclearization in Argentina and Brazil, see Solingen (1997a). On the Argentine Economy Ministry and its efforts to curtail the Atomic Energy Commission, see Carasales (1995: 48).

Group, an organization that Argentine officials had once labeled "the nuclear cartel of the North." The new foreign policy team aimed at transcending a reputation for supplying "rogue" regimes (such as Iran) with sensitive technologies. It thus canceled the legal sale of an experimental nuclear reactor to Syria with uncharacteristic flexibility to avoid costs to its reputation. In the old era, the Atomic Energy Commission had monopolized Argentina's nuclear policy and considered such exports as building up its own reputation, at home and abroad. In the new era the Under Secretary of Foreign Affairs Rogelio Pfirter acknowledged that "we found we were blacklisted by the international community for our aggressive policies and in the end found we had to cooperate with the netherworld of third-world countries" (quoted in Nash 1994).

Brazil's retreat from an internationalist agenda under Franco—never accused of implementing a coherent grand strategy—did not completely derail nuclear cooperation. On the one hand, Franco heeded statist-nationalist and military constituencies and endorsed statements on Brazil's sovereignty in nuclear matters that were more compatible with those of the preceding decade.[85] On the other hand, under heavy pressure from the Foreign and Economic ministries, Brazil's House of Deputies approved the mutual inspection agreements with Argentina in 1993 while retaining opposition to NPT ratification as a side payment to the statist-nationalist camp. The lingering power of this camp explains why no leading presidential candidate dared raise any future NPT commitments in the 1994 campaign.

Statist-nationalist pressures were far less successful in Argentina where, in a move that still forces many experts on Argentine politics to pinch themselves for a reality check, Menem ratified the NPT unilaterally in 1994, without a reciprocal Brazilian commitment. This step, which Argentina had resisted for decades even on a reciprocal basis, is compatible with the interstate coalitional dynamic explored in Chapter Three. A stronger internationalist coalition can maintain its strategy and help a weaker internationalist neighbor uphold cooperative postures, knowing the weaker ruling coalitions' shorter time horizons. Argentine leaders understood the requirements of an ongoing, if imperfect, internationalist strategy in Brazil, which increased Argentine confidence in a future Brazilian accession to NPT, as a move responsive to Brazil's own political considerations. Foreign ministries in Argentina and Brazil had become important bureaucratic actors with a clear conception of the organic links between an internationalist grand strategy and nuclear policies. Menem (1996: 36) himself specifically acknowledged these links when he declared that the NPT extension in 1996 and the Chemical Weapons Convention allow "countries like Argentina and entire regions like Latin America to make steady progress in economic growth and the solution of social problems without diverting resources to participate in costly and anachronistic arms races. Likewise, the creation of information-exchange mechanisms dealing with the import and export of conven-

---

[85] On the military's resentment over Brazil's commitment to IAEA inspections, see Tollefson (1996: 30).

tional arms will establish a more transparent and predictable framework which will make it easier to avoid false interpretations and suspicions about the interactions of other states."

In sum, the leap in economic liberalization was matched by a leap in bilateral cooperation, with effective integrative schemes, a mutual commitment to abide by Tlatelolco stipulations and international safeguards, and the replacement of three decades of nuclear ambiguity and competition. The deepening institutional links among liberalizers reinforced cooperation by reducing transaction costs and by facilitating the resolution of issues under dispute in different issue areas. Yet, given their congruent unilateral strategies, the need to monitor or punish noncompliance or improve information was far less compelling than it might have been under different independent strategies. The conditions for self-sustained rather than externally imposed regional cooperation were in place, exposing many elements of the generic interaction among strong internationalist coalitions identified in Chapter Three. As a result, internationalist agendas—otherwise labeled as "entreguismo" by the statist-nationalist opposition—propelled both countries to improved national standings, from the perspective of aggregate state power. These were not merely stronger economies better positioned to attract international investments but also transformed polities better positioned to attract international recognition and partnerships. Chile's consideration as a NAFTA (North American Free Trade Agreement) member, ahead of any of its neighbors, was but one instance of the new status that an internationalist revolution could yield. Individual country gains were always regarded in zero-sum terms by statist-nationalist neighbors and homegrown opponents but, in reality, added up to remarkable joint gains as a region. Internationalist coalitions viewed joint gains as favorable overall to their own domestic repositions, using competitive comparisons only to deepen liberalization further.

ONE HUNDRED YEARS OF (NON)DEMOCRATIC PEACE

Argentine-Brazilian relations have indeed evolved from guarded coexistence for over a century, with little economic interaction and a tacit nuclear competition until the late 1980s, to a denuclearized zone underpinning the economic integration of the Southern Cone in the 1990s. Despite the sharp differences in the fabric of relations over time, avoidance of war remained constant throughout (after the 1820s). The Chaco War came close to involving the two reluctant giants, with Brazil's chief of staff preparing to meet the threat of a sudden Argentine attack. The sustained absence of war between Argentina and Brazil can be traced to anything but democratic rule, as our historical overview suggests. Alternative theories must be marshaled to explain this long peace throughout successive democratic and nondemocratic regimes.

The Malvinas / Falklands war—not an intraregional war—is often interpreted as the outcome of a repressive Argentine junta in search of a unifying foreign adventure. Had a democratic regime attacked the British islands, the democratic peace hypothesis might have had to deal with another anomaly. Clearly, anomalies do not disprove an hypothesis postulating a high propensity among democracies to avoid war. Neither does the actual occurrence of a mixed dyad going to war provide any direct support for the democratic peace hypothesis. In particular, a long succession of mixed nondemocratic and democratic Argentine-British dyads did manage to avoid war until 1982. How certain nondemocratic (particularly military) regimes become involved in armed conflicts whereas others do not is beyond the scope of the democratic peace hypothesis. The enormous popularity of the Malvinas invasion among Argentines, however, does cast some doubt on the premise that dictatorships necessarily coerce their populations into unwanted wars.

Apart from the common avoidance of intraregional war by both democratic and nondemocratic regimes, have democracies made a difference in shaping relations between Argentina and Brazil in the last fifty years? Chapter Four suggested a potentially higher proclivity for democratic dyads to cooperate more extensively and intensely than nondemocratic ones. The evidence from the Southern Cone does not provide strong support for the view that democratic dyads are necessarily more cooperative. The relationship between regime type and conflictive or cooperative behavior here portrays a very mixed historical record. Perón faced democratic Brazilian governments (1946–1955), as did the military junta that replaced Perón (1955–1958) and the democratic presidencies of Frondizi (1958–1962), Guido (1962–1963) and Illía (1963), until Brazil's 1964 coup. Perón's policies—military purchases, nuclear and hegemonic ambitions embedded in his "greater Argentina" project—threatened all his neighbors. Brazil's postwar democratic regime under Dutra characterized Peronist policies as "imperialist geopolitics," and every subsequent administration remained wary of Argentina's regional designs, not only under Perón but also under the most statist-populist of the military administrations (Lanusse's).[86] The democratic administrations of Frondizi in Argentina and Kubitschek and Quadros in Brazil developed a rhetoric of regional fraternity not very different from earlier (and subsequent) foreign policy formulations by mixed democratic and nondemocratic interlocutors. Cooperation on River Plate Basin hydroelectric projects spanned the regimes of Illía (democratic) and Onganía (authoritarian) in the 1960s, and Perón (democratic) and Videla (authoritarian) in the 1970s.

Thus, the succession of various types of nondemocratic and democratic regimes in Argentina did not make a significant difference in the nature and depth of Argentine-Brazilian relations. In their overall international postures, it is true, one might find certain differences, with democratic regimes usually more identified with an independent position in the Cold War and greater openness to Third World alliances, and military regimes often more closely allied with the US against the Warsaw Pact. However, even there the record suggests that nondemocratic military rulers were as prepared as their democratic counterparts

---

[86] Hilton (1985: 33–35); Mares (1997). On Perón's pressures on weaker neighbors to "integrate" with Argentina, see Perón (1974: 81–96).

to maintain cooperative relations with US foes. Brazil's Foreign Ministry remained under effective civilian control after the 1964 coup, and revealed a convergence in civilian and military foreign policy objectives, much as in the Argentine case.[87] Such objectives were largely supportive of the statist-nationalist project, whose origins preceded the military regime. The assertion of civilian control over military niches under Alfonsín did not result in a radical departure from that project, either. Alfonsín did settle the Beagle conflict with Chile (which Peronists opposed) but refused to establish diplomatic relations with Britain. Moreover, Alfonsín sponsored missile development, not the kind of program that would reassure Chile or Brazil.

As to the military establishments in Argentina, Brazil, and Chile, on the one hand they exacerbated regional competition over resources and power, borrowing from Prussian and Nazi *lebensraum* theories to emphasize "vital spaces."[88] Their military academies imbued generations of officers and civilians with a geopolitical perspective that stressed security dilemmas, state sovereignty, territorial disputes, and zero-sum trends in oil resources, population growth, and technological capabilities. The concept of "ideological frontiers," for example, exacerbated Brazil's frictions with most of its neighbors. Military spending was privileged under Onganía's military regime—which in 1968 developed the first plans for invading the Malvinas—and under the 1976–1983 military regimes, which maintained the highest levels of military expenditures in decades and under which the Beagle and the Malvinas crises unfolded. On the other hand, old disputes among Southern Cone states—except for the Beagle—were more often resolved than exacerbated during the era of authoritarian military rule, as with the settlement of hydroelectric disputes among Brazil, Argentina, and Paraguay (1979). Coordination on border policies and natural resource exploitation increased prior to democratization, as well. Military regimes cooperated to suppress subversion at home, a pattern reminiscent of ASEAN, GCC, and of the nineteenth-century European concert. Finally, it was the military dictatorships of Videla and Figueiredo that undertook the first—albeit limited—steps toward nuclear cooperation.

This last point compels an examination of the nuclear interaction between Argentina and Brazil in relation to (democratic) regime type. Perón initiated the Southern Cone's nuclear competition with his dedicated efforts to develop independent nuclear capabilities with weapons potential. Although Perón's rule was not Dahl-style democracy, his regime was not wholly devoid of legitimacy either, and he did win an electoral majority in 1946. Following his ouster, electoral indicators continued to suggest broad Peronist strength. One might argue that Peronist affinity with the nuclear program—evident in unflagging support for the Atomic Commission—showed more than a compatibility between a democratic majority and a proclivity toward unsafeguarded nuclearization. Although this was also the case with other democracies facing Cold War security

---

[87] Barros (1984); Gordon (1984); Selcher (1984b); Varas (1989). On nationalist policy continuity between Galtieri and Alfonsín and on the latter's intransigence vis-à-vis the British on the Malvinas, see Escudé (1987).

[88] Pittman (1981); Child (1984); Selcher (1984a).

dilemmas, Perón and his successors had none that was external. Military regimes after Perón institutionalized the same nuclear objectives. The brief democratic interludes of Frondizi, Illía, Perón (1973–1976), and arguably Alfonsín, involved no serious attempt to reverse nuclear policy or to extricate it completely from navy control.[89] Indeed, nuclear efforts were unabated even when Argentina faced a democratic neighbor in Brazil. Reciprocally, Brazil's democratic regimes (1946–1964) aimed at matching Argentine nuclear progress, and the large-scale nuclear program the military embraced in the 1970s sustained this general trend by other means. The renewal of democracy in the 1980s did little to undermine Brazil's nuclear programs.

The beginnings of nuclear cooperation can be traced to the military regimes of Videla and Figueiredo. Yet neither mutual inspections nor commitments to the regional and international nonproliferation regimes materialized during common military rule. The democratic regimes of Alfonsín and Sarney continued building confidence but never reached denuclearization or adherence to NPT and Tlatelolco stipulations, and continued to defy international conventions regarding ballistic missiles. Only *internationalist* democrats—Menem, Collor, and Cardoso—eliminated the Southern Cone unequivocally from the international list of potential nuclear rivals.

Finally, the evolution of Argentine-Chilean relations shows a mixed record for the association between democratic regimes and regional cooperation. On the one hand, territorial disputes flared in 1960–1961 and 1964–1965, under the democratic dyads of Alessandri and Frei (Chile) and Frondizi and Illía (Argentina), but also under military dyads in 1978 and under mixed dyads under Perón and his military successors in 1958 and 1966–1968. On the other hand, mixed dyads (General Lanusse and President Allende in the early 1970s) were as eager to pursue legal solutions as their democratic predecessors. In fact, Alfonsín's spokesman declared in 1984 that Argentina's relations with military regimes were almost "idyllic."[90] Alfonsín signed a Treaty of Peace and Friendship with Chile's dictator Pinochet that year putting to rest the Beagle dispute, an achievement that democratic dyads were unable to claim.

The democratic nature of regimes thus has marginal utility for understanding peace and "deep" cooperation in the Southern Cone. The effects of democracy may become more apparent in the future, if the present democratic wave holds. If so, democracy may well strengthen patterns that internationalist coalitions have put in place; the initial conditions at the end of the twentieth century are significantly changed. Regional democratization may also provide a stronger guarantee against nondemocratic challenges to incumbent internationalists. Finally, the new vitality of regional institutions may contribute to the longevity of democracies and perhaps to the longevity of the long peace, even if the latter emerged out of other than democratic peace or regional institutional effects.[91]

---

[89] On the strong political connections of both Peronistas and Radicals with the nuclear program, and on the role of the program in their political platforms, see Sánchez-Guijón (1987: 378).

[90] Ibid., 379.

[91] MERCOSUR introduced a "democracy guarantee clause" that stipulates commercial sanctions on regimes that overturn democratic governments, a measure that frustrated a military coup in

THE TRIAD: ECONOMIC LIBERALIZATION, DEMOCRACY,
AND REGIONAL COOPERATION

First Democracy, Then the Market

Democratic regimes in Brazil and Argentina preceded the internationalist revolution of the 1990s, in contrast to South Korea and Taiwan and to the Arab Middle East. Alfonsín and Sarney inaugurated democratic regimes that clearly approximated Dahl's criteria, not the transitional forms evident in the most advanced cases of democratization in the Arab Middle East. Moreover, Menem, Collor, and Cardoso launched full-fledged internationalist strategies, akin to East Asian ones, of a kind not yet evident in much of the Middle East. The lagging economic liberalization and incipient democratization in the Middle East at the end of the century resembles Brazil's pattern in the 1970s and early 1980s (*de-estatização* and *abertura*, or opening).

Democracy was a temporal antecedent—but not an undisputed cause—of the economic transformation in Argentina and Brazil. The Chilean paradigm, instead, like that of its East Asian counterparts, followed the "authoritarian advantage" sequence discussed in Chapter Four. Argentina and Brazil helped buttress the competing "democratic efficiency" model, according to which political leaders rely on the legitimating quality of democracy to build support for economic reform. There is significant support for the view that the causal chain in Argentina and Brazil points to an intractable economic crisis as preparing the political ground for democracy first (in the 1980s), and for the inauguration of an internationalist coalition later (in the 1990s).[92] As Haggard and Kaufman (1995: 183) argued, the first democratic administrations after a lengthy authoritarian interlude were not responsible for the economic challenges with which their predecessors saddled them. The fact remains, however, that they were unable to initiate coherent stabilization programs or broader structural reforms, and that subsequent democratic administrations were apt to build on their democratic and nondemocratic predecesors' failures to initiate broad-based economic reform.

Politically important advocates of economic liberalization in Argentina and Brazil during the 1980s were also strongly supportive of democratization, with entrepreneurial associations playing a major role. The prodemocratic campaigns of Brazil's entrepreneurs and professional associations began with the manifesto against *estatizaçào*, a withdrawal of the state from the economy and from civil society. Similarly, Argentina's SRA and the UIA endorsed democratization in the 1980s. This had not been the case in the early 1960s, when Brazilian industrialists endorsed the 1964 military coup, or earlier in the 1930s, when Argentine economic elites withdrew their support for democracy. As Payne (1994) persuasively argued, industrialists are indifferent to regime type, and thus seek

---

Paraguay in 1996 (Calvin Sims, "Chile Will Enter a Big South American Free-Trade Bloc," *New York Times* 26 June 1996: C2).

[92] P. Smith (1991).

coalitional partners or provide passive or active support for regimes that can deliver political stability and stable investment rules. As for the armed forces, there were cleavages within them regarding both democratization and economic liberalization, although there was also a strong historical affinity with the statist-nationalist camp among large sections of the Argentine and Brazilian military, which prevailed for much of the last four decades in maintaining protectionist, mercantilist, and nationalist policies, including a vast military-industrial complex.

That the military cannot be classified a priori as an omnipresent partner in statist-nationalist coalitions is evident from the Chilean case, where the armed forces—under the centralizing control of Pinochet—opted institutionally for unqualified integration in the global economy. Whereas other military-authoritarian regimes in the Southern Cone accommodated inward-oriented groups, Chile's did not. Internal cleavages within the Chilean military were either limited or quickly muted, much as under Park in South Korea.[93] The absence of serious internal divisions among the political architects of Chile's internationalist strategy allowed technocratic teams to steer through economic crises and secure macroeconomic stability. Industrialists opposing economic liberalization could not mobilize a supportive coalition with a severely suppressed labor force, one that could challenge the cohesive coalition of financial conglomerates, technocrats, and the military. By the early 1980s new sectors backed the expansion of exports, privatization, export credits and competitive exchange rates, with export firms multiplying from 150 in 1974 to nearly 5,600 in 1995.[94] In sum, Pinochet spearheaded economic reforms that were neither popular nor necessarily compatible with at least some older institutional interests of the armed forces. The weapons-producing industrial fiefdom of the Chilean military was to play a subsidiary role—given budgetary constraints—while private firms thrived. Moreover, the Chilean military responded to regional challenges (notably, the Beagle) with utmost restraint to avoid endangering an internationalist strategy.

The "first democracy, then the market" sequence reveals important differences in the formulation and implementation of an internationalist strategy. Internationalist political entrepreneurs faced a dissimilar institutional context. Menem concentrated power at the expense of the congress and the Supreme Court and implemented reform through executive decrees. Argentina's two-party system allowed Peronists to embrace an internationalist agenda, leaving the other party to challenge it initially and eventually to endorse it mildly. Collor and Cardoso faced a highly fragmented institutional context (the 1988 constitution) that burdened coherent reform. Lamounier (1994) blamed the weakness of Brazil's political parties and party fractionalization for the unstable and tentative nature of transitions to both democracy and markets. Both sup-

---

[93] Haggard and Kaufman (1995: 75–82). Ames (1987: 238) discusses the influence of Chicago School sympathizers among the four military services.

[94] William R. Long, "Chile's Ship Comes In—With Foreign Sales," *Hemisfile* 7,1 (January–February) 1996: 3–4.

porters and opponents of economic reform blamed congress for being too corrupt and inept to carry out either of their respective agendas.

Internationalist revolutions in the Southern Cone also differed with respect to
attention paid to distributional effects. Menem's team seemed oblivious to such
effects, allowing liberalization to maintain a secular deterioration in income
distribution that preceding statist-nationalist and hybrid policies had reinforced.
The wealthiest Argentine decile increased its share of income from 32.5 percent
in 1983, when Alfonsín was elected, to 41.6 percent in 1989, before Menem.
The poorest 40 percent captured 15.7 percent of income in 1983 but only 11.7
in 1989. According to Cavallo and Mondino (1995) the share of the population
below the poverty line declined from 47.4 percent in 1989 to 19 percent by the
mid-1990s, although unemployment increased substantially. Collor's policies
intensified Brazil's historical pattern of dismal inequities, which had worsened
under the military and Sarney prior to effective liberalization.[95] Chile offers a
contrasting picture, with democratically elected Aylwin inheriting the successful
phase of reform from Pinochet. The economy had expanded by a 6.2 percent
average between 1985 and 1989, and exports by an average of 10.5 percent
(with a fiscal surplus of 1 percent of GDP in 1989). Elected on an antipopulist
platform, Aylwin's coalition could now broaden and shore up an internationalist
strategy, slashing import tariffs 30 percent to a uniform 11 percent in 1991 and
avoiding inflationary finance of social programs, but also applying improved
revenues to programs targeting disadvantaged sectors directly (rather than
through blanket subsidies). Brazil's Cardoso was in a far less advantageous
position than Aylwin's upon assuming power, but also attacked inflation as "the
cruelest tax on the poor" while investing in job creation, education, and health.

Finally, genuine economic liberalization in Argentina and Brazil was to come
about only in the 1990s, and not a decade earlier in the aftermath of the debt
crisis—a fact that questions deterministic perspectives regarding international
pressures. Not every coalition, democratic or otherwise, responded similarly to
external constraints and inducements. International pressures for trade liberalization and macreconomic adjustment did not bear fruit for many years among
the most intractable inward-looking coalitions. External support for internationalist coalitions improved these coalition's political credibility and overall
performance, and foreign investment helped them lower the political costs of
reform by financing expanded consumption, but also appreciating local currency and burdening exports.[96] The negative aspects of internationalization became evident with the 1994 Mexico crisis, which led to further market reforms,
deepening privatization, revenue collection, export promotion, and the strengthening of private banks, but also to a rise in tariffs in Brazil, to reduce current
account deficits. Argentina responded to the Tequilazo with a sharp fiscal program of higher value-added taxes, wage and spending cuts, and pension and

---

[95] UNDP (1996). Child mortality before age 5 was 233 children per 1,000 in Brazil (1992) as
opposed to 18 children in Argentina and 5 in Chile, in the same year.
[96] Naim (1995: 51).

labor market reform. Overall, internationalist coalitions stayed the course but exposed the vulnerability of reforms to international speculative trends.

First Democracy, Then the Market and a New Regional Order

The inception of democracy in Argentina and Brazil was followed by the lagged introduction of effective economic reform. Democracy, but more so the market, weakened the military and its associated industrial complex to an extent never before seen in the political cycles of the last five decades. The advent of democracy in itself failed to bring about these dramatic changes. Democratic regimes had spent less on military budgets than their authoritarian military counterparts in general, but only marginally. Moreover, democratic regimes ruled by either statist-nationalist or unstable coalitional hybrids had spent roughly the same (Perón 1973–1976) or more (Sarney, Allende) than their military predecessors.[97] Instead, a strong internationalist coalition under Menem executed the most radical contraction of Argentina's historically entrenched military-industrial complex. Clearly, a changed domestic political status for the military had favorable implications regionally. It was now possible to deprive statist-nationalist groups in the military and beyond from vetoing effective economic integration, effective downsizing of military personnel and industrial assets, and effective denuclearization.

Where economic liberalization preceded democracy, as in Chile, it laid the foundations for an internationalist grand strategy that the advent of democracy later reinforced. Chile's military expenditures after 1973 increased to nearly 7 percent of GDP but remained stable at that level despite unprecedented economic growth between 1974 and 1981 that doubled GNP per capita, and despite growing regional threats from statist-nationalist rivals in Argentina and Peru.[98] Despite its regional isolation and nationalist military ideology, the Chilean military resisted policies that might have endangered the economic miracle it helped engineered. Chile's military personnel thus doubled their real average income between 1970 and 1990, while Argentina's halved theirs. By the late 1990s, with a robust industrializing economy, Chile was posed for a considerable modernization of its air force, rendering support for the argument that internationalist agendas can end up strengthening military endowments and the wherewithal of their political carriers in the longer term.

There has been far more continuity regarding foreign policy and regional behavior between democratic and nondemocratic regimes than between coalitional variants. Foreign and defense ministries in Brazil and Argentina had been the main carriers of a rather stable pattern of external relations throughout civilian and military regimes, with policies gravitating within a set behavioral range on issues of independence, international defiance, and regional détente. State

---

[97] The Allende government increased real defense expenditures over the three years it held power (Scheetz 1992: 180). See also Zagorski (1992: 175). Illía (1963–1966) accorded high budgetary priority to the military and to health and education.

[98] Chile's private-sector arms production and exports developed in the late 1970s.

enterprises came to play a prominent role, as well, subsuming other foreign policy objectives to their individual gains. This was as much the case in nuclear policy as it was for the bartering patterns of Brazil's oil and military-industrial sectors. Only dramatic shifts in coalitional makeup in the 1990s led to a radical departure from this earlier foreign policy blueprint. The institutional partners in the new policy now included central banks and transfigured foreign and defense ministries, which liberalizers rescued from their historical subservience to statist-nationalist and military projects. Important architects of economic reform (Cavallo and Cardoso) started out as foreign ministers and later assumed the top economic post. The tradeoff embedded in the new strategy was clear: there was now an inverse relationship between maximizing the territorial reach of a missile and maximizing the reach of a stock exchange. The regional implications of the second path helped create a "new Southern Cone."

Democratic renewal in the Southern Cone is about a decade old. Although there are disagreements about the quality of democracy in each, democratic consolidation appears to have become a reality. The fate of economic reform is far more uncertain. Even here, however, there is considerable consensus that statist-nationalist (including military) challengers cannot build support for a reversal to the inflationary cycles and statist entrepreneurship that have characterized the region in the past. Consolidated democracies, as argued in Chapter Four, are less vulnerable to populist, highly nationalist, and military pressures than transitional ones, and thus more receptive to internationalist coalitions. The achievements of internationalist coalitions in building a new regional order have created new realities that can be undone only at high costs, in domestic and international terms. Clearly, a more consolidated democratic process steered by strong internationalist coalitions enhances the odds that the most cooperative regional order in the Southern Cone in decades will be maintained.

IMPLICATIONS FOR COALITIONAL ANALYSIS AND THE DEMOCRATIC PEACE HYPOTHESIS

The evolution of regional interactions in the last five decades yields the following general conclusions regarding the respective merits of coalitional analysis and democratic peace considerations.

1. Statist-nationalist populist coalitions in Argentina and Brazil presided over an era of guarded regional relations, limited economic exchange, and risky nuclear competition. This pattern helped consolidate the economic assets and political power of all partners to the coalition, and the military-industrial complex in particular. An international policy stressing independence, nonalignment, and frequent challenges to international economic and political institutions was useful for maintaining the coalitional balance tipped in favor of statist-nationalism.

2. Although the coalitions organized by Perón and Vargas were fairly consensual, subsequent statist-nationalist coalitions—mostly military—were far less homoge-

neous, particularly in Argentina. They expanded the statist and military infrastructure, frequently withdrew material populist benefits while exacerbating nationalist themes, and occasionally allowed short-lived episodes of trade liberalization and macroeconomic adjustment. These hybrid coalitions under heavy statist-nationalist pressure largely maintained the regional and international strategies they inherited. The occasional genuflections to US interests were either compatible with a domestic campaign to decimate opponents or with half-hearted attempts to attract resources from international institutions, particularly by weak would-be liberalizers that were to be quickly overwhelmed.

3. An entrenched statist-nationalist coalition in Argentina, which spearheaded this grand strategy in the region, including nuclearization, was the most prone to unleash military crises and mobilizations (Beagle) and eventually a war involving an extraregional actor (Malvinas). Neorealism can interpret Argentina's mistrust of Brazil and Chile, its nuclear buildup, and military swaggering against Chile and Great Britain in terms of a regional power's drive for hegemony. However, such a view fails to explain the birth of a radically different global and regional Argentine strategy in the 1990s. Instead, the protracted statist-nationalist and military fabric of its ruling coalitions from Perón onward goes further in providing a more complete understanding of its policies over time, as well as of differences between Argentina and its neighbors in their proneness to conflict.

4. The British response to the Malvinas invasion reportedly weighed in the character of Argentina's ruling coalition at the time. The British emphasized publicly the antidemocratic nature of the Argentine junta, but was no less oblivious to the statist-nationalist political makeup of its opponent, evident in the massive outpouring of support for Galtieri's brinkmanship. Highlighting these characteristic Argentine coalitional traits openly, however, would have improved—rather than undermined—the frail domestic support for Galtieri, a development British officials did their utmost to avoid.

5. Full-fledged regional cooperative strategies—effective economic integration and denuclearization—did not come about until internationalist coalitions assumed power in the 1990s. This unprecedented shift provides support for a coalitional perspective while questioning the hypothesis that democratic dyads are more prone to deepen cooperation. The democratic regimes of the 1980s did not create a radically different regional order than the one they inherited from their nondemocratic predecessors. Liberalizers did. However, the coalitional alternatives of the first generation of democratic regimes were shaped by the need to rebuild democratic institutions after a lengthy nondemocratic intermission. Menem's ability to piece together a conquering internationalist coalition might have been far more constrained had he been elected as the first democratic president after decades of dictatorship.

6. Neither can the democratic variable per se explain the strength of the commitment to an internationalist grand strategy—in its domestic, regional, and international dimensions—or the relative steadfastness in its implementation. Coalitional differences between Argentina and Brazil (in composition, degree of macropolitical consensus, and institutional framework within which the coalition operated) provide a better account of varying commitment and steadfastness.

7. Coalitional analysis thus helps capture the different texture of regional relationships under statist-nationalist and internationalist coalitions, including denuclearization. However, the absence of intraregional war as a constant, even under statist-nationalist and military regimes, compels alternative explanations for the long peace in the Southern Cone. Regional cooperation has more than one source and internationalist coalitions may not be necessary for the absence of war. At the same time, only internationalist coalitions produced intensive and extensive regional cooperation.

8. The dense regional institutional infrastructure in which the Southern Cone was embedded is often taken as a cue for the long peace. However, for all that density, regional institutions were frequently paper tigers when they aggregated statist-nationalist coalitions throughout the region. In fact, institutions provided opportunities—enhanced by a century largely free of wars—that were not exploited. They neither fulfilled their original missions nor created positive "spillover" cooperative effects; they simply "spilled around" (Ferguson 1984), reinventing themselves anew. Internationalist coalitions created fresh regional institutions (MERCOSUR, ABACC), or infused old ones (Tlatelolco, Rio Treaty) with new life, in order to underpin their domestic agendas and their global access. MERCOSUR was far more than a response to the idea of regional economic blocs and could have hardly come into being without the implementation of an internationalist grand strategy at home and vis-à-vis the rest of the world. Pointedly, the architects of MERCOSUR have adopted a minimal, flexible institutional structure, avoiding a tradition of excessive bureaucracy.

Beyond Argentina, Brazil, and Chile, internationalist coalitions throughout South America have put behind them even the most intractable ideological rivalries that engulfed the continent for many decades. The Bolivian officer who captured Cuba's revolutionary emissary Che Guevara in 1967—General Mario V. Salinas—disclosed in 1995 a best-kept secret: Che's burial site. Liberalizers in the Bolivian government intended to cash in on the site's tourist potential, making it part of a new attractive trail: "La Ruta del Che." Salinas broke his silence—he said—because it was time Bolivia and Cuba settled their differences. "If the Israelis and Palestinians can make peace . . . why can't we?"[99] It is to this near miracle in the Middle East—admittedly under stress after 1996— that I turn now.

[99] Jon Lee Anderson, "Where Is Che Guevara Buried? A Bolivian Tells," *New York Times*, 21 November 1995: A3.

CHAPTER SIX

The Middle East

COLD WAR and regional balance-of-power considerations, the centrality of Israel's security dilemma, and a zero-sum perspective on international politics
have dominated the literature on Middle East—particularly Arab-Israeli—relations for five decades. Yet, as in other instances of recent international change,
dramatic developments foreshadowing peace in the late 1980s and early 1990s
unfolded *before* the dominant approach could anticipate any revolutionary shifts
in the old regional order. Indeed, none of the main theoretical perspectives—
including institutionalist, world systemic, and cognitive—could effectively explain these changes on the basis of their core assumptions, and none could
anticipate the momentous Palestinian-Israeli convergence in 1993, its revolutionary effects throughout the region, and the forceful backlash they elicited. In
particular, looking through conventional theoretical lenses, cooperation in the
Arab-Israeli context was underdetermined. Yet, the domestic coalitional interplay between the internationalizing and statist-nationalist-confessional camps
suggested, all throughout the preceding decade, that the regional order was
pregnant with cooperative breakthroughs.

The Arab-Israeli conflict provides an exceptionally hard case—indeed a
"crucial case study"—for the general argument this book explores. Economic
liberalization is far more rudimentary in this region than in most others. Its
political carriers are therefore far less entrenched than would be ideal for them
to implement an internationalizing grand strategy. Further, the shadow of a long
noncooperative past is strong, setting up particularly difficult initial conditions.
Moreover, a regional institutional structure that might facilitate cooperation has
been altogether absent, and began to emerge only in the aftermath of initial
cooperative steps. Even worse, the foundations of a democratic zone of peace
could hardly be more lacking. Indeed, the endgame stage of the Arab-Israeli
conflict may be contingent on overcoming all these barriers, but it is more
likely to be shaped by coalitional dynamics than by any other process.

A coalitional approach does not merely make sense of recent changes in the
Arab-Israeli scene but also provides a useful perspective on a half century of
enduring rivalries and bitter wars throughout the Middle East. What follows is a
focused coalitional analysis of the Arab-Israeli conflict and inter-Arab relations
more generally during the last five decades. This is a reconstruction not of the
region's history but of a distinct source of conflict and cooperation that has
gained far less attention than deserved.[1] The first section reviews the statist-

---

[1] Korany and Dessouki (1991) and Barnett (1992) offer systematic comparative analyses of exter-
nal-domestic interactions.

nationalist-populist era and its regional corollaries. I turn next to the emergence and evolution of internationalizing coalitions and their implications for cooperative shifts in the early 1990s. The third section analyzes contemporary variants of statist-nationalist and confessional challengers. An outline of converging and diverging aspects of political and economic liberalization follows, ending with peculiar dilemmas that Middle East democratization presents for the peace process.

STATISM, NATIONALISM, MILITARIZATION, AND WAR

The Coalitional Profile

Much of the Arab world had embraced statist-nationalist variants by the late 1950s and 1960s with import substitution, state entrepreneurship, and national populism as their political-economic pillars. The armed forces and centralizing leaders played a key role in imposing this Werhrwirtschaft (war economy) model, invariably through authoritarian institutions, transforming the Middle East into a region with the highest levels of military expenditures and the largest military establishments relative to the general population.[2] Iraq (and Egypt up to the early 1970s) led the way with military expenditures as high as 51 percent of their GDP in the 1970s and 1980s, followed by Syria and South Yemen with 18 percent of GDP. Massive armies—half a million in Egypt by 1973, half a million in Syria, and three-quarters of a million in Iraq and Iran by the 1980s—consumed vast resources, as did high officers' salaries, travel, interest-free loans, and luxury housing. Strident pan-Arab nationalism, anti-Western rhetoric, and a war to extirpate Israel were regarded as essential coalescing ingredients. The strategy has survived in some Middle Eastern states to the end of the century, to an extent not evident in most other regions.

Statism and import-substitution implied massive nationalizations of oil in Algeria, Libya, and Iraq, of the Suez Canal in Egypt, and of other physical capital. Appropriating these assets meant funneling monopoly rents to the state and allowing it to convert them into sources of political support and to launch expansive populist programs.[3] Import substitution meant income transfers from the agricultural sector to developing infant industries under state aegis if not direct control. These strategies were designed to decimate political foes at home and throughout the region. State entrepreneurship combined with external revenues—oil sales, borrowing, foreign aid—strengthened the ability of statist coalitions to nurture their own political constituencies, particularly bureaucratic and military. These coalitions succeeded in suppressing private entrepreneurs throughout the Arab world—maintaining a much older Islamic and Ottoman tradition—and inhibiting the development of an independent bourgeoisie that might threaten the coalitions' hold on power by demanding economic liberal-

---

[2] International Institute for Strategic Studies (hereafter IISS) (1992); Hewedi (1989); Sayigh (1992); Sadowski (1993).

[3] Goldberg (1996); Richards and Waterbury (1990); Anderson (1987).

ization. Private entrepreneurs were thus sapped of economic and political strength by their own statist rulers and not by exposure to the global economy, as much of the dependency literature on this issue has claimed. Lacking their own state, Palestinians became a most dynamic private entrepreneurial force in the region and a source of "symbolic analysts" (teachers, managers, and scientists) to many a statist Arab regime. After three decades of statism, the typical Middle East state employed over 50 percent of the work force and accounted for three-fourths of industrial production.

Statist-nationalist Middle Eastern regimes have, for the most part, sought to legitimate themselves "less through references to financial statements than through manipulating nationalist, religious, and other symbols," notably pan-Arabism.[4] "Organic intellectuals" who dominated the educated strata refined pan-Arabism into a political tool to transcend divisive political and confessional allegiances. In some cases the military served as an instrument of control by a confessional minority or tribe, as with the predominantly Alawi military in Syria, the Saudi Sudairi clan, the Jordanian Hashemite officer corps, and the predominantly Takriti Sunni military command in Iraq. The religious minorities controlling Syria and Iraq resorted intermittently to pan-Arabism (*al-qawmiyyat al-Arabiyya*) or *raison de la nation*, and state nationalism (*wataniyya*) or *raison d'état*, as a way of papering over their own political control of the state. Pan-Arabism as a coalescing theme allowed Arab leaders such as Gamal Abdel Nasser to crush competing confessional visions, such as Islam.

The 1948 Arab-Israeli war was a catalytic historical event in the emergence of statist-nationalism throughout the region and in the demise of early republican and monarchist versions of liberalizers. The Palestinian cause—their exile and mounting socio-economic difficulties as dispersed refugees—provided a rallying point in the pan-Arab agenda. Although Palestinian despondency and uprootedness were very real and required effective action, most Arab rulers embraced it only rhetorically in a cynical use of the Palestinian plight for myth-making. The unwillingness to absorb Palestinian refugees, with a few exceptions, ensured that the coalescing issue of Palestine would keep the flame alive. At the same time, Arab rulers suppressed Palestinian nationalism when it made evident their own inability to deliver either pan-Arab goals or Palestine itself. Hypernationalism and calls for "drowning Israelis into the Mediterranean sea" were politically dominant among Palestinians, continuing a tradition set forth by Haj Amin al-Husseini, the mufti of Jerusalem who found in Hitler's Germany a favored political model. Armed struggle was the sole acceptable strategy, as captured in the Palestinian slogan "hawiyyati bunduqiyyati" ("my identity is my rifle"), because the United Nations–sanctioned 1947 partition between a Palestinian and an Israeli state was, as stated in the Palestine National Covenant, "illegal."[5] Efforts to outdo competing nationalist

---

[4] Bill and Springborg (1990: 31).
[5] This section on the PLO builds, inter alia, on Migdal (1980), Muslih (1988), Brand (1988), Selim (1991: 269–78), Hilal (1993), and Brynen (1995).

factions led to the fratricidal death of thousands charged with treason or lack of patriotic zeal. Terrorism at home and against others undermined latent international support for the Palestinian cause.

While courting the Soviet Union, the Eastern bloc, and radical Third World states, Fatah—the dominant political faction—embraced a nationalist rather than a class-based strategy, in contrast to its main ideological competitors in the Popular Front for the Liberation of Palestine (PFLP) and the Democratic Front for the Liberation of Palestine (DFLP). An inclusive populist appeal—coalescing the bourgeoisie, workers, and symbolic analysts—helped Fatah gain hegemony over Palestinian politics, relying on themes of full political and economic independence. The Palestine Liberation Organization (PLO) came into being in 1964 and by 1969 Yassir Arafat and Fatah dominated it as an umbrella for guerrilla groups and popular organizations of students, women, and professionals. The PLO developed a vast bureaucratic infrastructure operating welfare, industrial, and educational facilities, and an elaborate system of patronage and clientelism. Its revenues, administered by the Palestine National Fund (PNF)—the PLO's finance ministry—came mainly from contributions of Arab states and taxes on Palestinian workers. The PNF promoted a Palestinian industrial infrastructure, Samid (the "steadfast"), with activities throughout Arab and Third World countries. The PLO's militarization, natural for a national liberation movement, absorbed nearly 70 percent of expenses and helped forge its status as a state within other states, particularly in Jordan and Lebanon (where the PLO's budget rivaled that of its host state). This "statist" agenda—and its alliance with statist-nationalists throughout the region—led threatened Arab leaders to suppress the PLO by force, if necessary.[6]

Egypt after 1952 became a paradigmatic case of statist-nationalist populism. Nasser's revolution aimed at destroying the landed and industrial aristocracy through nationalization and at mobilizing middle-class technocrats, state managers, and professionals.[7] The promise of jobs in state agencies and enterprises created mass support for the statist project among an expanding young constituency. Land reform was perhaps Nasser's finest political hour, although it was Egypt's bureaucracy, not its small peasants, that inherited the power of the landlord, and land reform led to a decline in agricultural production, dependence on food imports, and increased indebtedness. By 1961 the entire banking, insurance, utilities, and foreign trade sectors were state-owned, as was most large-scale industry. The state employed over half of the nonagricultural work force. Government expenditures represented over 55 percent of the GNP by the late 1960s. Nasser's Perón-style populism leaned heavily on his own personal charisma. The military was his primary base of support and recruitment to administer the economic program.

Syria's first military coup d'état in 1949 initiated a succession of bloody

---

[6] For an interesting retrospective view on the lessons from PLO defeats in Jordan and Lebanon, see Haider 'Abdel Shafi, "The Jihad of the Self," *Palestine Report* 23 May 1997: 8–9.

[7] Issawi (1963); Waterbury (1983); Migdal (1988); Richards and Waterbury (1990); Owen (1992).

coups and countercoups. The Ba'th party took over in 1963, putting together a populist coalition of workers in trade unions, the rural peasantry, the military and security services, state bureaucrats and intellectuals, the salaried middle class, and import-substituting small-scale producers.[8] Following land reform, nearly 90 percent of Syria's large enterprises were nationalized in 1965. Many landlords and industrialists emigrated to Lebanon. The state employed over half the industrial work force and its share in industrial production reached 78 percent. The Alawite-controlled Ba'th forcefully subdued the Sunni-dominated Muslim Brotherhood in several uprisings, culminating in the 1982 massacre of 20,000 civilians at Hama. The strong pan-Arab bent of Syria's Ba'th gained it its reputation as "the beating heart of Arabism," always calling for war to liberate Palestine and against "reactionary" pro-Western kingdoms. The Ba'th also propagated the revival of a Greater Syrian space including Lebanon, Jordan, and Palestine. The most radical, messianic Ba'th revolutionary-nationalist strategy peaked between 1966 and 1970—leading to the Six-Day War—and collapsed with the ascent of Hafiz al-Assad in 1970. Assad's coalition included the armed forces, the Ba'th, the bureaucracy, and the public sector. It relied on both Soviet support and Saudi subsidies for a military buildup designed to maintain "strategic parity" with Israel. The Ba'th's historical animosity toward the United States culminated with the 1967 rupture in diplomatic relations. Resuming them later, Assad maintained a double game of supporting aggression against the US (in Lebanon, for instance) while seeking its support.

Iraqi regimes since the military coup of 1958, but mostly since 1964, approximated the inward-looking, statist-nationalizing, militarized ideal type rather well. Land reform, nationalizations, and Ba'thist state socialism brought land distribution but also increased bureaucratic regulation of agriculture, turning earlier self-support into food dependence (importing 70 percent of its needs).[9] Iraqi statism employed nearly half of the work force and accounted for over 62 percent of gross output in large manufacturing. The regime's survival can be traced to a combination of repressive totalitarian controls and successful redistributive policies. Saddam Hussein became the dominant political figure by 1979, transforming the state into a vast military machine with one of the highest levels of military expenditures worldwide. The external expression of Iraqi Ba'thism was a formal rejection of the international economic order and of the Camp David peace agreements, a reliance on the Soviet Union, advocacy of nonalignment, and a "hawkish" position within the Organization of Petroleum Exporting Countries (OPEC).

Iran under the Shah engaged both in primary and manufactured exports and import-substituting efforts, a rather unusual balance in the region at the time. Mohammad Mussadeq's populist attempt (1951–1953), backed by a rising professional middle class with heavy nationalist and anti-Western orientations,

---

[8] Nasser (1962); Migdal (1988: 211–12); Hinnebusch (1991, 1993); Heydemann (1993: 87).
[9] Marr (1985); al-Khalil (1989); Ahmad (1991); Kedourie (1992: 305). On oil nationalization and the Ba'th stragegy, see Hussein (1977).

failed under the combined pressure of Shah loyalists and Western support for the monarch. The Shah maintained an accommodation between state and private entrepreneurship (domestic and foreign), land reform, literacy, and profit sharing in industry. His military forces, including internal security, consumed 40 percent of the budget. The state employed about one-fourth of the non-agricultural work force, much less than in Iraq, Egypt, or Syria.[10] The Shah was no populist but he promoted a nationalist myth—around the "Aryan" (non-Semitic) ethnicity of Iranians—to differentiate Iran from its Arab neighbors. He never succeeded in building a coalition beyond the repressive military-security apparatus, and his reforms never broadened his support. His suppression of the ulama precipitated a formidable opposition that recruited easily among the impoverished and repressed, building up to the Shah's demise in 1979. The succeeding Islamic Republic of Iran acquired many characteristics of the radical confessional inward-looking statist ideal type. The new constitution stipulated state control and massive nationalization of all major industries, foreign trade, banking, mining, insurance, and transportation, effecting a national redistribution of wealth from the private to the public sector. Growing at 0.5 percent annually between 1980–1985, nearly 8 percent of GDP went to the military. The new populist rulers vilified Western economic and political regimes, attacked the Gulf states as Western lackeys, and exhorted Iraqi Shi'ites to revolt against Saddam Hussein.

Summing up, statist-nationalist regimes came into being in most Middle Eastern states—including Algeria, Libya, and South Yemen—often ridden with internal cleavages that weakened them, forcing a constant concern with "political survival" (Noble 1991: 50). Political competition, mostly through violent means, often pitted against each other alternative variants of statist-nationalist and confessional coalitions, which outbid each other in radicalizing the grand strategy. The overall strength of statist-nationalism relative to a feeble liberalizing camp allowed the unobstructed implementation of most domestic, regional, and international aspects of this grand strategy. Domestic rivals were frequently labeled agents of neighboring adversaries and Western powers. No effective liberalizing opposition was able to function for many decades under statist-nationalist regimes that were invariably dictatorial. Private entrepreneurs emigrated, were coopted into the statist protected economy in exchange for political compliance, or were simply too weak and politically repressed to coalesce around an alternative project. Intellectual dissent was feeble—more so than in other regions under similar repression—leading to a characterization of the Middle East intelligentsia as the "rhetorician of the state mission."[11] Some dissenters challenged the absence of political freedom but not the essence of the statist-nationalist grand strategy.

Israel's birth in 1948 marks the victory of statist Labor Zionism over other currents—including religious and Marxist—and of a developmental strategy

---

[10] Bill and Springborg (1990: 204); Amuzegar (1991); Abrahamian (1993).
[11] Waterbury (1994: 27).

combining statism and import substitution with dependence on foreign capital and agricultural exports.[12] Labor's coalition emerged out of the Yishuv (settlement) years and a socialist political infrastructure (kibbutzim and the trade union Histadrut) that succeeded in mobilizing the population in war and peace. At its peak, 80 percent of the work force was Histadrut-affiliated, and the state employed nearly 52 percent of the total work force. Ben Gurion's *mamlachtiut* (statism), emphasizing state autonomy and populist commitments, attracted wide support at the expense of Revisionists and Liberals, backed by politically weaker private entrepreneurs and antisocialist nationalists. Tempted by hegemonic political designs to dominate Israel's political life (Ben-Gurion 1955: 23–24), the secular and socialist Labor leadership sought a confessional mantle of legitimacy by including the National Religious party, Mafdal, in every coalition (1948–1977). Proportional representation and weak Knesset majorities endowed the small religious fringe with enormous coalitional bargaining power.

The regional environment secured a central role for the armed forces and budding military-industrial complex, as Israel was considered to be "the only state in history to be sorrounded by hostile countries that do not recognize its legitimacy as a sovereign state and that possess far greater demographic and material resources" (Schweller 1992: 265). The concern with the physical survival of the state was real—threats could be reported unedited from neighboring media—and underpinned a high popular willingness to endow the state with the resources required to foil such threats. The eventual strategic partnership (but no formal alliance) between Israel and the US since the late 1960s tends to blur this earlier historical reality of insecurity. The armed forces became privileged beneficiaries—indeed the essential component—of the statist model, with defense attracting up to 50 percent of government budgets from 1966 to 1975—or over 20 percent of GDP between 1969 and 1981—reduced to an average of 25 percent of the budget in the 1980s.[13] Nearly 50 percent of employees in the industrial sector—which employed a fourth of the work force—worked for defense-related industries.

Labor's grand strategy retained a rhetorical emphasis on self-reliance for many years, echoing the Holocaust experience, which provided a rallying theme across the political spectrum. However, the reality was one of extreme dependence on the outside world, particularly for weapons, which poured in from Communist Czechoslovakia in 1948 (not wholly unnaturally, given the political basis of Israel's Labor). Thus, the idea of ultimate weapons capable of overcoming that dependence began germinating in the 1950s, and accelerated with reported activities of Nazi scientists developing nonconventional programs in Arab states. Rigid Cold War alliances forced a redefinition of Labor's international policies toward French and German military support in the 1950s. United States military support (two-thirds of the total) and economic support began in earnest only after 1973. Despite a general orientation to the West during the

---

[12] Barnett (1992: 231); Shalev (1992); Harkabi (1986).
[13] Posen (1984: 28); Peri (1983: 22); IISS (1995): 265).

Cold War, there was little trust in Israel for international institutions, in which Third World majorities automatically endorsed Arab positions.

A Statist-Nationalist Cauldron of War

The regional coalitional landscape just described yielded a statist-nationalist zone of war par excellence, between Israel and its Arab neighbors, among the latter, and between Iran and its Arab adversaries. A study of armed conflicts between 1945 and 1995 portrayed the Middle East with the highest incidence of interstate and intrastate conflict, after Africa.[14] Five major Arab-Israeli wars were fought between 1948 and 1973. The 1948 war presaged a long series of encounters among statist-nationalist coalitions that grew stronger on all sides by the 1950s and 1960s. The Palestinians' *nakbah* or Israel's war of independence (1947–1949) ended with 300,000 to 700,000 Palestinian refugees and 1 percent of Israelis killed (6,000), leaving an indelible mark on all sides.[15] The zero-sum nature of this war provided—on both sides—fertile ground for statist-nationalist agendas, intense militarization, and the proliferation of myths that fueled nearly fifty years of intermittent war. Land (ownership over territory) was a central nationalist symbol, the object of competing claims for statehood.

Egypt under Nasser became the heart of statist-nationalism, and the nationalization of the Suez Canal provided a convenient justification in the hands of Egypt's adversaries to confront Nasser's grand strategy directly, through a British-French-Israeli military campaign unleashed in 1956. Israel justified the Suez campaign as a response to Egyptian sponsorship of terrorist fedayeen in Gaza and to Egypt's blockade against Israeli shipping in Aqaba and Suez. Nationalist rhetoric was high on all sides, lubricating the warpath. President Eisenhower forced the allies' withdrawal from Suez, and Nasser was able to convert military defeat into political victory, in a pattern that this region later perfected as no other. Challenging Israel and the West became central to the protection of grand statist-nationalist strategies, whatever the battle outcome.

The Six-Day War had similar roots—conforming to the dynamics described in Chapter Three—with statist-nationalist coalitions advancing their interests by exacerbating instability, challenge, and competition. Though these coalitions were not invariably interested in actualizing their war-fighting potential, the logic and risky behavioral corollaries of this strategy led them to stumble into war. Stressing national symbols, command over economic resources, territoriality, and self-reliance produced negative security externalities, unleashing processes that initiators could no longer control.[16] Nasser's swaggering closure

---

[14] Holsti (1995: 321). Ibrahim (1995: 35) estimated Middle East war-related casualties (1948–1992), including internal wars largely with outside intervention, to have reached at least 1.8 million. Arab-Israeli wars accounted for about 160,000 of the total.

[15] Bill and Springborg (1990: 310); Selim (1991: 262); Owen (1992: 88).

[16] On the eve of the Six-Day War Egyptian authorities covered Cairo with posters demanding "the death of the poisonous viper of imperialism, Arab reaction, and Zionism" (Jansen 1997: 158). On Nasser's view of the war, see Heikal (1973: 28–30 and 242–49).

of the Straits of Tiran to Israeli passage in 1967, his threats to destroy Israel, and his call to remove UN peacekeepers—which the UN quickly heeded—embodies much of this logic and led to Egypt's most devastating military defeat. As Quandt (1996: 13) argues, it was Nasser who "took the initiative to turn a relatively quiescent front of the Arab-Israeli conflict into a battlefield." To be sure, the domestic programs of all main protagonists in this war provided political ammunition in the hands of regional adversaries: extensive state and military entrepreneurship, policies of self-reliance and national exclusivity, and an emphasis on sovereignty, territoriality, and offensive deterrence, all of which were defining tools in their political arsenal.

Nasser's moves in May 1967 were no summer solstice gift for Israel's Prime Minister Levy Eshkol and his Finance Minister Pinhas Sapir, who had been nurturing an incipient liberalizing strategy within their own party, evident both in domestic political-economic proposals and in heightened international responsiveness to US pressures. On the one hand, Eshkol understood that the statist economy had run its course by the mid-1960s. On the other, he also understood that Nasser's steps had made war unavoidable, particularly as his cabinet members declared Israel's choice to be "to live or perish." Some military and political leaders regarded Nasser's actions as an opportunity to strike a fatal blow to his grand strategy. Under unprecedented pressure from the defense establishment, Ben-Gurion's statist party (Rafi), and extraparliamentary groups, hawkish General Moshe Dayan was appointed minister of defense in a National Unity Government. The war was to set back the clock in Eshkol's struggling agenda, and his ambivalence about the impending war was evident in his trembling voice during a radio address on the eve of the war.[17] The Six-Day War yielded Israel's occupation of Egyptian, Jordanian (West Bank), and Syrian territories.

The late 1960s and early 1970s represent the historical peak of statist-nationalism in the region. Domestically the strategy still reigned supreme in most Arab countries, with strong Soviet political and economic support. Renewed Israeli access to the West Bank (biblical Judea and Samaria) strengthened nationalist myths of a Greater Israel. Following Eshkol's death in office, territorial compromise was no longer clearly in the cards, as some leaders—notably but not uniquely from Likud—used the outcome of the 1967 war to further statist-nationalism at home. Nasser launched a "war of attrition" in 1969 to recover the Sinai Peninsula—a war that sacrificed over ten thousand Egyptian and over four hundred Israeli lives—only to maintain the status quo.[18] On the Jewish Day of Atonement (Yom Kippur) in 1973, Egypt and Syria attacked Israel across the Suez and in the Golan Heights. Their initial gains were quickly overturned, but the domestic reverberations of Labor's foremost strategic failure

---

[17] Eshkol (1969: 105–10). On Eshkol's moderate and compromising positions before and after the war, see Eshkol (1967); Brecher (1974: 334); Peres (1993: 167); Lustick (1993: 363). On domestic political pressures on Eshkol on the eve of the war, see Rabin (1979: 84–99) and Barzilai (1996: 59–82).

[18] *Ha'aretz* 18 August 1995: 28.

led, in time, to its first electoral defeat since independence. Likud's ascent to power in 1977 under Prime Minister Begin was prematurely heralded as the end of a statist era, but the continued dominance of statist-nationalism and confessionalism foiled this development, leading instead to economic stagnation and a new war, the Israeli invasion of Lebanon in 1982. Heralded by its architects as a legitimate response to terrorist attacks from Southern Lebanon, the war instead mobilized massive opposition within Israel. Following Begin's belated realization that his coalition had fallen captive to its political extremes, he retired into political oblivion, leaving a legacy of divisiveness and economic chaos.

Beyond the Arab-Israeli wars, an array of inter-Arab and Arab-Iranian rivalries erupted in armed conflict during these decades. Kerr (1971) described the 1950s and 1960s as an acute Arab Cold War. From 1955 onward Nasser sought hegemony over the Arab world but was often resisted, particularly by statist-nationalist competitors.[19] Syria's Ba'th support for a United Arab Republic (UAR) with Egypt in 1958 was a desperate move to avoid the prospects of a coalition with their domestic rivals. Some Ba'th officers feared an internal plot that would end their rule (supported by the private sector that resisted Nasserism) and sought Nasser out to strengthen their domestic hold on power. Their fears of external dependence were outweighed by their potential relative gains over domestic rivals. However, Syrian officers and civilian leaders were soon trying to cancel Nasser's UAR scheme, which collapsed by 1961. These events illustrate the interaction depicted in Chapter Three between a relatively weak statist-nationalist coalition pursuing an external integrative effort to strenghten its own position at home, and a stronger statist-nationalist partner ready to swallow it. The events following Yemen's coup in 1962, the new regime's appeal to Nasser, and Egypt's consequent five-year intervention in Yemen against Saudi Arabia followed a similar pattern.

The coalitional framework also suggests that statist-nationalist dyads often exhibit higher levels of armed conflict against each other than against internationalizing neighbors. Kerr's (1971) depiction of inter-Arab relations at the time provides support for this expectation: "Nasser's relations with his fellow revolutionaries tended to be more difficult than those with the 'reactionaries.' "[20] The latter—mainly Saudi Arabia and Jordan—bore that label for resisting much of the prevailing statist-nationalist grand strategy. Both kingdoms upheld Islamic principles, but their survival demanded a more internationalist approach. Syria's Assad embraced a détente with the pro-Western kingdoms—without prejudicing subversive operations against them—particularly as it secured a share of the Saudi oil windfall. Assad also upheld a liberalizing faction in Lebanon (the Maronites) in 1976, preventing the victory of a radical statist-nationalist coalition in its back yard. Assad's rule was less threatened by a Lebanon with resid-

---

[19] Noble (1991: 74); Walt (1987: 267); Levy and Barnett (1992: 32); Kedourie (1992: 308–9).

[20] See also Nasser (1962: 93), and Hudson (1977). On the war in Yemen, see Heikal (1973: 212–24). On his war on "reactionary" regimes, see Hussein (1992).

ual Christian influence than one led by its ideological kin, lest this presumed ally fall under competing (Ba'th) Iraqi influence and draw Syria into battle with Israel.

Iranian-Iraqi relations were also compatible with this pattern identified by Kerr. The 1958 coup pitted Iraq's Ba'th against the Shah, who supported the Kurdish revolt in Iraq. However, actual combat during the 1960s and 1970s was minimal, and in 1975 Imperial Iran—a pro-Western coalitional hybrid—and radical Iraq reached a modus vivendi. Indeed, Workman (1994: 87) described bilateral relations between 1975 and 1979 as "at their warmest." Not until the Iranian revolution did a major war of spasmic proportions erupt (in 1980–1988) leaving one million people dead and two million wounded. Islamic Iran's challenges to liberalizers and statist-nationalists alike were central to consolidating domestic zeal for its revolution and strengthening the ulama.[21] These policies, including an aggressive campaign against Iraq, allowed Saddam Hussein to initiate one of the region's bloodiest wars. Saddam's prospects of maximizing oil revenues to fund his grand strategy through the defeat of Iran backfired, depleting $35 billion in foreign reserves, escalating Iraq's external debt to $50 billion, and deepening Saddam's dependence on liberalizing neighbors and international institutions. This outcome might have deterred any would-be liberalizer from embarking on another similar venture, but it had the opposite effect on Saddam, who sought a new war—this time against Kuwait—to reverse the results of the earlier one and produce new resources. Noteworthy from the perspective of hypotheses advanced in Chapter Three is the fact that Iran and Iraq exhibited the most resolute import-substituting efforts of all in the region.[22]

Inter-Arab and Arab-Iranian wars confirm other characteristics identified in the analysis of interactions among statist-nationalist adversaries, such as the prominence of territorial issues and the rejection of persuasion, diplomacy, or economic inducements as favored strategies. As Noble (1991: 75) suggested, "Arab governments relied primarily on unconventional coercive techniques," including "strong attacks on the leadership of other states, propaganda campaigns to mobilize opposition, and intense subversive pressures, including cross-frontier alliances with dissatisfied individuals and groups. The aim was to destabilize and ultimately overthrow opposing governments." The financial and military trail of coalitional support across borders provides a flavor of the intricacies of regional policies. King Saud plotted to kill Nasser in 1958. Egypt attempted to destabilize King Hussein in 1958 and 1960. King Hussein aided Syria's Muslim Brotherhood against the Ba'th. Iraq's Brigadier Qasim executed domestic opponents with Nasserite allegiances. Later Iraq's Ba'th provided military assistance to Syria's Muslim Brotherhood and to Lebanese Christians against Syria. Syria backed Iranian and Iraqi Shi'ites against Iraq's Ba'th. Armed conflict, subversion, and wars among Arab states and Iran were frequent, resulted in many casualties, and escalated—unlike any Arab-Israeli

[21] Workman (1994: 52–54, 87–103); Gerges (1996: 128–29); Walt (1996).
[22] Richards and Waterbury (1990: 26).

war—into the use of poison gas (Iraq against Iran and Kurdish civilians, Egypt against Yemen).[23]

Finally, despite the rhetoric of integration, economic barriers among statist-nationalist Arab states never receded. Capital movements were small relative to outflows to the West, and intra-Arab trade never reached 10 percent of their total trade throughout the 1970s and 1980s. Regional economic institutions such as the Arab Common Market (1965: Egypt, Iraq, Jordan, and Syria), the Arab Cooperation Council (1989: Egypt, Jordan, North Yemen, and Iraq), and the many precursors to the Arab Maghreb Union (1989: Algeria, Libya, Mauritania, Morocco, and Tunisia) existed largely in paper, without much effective impact, much like their Latin American counterparts.[24] Integrative political schemes never lasted far beyond the declaratory stage. The Arab League epitomized the statist-nationalist fragmentation of the Arab world, becoming the theater where many Arab Cold Wars were played. In sum, regional institutions in the Arab Middle East lacked any solidity and were, according to Tripp (1995: 303), nothing but "a reflection of the internal organization of power within the states themselves."

Within this regional statist-nationalist expanse, a few incipient liberalizing anomalies stood out. Lebanon's ruling Christian-controlled coalition imposed few restrictions on foreign investments throughout the 1950s and 1960s and allowed private entrepreneurship to thrive. The army played a significant—albeit indirect—role between 1958 and 1970. Yet the army candidate was not elected in 1970 and the Chamber of Deputies investigated army corruption in 1972, exceptional events in a region where corrupt military regimes set the tone. Lebanon maintained an unusual (for the Arab world) modus vivendi with Israel during those years, which many thought made it ripest for an eventual peace with Israel. However, the precarious situation of a liberalizing island in a statist-nationalist sea became evident in the 1970s. The collapse of Lebanon as a state signaled the disintegration of its liberalizing coalition under the combined weight of domestic statist, confessional, and militarized factions and neighboring statist-nationalist intervention, particularly by Syria and Israel. Syria occupied Lebanon in June 1976 and prevented a victory by the PLO and Shi'ite radicals over the Christians who had ruled Lebanon since independence.

Transjordan's King Abdullah—King Hussein's grandfather—was another anomaly in the region, lukewarm to statist-nationalism and a liberalizer ahead of his times by the late 1940s. King Abdullah waged an unrelenting campaign to undermine nationalists like Jerusalem's Mufti Haj Amin al-Husseini and showed a readiness to negotiate an accommodation with Israel, which led to his assassination in the hands of a Palestinian radical in 1951. King Hussein retained his grandfather's tepid approach toward statism and populism, fighting a short-lived attempt in that direction by Premier Suleiman al-Nabulsi (head of the National Socialist party) in the mid-1950s. All the while, Jordanian Hash-

---

[23] Ahmad (1991: 194); Sayigh (1992: 120).
[24] Deeb (1989).

emites cultivated ties with the West as well as with the Muslim Brotherhood, which developed a vast system of patronage, including medical clinics, schools, and professional associations.[25] In contrast to Nasserite pan-Arab policies, which isolated Jordan during the 1950s and 1960s, Jordan's approach to the region was one of noninterference in the domestic affairs of other Arab states (Syria excepted) and of political accommodation with Israel. In the 1960s, Prime Minister Wasfi al-Tall—another early liberalizer—initiated economic reforms such as contracting the state bureaucracy and containing the military's expansion. Advancing a "Jordan-first" approach with full backing from the king, Tall aimed at disengaging from the Palestinian-Israeli struggle militarily, despite his principled and strong defense of the Palestinian cause. Not very receptive to such nuance, Palestinian terrorists killed Tall in Cairo in 1971. King Hussein could not fail to read the script and adjusted his coalitional efforts, as he would for the next two decades, navigating the perilous waters of regional coalitional politics. The 1970s and the surrounding oil boom led to Jordan's economic expansion in a statist direction, diverting it from a liberalizing path that would only crystallize after the 1991 Gulf War.

ECONOMIC LIBERALIZATION: THE ENGINE OF PEACEMAKING

Incipient Internationalizing Coalitions in the Arab World

The prospect of economic collapse and the overall dismal record of statist-nationalism—crawling per capita GNP growth, running inflation, budget deficits, and foreign debt—forced some ruling coalitions into a half-hearted grand strategic shift. By the 1980s, the Middle East had become one of the regions least able to feed its population and had some of the highest rates of infant mortality, illiteracy (particular female), unemployement, and income disparities.[26] Arab authoritarianism could not, as its East Asian counterparts could, claim economic miracles to soften its repressive image. The collapse of the Soviet Union reinforced the debacle of statist-nationalism and orphaned its old beneficiaries.

Egypt's Anwar Sadat was an early precursor of an internationalizing strategy. He initially mustered all that the infrastructure inherited from Nasser could yield politically, an effort that crystallized in the October 1973 military onslaught on Israel. Despite hailing the crossing of the Suez Canal as a victory, Sadat quickly realized the exhaustion of Nasser's model in its internal and external expressions.[27] Domestic economic and political bottlenecks compelled

---

[25] Dessouki and Kheir (1991); Tal (1995). See also speeches and memoirs of King Hussein and Crown Prince Hassan, in Hussein I (1962, 1969, 1994), and Bin Talal (1984, 1994).

[26] UNDP (1994, 1995). In one of the best cases, Syria's GNP doubled from $480 (1972) to $1,170 (1992), its budget deficit grew tenfold in that period (10 percent of GNP in 1980), and its external debt went from $400 million (1972) to over $16 billion (1988). On the legacy of statism in the region, see Richards and Waterbury (1990: 219–99) and Owen (1992: 139–65).

[27] Heikal (1975). Barnett (1992: 128–29); Karawan (1993); Dessouki (1991); Stein (1991). On Sadat as post-populist, see Hinnebusch (1985).

new directions, as did the robustness of Israel's presence in the region. A new grand Egyptian strategy required a compatibility between the domestic transformation and its international correlates. A policy of economic liberalization (*infitah*), accumulation, and growth, the need to convert military into productive assets and to foster a new political base of support all implied a wholly fresh relationship with the West and left little room for a regional policy that pivoted on military hegemony over the Arab world or war with Israel. A new anchor— "Egypt first"—would preclude threats to Egypt's integrity, while the task of reconstruction was under way. The historic visit to Israel and the Camp David accords (1979) were the natural corollary of this strategy.

Infitah required export-oriented foreign investment, financial assistance, and Western technology, as well as a commitment to privatization. The policy was as attractive to some business interests—including tourism, commercial agriculture, and *munfatihun* ("openers" to the global economy)—as it was threatening to the large Egyptian bureaucracy. Egypt signed a standby agreement with the IMF in 1976 committing it to reduce subsidies and lower deficits. Sadat reduced military expenditures from 52.4 percent of Egypt's GNP in 1975 to 13 percent in 1979, and demilitarized cabinets and governorships, 26 of which were held by military men in 1964, reduced to 5 by 1980.[28] He replaced Nasser's Arab Socialist Union with the National Democratic party. Following austerity measures, price increases, and violent demonstrations in 1977, the US and oil-producing Arab states buttressed Sadat's economic agenda through loans and grants. Egypt received over $35 billion in US aid after 1975. Foreign exchange from tourism, workers' remittances, and Canal revenues—activities made possible by peace with Israel—grew from $700 million in 1974 to $9 billion in 1981. Egypt's trade openness (imports plus exports as a percentage of GDP) increased from 39 percent in 1962 to 61 percent in 1977.

Sadat's internationalizing impulse notwithstanding, he failed to revolutionize Egypt's political economy. Inflation and budget deficits continued to rise. The entrenched Egyptian bureaucracy and many in the National Democratic party and organized labor resisted infitah, while its potential beneficiaries could not mobilize a powerful coalition to advance it. The military establishment forcefully resisted its own demise, succeeding in reversing Sadat's trend (1976– 1979) to privilege welfare and economic expenditures over defense. Military expenditures continued to decline from 13 percent of GNP in 1979 (in constant 1989 dollars) to 5 percent in 1989, yet Egypt imported $7 billion worth of weapons (1982–1986) just as external threats were the lowest in its modern history.[29] The military retained control of a vast network of industrial enterprises, much of which displaced the private sector. Foreign aid programs designed to promote reform instead strengthened patronage networks in the statist and military-industrial complexes. Infitah thus failed to stimulate production

---

[28] Springborg (1989: 137–38, 248–49); Waterbury (1983); Barkey (1992).

[29] ACDA (1991, table 1); Korany and Dessouki (1991: 38). On President Mubarak's aloofness from ministers advocating structural reform, see Waterbury (1992). Privatization has been nil, maintaining the benefits of 5,000 wealthy Egyptian managers of state enteprises (Cassandra 1995: 13).

and exports, and reinforced overconsumption, imports, high inflation, and indebtedness. In the 1990s both inflation and the budget deficit declined sharply and in 1996 a new effort at privatization, began with the sale of fourteen state companies. In his opening speech at the 1996 Cairo Middle East Economic Summit, President Housni Mubarak declared: "This year Egypt joined the global economy." However, the domestic political-economic dimension of Egypt's post-Sadat transformation has suffered from a credibility of commitment.

The regional pillar of Sadat's internationalizing strategy fared better than its economic one. Camp David marginalized his domestic opposition even if it radicalized the Islamic fringes. It was not a policy widely embraced at the outset, but one pushed through by a new team struggling to establish itself politically. Camp David helped remove Egypt's utmost external security threat, Israel, forcing it to endure an interlude of regional isolation from other Arab states, followed by a resumption of leadership by the late 1970s. The policy survived even though Sadat himself was assassinated in 1981 by an Islamic fundamentalist inspired to kill any Muslim ruler who collaborated with "unbelievers."[30] Ironically, after laying the groundwork for an eventual Jordanian and Palestinian rapprochement with Israel, Egypt restored some statist-nationalist themes partially to address its domestic Islamist challenges. The domestic weakness of Egypt's internationalizing strategy was at the heart of its cold peace with Israel. By the mid-1990s this weakness was brought into relief against the rise of a budding internationalizing coalition in Jordan.

Jordan is a small, natural-resource-poor, tourist-based, commercial agriculture, and munfatihun economy, with a fairly well-developed private sector. Although an inward-looking strategy was doomed at the outset, Jordan's incipient internationalists were fighting for survival for decades—in a regional sea of statist-nationalism—which explains some sharp turns in Jordanian grand strategy. In 1967 it reluctantly joined statist-nationalist Egypt and Syria in the Six-Day War against Israel, a decision King Hussein regretted taking in response to nationalist pressures.[31] Later Jordan was the first Arab country to end Egypt's diplomatic isolation in 1984 and to conduct secret negotiations with Israeli leaders. Subsequently Jordan was one of the few Arab states not to join the anti-Saddam Hussein coalition in 1990, a move that enraged Jordan's Saudi and Kuwaiti benefactors but helped King Hussein control mobilized populist sectors. More than most states in the neighborhood, regional instability and wars have spelled economic disaster for Jordan and forced a tormenting balancing act on the king and his allies, foiling their ability to pursue a coherent internationalist agenda. Attempts at economic reform in the late 1980s were forcefully resisted. Only in the aftermath of Desert Storm did a stronger internationalizing coalition emerge, skillfully tailored by the King and Crown Prince Hassan.

---

[30] On definitions of Islamic fundamentalism by As'ad AbuKhalil (1994: 677), see Chapter Two, note 89.

[31] "Jordan's King, in Frank Speech, Calls '67 War a Major Blunder," *New York Times* 6 June 1997: A9. On the political-economic dimensions of evolving Jordanian strategies see Bin Talal (1984: 86–104) and Hussein I (1962, 1969, 1994).

Iraq's defeat discredited populist, nationalist, and Islamist opponents and the threat of economic collapse swayed influential Jordanians into the internationalizing camp. The prospects of diminishing dependence on Gulf remittances and attracting foreign investment for genuine industrialization seemed better than ever before. The Islamic opposition in parliament plummeted from 32 members elected in 1989 to 18 in 1993. The opposition had focused its platform on the "affronts" of economic liberalization and the peace process—unsurprising themes, given the coalitional perspective advanced here.

Pent-up internationalist energies were unleashed in reformist legislation and formal policy statements that postulated a clear connection between economic reform and the peace process.[32] Many in the business community, hoping to create the necessary conditions to attract foreign investment, heeded the call.[33] Riad al-Khouri, director of Middle East Business Associates in Amman, articulated the internationalizing agenda typically: "Jordan's economic hopes are riding on the peace process. . . . A resolution of the conflict with Israel would also allow reduction of the country's defense budget (which accounts for more than 30 percent of government spending) and reconciliation with Saudi Arabia and the United States, from whom financial assistance is badly needed. . . . Against the background of the lingering Arab-Israeli conflict, it remains almost impossible to attract [foreign] investors. But if the peace process flourishes . . . Jordan will assume its rightful economic role. However, the vociferous fundamentalism unleashed by democratization is belligerent and xenophobic—opposed to both peace and foreign investment." Such statements would have been unthinkable during the statist-nationalist era. Jordan established formal diplomatic relations with Israel in the aftermath of the Palestinian-Israeli 1993 Oslo agreements.

On the economic front, parliament approved a new investment law in late 1995, the tax structure was revamped, and Jordan applied for World Trade Organization membership and free-trade arrangements with the European Union. Budget deficits declined from 24 percent of GDP in 1989 to 4.1 percent in 1996. Inflation decreased from 26 percent in 1989 to about 7 percent in 1996. GDP declined 13.5 percent in 1989 but thereafter grew steadily (11 percent in 1992, 5.7 in 1994, 6.5 in 1996). Foreign debt halved from 200 percent of GDP in 1989 to less than 100 percent in 1996. Food subsidies were replaced with direct financial assistance to needy families.[34] In 1996 the World Bank allocated a $1 billion credit to Jordan in support of its reform efforts.

The oil-exporting Gulf states—grouped since 1981 under the GCC (Gulf Cooperation Council)—comprise Saudi Arabia, Bahrain, Qatar, Oman, the United Arab Emirates (UAE), and Kuwait. These "rentier states" (Beblawi and

---

[32] See, inter alia, statements by Safwan Bataineh, economic adviser to the prime minister (Al Khouri 1994: 110ff.).

[33] Personal interviews, Amman (Jordan), 11–22 December 1995.

[34] *Jordan Times* 5 August 1996: 3; Amman Radio Jordan Network, 11 July 1996 in Foreign Broadcast Information Service—Near East and South Asia (hereafter *FBIS-NES*) 12 July 1996: 31–37.

Luciani 1987) controlled by extended royal families dominate the economy and polity via external oil rents rather than domestic taxes. Oil accounts for 60 percent of GNP, a fact that places the global economy at the heart of the rulers' considerations and coalitional preferences. The decline in oil prices has compelled them to restructure their relationship to the global economy by diversifying their export potential and liberalizing the domestic economy, which doubled the private sector's share of GDP by the 1980s. In Saudi Arabia, the al-Saud family had historically relied on revenues from a commercial class connected to global markets. The oil economy deepened dependence on foreign manpower and oil markets. The internationalized commercial class and the oil economy still underpin the power of the royal family, which retained a pro-Western orientation throughout decades of regional anti-Americanism. The royal family has preserved an Islamic mantle of legitimacy insofar as it does not impinge on internationalizing strategies. Better known for its commitment to the accumulation and consumption of wealth than for its devotion to ascetic Islamic lifestyles, Saudi rulers have attracted unrelenting criticism from the self-proclaimed "true" Islamic Republics (Iran and Sudan) and from fundamentalist challengers in the region.

Oil windfalls underpinned some distributive policies in GCC states, which may have so far foiled the decades-long prediction of their imminent demise. Yet domestic confessional pressures have remained, explaining some hybrid Saudi regional policies: formally severing relations with Egypt while supporting Sadat's efforts to undo Nasserism and statist-nationalism; countering accusations of Western "lackeyism" with the financing of militant Islam, secular Iraq (against the Iranian Shi'ite threat), and Syria's "steadfast" opposition to Camp David. Some GCC rulers—notably in Oman and Qatar—were at the vanguard of multilateral peace initiatives after 1993, and have hosted Israeli prime ministers and multilateral peace negotiations. Qatar, under its new liberalizing leader Sheikh Hamad ibn Khalifa al-Thani, exemplifies an iconoclastic regional approach geared to promote stability and cooperation by warming ties with Iran, Iraq, and Israel alike while hosting US warplanes and deferentially settling a dispute with Saudi Arabia.[35] Qatar's border dispute with Bahrein was on the GCC agenda for 1997. Of all the regional cooperative institutions in the Arab world, GCC has been considered the most effective and one of the most durable.

Recalcitrant statist-nationalist and confessional neighbors—Iran and Iraq— have done a great deal to consolidate GCC. Some GCC members have developed a modus vivendi with both regimes, even as all of GCC forcefully endorses UN sanctions on Iraq and condemns Iran's conquest of three UAE islands. Asked about President Rafsanjani's disposition to improve relations, the GCC secretary general welcomed it, but added: "Let me speak frankly. Deeds

---

[35] Hamad has also cut back government subsidies in housing, education, and automatic highly paid jobs. Douglas Jehl, "Persian Gulf's Young Turk: Sheikh Hamad, Emir of Qatar," *New York Times* 10 July 1997: A1; and Robin Wright, "Interview with Sheikh Hamad ibn Khalifa al-Thani," *Los Angeles Times* 22 June 1997: M3.

not words are the deciding factor in international relations. Dealing with Iran, no state can build relations on just the good words it hears. It would want to see that 'good' element implemented."[36] Previous aggression by the statist-nationalist-confessional giants of the North have strengthened GCC's military constituencies, who are opposed to curbing military expenditures and competition. Iraq swallowed Kuwait wholesale in 1991—and threatened Saudi Arabia with much the same—compelling GCC to rely on the good-willed hunter (the United States) to undo Iraq's Little Red Riding Hood strategy. Prior to 1990 the smaller Gulf kingdoms' military expenditures did not threaten their internationalizing strategy; moreover, they were high relative to the average in industrializing countries but not relative to statist-nationalist competitors in the region. The oil boom allowed Saudi defense expenditures to rise from $387 million in 1969 to $24 billion in 1984, or about 20 percent of its GDP, declining to 11 percent in 1994. Defense expenditures in the 1980s and 1990s were between 3 and 5 percent of GDP in Bahrain and Qatar, 5 to 7 percent in UAE, with only Kuwait's and Oman's rising above 9 percent. GCC's secretary general summarized GCC's efforts to stem military expenditures: "We do not want to enter into a process of amassing troops and arms as in the case of the cold war, when there was gigantic squandering of efforts. . . . The Gulf states hope efforts will be geared to development, particularly as economic power is the real power these days."[37]

Morocco and Tunisia pioneered internationalizing agendas in the region, promoting exports through preferential trade agreements with the European Economic Community in the late 1960s and stimulating private-sector and foreign investment. The state employed about one-fourth of the nonagricultural work force, far less than under statist-nationalist regimes elsewhere in the region. Morocco's balance-of-payment crisis and food riots in the mid-1980s led to a serious attempt to dismantle all state enterprises (except for six), attract foreign investment, and promote exports. Morocco's defense expenditures averaged 4 to 5 percent of GDP (1985–1994). Tunisia abandoned import-substitution by 1972 under Bourguiba. The state, although a dominant force, employed about 11 percent of the work force, far less than in Egypt, Iraq, or Syria. Zine el-Abidine Ben Ali deepened financial liberalization and foreign investment in Tunisia, promoted tourism, reduced the maximum tariff rate from 220 to 43 percent (1990s), and slashed defense expenditures from 5 to 1.4 percent of GDP (1985–1994). Both Morocco and Tunisia pursued accommodating regional policies and cooperation with Israel, playing a key supportive role in multilateral negotiations.

By the 1990s, all throughout the region private entrepreneurs with an eye on European Union markets and beyond increased their political access and prod-

---

[36] "Interview with Jamil al-Hujaylan, Secretary General of the GCC," *Al-Sharq al-Awsat* 1 January 1997: 2.

[37] "GCC Chief on Islands Issue, Policy on Iraq," *FBIS-NES* 28 October 1994: 19. On GCC ruling coalitions' interest in curbing military expenditures, see Sadowski (1993). On defense expenditures, see IISS (1995: 265).

ded their regimes to liberalize, finding unprecedented receptivity compared with previous decades.[38] In some cases state officials have been particularly active in drawing together potential beneficiaries of a new strategy, as in the organization of regional economic summits after 1994. The connecting link among these incipient internationalizing coalitions is an openness to international markets, investments, and tourism, and cooperative relations with international financial institutions and with fellow regional liberalizers—policies that make them natural opponents of statist-nationalist, radical Islamist, and Marxist groups. Their now assiduous attendance of World Economic Forum meetings, among other things, brought home in a direct way both the political advantages of East Asian models and the drawbacks of militarization.

An Ephemeral Internationalist Dyad? Israel and Palestine in Oslo

The logic of an opening to the global economy—and of its domestic and regional preconditions—has not escaped some Israeli politicians. Prime Minister (and former Finance Minister) Levy Eshkol and his finance minister, Pinhas Sapir, mark the substantive origins of an internationalizing strategy (1965–1966), including efforts to lower inflation, initiate privatization, restrain military budgets, and remove anti-export biases.[39] Eshkol was also quite sensitive to the political requirements of softening Israeli regional positions in order to improve its international status and economic access, particularly with the US. The period immediately following the Six-Day War included a 15 percent across-the-board cut in all tariffs (1968), a preannounced tariff-unification scheme, and an attempt to return occupied territories in exchange for peace and recognition. The untimely death of Eshkol helped doom an agenda that might have avoided the Arab-Israeli warpath, a path that led to the 1973 war and the unprecedented demise of Labor in 1977. The outcome of the Six-Day War and territorial expansion infused statist economic instruments with new life, after they had nearly run their course by the mid-1960s. With Dayan as the new defense czar, Sapir encountered fierce opposition to his attempts to restrain military budgets, which shot up, particularly after 1969 (Berglas 1986).

Sadat's strategic shift and Camp David somewhat alleviated the constraints on an internationalizing agenda by removing a key threat to Israel's security. Shrinking the state was high on Likud's electoral platform, which aimed at weakening Israeli bureaucracy, a traditional Labor fiefdom. For all its early developmental achievements, decades of statism were now translating into sluggish growth (1 percent a year since 1973), governmental behemoths, high inflation, the largest foreign per-capita debt, and heavy public-enterprise deficits. Prime Minister Menachem Begin's 1977 Likud coalition included the Democratic Movement for Change (DMC), which attracted rising private industrial-

---

[38] El Sayyid (1994), Ibrahim (1994).

[39] Earlier steps in 1952 (exchange rate) and 1962 (attempt to remove anti-export bias) were fairly limited (Bruno 1988: 233). On the 1966–1967 period see also Plessner (1994: 21). On Sapir's legendary attempts to control defense expenditures, see Peri (1983: 220–30).

ists, professionals, and some middle-class groups.[40] The DMC was the only coalitional partner with a somewhat coherent internationalizing agenda, not merely antistatist but also critical of Likud's uncompromising foreign policies, particularly regarding settlements. The DMC's influence quickly dissipated and Likud became shackled by commitments to rising nationalist, populist, and confessional groups, for whom economic liberalization was never a top priority. These commitments precluded an internationalist shift under Begin, both in its political-economic and regional aspects. Extreme nationalist leaders—Defense Minister Ariel Sharon and Chief of Staff Rafael Eitan—pushed Begin toward war in Lebanon, held by a former chief of military intelligence to have been the least justifiable of all Israeli wars.[41] Moreover, religious-nationalist leaders demanded a costly West Bank settlement policy with high political payoffs for Likud: fueling statist-confessional myths while offering Israelis cheap suburban housing.

Likud's regional policies and those relating to the West Bank in particular had become the heart of its political platform and electoral appeal, consistently undermining its proclaimed economic agenda. Annexing the West Bank was far more important to Likud and its allies than attracting foreign investment or dissipating the Arab boycott, estimated to have cost Israel over $50 billion since 1948.[42] A liberalizing economic agenda was never privileged; settlements and side payments to statist-nationalist coalitional partners were. Although trade liberalization had gradually proceeded—under Labor—since the late 1960s, Begin's coalition liberalized the capital account in 1977 without accompanying fiscal measures and other domestic reforms, thus converting an inflation rate of 20 percent in 1977 to 120 percent in 1979.[43] Governmental expenditure as a proportion of GNP grew between 1977 and 1983. Likud's policies maintained sluggish growth, from $4,100 per capita in 1977 to $6,850 in 1986, and were deemed to have unleashed far more serious macroeconomic instability than in any earlier period. The war in Lebanon cost over $4 billion and accelerated inflation from 101 percent in 1981 to 191 percent in 1983 to 445 percent in 1984, triggering hyperinflation and stagnation, with foreign reserves plummeting to a dangerous $1 billion, a foreign debt higher than Israel's GDP, and a 1984 budget roughly equal to its GDP. Likud had no alternative to a National

[40] Sharkansky (1993: 153); Arian (1989: 102).

[41] Harkabi (1986). See also Peres (1993). For Eitan's views on Arab-Israeli relations as "there are no choices. There is no compromise. Win or die," see Connie Bruck, "The Wounds of Peace," *New Yorker*, 14 October 1996: 17. On Likud's historical support for budgetary demands from the defense establishment, see Peri (1983: 226). On Begin's emphasis on military force and self-reliance, see Sofer (1988).

[42] Hufbauer, Schott, and Elliot (1990: 74) have estimated the annual cost to Israel of the boycott to have been 2.3 percent of its GNP (on average during 1951–1960) and 5.9 percent of GNP (1973–1980).

[43] On failed economic policies after 1977, see Bruno (1986: 301 and 1988: 238). On expansionary fiscal and monetary policies since 1969 as a source of inflation in Israel, and on economic policy as an outcome of military and security-related factors, see Barkai (1995). See also Razin and Sodka (1993) and Plessner (1994).

Unity Government (NUG) with Labor. Labor's Prime Minister Shimon Peres steered one of the world's most successful cases of stabilization and structural adjustment in 1985, with Finance Minister Modai (a Likud economic liberal) forcing a sharp budgetary contraction (the budget deficit declined from 16 to 1.3 percent of GDP between 1984 and 1986–1988), disciplined eradication of inflation (from triple digit to 16 to 20 percent), and currency stabilization.[44] A freeze on West Bank settlements was part of the austerity program. The NUG succeeded in reversing the economic collapse that Likud policies had engendered, raising GNP per capita steadily during the late 1980s. However, the deeper sources of the 1980s' political and economic crisis—a statist-nationalist agenda—were alive and entrenched, fueling a severe new crisis.

The intifada (Palestinian uprising) launched by Islamic Jihad and its political allies in 1987 was in tune with a logic of self-reliance (Israeli goods were boycotted), militarization, and mythical objectives of "freeing" Palestine. Paradoxically, this inward-looking nationalist convulsion—with its heroic symbolic achievements and catastrophic socio-economic results—paved the way for a strategic reversal. Sections of the PLO leadership, particularly Fatah, now opposed the indiscriminate and often fratricidal violence that undermined Palestinian survival and international support. The PLO formally recognized Israel's right to exist in 1988, while the intifada was still raging, harvesting an official relationship with the United States.[45] Henceforth the PLO was to manage the hard transition from a military—sometime terrorist—organization to incipient liberalizer. The Gulf War and the collapse of the Soviet Union had decimated the old PLO guard, lifting up supporters of an alternative strategy.

These shifts in the Palestinian camp were largely ignored by the NUG, particularly Likud, who also crushed a promising peace initiative by Labor's Peres and King Hussein. The former chief of military intelligence, Yehoshafat Harkabi—one of Israel's foremost experts on the Arab world—spearheaded the recognition of an incipient transformation in the PLO, but Likud leaders—and many in Labor—remained impervious to the regional prerequisites for transforming Israel's political economy. Likud subsumed all other objectives to maintaining populist, nationalist, and confessional support. It thus granted $250,000 benefits per West Bank settler family for the construction of bypass roads and ignored President Bush's threats to withdraw US loan guarantees for developmental projects if settler activities continued.[46] Meanwhile, Labor's political metamorphosis accelerated, with some prominent members meeting PLO leaders in contravention of Israeli law. Not until the 1992 elections did Labor, in coalition with secularist Meretz, muster enough support to initiate a comprehensive—domestic, regional, global—internationalizing shift. Backed by urban

---

[44] Plessner (1994) and Bufman and Leiderman (1995). On estimates of the economic costs of the 1982 war in Lebanon, see Peres (1993). This war accounts for a 2 percent jump in defense outlays relative to GNP, from 11.5 percent in 1981 to 13.2 percent in 1982 (Klieman and Pedatzur 1992: 59).

[45] Muslih (1988); Kimmerling and Migdal (1994: 251–75); Rubin (1994).

[46] "Israeli Premier Assails Jewish Settler's Costs," *New York Times* 22 June 1995: A7.

professionals, the middle class, highly skilled labor, export-oriented cooperative agriculture, and a vast pool of technical, scientific, service, managerial, and entrepreneurial groups poised to fuel a high-tech revolution, Labor-Meretz got a clear mandate: socio-economic renewal within the "green line" (pre-1967 borders) and a territorial compromise beyond that line.[47]

Labor-Meretz were singularly disposed to draw the explicit links between an internationalist strategy—building on a comparative advantage in internationally oriented entrepreneurs and symbolic analysts—and the requirements for a peaceful settlement of the Palestinian question. The business community's desertion of the Likud camp—which they now clearly associated with statist-nationalism and confessionalism—accelerated.[48] Prime Minister Rabin articulated the connection between widespread reform and regional stability. In a speech to Israeli business leaders he criticized West Bank settlers for imposing "enormous costs" on the state and for precluding investments in "hotels . . . industry . . . sciences."[49] Economy Minister Yossi Beilin explained the coalition's regional aims: not hegemony, but a peaceful transformation that would enable Israel to deepen its ties with the global marketplace. This objective also required becoming "a more welcome member of the international club."[50] Rewarding Labor-Meretz for its compromising regional policies, President Bush approved $10 billion in loan guarantees for investments in infrastructure and jobs. The approval was a windfall for a policy Labor favored anyway, including booming road and housing building within Israel—not in the West Bank—and credit to private businesses. The coalition emphasized the exigencies of economic survival, privatization, and international competitiveness, as well as the futility of military technological fixes for solving Israel's security dilemma. The promise of becoming an economic powerhouse had all too long been precluded

---

[47] Over 60 percent of GDP by the 1990s was accounted for by technology-based industry. The size of the highly skilled pool can be partially gauged by the fact that one Israeli worker in three has a university degree.

[48] Private interviews, Israel's Manufacturers' Association, Chambers of Commerce, Export Institute (Tel Aviv, December 1995–January 1996, May–June 1996). Benjamin Gaon, president of the Koor Conglomerate, stated: "There is an absolute link between politics and the economy. Israel's emerging economy cannot proceed without the peace process," *New York Times* 11 October 1996: A23). Investor Effi Arazi was similarly direct: "Peace treaties attract investment" (*Link* April 1977: 7). On the massive support for the peace process among Israeli entrepreneurs, see also Yaacov Yonah, "The Peace Process as an Employment Problem," *Ma'ariv* Saturday Special Annex, 19 January 1996: 24. About 97 percent of all businesses operating in Israel are small enterprises, according to the Israeli Chamber of Commerce. The perception that the peace process and an internationalist agenda are intricately linked is evident on the pages of *Link*, Israel's International Business Magazine founded by entrepreneur Stef Wertheimer. See, inter alia, the editor's page in April 1977: 4, where he connects economic malaise to a faltering peace process and calls for new elections.

[49] "Israeli Premier Assails Jewish Settler's Costs." On Rabin's consistent guidelines at cabinet meetings regarding lower budgets and less state intervention, see *Ha'aretz* 5 November 1995.

[50] *Haaretz* 1 November 1995: B2. See also Beilin (1993). Eric Silver, in the *Financial Times* 7 December 1992. Kemp (1994: 400) discusses European and Japanese reluctance to invest in Israel as a geopolitical risk. On Beilin's economic and peace strategies, see Beilin (1992: 263–68). As economy minister, Beilin created a Bureau of Society in Peacetime.

by an unstable regional environment, prone to erupt in violence at any time. Foreign Minister Peres hatched a corresponding peace offensive.

In September 1993 Labor-Meretz presented the Israeli public with the Oslo Declaration of Principles recognizing the PLO as the legitimate representative of the Palestinian people and a partner in peace negotiations. A three-to-two approval rate followed overnight, both among Israelis and Palestinians.[51] The newly created Palestinian Authority (PA) thus became the only Arab political institution ever to have regained Palestinian land, achieving what twenty-one Arab states with 200 million people and vast standing armies and weapons could not accomplish for decades. The PA faced the intractable challenge of developing an internationalist strategy in tandem with forging statehood itself. It was essentially born into a liberalizing economic agenda insofar as a dense international institutional overlay—including the World Bank, IMF, EU, and the UN—imposed administrative and economic targets as a condition for delivering aid. International donors imposed financial accountability and transparency in the allocation of funds—$3.4 billion pledged and $1.5 billion disbursed by 1997—and in tax collection.[52] However, the PA faced a Catch-22 dilemma: donors demanded stringent political and economic conditions before releasing funds, while the PA needed these funds to build the infrastructure required to satisfy those conditions. The PA committed itself to a balanced budget by 1997 and a surplus by 1998. Its revenue collection doubled (relative to 1993) and fiscal balances and financial accountability improved markedly. At the 1996 fourth annual donor meeting in Paris pledges exceeded the amounts requested by the PA. An export-oriented Gaza Industrial Estates investment initiative was established in 1996 with free access to European and US markets. In early 1997 the Palestine Stock Exchange came into being. The World Bank allocated over $300,000 to the PA for political risk guarantees, housing projects, water, and sanitation, and the development of a legal system.

Among the architects of the Oslo agreement were Ahmed Quray (Abu 'Ala) and Dr. Nabil Sha'ath.[53] Quray—the PA's first economy minister and head of a National Council for the Encouragment of Investment—committed the PA to support private entrepreneurship and low inflation. By 1995 the PA had enacted an investment law designed to attract foreign investors by offering tax exemptions of up to five years. Sha'ath, a former business professor in the United States, became technology and international joint ventures minister. In a statement remarkably in tune with the internationalist profile outlined in earlier

---

[51] Center for Palestine Research and Studies (Nablus), *Results of Public Opinion Poll* (September 10–11, 1993).

[52] Brynen (1996); *Palestine Report* 27 June 1997: 15. Aid disbursements as of October 1996—$1 billion—went to infrastructure and housing (33 percent), public finance (16 percent), education (15 percent), institution building (11 percent), with only 2 percent for the PA police force (*Journal of Palestine Studies* 26, 2 Winter 1997: 134). The European Union helped establish a Center for Private Enterprise Development in Ramallah.

[53] Peres (1993) and Makovsky (1996) highlight the centrality of economic considerations for Oslo negotiators, on both sides. On Israel's poor record in attracting foreign private investment, and motivation to engage in peace talks to resolve that problem, see Halevi (1993: 97).

chapters, Sha'ath proclaimed: "We [the PA] must prepare to become a manufacturing and exporting society. . . . We do not have the weakness of Third World countries. We have neither a bureaucracy to fight nor any outside debt to reduce, and our economy is principally based in the private sector. . . . Instead of setting up a government manufacturing sector which we would then privatize, we are starting with privatization," even in infrastructural areas like electricity and communications.[54] Sha'ath stressed that a global orientation and joint ventures would, in time, yield regional economic cooperation as well, reinforcing the contention that globalization is the engine of liberalizers' cooperative postures.

The PLO/PA's and Israel's Labor cooperative course in the early 1990s illustrates how internationalist coalitions stress the maximization of international and regional economic opportunities over the maximization of land. The lessons from territorial enclaves like Singapore and Hong Kong were not lost to Oslo negotiators: neither Greater Israel (Likud's myth) nor Islamic Palestine (Hamas's myth) had much affinity with an internationalist grand strategy.[55] The new partners understood the embedded requirements of regional stability and the enormous potential of knowledge-rich "virtual states" with a global reach. Arafat's historical ability to navigate the intricate paths of Arab coalitional politics was reflected in the massive vote of confidence he won in Palestine's first democratic elections in January 1996.

Labor's grand strategy unfolded with the globalization of Israel's economy at its heart. Defense spending—an important barrier to this transformation—declined from 24 percent of central expenditures (1986) to 16 percent (1996 Labor's projected budget).[56] Once-powerful defense industries (such as Rafael, IAI, and IMI) were downsized under dwindling governmental support, growing marketization, and a changed regional environment. An independent central bank strengthened internationalist policies as it deflected from Labor populist opposition to austerity while linking economic growth to the peace process.[57] Inflation in 1995—at about 8 percent—had declined to its lowest level in decades. GDP growth doubled from 3.5 percent in 1993 to nearly 7 percent in 1994 and 10 percent during the first seven months of 1995, the highest real growth rate in 22 years.[58] Unemployment was cut in half between 1993 and

---

[54] *Haaretz*, 1 November 1995: B2; "Quray' Says Development Plan to Be Implemented," *FBIS-NES* 31 October 1994: 7. Shikaki (1996: 15) identified three main pillars of Arafat's PA coalition when it came into being: wealthy senior PLO officials and professionals socialized in Arab countries outside Palestine, business leaders from the commercial class and big families, and Palestinian Liberation Army leaders. By late 1994 Fatah was massively absorbed into the military to neutralize Hamas.

[55] On Arafat's promise to turn Gaza into a Singapore, see *al-Ahram*, 29 June 1995: 5. On the PA's emphasis on Palestinian technical and entrepreneurial skills, see Sha'ath (1996: 31).

[56] Israel Information Service (Internet) (hereafter IIS) *News Flash*, 29 November 1995: 3–4. On the progressively unsustainable burden of arms industries and acquisitions, see Peres (1993).

[57] Jacob Frankel (Jaffee Center, Tel Aviv University, Aaron Yariv Annual Lecture, 18 January 1996). On the lowest inflation levels in 1995, see *Jerusalem Report*, 10 August 1995: 45.

[58] IIS *Economic Survey* 9, 15 and 26 November 1995. *Ha'aretz* 13 November 1995. Kanovsky (1997: 5) disputes the link between the peace process and economic growth, suggesting GDP

1995—from 11 to 6 percent—despite the influx of over 600,000 Russian immigrants into a country of 4.5 million. Privatization was less impressive beyond the case of Koor Industries (formerly Histadrut), involving two banks—Mizrahi and Igud—Shekem department stores, Shikun Ufituah (housing), Israel Shipyards, and Israel Chemicals. Revenues from privatization doubled to $1.2 billion from 1992 to 1993, but slowed down afterward. Exports grew by 12 percent in 1994. From 1992 to 1995 exports to Asia grew by 187 percent. Foreign investment in Israeli stocks more than doubled from 1994 to 1995—from $1 billion to $2.1 billion—with real direct foreign investment expanding from $100 million in 1993 to $300 million in 1994 to $1.2 billion in 1995.[59] Major hotel chains increased their presence in Israel from 5 chains and 11 hotels in 1992 to 14 chains and 61 hotels in 1997.[60] In late 1995 Standard & Poor raised Israel's credit rankings from BBB + to A −, an improved rating that facilitated Israel's subsequent sale of its new bond offering, its first without the backing of the US Treasury.[61]

The globalization of the Israeli economy was matched by a globalization of Israeli diplomacy. Formal relations with 90 states in 1991 grew to 126 in 1993 and 153 in 1995. Israel's reception within the United Nations changed radically after decades of alienation. Diplomatic and trade relations with previously lukewarm partners improved dramatically. The European Union's Essen declaration in December 1994 specifically linked the Middle East Peace process to the potential of Israel's improved status vis-à-vis the EU. An expanded and deepened "Treaty of Association" with the EU replaced the 1975 agreement in 1995, as Israel became a full member of the EU's Fourth Framework Research and Development program, the only non-EU member with that status apart from Switzerland. Japan's Tomiichi Murayama visited Israel, a first by a Japanese prime minister. Embassies and markets for Israeli goods opened as far away as China, Indonesia, Japan, Korea, and India. The strategic behavior of victorious constituencies in the 1992 elections had yielded the expected fruit, but also unintended consequences.

---

growth in 1993–1995 was somewhat lower than in the three preceding years. However, his account lumps 1993—most of which preceded the Oslo agreement—with its aftermath, and uses lower real growth rates for that period than most other estimates.

[59] *Link* May–June 1996: 8; IIS *Economic Survey* 15 November 1995: 4 and 26 November 1995. The following foreign firms have purchased Israeli firms, entered joint ventures, or established research and development centers in Israel in 1995 and 1996: Intel ($1.6 billion in a new plant); Motorola ($1 billion in car electronics); Hewlett-Packard, Siemens, Applied Materials, Nestle, Danone, Microsoft, Lauder, Unilever, NEC, Volvo, and Volkswagen (the first major German investment in Israel), among others (*Globes* 1 January 1997: 37). Disney's Shamrock Holding acquired 22.5 percent of the Koor conglomerate ($252 million).

[60] The general manager of a major international hotel chain acknowledged that they "wouldn't have decided to come into Israel if there wasn't change on the horizon" (*Jerusalem Report* 10 July 1997: 40). On the explosion of tourism as an outcome of the peace process, see *Link* April 1997: 14–15.

[61] *Ha'aretz* 7 December 1995: 3. In 1995 there were more high-tech companies from Israel on the New York Stock Exchange than from any other country except Canada (Thomas Friedman, "I Dial Therefore I AM," *New York Times* 29 October 1995: 13).

The near-revolutionary changes placed domestic opponents of the internationalist strategy on a political war footing, allowing unprecedented personal political attacks on government officials and progressively more violence-prone demonstrations. These threats from militant nationalist, populist, and religious settlers triggered a large propeace, antiviolence demonstration on November 4, 1995, with nationwide participation.[62] At the very end of this event a fundamentalist Jewish extremist assassinated Prime Minister Rabin. The second onslaught on the internationalist revolution was delivered by opponents of the PA, Labor-Meretz's partners in the Palestinian camp. Endangered by peace and the PA's internationalizing stragegy alike, Islamic terrorists murdered dozens of Israeli civilians in early 1996, actions Likud and its allies used to undermine the peace process and its architects. Israeli and Palestinian statist-nationalist confessionalism acted as two jaws of a pincer movement that succeeded in stalling internationalist advances in both Israel and Palestine.

The terrorist chain and its political implications threatened the PA, derailing its economic and peace program at once. State-building had an inherent potential for expanding a clientelistic bureaucracy at the outset, but Israeli closures and the paucity of foreign private investments exacerbated the use of public-sector employment as patronage, explaining its growth from 20,000 employees in 1993 to 68,000 civilians and 30,000 policemen in 1996. Nor was the PA immune from exchanging monopolistic economic rights for political support, allegedly in the import of automobiles, cigarettes, cement, gravel, iron and steel. The PA pledged to the IMF that it would dismantle import monopolies by the end of 1998.[63] Under pressure from international donors and the Palestinian Legislative Council the PA activated an internal auditing by its Monitoring Institution to probe into financial mismanagement in some ministries. The PA struggled to build modern political and economic institutions from scratch— from a Palestinian central bank to new legal market-oriented frameworks—but also ended up with an expansive military apparatus. Moreover, no viable export-oriented strategy could be implemented with rampant unemployment, Israeli closures, and a weak transportation, communications, and energy infrastructure. Islamist terrorism contributed in foiling incipient stability and private investment, provided a justification for sprawling military agencies, and triggered further closures which—in a vicious circle—limited Palestinian access to

---

[62] Industrialist Jean Frydman, a personal friend of Shimon Peres, reportedly financed public transportation (800 buses) for this event, also supported by Dov Lautman (former president of Israel's Industrialists Association), among others. In the aftermath of the assassination, Lautman, Dani Gillerman (president of Israel's Chamber of Commerce), and others established a supportive relationship with a new local NGO, "Dor Shalom" (The Peace Generation).

[63] See *Palestine Report* 30 May 1997: 1, 3; Douglas Jehl, "Frustrated Gaza Increasingly Faults Its Rulers," *New York Times* 2 February 1997: 1; Daoud Kuttab, "Live from Ramallah," *New York Times* 6 June 1997: 19. On employment figures, see *Palestine Report* 2 May 1997: 15 and *Palestine Economic Impulse* (http://www.palecon.org/pulsedir/november/pulsnov2.html). Municipal employees in Gaza grew from 800 to 1,269 between 1994 and 1997. See also Palestine National Authority Official Website (http://www.pna.net) and United Nations Office of the Special Coordinator in the Occupied Territories Website (http://www.arts.mcgill.ca/programs/icas/icas1.html).

70,000 jobs in Israel, to foreign markets, and to industrial inputs.[64] Per capita GNP had dropped 8.5 percent in 1995 and unemployment grew from nearly 20 percent in 1995 to over 30 percent in 1996. Meanwhile Islamist charities mobilized local support through their internationally funded educational, health, and social networks. This internal Palestinian coalitional contestation had, of course, regional referents, with internationalizing partners endorsing PA efforts and statist-nationalist and confessional opponents (Iran, Syria, Iraq, and Sudan, as well as challengers of ruling internationalizers) aiding the Islamist resistance.

The subsequent fragility of internationalist coalitions in Israel and Palestine, and their mutual interactive effects, exposes the open-ended fate of the strategies they have unleashed. However, this dyad's brief internationalizing interlude (1993–1995) effected changes with dense spillovers onto the region as a whole.

Interim Achievements of an Internationalizing Cluster

The regional impact of internationalist coalitions is often a function of their political strength and related ability to fulfill all aspects of a grand strategy. To some extent Camp David was the product of frail internationalizing efforts in the 1970s. However, the coalitions represented at the Madrid Conference in 1991 were shackled by strong statist-nationalist and confessional pressures; most would have not been there without forceful US persuasion. Indeed, Madrid's immediate results were limited, although they did set in motion a process that internationalist coalitions were later able to transform into a remarkable institutional arena for multilateral negotiations.

Oslo created some of the conditions depicted in cell 1 (Figure 2) with incipient internationalizers addressing progressively deeper layers of conflict resolution, both in bilateral and multilateral contexts. The multilateral venue included unprecedented arms control negotiations, as well as comprehensive discussions on converging approaches to economic, environmental, water, and refugee issues. These negotiations superseded—to some extent—decades of regional balance-of-power politics and planted the seeds of potential future multilateral collective security arrangements.[65] This cooperative approach did not merely imply a passive acceptance of mutual concessions in the realm of security in exchange for economic advantages, as their opponents at home often argued. The domestic consequences of these cooperative policies were no less attractive: such policies were expected to free resources to address the results of declining oil prices, bloated bureaucracies, economic mismanagement, overpopulation, militarization, and foreign-policy adventurism on all sides.

The boldest cooperative breakthroughs were clearly more a product of these coalitions' strategies than of external imposition. The Oslo agreements bypassed the formal negotiations under US sponsorship, even though ensuing negotiations between the PLO (and later the PA) and Israel's Labor required occa-

---

[64] Abed (1994: 45–49); Brynen (1996).
[65] Toukan (1995); Sayigh (1995); Solingen (1995).

sional US interventions. Yet many more difficulties were resolved at the time without external pressures, suggesting a joint commitment to the peace process that did not feed merely on outside coercion. Similarly, the internal logic of the 1994 Jordanian-Israeli rapprochement is evident, among other things, from public meetings held at their mutual border even prior to White House meetings between King Hussein and Prime Minister Rabin. The US undoubtedly played an important role as moderator and guarantor in most of these unprecedented peace negotiations, particularly in the Syrian-Israeli context. Assad's continued subservience to statist-nationalist and military constituencies precluded the kind of grand strategic reversal observed in Jordan, Palestine, and Israel. Internationalizing coalitions occasionally attracted a more visible statement of international support when fundamentalists on both camps threatened the peace process. An impressive international representation—over seventy heads of state and foreign ministries—attended Prime Minister Rabin's funeral in 1995, and a similarly well-attended international antiterrorist conference took place in Sharm al-Sheikh in 1996.[66]

The architects of the peace process converged in advancing the globalization of their domestic political economies. At the top of the agenda at the Casablanca and Amman economic summits was the expansion of private-sector investment, revealing a conviction that peace and regional cooperation will trail progress, or lack thereof, in economic liberalization. In the direct style of slain Prime Minister Rabin: "To produce, to sell, to market, and to profit. None will come here [to the Middle East] because of our winning smiles; they all want to make money."[67] These summits became an opportunity for private entrepreneurs from the whole region and beyond to explore increased international and regional economic ties, as stipulated in the Casablanca Declaration in 1994: "Business leaders recognize that governments should continue to forge peace agreements and create foundations and incentives for trade and investment. They further recognize the responsibility of the private sector to apply its new influence to advance the diplomacy of peace in the Middle East and beyond. Governments affirm the indispensability of the private sector in marshalling quickly adequate resources to demonstrate the tangible benefits of peace."[68]

Casablanca laid the foundations of a future economic community connected by the free flow of goods, capital, and labor, endowing a Regional Economic Development Working Group with the task of steering multilateral economic cooperation. The Amman summit in 1995 created a regional Economic Development Bank. Economic cooperation was sometimes burdened with calculi of relative gains, particularly from those who—while wielding statist-nationalist considerations—aimed in fact at protecting potential private or public casualties of new economic arrangements.[69] Overall, however, there was unprecedented con-

[66] The people who attended this conference were labeled "Hamas's enemies" by Dr. Abdul Azeez al-Rantisi, a leading Hamas figure in Gaza (*Palestine Report* 2 May 1997: 10).

[67] Quoted in IIS *Policy Paper* 29 October 1995: 5. See also Rabin (1994).

[68] *FBIS-NES* 2 November 1994: 8–9 (Rabat Television Network).

[69] Personal interviews with representatives to multilateral economic negotiations (Athens, No-

vergence on the merits of global and regional openness. Tourism increased by about 20 percent in Jordan, Egypt, and Israel in 1995. Even though there was a realization that the economic integration of the Middle East was in its infancy, there were discussions about the possible paths such integration could follow. The shadow of the past could preclude either the Big Bang model of integration (which often follows an overarching political event) or a Hub-and-Spoke model (whereby the smaller countries integrate with the major market) that placed Israel as a hub.[70] Those most threatened by economic liberalization articulated the "threat" from Israel's economic hegemony while others built on expanding regional opportunities across borders, eschewing political considerations. Some Arab leaders discussed Israel's own Hub-and-Spoke experience—a free-trade area with the European Community and the US—as far more promising in minimizing political opposition at home. Israeli businessmen, for their part, had their eyes on expanding Asian markets, a result of Israel's increased attractiveness after Oslo. And yet the Israel Export Institute, the Israel Manufacturers Association, and the Federation of Israeli Chambers of Commerce also pursued economic cooperation with GCC countries, involving major conglomerates like Koor, the Dankner Group, and the Israel Corporation.[71] By 1997, as I discuss next, these economic scenarios had become far more hypothetical.

The expected cooperative orientation of internationalist coalitions gains confirmation in a most unlikely domain. Nuclear policies—presumed to be quintessential outcomes of security dilemma considerations and thus the toughest dependent variable, from this book's perspective—have also evolved in tandem with coalitional trends.[72] Statist-nationalist coalitions launched nuclear and ancillary programs with weapons applications in the 1950s and 1960s. Nasser attracted scientists with experience in Nazi Germany's missile and related projects, and his influential pro-Soviet advisers—Ali Sabri, Ahmed Sidki, and Hasnein Haikal—were Egypt's most fervent advocates of nuclear weapons.[73] In Israel, a small group around Prime Minister Ben-Gurion—who embodied statism—developed a nuclear program although Israel never acknowledged the possession of nuclear weapons. Statist-nationalist Iraq, Libya, Syria, and Iran have pursued weapons of mass destruction as redeeming tools. Iraq's nuclear program employed over 20,000 people and became a crowning symbol of statism and self-reliance. Although a UN Special Commission has partially neutralized aspects of this program, effective Iraqi denuclearization—and rejection of chemical and biological weapons—will be more likely under a radically

---

vember 1994; Amman, December 1995 and August 1997; Jerusalem, January 1996 and August 1997; Bahyat el-Brid, August 1997).

[70] Hufbauer and Schott (1994: 131–32).

[71] *Globes* 17 June 1997: 62–63. Personal interviews at the Institute, Manufacturers Association, and Chambers of Commerce.

[72] Solingen (1994a and 1994b).

[73] Jabber (1971: 141); Perlmutter, Handel, and Bar-Joseph (1982: 33). For the views of M. Hasnayn Heikal, an adviser to Nasser and editor of Egypt's influential *Al-Ahram*, see his article in *Al-Ahram* 23 November 1973 reported on *Foreign Broadcast Information Service* (Nonproliferation) 26 November 1973: G1, G2.

different domestic coalitional landscape. Both Iraq and Iran violated their formal NPT commitments by actively pursuing nuclear weapons in the 1980s and 1990s.

Strong opponents of a policy based on nuclear deterrence in Israel included Prime Minister Eshkol and Finance Minister Sapir, early proponents of an internationalizing strategy.[74] Other precursors of such coalitions—notably Egypt under Sadat—spearheaded a Middle East nuclear-weapons-free-zone (NWFZ), suggestively in the same year that Sadat launched infitah (1974). Most internationalizing coalitions throughout the region have ratified and abided by the Nonproliferation Treaty. Israel has not signed it but has endorsed a regional NWFZ based on mutual inspections. Labor coalitions have been more receptive to international institutions, territorial compromise, regional regimes, and arms control agreements, and most influential Labor leaders have favored a NWFZ. Yet the old statist-nationalist regional context—with its rigid Arab refusal to recognize Israel's existence—made unilateral denuclearization politically prohibitive for any coalition. Menachem Begin's Likud—under radical nationalist Rafael Eitan as chief of staff—bombed Iraq's Osirak reactor (during Israel's 1981 electoral campaign). Important Labor leaders such as Shimon Peres— sensitive to responses by international allies and institutions—opposed this defiant step and sought more time for diplomacy. Prime Minister Rabin declared in 1974—in response to Defense Minister Moshe Dayan's call for nuclear weapons—that "attempts to rely on mystical weapons are negative trends."[75] Although prominent Likud-associated leaders opposed a NWFZ—notably Sharon and Eitan—the party has no declared policy on this issue and former Prime Minister Shamir supported the NWFZ proposal. At the same time, supporters of Likud and its allies justify the use of nuclear weapons by a larger margin (46 percent in Likud, 57 percent among its allies) than supporters of Labor and its natural partners (43 and 36, respectively).[76]

The region's nuclear future created tension within the Arms Control and Regional Security working group in the multilateral negotiations in 1955. Egypt demanded that nonconventional weapons be discussed at the outset, whereas Israel demanded that they be discussed last. Prime Minister Peres declared that Israel would endorse regional denuclearization two years after a comprehensive peace settlement was signed.[77] This commitment was unprecedented and cost the prime minister political headaches at home—readily used by political opponents—considering the outstanding obstacles to regional peace, as represented by Iraq and Iran and their separate pursuit of nonconventional weapons. The epilogue of Middle East denuclearization has yet to be written, and coalitional balances—as we see next—will be likely to affect the script.

---

[74] On the politics of Israel's nuclear program, see Flapan (1974: 46–54); Evron (1974); Feldman (1982).

[75] Inbar (1986: 61–78).

[76] Arian, Talmid, and Hermann (1988: 72). On the positions of Sharon, Yuval Ne'eman, and Rafael Eitan, see Nimrod (1991: 15–18) and Bar-Joseph (1982: 205–27).

[77] Israel TV Channel 2, 24 December 1995.

A CONFESSIONAL BACKLASH? THE QUICKSANDS OF PEACEMAKING

Statist-populist and radical confessional challengers have claimed the ground as the main alternative to ruling internationalizing coalitions throughout the region. These challengers are inspired and often funded by neighboring political allies—in the best tradition of transregional coalitional intervention described earlier—but have developed rather strong native roots. Islamist blocs and movements differ in their composition but are often backed by segments of small business, rural agrarian capitalists, notables and estate-owners, state bureaucrats, the underemployed intelligentsia, and students.[78] Islamist business interests are often thickly intertwined with state entrepreneurship, bureaucracies, and the military. When in power (as in Sudan and Iran) or as the main opposition, Islamist leaders propose a political economy rooted in what they define as core Islamic principles, rejecting most international economic regimes and their alleged associated scourges: inequality, corruption, unemployment, and enslaving indebtedness.[79]

According to this neodependency populism, the West denies Islamic peoples self-determination, self-sufficiency, and control over their own resources. As articulated by Sheikh Fadlallah, leader of the Iranian-backed Lebanese Hizbolla, "it is the political and economic West with its monopolistic corporations that we oppose."[80] The strong economic foundations of this confessionalism are evident in Fadlallah's own clientelistic networks, which endow him with a fifth of the community's annual profits (*al-khums*), a legally prescribed alms tax (*zakat*), and other donations. Such confessional political entrepreneurs—from Iran to Sudan and beyond—thus fear a modern, efficient, and internationalized state that could undermine their homegrown economic structures: "We refuse that our economy or our independence should be taken over," in Fadlallah's clear formulation. Internationalist coalitions aim at shrinking many functions of the state, whereas confessional leaders aim at capturing and expanding it to promote their agenda.

In the new socio-political order against what Fadlallah defines as "the forces of World Arrogance, the forces of Western Arrogance, and the Forces of Zionist Arrogance," these coalitions have shown little space for deviants. Internal repression of dissent in Iran, Sudan, and among fundamentalist movements throughout the region leaves little room for a policy of regional reconciliation with "apostates," let alone with non-Muslims. Militant Islam has thus remained overwhelmingly opposed to the Arab-Israeli peace process. Fadlallah (1995: 74–75) has declared Israel's complete illegitimacy and has acknowledged "that we remain entrenched in our positions that may appear extremist holdout positions by today's standards." Jordan's Islamist bloc has built its political strategy by targeting a double evil: the peace process and IMF-induced economic re-

---

[78] Binder (1988); Springborg (1989: 63–69); Waterbury (1994: 28).
[79] Kuran (1993).
[80] All quotes from Fadlallah (1995: 64–67).

form. Even Egypt's Muslim Brotherhood has condemned every cooperative step from Camp David through Madrid and Oslo.[81]

In dissecting the affinity between Arab nationalism, Marxism, and Islamic fundamentalism, Rouleau (1993) identifies the latter as essentially political rather than merely concerned with ethical lifestyles. Islamism has replaced the content of pan-Arab nationalism with a different, now confessional but still populist, essence. This affinity is written into the Charter (1993: 125) of Hammas ("zeal"): "Nationalism . . . is part and parcel of religious ideology. There is not a higher peak in nationalism or depth in devotion than *Jihad* when an enemy lands on the Muslim territories." In Sudan's al-Turabi's words: "The only nationalism that is available to us, if we want to assert indigenous values, originality and independence of the West, is Islam. . . . It is the only doctrine that can serve as the national doctrine of today."[82] The use of violence by radical Islam to undermine domestic and regional adversaries is widespread, although repression may have contained its scope of action.[83] Radical Islamist states and movements have thus far captured Islam's mobilizing potential from more moderate alternatives. Yet, Islamism is not an ideological monolith; its political and economic themes vary, as do their approaches to the West. Moderate movements exist but their influence has been limited. Salamé (1993) and Razi (1990) have argued that moderates and militants play a political game that reinforces their respective bargaining power.

Islamist economics have nowhere resulted in more just, more equal, more productive, or more innovative societies.[84] Moreover, securing welfare and redistribution requires preserving the export-oriented rentier state and ties to the world economy. Even radical Islamist regimes have thus experienced liberalizing pressures. The "economy first" or "pragmatic" faction in Iran—represented by President Hashemi Rafsanjani and backed by Teheran's *bazari* (bazaar) merchants and money lenders—seeks privatization of an extensive network of state-run factories and power plants, increased trade with Europe and Asia, and a utilitarian (nonconfessional) approach to foreign policy. Opposition to Rafsanjani's liberalizing efforts from bloated Islamist bureaucracies and foundations (*bunyods*) and import-substituting interests have prevented economic reform.[85]

---

[81] Egypt's Mustafa Mashhur, deputy general guide of the Muslim Brotherhood, urged confrontation with the "enemy" ("Freedom, Elections, and Enemies," *al-Sha'b*, FBIS-NES 16 March 1995: 11). On Jordan's Islamist bloc policies, see declarations by spokesman Hamzah Mansur, in "Islamic Deputies, Others Denounce Peace Treaty," *FBIS-NES* 26 October 1994: 38–39. On racism in the Islamist opposition, see "Opponents of Peace Accord Escalate Verbal Attacks," *FBIS-NES* 27 October 1994: 32–33 (from *Jordan Times*).

[82] Viorst (1995: 54–55). On Islamism as nationalism and populism, see Leca (1994) and Budeiri (1995).

[83] Haeri (1991); Sisk (1992). On militant Islam's readiness to use violence, see Deeb (1992).

[84] Roy (1994); Kuran (1997).

[85] "Iran: Majles Sessions," *FBIS-NES* 20 October 1994: 1–15; "Taki Tarabi on Central Bank, Independence, Policies" and "Hoseyn Abrandabadi Editorial on Current Banking Problems," *FBIS-NES* 24 October 1994: 1ff., 23ff.; *New York Times* 31 January 1993: 6. On Khamenei and radical clerical opposition to Rafsanjani's efforts at privatization, deregulation of currency controls, and the

The Islamic constitution forbids foreign concessions and requires Majlis (National Assembly) approval of foreign loans. The unresolved contest between feebly liberalizing and strong radical Islamist camps helps explain the unclear and unstable nature of Iran's regional postures. 'Ali Akbar Velayati—the revolution's permanent foreign minister until 1997—highlighted Afghanistan, Palestine, Bosnia, Karabkh, and the Caucasus as Iran's major foreign-policy achievements.[86] A secret report by Iranian liberalizers from the Plan and Budget Organization, leaked to London, draws the explicit links between "normal" and positive relations with the outside world and the successful implementation of economic reform: "If our political relations with various countries are not based on mutual understanding and the elimination of disorder, the possibility of selling goods on the world's markets will be quite limited. . . . If we want to export $10–20 billion annually, naturally the existing diplomatic foundation is a very restrictive bottleneck."[87] Rarely does one get as clear a snapshot of political activities—in an authoritarian context—geared to make explicit the requirements of an internationalizing strategy. The rise of Sayed Mohammad Khatami in 1997 signaled a possible exhaustion of the radical statist-nationalist-confessional wing but not quite an internationalist shift, as we shall see below.

The opposition to Islamist statism is even weaker in Sudan. Islamist challengers elsewhere in the region lead the offensive against ruling would-be internationalizers, and have found convenient partners in secular remnants of old statist-nationalism. Egypt's Labor Socialist party, National Progressive Unionist party, and Liberal Socialist party joined in opposing an internationalizing agenda at home and in the region, upholding the interests of the "national bourgeoisie."[88] The Mubarak regime has alternated between conciliatory and repressive policies, maintaining austerity measures, export promotion, some privatization, and foreign investments, while publicizing Egypt's pressures for Israeli concessions to stem statist-nationalist criticism. Jordan's King Hussein faces a similar oppositional makeup, with the militant Islamic Group joining old secular statist-nationalists in a fierce rejection of the peace process and of economic liberalization. The Islamic Group's parliamentary strength decreased from 32 in 1989 to 18 members in 1993, but Islamist radicals have ·captured politically influential professional organizations. The state bureaucracy and symbolic analysts in professional, educational, and small-scale commercial enterprises have provided fertile ground for the opposition to economic reform and peace initiatives, the two of which are often perceived to be linked by prospects of open

---

end of food and gasoline subsidies, see Chris Hedges, "Islamic Hardliners Said to Gain Ground in Iran," *New York Times* 3 August 1994: A3. The holdings of just one bunyod—the Foundation for the Oppressed—is estimated at $12 billion. Iran's share of global GNP dropped in a single year from 0.69 (1988) to 0.40 (1989) (*IRNA* 12 August 1996 in *FBIS-NES* 14 August 1996: 57).

[86] *IRNA* 31 July 1996: 10 in *FBIS-NES* 6 August 1996: 82.

[87] *Keyhan* (London) 27 July 1995: 4, in *FBIS-NES* 26 September 1995: 1.

[88] On attempts by retired military officers to establish a new October party, aimed at economic self-reliance and war preparations against Israel, see *al-Hayah* 13 August 1996: 5 (*FBIS-NES* 14 August 1996: 8).

borders. Arafat's PA has faced challenges from Hamas and Islamic Jihad. At the height of the peace process from 1994 to early 1996 polls and Palestinian election results (in 1996) suggested that confessional and secular opponents of an internationalist strategy were weaker in Palestine than elsewhere in the region, including Israel. However, the 1996 coalitional reversal in Israel has done miracles to revive the political wherewithal of Palestinian radical counterparts.

In Iraq, the entrenched power of state enterprises and bureaucracies, the military-industrial complex, import-substituting interests, and their respective beneficiaries have obstructed anything more than limited economic reform.[89] Statism has increased, even prior to the Gulf War, with the state controlling over 80 percent of GDP in infrastructure, manufacturing, trade, and services and with military expenditures absorbing nearly 26 percent of GDP ($17 billion in 1993 constant prices) in 1985. Saddam Hussein (1979, 1992) has made Iraq among the most war-prone states in the last two decades, unleashing a bloody war with Iran in the 1980s and annexing Kuwait in 1990. According to Niblock (1993: 77), Iraq's "economy-based incentive to attack Kuwait came from the determination to maintain heavy state expenditure (on both economic and defence projects), and the lack of sufficient funds to meet this expenditure."[90] Kuwaiti oil assets would have provided the Iraqi regime with the economic wherewithal to maintain a statist and militarized grand strategy, one that was devoted extensively to military programs ($85 billion between 1980–1988 against a 1985 GDP of $47 billion).[91] This war recalls our characterization of a strong statist-nationalist coalition (Iraq) riding roughshod over its weak internationalist opposition at home and over a similarly weak ruling neighbor (Kuwait). Such conditions whet the appetite for external aggression, where the strong statist-nationalist coalition is positioned to extract vast resources from society and to convert them into a powerful military machine that, in turn, is able to extract resources from the neighborhood. Iraq's acceptance of US military support during its war against Iran, and its courting of Western Europe and Japan as relations with the Soviet Union declined, should not be confused with a grand strategic shift. All elements of the statist military regime, complete with resilient pro-Soviet constituencies, were in place. The total grip of the military-industrial complex over the Iraqi economy—deepened by nonconventional weapons programs—has been stronger than anywhere else in the region. Saddam's partnership with a statist military has been inextricable, rising together and, quite likely, falling together as well.

[89] Richards and Waterbury (1990: 255–57); Owen (1992: 152–53). On defense expenditures, see IISS (1995): 265.

[90] Against Chaudhry's (1991) thesis that privatization led to the invasion of Kuwait, Niblock argues that the social problems spawned by a very incipient economic liberalization were significant, but did not lead to Kuwait, and could have been solved if the government's attention and resources had not been directed elsewhere. Ibrahim (1994: 79) explains the invasion as a response to domestic threats from a new middle class, a modern working class, and the urban proletariat.

[91] Iraq's Foreign Minister Tariq Aziz acknowledged the impact of accumulated debts from the war with Iran and of declining oil revenues on the invasion of Kuwait. "We were near the point of economic collapse," he argued (Viorst 1991: 66).

A similar but milder syndrome has afflicted Syria's Assad. The pervasive Ba'th-run state has proven to be most resistant to reform and, despite incipient liberalizing steps, the state expanded in tandem with a "military-mercantile complex" of state firms and private contractors.[92] Even after the second "infitah" in the 1980s, the state accounted for nearly 50 percent of GDP, although the planned economy was in retreat. The collapse of the Soviet Union weakened the domestic pillars of bureaucratic statism, import-substitution, and the military-industrial complex, all of which retained economic ties with the former Eastern bloc, North Korea, and Cuba, while countering nascent private commercial and industrial groups. Students and the underemployed intelligentsia have largely remained within the statist-nationalist coalition, while a merchant class has endorsed selected aspects of an internationalizing agenda that would restrain military and statist interests and join the bandwagon of the peace process.[93] The coalitional struggle, including confessional aspects of Alawite-Sunni competition, helps to explain Syria's meandering in regional politics and its resistance to join the multilateral peace process. A Greater Syria project—retaining Lebanon and defying peace with Israel—has served the statist coalition well, as have intermittent threats against the PA, Iraq, Jordan, and Gulf states.[94] In Perthes's (1995: 264) successful formulation: "Syria's posture as a 'credible' enemy to Israel is not only of ideological and legitimatory importance. It has also been, as shown, a crucial element of the country's political economy," enabling societal mobilization, the maintenance of a huge army, and the flow of strategic rents from wealthier Arab states and ocassionally Iran. A commitment to the peace process advances an internationalizing agenda of increased foreign investment and trade. As Quandt (1995: 50) argued, "the Assad-style regime no longer gets any sort of legitimacy . . . from its sponsorship of Arab nationalism . . . that's a waning asset."

Statist-nationalist and confessional coalitions have once created the conflict-prone order described earlier in this chapter and have re-created it again at the end of the twentieth century, as they resist the inroads made by incipient internationalist strategies. "Islamic countries are beset by internal squabbles. Muslims are fighting more wars among each other than they fought against Israel. A few square meters of land here or there could lead to war between one Islamic country and the other." These are not the words of a critic of Islamism, but of none other than Sheikh Fadlallah (1995: 62), who ascribes this state of affairs—not unexpectedly—to Western designs and local proxies. Ironically, this

---

[92] On Assad's granting of broad administrative priorities to public-sector enterprises in 1994, see "Text of Legislative Decree on Public Sector," *FBIS-NES* 21 October 1994: 47–53 (from *Al-Ba'th*); Hinnebusch (1993); Heydemann (1993); Sadowski (1993: 35) Perthes (1995). On defense expenditures, see IISS (1995): 265.

[93] According to Hinnebusch (1996: 46) many in the Syrian bourgeoisie fear the prospects of Israeli competition in domestic Syrian and Gulf markets, and have therefore not pressured Assad on the peace front. On public sector managers, the military and "Eastern connections," see Lawson (1994).

[94] Noble (1991:80). On the Ba'th, the bureaucracy, and the Alawi "security barons," and their rejection of peace talks and economic reform, see Perthes (1995) and Hinnebusch (1996: 45).

is the same Fadlallah who attacked the Egyptian regime for attributing its own domestic challenges to "machinations of foreign circles." Sudan's coalition of the military and Hassan Tourabi's Islamic Front—one with little affinity with economic reform—launched an onslaught against Sudanese Christian and animist dissidents and escalated conflict with Egypt, Eritrea, and Uganda. In the early 1990s, Sudan was in a virtual state of war against *all* its neighbors, mobilized 500,000 volunteers besides its regular forces in 1995 to counter an alleged US invasion, and was under UN sanctions in 1996 for its suspected support of international terrorism.[95] Finally, all statist-nationalist-confessional regimes have hosted and funded violent opponents of the Arab-Israeli peace process, and none has joined the regional multilateral peace negotiations, let alone efforts to create a Middle East nuclear-weapons-free-zone (NWFZ). Indeed, following the Islamic revolution in 1979 Iran discontinued its active role in promoting a NWFZ. Although formally a party to the Nonproliferation Treaty (as is Iraq), Vice-President Sayed Ayatollah Mohajerani argued in 1992 that "we, the Muslims, must cooperate to produce an atomic bomb, regardless of UN efforts to prevent proliferation."[96] Operational steps by dedicated agencies have left Iranian footprints in illegal purchases of inputs for nonconventional weapons, largely from European countries. Iraq has continued to pursue these objectives even under supervision of the UN committee entrusted to dismantle them.

The challenge to Labor's grand strategy within Israel has come from Likud and its religious and secular statist-nationalist partners. As argued, Liberals within Likud represented free enterprise liberalism in Israel's early years, but Likud has progressively relied on populist and confessional support. Moreover, although historically a secular party, Likud has become the political vehicle of confessional and nationalist fundamentalism opposed to territorial compromise. Some politicians within the Likud camp favor economic liberalization, but the party has consistently sacrificed this objective in recent decades to privilege a larger populist and confessional constituency that includes: the West Bank settler movement; opponents of privatization, trade liberalization, and the contraction of the military-industrial complex; and sectors threatened by possible economic competition from liberalized regional arrangements with Arab neighbors and with the rest of the world.[97] Likud's economic policies, dictated

---

[95] Ibrahim (1994: 86); *FBIS-NES* 8 March 1995: 19–21.

[96] Hoodbhoy (1993: 43). On Iranian nuclear purchases, see KCET *Frontline*, no. 1116 "Iran and the Bomb," 13 April 1993. The chairman of the UN commission in charge of dismantling Iraq's nonconventional weapons declared as late as 1997 that "Iraq still has biological weapons sufficient to inflict casualties on the order of a nuclear attack," Barbara Crosette, "Australian to Head UN Effort to Monitor Curbs on Iraqi Arms," *New York Times* 2 May 1997: A5.

[97] Threatened sectors include construction, wood, air and land transportation, shipbuilding, metalwork, textiles, fishing, food processing, and agricultural farms, particularly moshavim. Yaacov Yonah, "The Peace Process as an Employment Problem," *Ma'ariv* (Saturday Special Annex), 19 January 1996: 24. On populist sectors' proclivity to regard the threat of war as more highly probable than peace, see Arian, Talmud, and Hermann (1988: 72). On the socioeconomic profile of voters for Likud and its political allies on the one hand, and labor and the left on the other, see Arian (1998).

by expansionary demands from these populist, statist, and confessional partners, have alienated the bulk of Israel's globally oriented entrepreneurs, symbolic analysts and technicians, a vast corps of highly skilled labor, and service firms. In 1991 Likud forfeited US loan guarantees that would fuel economic modernization (but precluded investments in the West Bank) in order to retain settler support. It relied on myths of self-reliance, military prowess, and high mistrust of international "allies" and institutions, as articulated by Tzomet Minister Rafael Eitan: "what the world thinks does not matter at all."[98] The assassination of Prime Minister Rabin was a symptom of a deeper tendency in extreme religious groups—massively favoring Likud's Benjamin Netanyahu—to impose a fundamentalist content on the Israeli state.

The May 1996 elections strengthened these patterns, with a dramatic decline of the secular Likud in the Knesset elections and rise of orthodox religious parties and moderately religious populists, mostly Sephardic, represented by Shas. Following an electoral reform, Netanyahu won the first direct elections for prime minister by less than 30 thousand votes, and crafted a coalition that favored statist, ultranationalist, and confessional partners over a frail (proto)liberalizing wing, represented by Finance Minister Dan Meridor, whom Netanyahu initially excluded.[99] Even secular ministers such as Foreign Minister David Levy (Gesher faction) and Infrastructures Minister Ariel Sharon share a statist-nationalist agenda, imposing deficitary construction and settlement projects in the West Bank while opposing budget cuts designed to attract foreign investors. Religious parties, for their part, have always excelled at rent-seeking, expanding government budgets to service the social, educational, and political institutions of their rapidly proliferating constituencies within and beyond the Green Line.[100] None of the four ministers representing religious constituencies voted in favor of the budget cuts proposed to the cabinet for the 1998 budget. Private entrepreneurs were not swayed by Netanyahu's lip-service campaign rhetoric of macroeconomic stability and reform, and read his coalition's likely economic

---

[98] Dvorah Getzler, "World Criticism Doesn't Matter," *Jerusalem Post International Edition* 12 March 1988: 6. On the anti-Western element among some fundamentalist groups in Israel, see Joel Greenberg, "Settlement Vows Fight on Peace Plan," *New York Times* 21 February 1994: A4. On how cultural elements of globalization associated with Labor policies mobilized the orthodox vote overwhelmingly toward Netanyahu, see Thomas Friedman, "The Ghetto or the Global Village?" *New York Times*, 22 September 1996: 13.

[99] Likud activists imposed Meridor on Netanyahu's cabinet. On Meridor's eventual departure from the coalition and on how his views diverge from those of Netanyahu on Arab-Palestinian relations, see *al-Shark al-Awsat* 6 July 1997: 3. On Netanyahu as the candidate of those who favor the old welfare state and the new fundamentalists, see Zeev Hafets, "Lightning vs. God's Gift," *Jerusalem Report* 26 June 1997: 21.

[100] On their support for bread, cigarettes, and gasoline subsidies, see *Hatzofeh* 2 July 1997. On their veto of budget cuts, see *Ha'aretz* 15 August 1997: A2. On a religious party's demand for a half billion new Israeli shekels allocation for its institutions, see *Ha'aretz* 18 October 1996: 1. On pressures from Levy's faction (Gesher) for increased subsidies to his constituents, see *Ma'ariv* 14 July 1997. On Sharon's and Levy's statism, see Yossi Melman, "Sharon gets His Cabinet Post, but His Power Is Diminishing," *Los Angeles Times*, 14 July 1996: M2. On Sharon as working "to increase government involvement in the economic sectors for which he was responsible," see *Ha'aretz* 3 June 1996.

performance differently when they cast their votes for Labor. During his first weeks in office Netanyahu proclaimed his administration to be at the vanguard of genuine economic liberalization. However, he quickly gravitated toward the statist and nationalist agenda of coalitional partners that clearly undermined the bulk of such reforms. Business leaders were reported to urge him to show moderation on security issues, fearing his coalition would doom domestic and foreign investment.[101]

Islamic terror in early 1996 had derailed Labor's strategy politically and economically. Labor allowed public-sector salaries to rise in a pre-election period, leading to a NIS (New Israeli shekels) 3 billion budget deficit. In four months Netanyahu deepened this deficit by 50 percent—to NIS 4.5 billion—and by the end of 1996 the budget deficit had ballooned to 5 percent of GDP. In 1996 and early 1997 the Israeli economy was still fueled by the positive shocks of the preceding two years. Foreign investment flows continued, and the independent central bank governor Jacob Frankel imposed fiscal restraint and macroeconomic stability. However, the 4.5 percent GDP growth rate—in annual terms—in the first half of 1996 (under Labor) declined to 2.7 in the second half of the year (under Netanyahu). By 1997 the crisis of confidence unleashed by Netanyahu's coalition had damaged a thriving economy. Israel's economic growth for 1997 plummeted to 2.2 percent, an effective 0.5 economic contraction and less than half of the average growth rate for much of the 1990s. Unemployment surged to its highest level in three years (8 percent). The Jerusalem Business Conference—held annually since 1992 with great success—and others like it, were canceled in 1997 due to the difficulties of attracting participation "in the current atmosphere."[102] The wave of privatizations started under Labor-Meretz continued with the sale of Israel Chemicals and of government shares in Bank Leumi and Israel Discount Bank. Privatization provided an opportunity to dispose of agencies and firms associated with Labor, such as the Egged bus cooperative and the Israel Broadcasting Authority. The latter's TV Channel 1 had disclosed the damaging Bar-On affair that engulfed Netanyahu's coalition in early 1997. Once again—as with the 1982 war in Lebanon and the intifada—the corollaries of Likud's policies brought about severe dips in Israel's tourism.

A report from Israel's independent central bank blamed slower growth on political and security uncertainty, in addition to lower immigration and a decrease in demand by the public sector. Israel's Manufacturers Association's Strategic Planning Committee formulated a position paper calling on Netanyahu to adopt more policies promoting economic globalization. Israeli exports to Japan—which had grown by 50 percent since 1993 to $1.1 billion by 1996—declined by 14 percent in the first nine months of 1997. Netanyahu's trip to

[101] Joseph Berger, "Israeli Executives Urge Moderation on Netanyahu," *New York Times*, 8 June 1996: 3.

[102] *Jerusalem Report* 26 June 1997: 6, 17–22. Quarterly data on GDP growth rates are from *Ha'aretz* 7 November 1997: 6; *Link* March 1997: 18; and data on declining tourism from *Link* April 1997: 14–15.

Japan attracted more criticism than investments, allowing Japan's Foreign Ministry officials to remind Netanyahu that large Japanese companies would not invest in Israel until regional diplomatic issues were settled. Herein lies the weakest link in Netanyahu's proclaimed endorsement of free markets: his regional policies are perceived to be a main obstacle in the road to Israel's effective internationalization. In the words of key foreign investor Stanley Gold of Shamrock Holdings, Inc., the Disney family holding company, and chairman of the board of Israel's most successful conglomerate Koor, Shamrock's enthusiasm has been checked by "the breakdown, halt, or at least a delay in the peace process," and by doubts about the country's economic mismanagement.[103] One barometer of Israel's relative economic attractiveness—the World Competitiveness Scoreboard—demoted it from 24th to 26th place in the global ranking between 1996 and 1997. Rankings are performed during the first half of every year, so 1996 still addresses a Labor-led economy (Likud assumed power in June of 1996). A more disaggregated ranking shows Israel upgrading its "internationalization" score from 22nd place in 1995 to 18th place in 1996 (under Labor), with the Likud coalition downgrading it to 34th place after one year in power. On the "government" ranking category—a cluster able to detect levels of "statism"—Israel improved from 38th to 31st place (1995 to 1996, under Labor), only to decline to 36th place in 1997. In "finance" there was a stellar improvement between 1995 and 1996, from 32nd to 24th place, overturned by 1997 to 30th place.[104] Although these rankings should be read with great care, as they also reflect other states' performances, they build on the most comprehensive set of variables that might be summoned to evaluate the depth of internationalist (and conversely, of statist-nationalist) policies. Moreover, it might be argued that given the relative stability of a key competitiveness factor—a dynamic high-tech sector—Israel's decline in merely one year had been particularly dramatic.[105]

The economic slowdown was matched by Netanyahu's erosion of all cooper-

[103] Michael Eilan, "Not a Pretty Place to Invest, Not a Pretty Place to Support," *Link* 6,56 (May–June 1997): 45. On the Central Bank's report, see IIS *Economic Survey*, 17 November 1997: 2. See also Central Bank Governor Jacob Frenkel's statement: "I think there is no doubt that the position of the Israeli economy today in the world capital markets has improved significantly with the peace process. Israel attracted foreign investment and its rating as sovereign borrower was significantly upgraded" (Avi Temkin and Michael Eilan interview with Jacob Frenkel, "Frenkel's Long-Term Targets," *Link* 6,5 (September 1996): 22–23. On Netanyahu's Japan visit, see *Jerusalem Report* 18 September 1997: 6.

[104] International Institute for Management Development (1997). The "internationalization" ranking builds on the following factors: openness, national protectionism, balance of payments, exports and imports of goods and services, foreign direct investments, exchange rates. "Government" includes: national debt, government expenditures, fiscal policies, state efficiency, state involvement, justice and security. "Finance" includes: banking sector efficiency, stock market dynamism, availability and cost of capital.

[105] A year into his tenure, this economic reality has come to haunt Netanyahu, who now warned his cabinet of lower credit ratings in the face of budget deficits and a stagnant economy. See "Prime Minister's Comments before Cabinet Meeting to Cut 1997 Budget," *Israel Economic Update* 25 July 1997: 1.

ative regional frameworks, in spite of some initial leeway granted him by his Arab interlocutors. Netanyahu consistently undermined the PA, proclaimed and executed renewed West Bank settlement growth, and aggressively exacerbated tensions over Jerusalem's future status. These policies induced a new level of violence in September 1996, now between armed PA police and Israeli soldiers. A deepened hostility with Syria revived the possibility of war, exacerbating further a growing gap between Netanyahu's coalition and military officers.[106] The armed forces (IDF) have not remained aloof from broader internationalizing socio-political and economic changes centering on the peace process, and have been adjusting to what Ehud Barak, former chief of staff and Labor's leader in 1997, labeled "a smaller and more clever I.D.F."[107] Statist-nationalist grand strategies had lost out massively among IDF rank and file.[108] The peace process was in virtual coma by 1997, reaching its deepest valley since the intifada, which now showed signs of revival. Indeed, Netanyahu brought US-Israeli relations to new lows as well, despite a Clinton administration that had shown support for Israel as no other US president before. Netanyahu's American upbringing has not precluded him from steering his coalition away from US preferences, as a condition for holding the coalition—and his power—together. On Israel radio he declared defiantly: "Although relations with the US are a strategic asset of the utmost importance, they are not the supreme asset of the State of Israel. . . . The supreme asset is our security. The supreme asset is things holy to us like Jerusalem."[109] The confessional rhetoric had overtaken an otherwise secular political entrepreneur even in the revered domain of US-Israeli relations.

As expected, Netanyahu's policies galvanized analogous political forces throughout the Arab world, leading to a politically debilitated PA and a revitalized Islamist opposition, a redeemed Syrian regional status, the first Arab Summit in six years, and increased nationalist and fundamentalist pressure on Arab leaders associated with the peace process. Incipient business contacts with GCC states were reversed and a June 1997 meeting in Cairo all but reinstated boycott mechanisms (straw companies, the use of third countries).[110] The Fourth Economic Summit in November 1997 in Qatar reflected the complete reversal of previous multilateral achievements. The PA, still struggling to define the economic and political parameters of the state-in-the-making, began progres-

---

[106] There have been reported contacts between independent Israeli businessmen and Syrian officials to restart bilateral negotiations, suggesting a new level of political activism by resourceful internationalist constituencies threatened by Netanyahu's policies. Netanyahu denied they were acting on behalf of his government (Israel, Cabinet Communique, Israel Foreign Ministry Information Division 6 July 1997, via Internet).

[107] Clyde Haberman, "Israelis Deglamorize the Military," *New York Times* 31 May 1995: A9.

[108] For public endorsements of the peace process signed by dozens of top-ranking former military officials during the 1996 elections campaign, see *Ha'aretz* and *Jerusalem Post* 27–29 May 1996.

[109] *Jerusalem Report* 17 October 1996.

[110] Qatar had previously allowed Israel to open a trade office but Arab pressure against Netanyahu's policies forced Qatar to freeze relations with Israel (Douglas Jehl, "Arabs Cool on Meeting with Israel on Closer Ties," *New York Times* 11 July 1997: A3.

sively distancing itself from earlier policies. Meager private foreign investment flows into Palestine and Israel's closure of Palestinian territories—both a result of Islamist terror—could not broaden domestic constituencies favorable to the PA's initial policies. The PA began alternating between repressing Islamist activists and unleashing them in response to Netanyahu's provocations, between proclaiming a privatized economy and building up a centralized and militarized one, between promoting a strategic endorsement of peace and mobilizing violent protests against Netanyahu's policies. In sum, Arafat was now the subject of a "double whammy" syndrome identified in Chapter Three (quadrants 2_{II} and 4_{III}). An incipient—indeed feeble—internationalist coalition under assault by statist-nationalist confessionalism at home and in the region had turned to the themes of its domestic opposition to advance its short-term survival while threatening its long-term interests, at home and abroad. This scenario heightened the potential for militarized hostilities.

This overview suggests that statist-nationalist and confessional challenges to internationalizing coalitions—from within and without—are strong throughout the region. This opposition is effectively organized, poses a formidable barrier to economic reform and peace, and fuels the rise of political clones across borders. The emergence of nascent collective security mechanisms within the internationalist camp had created a balance of power between it and the statist-nationalist-confessional camp, now shattered by the return to power of Israel's statist-nationalist-confessional coalition. These reversals emphasize how misleading it is to conceive of regions merely in classical interstate balance-of-power terms with relatively fixed geostrategic characteristics. Tracking domestic coalitional formations and their projection in the region seem far more useful. The balance of power is coalitional, and is played out domestically and regionally. Both economic reform and the peace process hang on this balance.

THE DEMOCRATIC PEACE: SOME MIDDLE EASTERN DILEMMAS

It is now time to examine the impact of democratization on the peace process in light of the hypotheses suggested in Chapter Four. To begin with, the debate over the democratic peace phenomenon strictly considered is not pertinent here, for the following reasons: First, in general terms, although with some caveats, Arab-Israeli relations in war and peace as analyzed so far have involved a single democracy (Israel) facing an array of nondemocratic regimes.[111] We essentially lack the building blocks of the democratic peace hypothesis: two inter-

---

[111] By Dahl's (1989: 221) definition, only Israel within the 1967 borders can be considered democratic, and even there coalitional politics have yielded some success to the attempts of religious fundamentalists to undermine democratic standards (Sprinzak and Diamond 1993). No Arab state meets the bulk of Dahl's criteria, but a slow movement toward some of the institutions of polyarchy was evident in Jordan, Tunisia, Morocco, Egypt, Mauritania, Kuwait, Yemen, and most recently, Palestine.

active democracies.[112] Second, the absence of democratic dyads was correlated with military conflict and with a more or less permanent war potential since 1948 and even earlier. However, the very same dyads that waged wars for decades shifted gears, beginning with Egypt and Israel in 1979, and followed by Israel and the PLO in 1993 and Israel and Jordan in 1994. These dramatic reversals toward cooperation have not taken place in the domain specified by democratic peace thinking: the onset of peace negotiations cannot be traced to democratic partners in action, although Jordan-Israel comes closest to that case. Third, these shifts toward cooperation do not necessarily harm the democratic peace theory, which only holds that democracy is generally sufficient—but not necessary—for the avoidance of war. Fourth, in 1996 elections placed Palestine, together with Jordan, at the forefront of democratization in the Arab Middle East. This uneven, slow, and incipient process may alleviate somewhat the problem of little variance in the independent variable (long-standing non-democracies in the Arab world), and allow us to gauge the preliminary impact of change toward democracy on the foreign policy of democratizing Arab states.

Democratization in the Arab world—wherever it is happening—has been characterized by two main features, both of which arguably pose a dilemma for the sustainability of the peace process: "first above, then below," and "first democracy, then theocracy?"[113]

First Above, Then Below. "Democratization from above" originates with state officials seeking to coopt influential actors while regulating the expansion of political rights.[114] Sadat in the 1970s and Mubarak in the 1980s initiated such incremental reforms, and Ben Ali of Tunisia and King Hussein of Jordan gathered key figures to work out national pacts (rules of procedure and limits to oppositional activity). Saudi Arabia's king chose sixty members for a newly established Consultative Council (Majlis al-Shura) in 1993, revealing the narrow boundaries of political openness there. Kuwait held elections for the National Assembly in 1992 after a suspension of that body since 1986, in a first wave of political reform. In Tunisia, Algeria, and Egypt control over the content of political programs and party policies, party registration, permits for meetings and rallies, and other political activities have yielded sometimes 95 percent support for incumbent regimes. An exception to the general trend of democratizing from above were developments in the Palestinian camp, where

---

[112] Hudson (1995) argued the counterfactual: even if Arab states had been democracies throughout the last decades, they would not have pursued peace with Israel. This position is compatible with a coalitional argument: not the absence of democracy but the presence of strong statist-nationalist coalitions helps account for half a century of wars and conflict.

[113] For bibliographic references and an expanded treatment of democratization in the Arab world, see Solingen (1996a).

[114] This section builds, inter alia, on Vandewalle (1992), Pool (1993), Ghabra (1994), Harik (1994), and Norton (1995). See also *FBIS-NES* 10 March 1995: 23 and 14 March 1995: 12.

pressures from below operated very forcefully to implement scheduled elections in January 1996.[115]

Democratization from above has four main implications for democratic stability and for the peace process. First, systematic comparative research suggests that democratization through pact making among relevant elites appears better able to secure peaceful transitions to a stable democracy than transitions involving violent uprisings.[116] Such aggregate evidence bodes well for processes at work in Jordan and Palestine, despite intermittent difficulties. Second, Mansfield and Snyder (1995) suggest that former authoritarian states in which democratic participation is on the rise are more likely to engage in wars than are stable democracies or stable autocracies. Moreover, states that make the biggest leap into extensive mass democracy are nearly twice as likely to fight wars in the decade after democratization as are states that remain autocracies. Democratization from above may cushion some of these effects. Third, the peace process itself—Oslo and its diplomatic aftermath—was constructed "from above" on all sides. "Peace from above" does not make peace undemocratic if incumbents eventually face the electoral outcomes of their foreign policy decisions, as Israel's Labor-Meretz have. Fourth, when democratization stalls and falls short of delivering on broadened civil, political, human, and economic rights, such failure undermines leaders associated with the peace process. Under such conditions political challengers have conveniently draped their opposition to peace in prodemocracy rhetoric.

First Democracy, Then Theocracy? This potential sequence has presented some ruling coalitions with an excruciating dilemma: will democratization lead to democracy or to Islamic theocracies? An extensive scholarship and exegesis has not reached any consensus on the compatibility between Islamic doctrine and democracy.[117] Beyond this philosophical debate, the actual behavior of extant regimes in Iran and Sudan does not bode well for democratic stability under their brand of Islamism. These theocratic states leave little room for dissent, deny basic political and human rights, and have aimed at physically eliminating selected ethnic and religious minorities (such as Kurds, Baha'is, Christians, and animists) and political adversaries. Only Iraq has a worse record of ethnic and political "cleansing." The platforms of most Islamist challengers include the establishment of an Islamic state as their central declared objective. The 1991 Algerian coup exemplified a dilemma between two authoritarian outcomes, one theocratic, the other military. Islamic Salvation Front preachers (not just the Armed Islamic Group) were openly disdainful of democracy and unwilling to guarantee elections beyond 1992.[118] Palestinian Islamists dismiss de-

---

[115] Shikaki (1994); Muslih (1995).

[116] O'Donnell, Schmitter and Whitehead (1986); Karl and Schmitter (1991).

[117] For a sample of arguments on both sides, see Voll and Esposito (1994) and AbuKhalil (1994). On Islamic liberals and their affinity with democracy, see Binder (1988) and Ayubi (1991: 201–13).

[118] Dunn (1994); Quandt (1994: 5); Sivan (1995).

mocracy as "a Western concept with no place in a Muslim society."[119] The editor of *al-Hayat*, Jihad al-Khazen, argued that "Muslim fundamentalist parties are undemocratic, no matter what they say."[120] Clearly, a strong democratic Islamic current has not become evident yet, beyond tactical reliance on elections as a springboard to power.

Even if democratic tendencies within Islamist movements are weak, extant evidence suggests that democratic inclusion can moderate such movements where they exist, while marginalizing their radical fringe. Democratic inclusion has resulted in Islamist gains of no more than 30 percent of the vote and appears to have led to diminishing political returns for Islamist movements, as their declining electoral performance in Jordanian (1989, 1993) and Palestinian (1995, 1996) polls and elections suggests. Sudan's National Islamic Front never won more than 20 percent, while Tunisia's Mouvement de la Tendence Islamiste (renamed Hizb al-Nahdha or Renaissance party) captured about 14 percent in 1989. Candidates affiliated with Islamist groups won only six of eighty-eight seats in the 1996 Palestinian elections. These trends vindicate what might be labeled the "balloon theory" of radical Islam, premised on the view that rank-and-file supporters are "remarkably mobile in terms of granting and withdrawing their allegiance."[121] Some Middle East regimes—notably Algeria and Egypt—have not risked potentially unfavorable outcomes and have thus contained the Islamist opposition through repression, imprisoning members presumed to support violence, attacking fundamentalist strongholds, and (in Egypt) suppressing Islamist candidates in legislative and union elections.

The theocracy-follows-democracy sequence—a contested hypothesis—has implications for the peace process. Scholars who are persuaded that this sequence is quite likely have warned that where radical Islamist leaders hijack democratization and establish theocracies, democracy itself will wither away and so will peace. They base their judgment on the public record and on expressed political agendas of the radical Islamist opposition and of regimes in power in Sudan and Iran. Aggregate studies have also shown that changes toward autocracy, including reverting to autocracy after experiments with democracy, increase the probability of war. As Mansfield and Snyder suggest, this pattern reflects the successful use of nationalist formulas and of democratic openings in order to develop populist legitimacy, while dismantling the democratic process itself. Others do not regard the sequence democracy-theocracy-war as inevitable or most likely, and advocate Islamist inclusion and greater attention to nonviolent Islamist movements. Without their combative, messianic, and radical overtone, there is little indication of the political appeal such movements might have. For now, even presumed moderate strands such as Tunisia's Rashid Ghannouchi's

---

[119] Abu-Amr (1993: 18).

[120] Al-Khazen (1995: 71).

[121] Norton (1995: 2). Rouleau (1993: 45) described Hamas as "a balloon that will deflate the moment the PLO gets something significant from the Israelis." On potentially inflated claims of fundamentalist support throughout the region, see Kuran (1997) and on democratic inclusion, Mottahedeh (1995) and Razi (1990).

retain struggle with "the other" as the pivotal conceptual and programmatic component in Islamism.[122] At the same time, preliminary evidence suggests that democratic inclusion can tame these movements' modus operandi—if not their strategic objectives—while deflating some of their appeal.

At least four scenarios connecting democratization, radical Islamist challenges, and the peace process have emerged:

1. Where democratization leads to a radical Islamist takeover—as in Iran and Sudan—the prospects for peaceful regional accommodation seem weakest.

2. Where democratization allows the expression of Islamist movements—and is able to deflate their oppositional potential, as in the Jordanian and Palestinian elections—continued support for the peace process seems more viable. Chairman Arafat entered Gaza in 1993 with only 41 percent of Palestinians supporting the peace process, and democratically elected President Arafat collected over 80 percent of the vote in 1996. Hamas was decimated in the elections, as the "balloon theory" predicted, counter to Likud's perennial bet on scenario 1.

3. Where democratization is selectively extended to coopt important secular political groups previously excluded, while keeping Islamist forces at bay—as in Tunisia—regimes can also sustain their commitment to the peace process, but under greater constraints than in scenario 2.

4. Where democratization stalls, failing to coopt important secular groups, regimes may aim at the physical elimination of the radical Islamist opposition—as in Egypt—but also fail to broaden support for the peace process.

Fundamentalist threats hover over Israel's democracy as well, but democratic institutions there are half a century old and deeply rooted.[123] As in the Arab camp, there are philosophical exponents of theocracy—even in academia—as well as terrorist practitioners, such as Prime Minister Rabin's assassin and settler Baruch Goldstein and their sympathizers. Extreme ultranationalist messianic movements, for whom the maintenance of Greater Israel overrides the legitimacy of Israel's elected government, are a growing danger to both democracy and peace. Their electoral strength is low, although rising "moderate" wings have not always effectively dissociated themselves from their antidemocratic partners. Their joint political game sometimes parallels the one Salamé identified for the Arab world. The first year of Netanyahu's coalition provides forceful evidence of the capacity of Israeli fundamentalism to wreak havoc and violence throughout the outstanding Palestinian-Israeli negotiations. This coalition has also reversed the deepening of Israeli democratic institutions under Labor-Meretz, which strengthened constitutionalism and civil—including Arab—rights. The Human Dignity and Freedom Act and the Freedom of Occupation Act of 1992 were building blocks of a Bill of Rights, granting the Supreme Court powers to overturn legislation that violated those rights. Under Netanyahu, Supreme Court judges have become subjects of assassination

---

[122] Filali-Ansary (1996: 78).

[123] These threats are analyzed in Sprinzak (1991), Liebman (1993), and Lustick (1994).

threats from religious fundamentalists, leading to no coherent governmental attempt to draw a sharp line in defense of democratic institutions.

The Triad: Economic Liberalization, Democratization, and Peace

The most important interactions among economic liberalization, democratization, and peace in the Middle East context can be summarized as follows.

First the Market, Then Democracy. Unlike sequences between political and economic liberalization elsewhere (in Latin America, for instance) economic liberalization in the Middle East preceded democratization, although in some cases the twin reforms were initiated more or less concomitantly. Morocco initiated economic reforms during the second half of the 1970s and followed up with selective steps at democratization. In 1993, Morocco's freest parliamentary elections since the 1960s came in the wake of a new wave of extensive privatization efforts. Egypt began its return to multiparty politics in 1976, trailing infitah, which was launched in 1974. Economic liberalization and privatization in Tunisia began under Habib Bourguiba and were followed by Zine al-Abidine Ben Ali's political opening. Transitions to multiparty systems in Algeria, Yemen, and Jordan in the late 1980s similarly followed incipient economic liberalization in the early 1980s. Qatar's Sheikh Khalifa al-Thani introduced major changes in the family's traditional economic control of the state, proceeding to abolish censorship, institute freedom of the press, and schedule unprecedented municipal elections, allowing women to vote. Lebanon's pre-1970s brand of democracy operated against the background of a minimal state and a more or less laissez-faire economy dominated by bankers and merchants.

The political logic behind this sequence may be stated as follows: economic liberalization leads to austerity programs, which in turn leads to public protest fueled by Islamist radicalism, which forces political liberalization.[124] The experience of Egypt in 1981, in Tunisia 1987, Algeria in 1988, and Jordan in 1989 appears to support this interpretation. The theory of "democratic efficiency" reviewed in Chapter Four might be marshaled to explain this process. Accordingly, authoritarian leaders realize the need to democratize—even if at an exceedingly slow rate—to enable economic reform, without which their grip on power would wane. Dependence on electoral support arguably forces politicians to consider the general welfare more seriously than in the absence of such dependence. Moreover, political liberalization can help build new political coalitions to counter the lingering power of state bureaucrats and other opponents of economic reform, as Sadat and Ben Jadid clearly had in mind. The drive for economic liberalization also requires a good image abroad, adding to the pressure for democratization.[125] Political motions in the direction of democratization

---

[124] El Sayyid (1994).
[125] Niblock (1993).

do not necessarily cancel the ability to impose economic liberalization from above.

Given the piecemeal and incipient stages of both political and economic liberalization, the Arab world in the early 1990s seems suspended between the "democratic efficiency" and the "authoritarian advantage" models, with different regimes leaning to one side or the other. If the former model has it right, deepening economic liberalization may underpin deepening democratization. However, even if markets are a necessary condition for democracy—they create conditions for sustained economic growth in the long term while diffusing economic and political control over resources—they are certainly not sufficient.[126] In fact, as an earlier discussion on myopic economic reform suggested, unleashing market forces without attention to distributional consequences can have detrimental political effects on the democratic process. Ruling coalitions pursuing economic liberalization throughout the region are often oblivious to these effects. The second model does not seem viable—at least not at a low political cost—for those regimes that have already set themselves on the road of democratization. At any rate, either model presumes an effective commitment to economic liberalization, a commitment that has so far been more rhetorical than practical throughout the region. Egypt provides a paradigm for little structural adjustment, regulatory reform, privatization, or trade liberalization, whereas Jordan began moving forward more swiftly on all fronts.[127]

Considering the Middle Eastern regimes that have *not* democratized renders further credence to the link between economic liberalization and democratization. Those found to be most resistant to economic liberalization are also most resistant to democratization. First, Syria's personalistic authoritarian state has battled most demands for democratization with unusual brutality. The Ba'th-dominated National Progressive Front won two-thirds of the parliamentary seats in 1991, with elections limiting political competition mostly to rival groups within the dominant coalition. Second, Iran's Fourth Islamic Majlis elected in 1992 was no more than a regulated factional rivalry between religious power blocs: Rafsanjani's Ruhaniyat and the opposing Ruhaniyoun. Candidates without a "practical commitment to Islam and to the Islamic government" were barred from running, a Council of Guardians checked the "credentials" of prospective candidates, and the armed forces are required by law to defend the Islamic regime, rather than merely Iran's territorial integrity.[128] Repression and violence have been central instruments of state policy in Iran, despite a relatively lively press. The 1997 election of "moderate" Khatami could signal a move toward greater political and economic openness. Slow economic growth and high inflation seem to have played an important role in swaying the electo-

---

[126] Nelson (1994); Maravall (1994).

[127] Cassandra (1995: 13). Fahed Al Fanek, "Economy to Grow by 20 percent in 3 Years." *Jordan Times* 17 December 1995: 6; Suleiman Al Khalidi, "Cabinet Approves Key Foreign Ownership Law." *Jordan Times*, 19 December 1995: 8.

[128] "Complete Regulations of the Islamic Republic of Iran Armed Forces," *FBIS-NES*, 27 October 1994:14–16.

rate toward Khatami. However, the essentially authoritarian nature of Iranian politics remains evident, as Ali Khamenei—the spiritual but unelected leader—remains the ultimate decision-making authority.[129] Third, any meaningful effort at democratizing a brutal regime has evaded Iraq so far. Finally, Sudan's military-Islamist coalition has *reversed* democratization, and ruled through harsh authoritarianism, despite mock elections.[130] In sum, all four regimes have defied pressures for economic liberalization and democratization alike.

First the Market, Then Peace and *Democracy?* Economic liberalization has been generally conducive to the inception of democratization in the Middle East, and the reverse sequence does not seem to have seized this region yet. Efforts to liberalize the economy accompanied by moves toward democratization from above have also been on the whole propitious to peace. Islamist radicalism has not been able—as of 1997—to gain electoral support for a reversal of incipient economic liberalization or the peace process. Secular opponents of economic liberalization and the peace process in Jordan or Palestine have not attracted large-scale populist support against either. However, the affinity between transitional democracies and populism identified by Kaufman and Stallings (1991) cannot be discounted. Some opponents of economic reform and the peace process in the 1990s are political successors—now committed to democracy—of an old political and economic Arab nationalism with a rather poor historical record vis-à-vis democracy.[131] As Harik (1994: 45) argued: "During this century, Arab nationalism has shown itself to be less tolerant and has allowed less room for democracy, both in theory and in practice, than Islam. Concerned mainly with vindicating communal identity and winning freedom from colonialism, Arab nationalism has long stressed political unification and uniform national character, allowing very little room for diversity." While retaining anticolonial rhetoric, now defined as antiglobalization, these political groups are an integral part of statist-nationalist and confessional coalitions. Where these coalitions rule—Syria, Iraq, Iran, and Sudan—there is the highest resistance to democratization, economic liberalization, and peacemaking. No leaps into high levels of mass participation—the prospects of any of these autocracies turning fully democratic in rapid sequence—seem in the immediate offing. Yet stable autocracies are not a good bet for stable peace, either.

Insofar as economic reform has imposed a dramatic contraction of military budgets and of the military-industrial complex as a whole, the potential for the Middle East to overcome half a century of militarization is significant. This process is intrinsically related to the prospects for both democracy and peace.[132] The fit between incipient efforts to liberalize the economy, democratize the

---

[129] Stephen Kinzer, "Many Iranians Hope Mandate Brings Change," *New York Times* 26 May 1997: A1.

[130] Harik (1994: 52); *FBIS* 8 March 1995: 21–22.

[131] Salamé (1994). On how the prevailing populist discourse in the Arab world has stunted the growth of pluralist democratic currents, see al-Azmeh (1994).

[132] Goldberg (1996); Crystal (1994); Hudson (1996).

polity, and endorse the peace process has thus been rather significant, and particularly evident in Jordan, Palestine, Tunisia, Morocco, Qatar, and to a lesser extent in Egypt.[133] The more consolidated democratizing regimes become, the less likely they are to experiment with populism and war. However, the feeble nature of both democratization and economic liberalization, and the unintended effects of both (Islamist activism and socio-economic upheaval), have posited serious dilemmas for ruling coalitions and endangered their peace strategies. The consolidation of a genuine democratic opening, and one sensitive to the distributive impact of economic liberalization, is a necessary condition for sustaining a peace negotiated from above.

Finally, Israel is no less subject to mutual interactions between economic reform, democracy, and the peace process. All in all, the three processes have progressed in tandem during the brief internationalist Labor-Meretz interlude and regressed—to differing degrees—in the aftermath of the statist-nationalist-confessional reversal of May 1996. Given the unwieldy nature of Israeli coalitions one cannot dismiss the potential for dramatic changes in either direction. These may include a redefinition of the Likud party's political strategy by Netanyahu, given the exhorbitant price exacted thus far by his religious allies along all three dimensions: economic reform, Israel's democratic essence, and the prospects of peace.

IMPLICATIONS FOR COALITIONAL ANALYSIS AND
THE DEMOCRATIC PEACE HYPOTHESIS

The Middle East is likely to become a critical testing ground for the democratic peace hypothesis if, in a historically highly belligerent regional context, peace takes root in tandem with democratic political structures. However, only preliminary lessons can be learned thus far, with progress far too tenuous to sustain a methodologically sound analysis of that hypothesis in this region yet. Moreover, the dismal failure in predicting Eastern European democratic revolutions should remind us of our limited ability to anticipate such transformations more generally. Predictions are hindered by a phenomenon that may be only marginally different for the Middle East of the mid-1990s than it was for the Soviet Union and Eastern Europe in the mid-1980s, namely, what Kuran (1991) has labeled "the predictability of unpredictability." The imperfect observability of real private preferences in much of the Middle East—where both state and societal coercion encourage preference falsification—can conceal "bandwagons in formation." Some analysts see bandwagons forming along Islamist tracks. Others, including Kuran himself, warn against assuming a conquering Islamist revolution. This last view is supported by evidence from a partial window into private preferences in the form of preliminary unimpressive electoral performances of Islamist blocs in selected Middle East contests. This evidence is

---

[133] On Jordan, Morocco, and Tunisia as the most prone to liberalize their economy, see Barkey (1995).

compatible with the "balloon theory" on the volatility of political commitment to Islamist parties.

Some preliminary lessons about converging and diverging elements of coalitional analysis, democratization, and peace in the Middle East include the following.

1. The Middle East has been dominated by statist-nationalist coalitions for many decades, leading to a war zone par excellence. These wars and militarized disputes spanned the Arab-Israeli, inter-Arab, and Arab-Iranian cleavages in the region. A pattern of domestic and regional outbidding among statist-nationalist competitors radicalized the generic statist-nationalist grand strategy, escalating conflict across all categories.

2. The beginnings of cooperation in the most intractable—Arab-Israeli—conflict follows the inception of internationalizing coalitions struggling to consummate their complementary grand strategies, including a contraction of the military-industrial complex and an expansion of markets and international political-economic access.

3. Piecemeal market-oriented policies have for the most part not yet led to improved growth rates, reduced unemployment, price stability, or diffuse (rather than concentrated) benefits. Without these, internationalizing coalitions have found it hard to gain and maintain a broad political base. Neither the slow pace of economic reforms nor the scant attention paid to distributive outcomes bodes well for either democracy or peace. Lagging economic liberalization has strengthened statist, nationalist, populist, and confessional coalitions, often allied with the military-industrial complex. However, even limited economic reforms have weakened the "*mukhabarat* [internal security and intelligence services] state," and with it, the ability of this critical partner in statist coalitions to revert to the war-making patterns of the past.

4. The brittle foundations of peace in the region can hardly be traced to the brittle foundations of democracy, particularly where the latter trailed peace agreements, as in Palestine. Moreover, democratization has been slow, and many fear serious challenges if not a complete reversal.[134] At the same time, ruling coalitions whose behavior accords with the "democratic efficiency" theory have improved the chances for both continued democratization and for economic liberalization more attentive to equity considerations. Progressive democratization from above has facilitated the task of civic inclusion of confessional movements, even if it has not completely dissipated concerns with an Islamist reversal of democracy. Inclusion has neither emasculated democracy nor shelved peace overtures, thus far.

5. Despite a significant empirical fit between democratization, economic liberalization, and peacemaking, no linear progression along all three dimensions is guaranteed. Democratic opponents of both peace and economic reform—in essence a democratic statist-nationalist-populist coalition—could prevail in the absence of effective distributional efforts. Such transitional democracies are more likely to be belligerent within their region and beyond, although their actual war-fighting capability will be far more limited than in the past, given emaciated military partners.

---

[134] El Sayyid (1994).

6. In the only stable democracy in the region, Israel, the following two relationships among democracy, coalitions, and peace can be observed: first, attempts to improve democracy and strengthen the peace process went hand in hand under Labor-Meretz's internationalist coalition; and second, democracy itself provided a statist-nationalist and confessional coalition the opportunity both to overturn the peace tables and weaken a political-economic revolution. Netanyahu's coalition has obliterated an emerging cooperative order while tolerating unprecedented threats to Israel's democracy.

7. The expectation that mixed regional clusters will find it hard to engage in collective denuclearization is borne out in the Middle East. Internationalizing coalitions have indeed been more prone to embrace measures toward denuclearization, although the history, capabilities, and intentions of neighboring nuclear-prone statist-nationalists has thus far defied the region's effective denuclearization.

8. Two key leaders of internationalizing coalitions—Egypt's President Sadat and Israel's Prime Minister Rabin—who pioneered changes toward peace were assassinated by homegrown fundamentalists whose rationale was eerily identical. The leaders' commitment to an internationalist strategy—at home and in the region—was the sole justification for the murder. In neither case have coalitional balances been dramatically altered in an internationalist direction as a result of the murder.

CHAPTER SEVEN

The Korean Peninsula

> It is no exaggeration to say that the successful modernization of Korea serves
> as a compass indicating the direction of peace and security in East Asia.
> —*South Korea's President Park Chung Hee* (1971: 138)

THIS CHAPTER surveys the evolution of coalitional interactions between North and South Korea over the last four decades. On the one hand, different variants of realist and neorealist analysis have dominated the study of the relationship between the two states in the Korean peninsula. On the other hand, the massive literature on industrialization strategies in South Korea and East Asia in general has evolved largely aloof from the security implications of such strategies.[1] This disconnectedness has precluded an effective understanding of coalitional dynamics, grand strategies, and regional orders in the Korean peninsula.

Neorealism is a natural theoretical contender in studying a region in which anarchy and self-help appeared to have dominated the Cold War years. The Korean peninsula's security context indeed loads the dice in favor of neorealism, turning it prima facie into a case least likely to support a coalitional approach as a conceptual alternative. The evolution of the Korean War can hardly be understood without reference to the Cold War, as the vast literature on this topic suggests. However, the very outbreak of the war requires far closer attention to Kim Il Sung's grand strategy at home and in relation to his southern rival. Moreover, neorealism cannot explain shifts away from war since the 1950s, the North-South modus vivendi of the 1970s, and an incipient economic and security cooperation toward the late 1980s and early 1990s. Much as in the Israeli-Palestinian Authority relationship, no neorealist device can explain South Korea's willingness to buttress the North's economic wherewithal (through investments) without violating the theory's basic tenets.

Nor is neorealism a reliable guide for understanding why South Korea opted for unilateral denuclearization early on, while its opponent in the North did not, or why the North reversed itself several times on this issue in the early 1990s. The phenomenon of an extremely vulnerable state—the South in the early 1970s—giving up the alleged best option to secure its own survival is not easily explainable by US security guarantees or coercive pressure alone. These guarantees were not foolproof in the eyes of most South Koreans, and they can

---

[1] Security aspects—mostly the US role—have entered this debate only marginally as an independent variable influencing industrialization strategy, generally treated in passing. The regional security *implications* (as a dependent variable of industrialization strategy) have gained far less attention.

never be so within a neorealist framework of self help, by definition. Moreover, US pressures elsewhere did not invariably yield their denuclearizing objective, as the cases of South Africa, Egypt, Pakistan, India, Israel, the Southern Cone, and North Korea for many decades, clearly show. Finally, changes in North Korea's external behavior throughout the last two decades must be explained against a constant: the continued presence of nearly 40,000 US troops in South Korea. The imputed long-standing heart of the North's security dilemma remained largely unaltered while North Korea's policies evolved—although in anything but linear fashion—from highly conflictive to more cooperative.

The absence of a regional institutional infrastructure or of democratic interlocutors denies institutional and democratic peace approaches an explanatory role in either the evolution of a modus vivendi between North and South or in the South's denuclearization in the midst of continuous rivalry. A coalitional analysis, instead, sheds lights on historical shifts away from war, on the evolving nature of North-South relations throughout nearly five decades, on cooperative overtures including the South's willingness to help develop the North, and on the reasons why the two sides chose different nuclear postures in the 1970s and 1980s, but more converging ones in the 1990s.

The next section dissects the inward-looking strategies of North and South Korea in the 1950s and early 1960s while distilling the regional consequences of prevailing coalitional strategies. I discuss the Korean War as a logical outcome of such strategies, an emphasis that precludes an in-depth treatment of the war through the more conventional lenses of East-West competition. Next I explore the much-studied South Korean internationalist shift, which may have been far more connected to the ruling coalition's domestic and regional security requirements for stability than is usually recognized. As one of the strongest internationalist coalitions in the industrializing world, South Korea provides a critical case for testing this book's general argument, since problems of coalitional thresholds are of less concern in this case than elsewhere. The following section examines the evolving regional interaction between a nearly prototypical internationalist coalition controlling the South and a nearly prototypical statist-nationalist coalition controlling the North. Nuclear politics played a central role in these dynamics, and progressively so in the 1990s. I subsequently extend the coalitional argument in an exploratory rather than exhaustive fashion to other East Asian cases—Taiwan and ASEAN—whose grand strategies were largely comparable to South Korea's. This section also discusses the essential irrelevance of the democratic peace theory to understanding the history of regional conflict and cooperation in all these cases.

ECONOMIC INSULARITY, *JUCHE*, MILITARIZATION, AND WAR

The Coalitional Profile

Korea's division in 1945 along the 38th parallel resulted in two new states: the Republic of Korea (ROK) in the south and the Democratic People's Republic of Korea (DPRK) in the north, both founded in 1948. North Korea quickly became an indigenous adaptation of the Soviet and Chinese models, and one of the most long-lasting statist-nationalist coalitions in power, surviving beyond the disintegration of its original models. A decentralized ruling coalition of "people's committees" was in place in 1945–1946. Three communist factions—the Soviet, the Kapsan, and Yenan groups—merged into a unified North Korean Workers' party in 1946. This coalition absorbed the South Korean Workers' Party in 1949 and aimed at undermining the domestic North Korean (*kungnae*) communist bloc. By 1948 Kim Il Sung's dominance was significant, allowing him to continue purging potential competitors in Stalinist fashion.[2]

Kim Il Sung and his family came to control the political and economic pillars of the regime in a pattern similar to Saddam Hussein's Tikriti extended family. Kim forged a state characterized as "ideologically paternalistic, economically collectivist, ethnically racist, diplomatically isolationist, and culturally nationalist," a faithful representation of the statist-nationalist blueprint depicted in Chapter Two.[3] This highly militarized state came to control every aspect of economic activity. Outright autarky and self-sufficiency (*juche*) were cornerstone strategic principles for the rulers of the "hermit kingdom," leading to one of the lowest levels of foreign trade worldwide. In Kim Il Sung's words, "self-reliance in the economy (*juche*) is the material basis of *chajusong* (all-round independence in international relations)," and "economic dependence leads to political subordination."[4] A "self-dependent national economy" was to produce virtually everything, with guided foreign economic relations, overwhelmingly with the Soviet Union filling some minor gaps. Kim Il Sung, the Korean Workers' party (KWP), and the North Korean People's Army would thus deliver invulnerability to the Korean people, a highly valued political goal for a population subjugated to ruthless Japanese rule for decades. Juche was the path to reinforce *minjok tongnip* (national or ethnic independence) and to weaken Kim's domestic opponents, including pro-Soviet and pro-Chinese factions.

The nationalist character of juche is evident in the fact that the concept came to replace Marxism-Leninism, first tacitly but progressively more forcefully and openly. Juche and "Kimilsungism" became the "solely correct revolutionary theory" that substituted for universal Marxism.[5] The independence inherent in juche led to friction with the Soviet Union, which nonetheless allowed North Korea's selective participation in the COMECON (Council for Mutual Economic Assistance). Juche approximated a confessionally based unifying national fabric—Kim Il Sung's rendition of Moses' delivery of the Hebrew laws—and the basis for Kim's own mythification and adulation by the masses,

---

[2] On his political program at the time, see Kim Il Sung (1975a: 146–48); Cumings (1990: 291–324); Lee (1963); Paige and Lee (1963); An (1983: 8–12).

[3] Park (1996: 2); Cumings (1993: 204–7, 214–15, 223–24).

[4] Smith (1994: 100); Mikheev (1996: 92); An (1983: 35–71). Juche was already in use by the 1940s but the term became far more prominent later. See Kim Il Sung (1975a).

[5] Mikheev (1996: 89–90); Scalapino (1963). On how the use of nationalism in the North overwhelmed its use in the South, see Koh (1984: 235).

closely resembling the religious submission of many Iranians to the Ayatollah Khomeini. Beyond juche and the cult of leadership, another central political instrument of mythmaking was the *sadaejuui* (mercenary, flunkey, "puppet") nature of South Korea's political leadership. The latter was depicted as a proxy of "imperialist USA" (Kim Il Sung 1975b: 157–72) with a joint proclivity to initiate wars, as they were imputed to have done in 1950. Vilification of US imperialism was central to the North's strategy, while the nonaligned movement provided an appropriate international context for the exercise of juche. Even the Sino-Soviet competition offered the opportunity to advance juche and the national uniqueness of North Korea's path to communism.

Statism was a pillar of economic self-reliance and juche indoctrination. Initial recognition of the concept of cooperative—as opposed to state-owned—property quickly led to its dismissal in favor of state control, both in industry and agriculture. Kim Il Sung's Kapsan faction purged opponents of heavy industry and the collectivization of agriculture.[6] State enterprises offered a more effective tool for concentrating power and implementing party directives. Moreover, North Korea's relatively advanced industrial infrastructure—built during the Japanese occupation and feeding its war-mobilized economy—provided the foundations for an emphasis on heavy industry. By 1946 the regime nationalized more than 1,000 industrial enterprises, or 90 percent of all North Korean industry. This statist economy was molded to serve North Korea's militarization, an objective built into the leadership's grand strategy as a core basis of legitimacy. The military was Kim Il Sung's political backbone, and it enjoyed privileged resources (one-third of the budget, one-fourth of the GNP, more or less consistently since the 1960s) and considerable autonomy. The North Korean People's Army came into being in 1945, and after extensive training with Soviet help it officially became the regular army in 1948. By 1950, a 200,000- to 300,000-strong force (24 divisions) with heavy weapons and tanks had been assembled in preparation for invading the South.[7] In time, the readiness for war as a mobilizing tool had yielded a genuine fear of invasion, intensified by the South's threats to launch a "northern expedition."

The ROK, under US influence, endured a period of internal turmoil between 1945 and 1950, including a bloody uprising in 1946 that overturned the Korean People's Republic. The domestic pillars of Syngman Rhee's First Republic were the military and the Korean National Police, his Liberal party, and former colonial bureaucrats. Conservative absentee landlords and a group of industrialists organized in the Korean Democratic party (KDP-Hanmindang) challenged Rhee's control of the bureaucracy. They came to dominate the bureaucracy, however, and were de facto members of Rhee's coalition and major beneficiaries of import-substitution and widespread corruption.[8] Among the prominent anticommunist leaders allied with Rhee was the extreme nationalist Yi Pŏm

---

[6] Kuark (1963).

[7] Chung (1963: 110).

[8] Cumings (1984, 1990: 185–290, 1993: 224), Cheng (1990), Jang Jip Choi (1993), Haggard and Moon (1993).

Sok, leader of the one million-strong Korean National Youth. Yi relied on exaltation of the nation and the state (*minjok chisang, kukka chisang*, or nation first, state first), on opposition to reliance on foreigners (*sadaejuui*), and on racial purity (*hyolt'ong*), in ways that summon not only 1930s European fascism to mind but also Kimilsungism. Yi became the ROK's first minister of defense and prime minister. Guerrilla war and radical popular nationalist uprisings (in Cheju, South Cholla, and South Kyongsang, among other places) fueled political polarization and challenged Rhee's First Republic.

The 1948 constitution—characterized as one with a "socialist bent"—institutionalized state control over planning, trade, and heavy industry. Governmental expenditures were relatively high throughout the 1950s compared to subsequent decades. Economic bureaucrats were not free traders, but students of Friedrich List and even Karl Marx, concerned with controlling and guiding capitalist competition.[9] Rhee opposed US pressures for privatization and conservative fiscal and monetary policies that would undercut the Liberal party's patronage system. Labor (workers and farmers) remained completely excluded from this weak ruling coalition. Not so the military which, although occasionally at odds with Rhee, had become the core component of South Korea's coalitional landscape. With vast US military aid, the ROK's militarization during these years grew exponentially. The 75,000-strong standing army of 1950 became nearly 600,000 by the end of the Korean War.

The Korean War and Its Aftermath

The Korean War unfolded against the background of parallel efforts at statist-nationalist consolidation. Rhee's regime promoted the aggressive motto of "Let Us March North," while Kim Il Sung geared his political and economic resources to an inexorable attack on the South, proclaiming the need to overthrow Rhee and unify Korea. Kim was convinced that the invasion would quickly ignite an uprising against Rhee, leading to Northern control of the entire peninsula. The die was cast when Stalin approved Kim Il Sung's "Korean People's Army Preemptive Strike Plan." North Korea invaded the South on June 25, 1950, and forced a sharp retreat of South Korean forces. Military victory was the North's intended instrument to build legitimacy for its revolution.[10] This was no accidental sliding down the slippery slope toward war, as some might argue about Nasser's steps in May 1967. Overwhelming the South militarily was as deliberately planned and implemented as Iraq's invasion of Kuwait, with very similar initial results (conquest of the adversary's territory), eerily comparable

[9] Chang (1994: 125); Amsden (1989: 43–46).

[10] Walt (1996: 319–23). On the belligerent rhetoric and near-war footing of North Korea since Soviet troops departed in 1948, see Cumings (1990: 374). On Stalin's approval, see "Kim Country: Hard Times in North Korea," *New Left Review* 198 (March 1, 1993: 25–26). On Stalin's wavering and Kim Il Sung's commitment to launch a war, see Goncharov, Lewis, and Litai (1993: 136–45). On Rhee's concentration on reunification, anti-Japanese nationalism, and short-term economic objectives rather than on a coherent industrial strategy, see Jones and Sakong (1980: 40–77).

miscalculations about the resolve of the adversary's allies, and the significantly analogous use of the ultimate defeat to build up domestic support for a "heroic" leadership capable of confronting an imperialist hegemon.[11]

The United States pulled together UN support for the South under the principle of collective security, leading to a reversal of battle, an invasion of North Korea, and an eventual return to the territorial status quo ante bellum. North Korea's military debacle and an impending threat from US forces had compelled China to enter the war, reversing its course. The war lasted more than three years and consumed the lives of 212,000 South Korean soldiers, 34,000 US soldiers (and 100,000 wounded), and an estimated one million North Koreans.[12] About 700,000 civilians were killed and millions displaced and maimed by the time the armistice agreement was signed in 1953. Rhee's maximalist claims included the North Korean Army's surrender to the ROK and ROK military control of North Korea. As with the 1948 Middle East war, the Korean War would leave an indelible imprint on subsequent coalitional dynamics in the region.

In the war's immediate aftermath Kim Il Sung's Kapsan faction eliminated any residual influence of other party factions, notably those who had opposed heavy industry. The party then embraced a First Five-Year Plan (1957–1961) emphasizing heavy industrial sectors in order to "flesh out the skeleton," accelerated house construction and the provision of basic needs, all of which contributed to a remarkable GNP growth, arguably 22 percent yearly (1953–1962).[13] Rather than diluting military efforts, the outcome of the Korean War provided a convenient springboard to deepen militarization and juche. In Kim Il Sung's own words: "We are producing as many weapons as we can to arm the entire people" (1975: 373). The Fourth Workers' party (Rodongdang) Congress in 1962 adopted the "four great military policy lines": "arm the entire people, fortify the entire country, cadetify the entire army, and modernize the entire army."[14] The military was allocated self-sustaining economic fiefdoms including foodstuff production, irrigation, and other massive projects. Military expenditures during the late 1950s were thus reduced, coinciding with the North's most significant episode of postwar economic growth. Soviet military assistance helped build the military-industrial complex, with the vast majority of North Korea's top one hundred engineering enterprises linked to that complex. Army personnel grew to over 600,000 by 1958 and the air force to 900 planes, turning North Korea into one of the largest military machines in the industrializing world at the time.

The Korean War had "rescued" the South's weak coalition under Rhee, but

---

[11] On Kim Il Sung's contention to Stalin that the war could be quickly won before the US had time to intervene, see Foot (1990: 41) and Stueck (1995: 11–29). Kim had expected the weakness of the South's ruling coalition—with Rhee collecting barely a third of the vote in the May 1950 elections—to facilitate a blietzkrieg.

[12] Koh (1984: 210); Park Chung Hee (1971: 83).

[13] Kim (1988: 137); Kuark (1963); Amsden (1989: 40).

[14] Baek (1988: 168–69); Chung (1963: 119–20); Trigubenko (1996: 146–49).

not for long. The war eliminated the landowners' economic base, redirecting them to urban activities. By 1953 Rhee had embraced import-substitution and an overvalued exchange rate, bolstering the economic rents of privileged importers and speculators in exchange for political financing. Rhee's tight control of US aid—70 percent of government revenue at the time—lubricated this pact. As Amsden (1991: 286) argued, "the exemplary East Asian states after the 1960s were egregious rent seekers in the 1950s—to wit, Chiang Kai-shek in Taiwan and Syngman Rhee in South Korea." In 1954 the US conditioned its assistance to Rhee on privatization of state enterprises and banks, a realistic exchange rate, ceilings on South Korea's military, and anti-inflationary stabilization programs. However, severe poverty, stagnation (GNP growth rates declined from 8.8 percent in 1957 to 2.3 percent in 1960), unemployment, and political uncertainty remained this period's defining characteristics. Rhee had failed to put together a coalition with a coherent strategy, except for relying on anticommunist rhetoric to control political mobilization.[15]

Rhee's relationship with the US was punctuated by mutual distrust, with the US coming very close to deposing him over his independent approach to the North, his release of war prisoners in 1953, and his unmitigated hostility to normalization with Japan (a key component in the potential development of a South Korean internationalist strategy). Although it opposed Rhee's statism and import-substitution, the US found no other coalitional alternative for rebuilding a devastated South Korea at the time.[16] A wave of student protests culminated in the April 19, 1960, uprising forcing Rhee's resignation. Myon Chang was Prime Minister under the short-lived Second Republic, which was characterized by abortive liberalizing steps, including exchange-rate devaluation, reform of state enterprises, and the creation of a "superministry" to rationalize economic policy. The program failed with Chang's inability to marshal military and corrupt bureaucrats and entrepreneurs into the reform plan. Protests escalated, with communist groups now active in demanding unconditional negotiations with the North at Panmunjom. A military group around Park Chung Hee, which had began plotting the ouster of Rhee, would now seize the threat of a communist takeover in 1961 to take power into its own hands.

All throughout this period North and South Korea were locked in a race to consolidate a domestic coalition and a regional strategy, while reciprocally threatening the renewal of hostilities in the name of making the Korean nation whole. By the end of the decade, Kim Il Sung's coalition had the upper hand in political and economic consolidation, a perception that would trigger a response within South Korea.[17]

---

[15] Rhee (1956); Haggard, Cooper, and Moon (1993: 294–96); Stueck (1995: 27); Cheng (1990: 148).

[16] Even powerful hegemons are constrained by the extant coalitional infrastructure of small states, as the US was to relearn in Somalia five decades later. On the failed US attempt to organize a "moderate center" into something called the Coalition Committee, see Cumings (1990: 220) and Stueck (1995: 23).

[17] Scalapino (1963); Kuark (1963: 63).

THE SOUTH KOREAN "MIRACLE": FROM MILITARISM TO MONETARISM

The coup led by General Park Chung Hee in 1961 planted the seeds of a new grand strategy in South Korea, where national security and rapid economic growth became more intricately and coherently intertwined.[18] The shadow of a North Korean economic performance that was particularly remarkable in relation to the South, triggered the emergence of a ruling coalition far stronger than that of the preceding decade. Park and his allied junior officers purged the bureaucracy, the old political leadership, and the military itself. The junta initially favored farmers and small to medium sectors over "parasitical" urban industrialists. This inward-looking phase—import licenses, high tariffs, and a multiple exchange rate—lasted until 1963, when an inflationary and balance-of-payment crisis favored the introduction of an export-led strategy.

The new policies included a major devaluation to create a competitive real exchange rate, the unification of exchange rates, a gradual reduction in tariffs and import licensing requirements, strong incentives to export-oriented firms, guarantees for foreign investments and loans, and improved tax collection. Both US pressures and domestic conditions pushed toward an export drive.[19] Choices were rather constrained, with dipping balance-of-payments deficits and accelerating inflation forcing incremental responses. Facing both the exhaustion of import-substitution and US and multilateral (IMF) pressures in the same export-led direction, Park could read the script of his regime's survival on the wall. In his own words: "For a country like Korea, unendowed by nature and saddled with minuscule markets, only an external-oriented development strategy, making full use of the abundant human resources but aimed at exports, appeared relevant" (1979: 72). A successful internationalist strategy had the potential of building domestic support for a weak regime with an unremarkable record. Only a successful implementation could stem the combined challenge by Park's emboldened domestic and North Korean foes. The regime's motto became: "Nation Building through Exports," and "Think Export First!"[20]

This "sword-won" coalition included military administrators, state technocrats (particularly in the newly created Economic Planning Board—EPB), and industrialists.[21] Park centralized power and decision making in the Blue House, the president's residence. The EPB controlled the Finance Ministry (and consequently, the Bank of Korea) and all ministerial and state agencies. Park coerced the business class into the new project, first arresting and parading the beneficiaries of import-substitution as "parasites," and then demanding total compliance

---

[18] Park (1971, 1976, 1979).

[19] Haggard and Moon (1993); Cumings (1984); Cooper (1994); Haggard, Cooper, Collins, Kim, and Ro (1994).

[20] On Park's popularization of the export-led strategy, see Ogle (1990: 40).

[21] Cheng (1990: 158–59). On the decisive role played by the military in the switch from import-substitution to export-led growth, see Cumings (1984: 26), Johnson (1987: 153) and Amsden (1989: 48–52). On the need to avoid purely statist or societal interpretations of South Korea's political economy in favor of a dynamic coalitional perspective, see Moon (1990).

with new directives. He sustained their compliance by manipulating credits and loans from nationalized commercial banks. Emerging industrial concerns (*chaebols*) received subsidies and financial assistance in strict exchange for efficiency, turning rents into a highly contingent and dynamic currency in the coalitional bargain between private entrepreneurs and state technocrats. Park also protected and subsidized a conservative rural constituency (*saemaul*), while excluding labor (workers and farmers), small businessmen, middle-class bureaucrats, and intellectuals. The Korean Central Intelligence Agency was a powerful guarantor of the political-economic order—particularly after 1971—penetrating all aspects of society to a degree comparable to Middle East "mukhabarat" states. The military was not particularly threatened by the macroeconomic requirements of an export-led (and, more broadly, internationalist strategy); its own institutional growth and political leverage in the early 1960s were enhanced by massive US military aid. Thus, internal cleavages within the military were successfully suppressed or muted after 1964, in sharp contrast with the Argentine military.[22]

Macropolitical consensus within the coalition was strong, ensuring the strategy's stability and decreasing domestic and international uncertainty.[23] The absence of serious intracoalitional divisions allowed technocratic teams to steer through economic crises and to reorient—in cumulative steps—the country's political economy. The short duration of import-substitution had prevented the political entrenchment of beneficiaries, facilitating export promotion and its required exchange-rate structure. Political repression of a weak labor movement and associated political parties facilitated steadfast implementation and stable macroeconomic policies (a condition for private investment), in a pattern highlighted by "authoritarian advantage" theories of industrialization. Centralized control over fiscal policy helped maintain macroeconomic stability, a core objective outlined in EPB plans.[24] Despite selective protection, export subsidies, state entrepreneurship, and support for private cartels, the incentive system was not weighted heavily in favor of domestic production or state entrepreneurship.[25] Some import restrictions remained, but not enough to create "wrong" inducements for major industries. State enterprises were not allowed to smother private ones and to create rents that might endanger exports. Of the ten largest companies that emerged, nine were private chaebols, accounting for over 63 percent of GDP in 1987. State enterprises—even during a statist-nationalist interlude—accounted for only 10 to 15 percent of total industrial employment and 25 percent of industrial output (compared, for instance, with Syria's or Egypt's figures of 50 percent and 75 percent, respectively). This active but "market-conforming" state (Johnson 1982: 318) thus nourished an interna-

---

[22] Haggard and Kaufman (1995: 75). On the military's commitment to private enterprise, see Amsden (1989: 49).

[23] Jones and Sakong (1980); Ogle (1990: 33–34); Moon (1994: 146).

[24] Haggard, Cooper, and Moon (1993: 311–12).

[25] Gereffi (1990); Amsden (1991); Byung-Sun Choi (1993).

tionally competitive private sector and displaced it to a far lesser extent than import-substituting states in Latin America and the Middle East.

The strategy leaned primarily on foreign markets, capital, and technology, with a focus on global rather than regional markets. An interministerial subcommittee that included private-sector peak associations and chaebol-owned General Trading Companies became core instruments in the export drive, with Park directly overseeing export performance by firm and sector. Exports grew from $87 million in 1963 to $250 million in 1966, and $882 million in 1970. Exports (mostly of industrial goods and services) as a share of GDP nearly tripled from 4.8 percent in 1963 to 14.2 percent in 1970, doubling again to 29.1 percent in 1973. Trade openness (exports plus imports) doubled from 20 percent of GDP in 1963 to 40 percent of GDP in 1970, in merely seven years. Manufactured goods—17 percent of exports in the early 1960s—rose to 83 percent a decade later. To the vagaries and growing protectionism of global markets in the late 1960s Park responded with greater cooperation with raw material and technology suppliers and higher labor productivity.[26] External borrowing allowed high levels of investment and savings. By the early 1960s large-scale US loans and grants had declined sharply and efforts to attract Japanese capital and technology intensified. Overriding nationalist opposition, Park ratified a treaty normalizing relations with Japan in 1965 in exchange for $800 million in Japanese grants, loans, and credit. South Korea's foreign loans increased tenfold between 1965 and 1970, while reliance on IMF funds grew from virtually nil in the early 1970s to about 300 percent of its quota a decade later. By 1988 South Korea had exhausted its borrowing potential from the IMF and had repaid all its debts.[27] Only with a reconstructed economy did South Korea encourage foreign direct investment, and even then at a slow pace and in consonance with its preference for joint ventures over wholly owned subsidiaries. A massive diplomatic offensive accompanied the drive to broaden international access to markets, capital, and technology.

By the early 1970s both growing global protectionism and US plans to withdraw ground forces from the region had strengthened statist-nationalist constituencies, including import-oriented firms and proponents of a more self-reliant military-industrial complex. Labor strikes in 1969–1970 culminated in the immolation of a textile worker and protests in Kwangju. Park followed the disappointing results of the 1971 elections with more expansionist fiscal and monetary policies in 1972, responding to the opposition's populist platform, which stressed equity issues, agricultural reforms, and the Cholla provinces' relative disadvantage vis-à-vis Park's native Kyongsang. IMF stabilization efforts between 1970–1972 had slowed real growth and export expansion, adding to Nixon's economic shock in August 1971 and new limits on Korean textile exports to trigger a demand by the Federation of Korean Industries (FKI)—repre-

[26] Park (1971: 172–73); Bradford (1990: 38). On export figures, see Krueger (1995: 19).

[27] Park (1971: 172–73); Cooper (1994: 267, 279); Byung-Sun Choi (1993: 27–29). On Park's own determination to use the Japanese card in his internationalist strategy, beyond US pressures in that direction, see Koh (1984: 215).

senting the largest firms—to end economic contraction.[28] Park responded with emergency measures (1972) that reversed financial liberalization, reinstated price controls, and introduced the "October Revitalizing Reforms" (Siwol Yushin), wrapped in juche and national identity rhetoric in an uncanny—if short-lived—convergence with North Korea's assiduous manipulation of the term.

A new Industrial Rationalization Council controlled by the prime minister now provided subsidies and protection for (mostly) large chemical and heavy industry conglomerates in iron and steel, shipbuilding, oil refining, and petrochemical industries, among others. Tax and financial incentives and foreign (particularly Japanese) loans and technology were designed to attract private firms to this endeavor. Economic nationalists in the state bureaucracy, including the Ministry of Commerce and Industry and the Korea Development Bank (KDB)—bypassed the EPB and the Ministry of Finance, often associated with neoclassical approaches opposed to industrial deepening. The turn toward heavy industry—embedded in the 1971 Third Five-Year Plan, 1971–1976— provided evidence of state officials' ability to steer private economic activity rather than merely being shaped by it. Yet, not coincidentally, industrial deepening (and KDB loans) followed the return to authoritarian rule and the need to maintain support from chaebols, the conservative rural saemaul (New Village) movement, and military sectors favoring a homegrown military-industrial complex. The latter brandished Nixon's 1969 Guam doctrine and the 1971 withdrawal of an infantry division from South Korea to promote self-reliant policies.[29] Their expected benefits from the Heavy and Chemical Industry Plan materialized in higher military expenditures, rising from 23 percent of the budget in 1970 to 32 percent in 1978. A Force Improvement Plan increased the percentage of GNP devoted to the military from 5 to 7.5 percent yearly during the 1970s. The US and the World Bank opposed deepening, but were unable to overturn the policy, even using political and economic coercion.[30]

Even during this deepening interlude, Park prevented fiscal costs from threatening macroeconomic stability, warning that rising prices often threaten workers' income, shake the consumer order, and "lead to weakened international competitiveness, which in turn discourages production and exports" (1979: 98– 99). At its peak, inflation was not nearly of the order of magnitude that affected statist-nationalist regimes in the Middle East and Latin America; rather, inflation was contained at modest levels compatible with the avoidance of pernicious effects. Government expenditures—13 percent of GDP with the inception of deepening—rose at most to 17 percent (in 1978). Budget deficits relative to GDP declined from 2.9 percent in 1976 to 1.4 in 1979, and went to

---

[28] Haggard (1994a: 28–42).

[29] On the logic of national security behind Yushin, see Jang Jip Choi (1993: 32). On Nixon's Guam doctrine of lowering US military commitments in Asia while urging Asian states to rely on their own military resources, see Reiss (1988: 81).

[30] Cumings (1984: 33); Haggard (1994a and 1994b).

finance government investment or private-sector lending.[31] The large external
debt of the mid-1980s could not be traced to general budgetary support. The
overall rate of effective protection in the 1970s was 10 percent.[32] Sustained
growth, stable prices, and improved balance of payments upheld an expansionist policy (1975–1978). Total exports grew from less than $1 billion in 1970 to
$17 billion in 1980. Marketing and licensing agreements with foreign firms and
joint Korean-American enterprises, as well as growing US direct investment,
underpinned this expansion of exports.

The 1970s oil crisis unleashed pressures that activated the opposition around
Kim Dae Jung, backed by textile workers, small business, domestically oriented
firms, the most deprived urban and rural workers, and others adversely affected
by *yushin* (reforms) and the heavy-industry drive. By the end of the decade
rising inflation and declining exports reinvigorated the power of liberalizing
reformists in the bureaucracy against the architects of deepening. The EPB and
a renewed emphasis on stable prices, import liberalization, and adjustment returned through Comprehensive Measures for Economic Stabilization in 1979.
However, Park's assassination in October 1979 aggravated instability (including
18 percent inflation). In the midst of severe political turmoil, shattered macropolitical consensus, rising unemployment, and current account deficits that
threatened the continuity of an internationalist grand strategy, General Chun
Doo Hwan captured the military in 1979, the Korean Central Intelligence
Agency, and the state (in 1980), as he massacred workers in Pusan and Inchon,
miners in Sabuk, and students. Over nine hundred strikes in the first half of
1980—more than during the entire Yushin period—revealed an unprecedented
challenge to reigning coalitional arrangements.[33] The introduction of martial law
led to the Kwangju insurrection and allowed its bloody repression. In its aftermath Chun increased funding for public works to relieve unemployment, and
lowered interest rates and the special consumption tax. These instinctive responses resemble much of Onganía's rejoinder to the Cordobazo in Argentina.
Chun quickly abandoned welfare initiatives as the EPB and liberalizing economic advisers gained the upper hand.

Strains between Chun's technocrats and large chaebols grouped in the FKI
became evident in a FKI press conference, where the latter refuted accusations
of corruption. The regime's selective cooptation of chaebols in a strategy of
"divide and rule" had weakened the FKI. Chun's emphasis on macroeconomic
stability was designed to attract what had become the largest political constituency: a middle class of small and medium-sized firms, professional, managerial
and technical workers, consumers, and savers.[34] This constituency had signaled
its coalitional proclivities by supporting—however reluctantly in the absence of
democratic reform—the regime's political-economic thrust over its potential

---

[31] World Bank (1993a: 6); Cooper (1994).
[32] Haggard (1995b: 129).
[33] Jang Jip Choi (1993: 29–30); Haggard and Kaufman (1995: 83–93).
[34] Moon (1994: 146–47).

demise by student-led demonstrations. Thus, in an effort to restore a failing internationalist strategy, and facing a $5 billion current account deficit, Chun's technocrats turned to Euromarkets and the IMF. Monetary, fiscal, and exchange rate policies remained expansionary until 1982, partly to overcome the deep recession of 1980.

The strong adjustment of 1983–1984, including sharp bureaucratic downsizing and wage freezes, consolidated earlier gains in the form of sustained (about 5 percent) GDP growth, low inflation (down to an annual average of 6 percent), and lower external debt.[35] Restructuring also aimed at reducing industrial concentration (trimming chaebols) while encouraging small and medium-sized firms. Central to Chun's reforms was financial liberalization, which included privatization of commercial banking, freer interest rates, and a gradual opening to foreign banks and foreign investments in the financial sector. Liberalized trade and investment were not merely a response to US pressures but highly consistent with Chun's (ultimately futile) objective of restraining chaebol growth, concentration, and political power. Average tariff rates declined from 23.7 percent in 1983 to 18.1 in 1988, and items subject to quantitative restrictions decreased from 20 to 5 percent in the same period.

Opposition to growing international openness rallied small and medium-sized businesses, the agricultural sector, and the student-worker movement. However, the coalitional base supporting an export-driven strategy was stronger than ever by the 1980s, including chaebols, the middle and even the working class, who had seen remarkable real wage increases.[36] Foreign trade (imports plus exports) amounted to over 50 percent of GNP in the late 1980s. Even the opposition supported financial liberalization, reduced state intervention, and central bank independence. The political opening of 1987, however, had led to labor disputes and a decline in EPB and executive centralization at the expense of politicians and captive bureaucracies. The legacy of the Fifth Republic—the 1980 coup, corruption, and repression—fueled the opposition's campaign. By 1987 the large middle class no longer faced the dilemma of undermining the authoritarian regime they despised without wrecking the internationalist strategy they endorsed. Democratization could now consolidate a stable strategy. Roh Tae-Woo—assuming power in 1988 after relatively fair elections—largely maintained Chun's emphasis on exports, macroeconomic stability, and restraining chaebols. Roh's *botong saram* (ordinary people) policies led to a vast housing program, increased social spending, and increased responsiveness to wider societal forces.[37] Roh organized a Grand Conservative Coalition—controlling two-thirds of the legislature—by merging his own party with the Reunification Democratic party and the New Democratic Republican party. The new Demo-

---

[35] Chun charged against inflation in his "purification" (*jonghwha*) campaign (Chun 1984; Haggard and Collins 1994).
[36] Jang Jip Choi (1993: 29–32, 44–46); Byung-Sun Choi (1993: 42); Haggard and Kaufman (1992: 334 and 1995: 230).
[37] Chung-in Moon (1994: 153–57); Haggard and Kaufman (1995: 238–39).

cratic Liberal party became the grand coalition upholding an internationalist strategy, now invested with democratic legitimacy.

South Korea's internationalist grand strategy had survived the challenge of transition to democracy with widening support, although demands for greater democratization grew stronger. Attacks on international economic openness, alignment with the US, and elusive reunification with the North waned without ever disappearing completely.[38] The relative weakness of this opposition was acknowledged even in unexpected quarters: as early as 1964 Kim Il Sung registered the weakness of revolutionary potential in the South.[39] This recognition was not to be confused with resignation: North Korea maintained its attempts to undermine the South from within, in classic Middle East fashion. This challenge, backed by massive military force, makes the relative stability, growth, and consolidation of the South's internationalist strategy all the more remarkable.

In principle, the perceived threat to South Korea's existence provided its military with ammunition to maintain both its own political centrality and its industrial complex. The potential for military expenditures to derail an internationalist strategy was real. After all, developing a modern military with a deterrent capability would arguably have healthy effects on the regime's reputation and commitment to regional and domestic stability. Yet this objective was never allowed to undercut the integrity of the internationalist strategy introduced in the 1960s. Upon taking power, General Park brought in technical and economic experts with the intention of checking "the arbitrariness and rashness of the military officers."[40] Cultivating national strength, argued Park, means "doing away with those activities that tend to drain or waste our natural resources in a broad sense." Even during the consolidation of the export-led strategy (1962–1972) expenditures for economic development were higher than for defense.[41] Defense absorbed 4 percent of the GDP on average before 1975, while US military assistance was extensive (1953–1973). This assistance declined drastically in the early 1970s, ceasing completely in 1978, which raised South Korea's average military expenditures to 6 percent of GDP initially; it later decreased to 5 percent in 1985 and 3.6 percent in the 1990s.

As a percentage of GDP, military expenditures were close to the industrializing world average (about 5 percent) and far lower than in other high-conflict regions—notably the Middle East—where expenditures ran as high as 20 percent of GDP in the 1970s and 1980s. Moreover, although South Korea's GDP grew 10 percent on average between 1965 and 1989, military expenditures as a percentage of GDP remained largely constant. Only decades later did 3.6 percent of GDP amount to a more significant military investment ($12–14 billion

---

[38] Vogel (1987: 59).

[39] Baek (1988: 167).

[40] Park (1971: 107 and 1976: 171). On how the coalition agreed not to dissipate resources crucial to growth in satisfying short-term interests, see Jones and Sakong (1980).

[41] ACDA (1990); *IISS* (1995: 266); Koh (1984: 210–11), Moon and Hyun (1992), and Ball (1988: 54).

by the mid-1990s), given a GDP of \$332 billion in 1993. At the same time, military expenditures relative to GDP were comparable to those of Argentina in the late 1970s, in a region characterized by the lowest threat perceptions worldwide. At their peak South Korea's military expenditures accounted for 27 percent of the budget (in 1974), not much higher than Brazil's—often considered a low military spender—where they absorbed 20 percent of the budget on average between 1967 and 1973. South Korea's armed forces remained stable since 1971 at about 600,000 men.

From this section's analysis of the domestic and international underpinnings of South Korea's grand strategy I turn to its regional implications and requirements. This strategy was to become—in the words of its pioneer agent, President Park—the region's "compass of peace."

THE INTERNATIONALIST TIGER VERSUS THE STATIST-MILITARY BEAR

A *Modus Vivendi* and Its Unraveling

The maintenance of an internationalist strategy—and of economic stability—required avoiding regional wars "by all means," and "under any circumstances," leading Park to stress that "instability is an anathema to . . . development and progress."[42] In effect, successive internationalist coalitions pursued the least confrontational policies possible under a highly adversarial regional context, stressing war prevention as their undisputed first strategic principle. Park quickly abandoned the old "Let Us March North" slogan and sought to reduce tension and pursue unification through peace and gradualism: "However pressing and urgent . . . unification may be, the goal must never be pursued by means of violence or military force," Park declared in 1975, while adding a self-binding commitment: "I take this opportunity to make it clear once again to the north Korean side that violence or military force will never be employed by us in the pursuit of the goal of unification. That has been, and will continue to be, our fundamental position" (1976: 125). In regions with comparable levels of threat perceptions—the Middle East and South Asia—such a straightforward commitment to avoid war was rare and threats to use force prevailed.

With South Korea geographically surrounded by adversarial statist-nationalist regimes—in the North, China, and the Soviet Union—staying the course of an internationalist strategy was no meek political effort, particularly in the early years. In 1965 Park had little choice but to deploy a 50,000-strong contingent in Vietnam to support his ruling coalition's main benefactor, the US, against their common statist-nationalist rivals in the region. This was historically the first— and only—Korean intervention in a foreign war. For all the military and economic support, the South faced uncertain US commitments. Nixon's 1971 shock, phasing out the fixed exchange rate system, was no less of a threat to the Park regime than was US policy vis-à-vis China and generalized fear of US

---

[42] "Let Us Move Forward in Stability" speech (Park 1976: 29–33, 1979: 94, and 1976: 118).

disengagement from the region in the post-Vietnam era.[43] Less than a decade after launching an internationalist strategy, these threats compelled Park to adjust through the 1970s deepening and military buildup. At the same time, his Open Door policy sought to strengthen global access through economic and political relations with virtually any state, regardless of ideological stripe. Park aimed at conveying a new image of South Korea, departing from the past "unfavorable impression of being an extremely obstinate and inflexible anti-Communist state," and now moved by a desire "not to run counter to world trends in this new era of hoped-for detente" (1979: 139).

Soon after the birth of South Korea's internationalist strategy in 1960s and threatened by its incipient success, North Korean leaders escalated hostilities toward the South—from 88 incidents in 1965 to 985 in 1968—and attempted to assassinate Park.[44] The North also seized the *USS Pueblo* in 1968 and downed a reconnaissance plane in international waters (1969). In tandem with this inveterate revolutionary component in the North's regional and international behavior, a more pragmatic strand evolved. Without relaxing the military buildup or the revolutionary path to unification, Kim Il Sung tested a policy of "autonomous" peaceful unification. Juche had become routinized by the 1960s as the all-encompassing principle of political organization, rendering greater stability to the revolution than ever before. Even as it maintained political supremacy and budgetary privileges, the military avoided actualizing its war-fighting potential, lest it be decimated by a maturing rival with an overwhelming patron. Instead, infiltrating guerrillas into the South, assassination attempts on South Koreans, and digging tunnels under the demilitarized zone—actions imputed to security agencies rather than to an articulated policy—were safer means of defiance.[45] Signs of relative coalitional stability and of an embryonic influence of liberalizers were evident in the North's relaxation of its economic arm's-length relations with the West in the 1970s. Western imports doubled to about 54 percent of all imports, with Japan becoming the second largest trading partner by the mid-1970s. In the early 1970s Kim Il Sung was sending clear signals via Japan, seeking direct negotiations with the US and advancing a political campaign to expand North Korea's diplomatic recognition. In 1971 Kim also withheld earlier preconditions for a dialogue with the South—the removal of US troops—thereby ushering in the North-South dialogue.

With both the South's internationalist and the North's inward-looking strategies in place by the early 1970s, a certain regional equilibrium had emerged. The political rivalry between the two states was expressed in a regional context of tension and mistrust, but not of open military conflict. At the heart of the

---

[43] On the impact of the withdrawal of the US infantry division on President Park, see Park (1979: 48, 132). On the political and economic gains from South Korea's participation in the Vietnam War, see Koh (1984: 154–55).

[44] Baek (1988: 167). Koh (1984) reports 50 incidents in 1965, rising to 629 incidents in 1968.

[45] Smith (1994: 106). On the consolidation of juche in the 1960s, see Mikheev (1996) and An (1983). On Kim Il Sung's depiction of "foreign trade personnel" as "flunkeyists," weakly imbued with Party spirit, and "infected by revisionism," see Kim Il Sung (1975a: 448–58).

competition was a symmetry: both parties developed a strategy wherein unification would be viable only following their respective domestic transformations. For the North, the South had to undergo "the south Korean revolution" first; for the South, the north had to undertake "the internationalist revolution" prior to unification.[46] This symmetry implied that undermining each other's regimes was acceptable, although the war option was to be relegated to a secondary role (for the North) if not a very last resort (for the South). By renouncing the direct use of violence—if not of aiding in prospective revolutionary takeovers—this symmetrical strategy consigned the violent option to marginalized domestic challengers in each state. These conditions alleviated pressures for war between strong adversarial coalitions even in a regional context ridden with competition and threats.

"Peaceful competitition," a policy launched by Park in 1970, and Kim Il Sung's withdrawal of preconditions, led to 1971 meetings between their respective Red Cross societies. The 1972 July Fourth Joint Communiqué and the formation of a North-South Coordination Commission became milestones in the development of a modus vivendi, with peaceful unification at its heart. This "dialogue of reconciliation" was unprecedented even if it never moved beyond preliminary discussions of confidence-building measures on humanitarian issues such as family reunification. In 1973 Park followed with a Foreign Policy for Peace and Unification, searching for a formula that would address reunification while preserving stability, domestic and regional. "We should guard," he warned, "against the theory that [unification] should be attained whatever the costs."[47] "What meaning would unification have, if what we united was just a heap of debris? Only through peaceful means could the goal of unification coincide with the nation's objective of bringing about development and prosperity. . . . Put succinctly, our policy is peace first, unification second." A mutual nonaggression pact, people's exchanges, and economic cooperation were Park's most frequently invoked policy instruments. To domestic constituencies weary of economic hardship, of the division of Korea, and of a possible invasion by the North, Park presented the North-South dialogue as the complementary requirement for "strengthening national power," lest his rejection of the war option be interpreted as a sign of weakness at home. Emphasizing the connection between the domestic and regional pillars of his grand strategy, he advanced the notion that "efforts to strengthen the fabrics of peace serve the very cause of our nation's progress and prosperity and the eventual unification of the fatherland by peaceful means." Put differently, sacrificing for "prosperity" (that is, through integration into the global political economy) was a sacrifice for strength and unification as well.

Just as Park prevented military investments from compromising his strategy in macroeconomic and political terms, he prevented the conflict with North

[46] Park (1971: 166); Baek (1988: 165–67). On the symmetrical competition between North and South for the goals of legitimacy, security, and development, see Koh (1984).

[47] Quotes in this paragraph from Park (1979: 120–24 and 1976: 125–26). On Kim Il Sung's openness to negotiations in 1972, see Kim Il Sung (1975b: 143–56).

Korea from being overtaken by militarized means. He skillfully used Northern threats to mobilize and consolidate domestic support for his strategy, as well as to suppress internal dissent, while steering competition to maintain that strategy's requirements without conveying external weakness or resignation. "I have proposed to north Korea to accept peaceful competition between our free system and theirs to determine which system can give the people a better life," argued Park (1979: 94–96), adding that the South was emerging victorious from this competition through its rising living standards. His strategy's added advantages included "the need . . . to maintain a position superior to north Korea. . . . Unless a policy of high economic growth is sustained, there will be no way to meet increased defense spending." Even after taming recalcitrant military elements into embracing an internationalist strategy, Park was not oblivious to his fellow officers' concerns with another onslaught from an overzealous counterpart in the North. Bowing to these concerns, Park (1979: 201–7) stressed military preparedness, bolstering defensive capabilities, readiness to "meet force with force," and to "forge a formidable military might that the Communists will respect." Military exercises with the US after 1969—which became the annual "Team Spirit" exercises in 1976—were an important tool in displaying preparedness against external threats.

By 1975 North Korea was unable to repay a $2 billion debt to mainly Western creditors, and its imports and exports (mainly minerals and ores) dropped dramatically relative to the early 1970s. The oil crisis had dealt a heavy blow to an incipient effort at increasing economic openness—the six-year plan in 1971–1976—which had led it to double its trade with capitalist countries (Koo 1992: 151–53). The North-South Coordination Commission ceased to meet in 1975, after three meetings (and the assassination of Park's wife by a North Korean envoy in 1974). Yet the preliminary fruits of Park's grand strategy reinforced his sense that South Korea's economic vitality, regional stability, and the positive "recognition in the world community" were intrinsically connected. Asked about his most significant political achievement, Park highlighted the South's economic triumph over the North while avoiding a war of aggression.[48] He regarded the crossing of the $10 billion threshold in manufacturing exports in 1977 as a milestone in a strategy that lifted South Korea's economy from 72nd place in 1962 to 28th place in 1976. Park carefully emphasized that South Korea had achieved that target in a shorter span than West Germany and Japan. As the strategy evolved, a stronger domestic constituency backing its regional and international requirements evolved with it. Decision makers were extremely sensitive to the expectations of a growing exporting sector, which increased its exports to the US fivefold (in constant prices) between 1968 and 1978. The logic of global access had clear corollaries for regional policies, beyond the unchallenged principle of war avoidance. Park (1979: 56) advocated "active participation in the shaping of a new world order" in order to stimulate international conditions favorable to Korea's peaceful unification under the South's initiative.

---

[48] Interview with *Time* (30 June 1975).

South Korea's attempts to revive the North-South dialogue in 1979–1980 and 1981–1983 failed despite Chinese, Soviet, and US support for downgrading military competition in the peninsula. The North had cut itself off from negotiations with Chun following the Kwangju massacre, which the North hoped would rekindle revolutionary activities against Chun. Yet Chun maintained the cooperative thrust toward the North, offering to invite Kim Il Sung to Seoul in 1981 and to meet him anywhere for direct negotiations. He followed Pyongyang's rejection with another diplomatic offensive, the National Reconciliation and Democratic Unification proposal, clearly matching his commitment to an internationalist agenda at home with a similarly forceful one to secure regional stability through cooperation. The strategy had the additional advantage of deflecting domestic instability: Chun coopted the reunification theme—revived by the student-worker movement—while decimating the opposition. He also toured ASEAN countries, gaining the endorsement of fellow East Asian internationalizers in his conflict with the North. The meetings consolidated a common strategic outlook and a burgeoning economic relationship between South Korea and ASEAN.

Meanwhile, the North was under the grip of a leadership struggle, in a pattern that recalls Iranian policies a decade after the Islamic revolution.[49] Harrison (1994: 18) depicts liberalizers as "pragmatists," "cosmopolitan," and "technocrats" who advocated a significant opening of the economy and a reduction in defense spending. The "old guard" arrayed against liberalizers was centered around the armed forces, the military-industrial complex, and the nuclear establishment. The apparently inchoate cohabitation of aggressive actions and compromising initiatives by North Korea in the early 1980s were nothing but a reflection of this growing domestic struggle. In the midst of an economic drive to expand exports, the North submitted a proposal to the South in 1980—unprecedentedly addressing it to the Republic of Korea, the South's official name—including nonaggression commitments, troop reductions, and the withdrawal of foreign troops and nuclear weapons from the peninsula. However, following domestic turmoil in the South and Chun's takeover, Kim Il Sung revived his proposal for a Democratic Confederal Republic of Koryo to the party's Sixth Congress, emphasizing revolutionary action rather than negotiations. China's economic opening in the early 1980s buttressed the North's liberalizing camp, encouraging small private agriculture and services and foreign capital in special export zones. In 1984 North Korea's new foreign investment law to attract Western and Japanese capital and technology boosted embryonic liberalization. By the mid-1980s these changes were reflected in a more conciliatory approach toward the South as a means to advance tentative liberalization in the North.[50]

Yet the trickle of economic reform at this time was no shift in paradigm. To

---

[49] Banchev (1996: 203) speaks of a "red" and "expert" political divide within the North Korean leadership; Hayes (n.d.: 8–10) of a "conservative" and "pragmatic" divide.

[50] Kwak (1988). On the failure of these early liberalizing steps, see "Kim Chong-il's 'Pragmatist Diplomacy' Analyzed," *FBIS-EAS* 20 October 1994: 41 (translated from Chungang Ilbo, Seoul).

begin with, North Korea's foreign trade amounted to only 13 percent of its GNP, with exports limited to military systems and primary products (about 80 percent of total exports), and imports dominated by oil and derivatives.[51] Military exports to the Middle East—a portion of which was bartered for oil—included sensitive nonconventional technologies and missile systems to statist-nationalist partners such as Iran, Iraq, Libya, and Syria. The old statist-nationalist guard in North Korea held these exports to be an important guarantor of its own economic, political, and military wherewithal, as part of a policy that preserved juche and Southern "collective self-reliance." Reforms were also foiled by the reigning import-substituting model, with built-in impediments that forced North Korea to discontinue paying its foreign debts, limiting its access to additional capital. Moreover, limited reforms were overshadowed by Kim Il Sung's visits to Moscow in 1984 and 1986, and the resulting Soviet aid that strengthened centralized state bureaucracies. The old guard maintained violent tactics toward the South, bombing and assassinating South Korean ministers in Rangoon in 1983, and destroying a South Korean civilian aircraft in 1987.

A round of North-South negotiations on humanitarian, economic, parliamentary, and sports issues took place in 1984–1985. Team Spirit 1986 exercises, however, allowed the military to prevail within North Korea's leadership and to end the dialogue.[52] The North's military infrastructure was not merely vast but growing, with the Korean People's Army, the People's Guards, and the Soviet Red Army militia amounting, arguably, to a quarter of the total population (about 5 million). The People's Army grew from 838,000 in 1985 to over 1.1 million in 1994. Military budgets by the end of the 1980s amounted to an unwieldy 20 to 25 percent of GDP ($4.5 to $5.4 billion of a $21.1 billion GDP). These levels were particularly astonishing, given a foreign debt that kept North Korea at the world's bottom in credit standing. The historical pillars of North Korea's grand strategy—the Workers' party and the statist and military-industrial complex—revealed remarkable staying power in the midst of a rapidly changing East Asian region, which had become the locomotive of a global export-oriented bandwagon.

In the South, Roh Tae Woo sustained the cooptation of reunification from populist rivals, and aimed at strengthening the North-South dialogue in tandem with a program of deepening global trade, investment, and technology relations. Against the strong export performance of the late 1980s and a politically inclusive social agenda, Roh announced in mid-1988 a Nordpolitik of dialogue with the North and normalization with the Soviet Union and China. There was widespread support for Roh's approach to reunification, and technocrats, the military

---

[51] Andrew Pollack, "North Korea Said to Dip into Rice Reserves to Bar Unrest," *New York Times* 18 July 1994: A3. On exports plus imports representing about 10–15 percent of GDP, see Krause (1995: 10). On military exports, see Hayes (1993a).

[52] Even at this low point in the modus vivendi, observers—including a former US ambassador to Seoul—estimated that a war between North and South was unlikely, as was reunification. See Han and Myers (1987), particularly Gleysteen (1987: 42). On the North's military, see Sakai (1996: 120); *IISS* (1995: 266).

establishment, and chaebols helped conceive of Nordpolitik as an important tool of South Korea's dominant grand strategy. In 1989 Roh formulated an "Economic Commonwealth" policy toward the North, including direct trade and investment. South Korean conglomerates had become increasingly interested in shifting their labor-intensive operations to the North.[53] Such investments were compatible with South Korea's encouragement of the North's "soft landing" (China-style), a process resisted by the North's weakened statist-nationalist coalition. This incremental cooperative pattern, embraced by the South in spite of its overwhelming power resources over the North, was a natural extension of a strategy premised on domestic and regional stability and peaceful change, all of which were key to the survival of an internationalist project.

By the early 1990s, the collapse of the Soviet Union and its allies widened the cracks in the North's statist and military-industrial complex to the point of breakdown, much as in Syria at this time. These external changes, including the fate suffered by some Eastern European leaders, impacted North Korea's leadership directly. For some, they brought home the need to address consumer demands and the transformation of the reigning model. The marketization of economic exchanges with the Soviets in 1991 now required payments in convertible currency, which the statist structure was unable to yield. Blaming the Soviets and perestroika for North Korea's predicament had both the potential of clearing the leadership of responsibility, and providing a convenient subterfuge for courting old enemies, primarily Japan and the US. The liberalizing camp included the former deputy premier and foreign trade minister Kim Dal Hyon and his successor Kim Jong U, former Premier Yon Hyong Muk, the chair of the Koryo National Industrial Development Council Yi Song-nok, and Kim Jong Il's sister and party secretary for Light Industry, Kim Kyong-hui.[54] The strategy of Northern liberalizers was certainly not based on the idea of quick reunification with the South under capitalist rules, a policy that would have doomed them politically. Rather than "if you can't win them, join them," theirs was a policy of "if you can't win them, emulate them," with the prospects of turning North Korea into yet another tiger in the East Asian neighborhood. This strongly internationalist region—with its attractive markets and burgeoning institutions—came to play no small role in narrowing down the options of the North's leadership, as expected from the regional interactive framework proposed in Chapter Three.

Renewed negotiations in 1990–1992 up to the prime ministerial level yielded the 1991 Agreement on Reconciliation, Nonaggression, and Exchanges and Cooperation, and the Joint Declaration for the Denuclearization of the Korean peninsula. North Korea had moved closer to accepting the "One Country–Two

---

[53] Choi (1993: 42–43).

[54] See "Source on ROK Firms outside of Special Zones," *FBIS-EAS* 31 October 1994: 56–57; "Can Kim's Son Rule—and Last?" *World Press Review* 49, 9 (September 1994: 16–21); "Hyundai 'Secretely' Meets North Officials in PRC," *FBIS-EAS* 24 October 1994: 59–60; "Business Prepare for North South Economic Cooperation," *FBIS-EAS* 27 October 1994: 35; Shim Jae Hoon, "Lethal Legacy," *Far Eastern Economic Review* 21 July 1994: 15.

Regions" solution—in effect two sovereign states—at least during the transition toward unification. Improved relations with the West, normalization with Japan, and some flexibility on nuclear issues bear the marks of a heightened liberalizing influence in the North. In a dramatic historical reversal, North Korea accepted separate UN membership for North and South in 1991. North Korea's trade had plummeted from $4.6 billion in 1990 to $2.6 billion in 1991, weakening the viability of the old model and sharpening the recognition that the military burden was foiling economic reconstruction.[55] In 1992 liberalizers had become strong enough to introduce a new foreign investment law and to seek the expansion of special export zones. One of the most revealing aspects of this evolution in North Korea's behavior is the fact that nearly 40,000 US troops remained in South Korea, even while the North shifted from an intractable position to more flexible cooperation. The imputed long-standing heart of the North's security dilemma remained a constant while its policies changed.

This strategic adjustment was accompanied by a peculiar political succession from Kim Il Sung to his son Kim Jong Il, which had started in the 1970s but moved to the core of the political process by the early 1990s. Kim Jong Il enjoyed support among 170,000 Small Team Campaign young cadres he had mobilized into industrial leadership positions in the 1970s, among the mass movement called Comrade Oh Jung Heup, which included some young army leaders, and among some of his father's comrades-in-arms. Kim Jong Il planted political allies in key positions, including the Prime Ministry, the Foreign Ministry, the Central Committee Secretary for Unification, and heads of police.[56] Opposition to Kim Jong Il centered on the older military generation that could not prevent his appointment as Supreme Commander in 1992 and Supreme Leader in 1994. Upon Kim Il Sung's death, Kim Jong Il's political entrepreneurship was to face a historic test. The preliminary—scattered—record suggests that the younger Kim chose to straddle the coalitional divide without consolidating a coherent supportive coalition, a personal survival strategy he had embraced for decades. Kim Jong Il was connected with attempts to cajole the most rabid conservative factions by planning and executing the murder of two American soldiers in the demilitarized zone, the 1983 bomb in Rangoon, the 1987 bomb on Korean Airlines, and the 1993 withdrawal from the Nonproliferation Treaty, among other initiatives. At the same time, he was credited with spearheading special economic zones and other policies endorsed by his liberalizing allies as well as endorsing the 1994 nuclear framework agreement.[57]

The succession process accelerated the political collapse of North Korea's leadership after 1992, deepening coalitional competition and shattering the relative stability of the North-South modus vivendi. Both domestic factors (politi-

---

[55] Park (1996: 226); *FBIS-EAS* 24 February 1992: 18.

[56] Mikheev (1996).

[57] On Kim's supportive coalition, see Sakai (1996) and Kanin (1989). On his leanings toward the liberalizing camp, see Mazarr (1995: 166–67), Gills (1996), and "Kim Jong Il's Inheritance," *Economist* 16 July 1994: 19. On his role in the bomb incidents and the NPT withdrawal, see Ahn (1994: 96) and "Who Is Kim Jong Il?" *World Press Review* 41,9 (September 1994: 18–20).

cal-economic debacles and natural disasters) as well as international ones
(mainly the disintegration of the Soviet Union) had exacerbated the cleavages
between the old guard and liberalizers, leading to a mixed pattern of cooperative and highly conflictive interaction in the Korean peninsula. The North's
confusing response to the dramatic changes of the early 1990s recalls conditions discussed in Chapter Two, in which neither coalition prevails politically,
thus dooming any coherent grand strategy. North Korea's closure (matched perhaps only by that of the old Albania) burdens the ability to trace the precise
dynamics of domestic competition and the resulting coalitional landscape. Yet
there is evidence that a condominium emerged between those who upheld the
ancien regime and incipient liberalizers, and that the two divided up the state
(and policy areas) into coalitional jurisdictions. The result of this equipoise was
the sharpening in the 1990s of an older schizoid pattern in foreign policy, evident across the regional-global and political-economic spectrum. The contours
of North Korea's grand strategy were far less coherent by the mid-1990s than in
the previous five decades, to say the least, and this became most evident in the
nuclear crises.

To the Nuclear Brink and Back

Nuclear politics offer a window into the coalitional dynamics that shaped
North-South relations in the last three decades. Even as the North was allegedly
developing a nuclear weapons program by the early 1960s, South Korea signed
the Nonproliferation Treaty in 1968, during the early phases of its internationalist shift. Park's new strategy had not yet yielded sustained results or broadened
his regime's legitimacy due to economic hardship, resentment over rapprochement with Japan, and the lingering ferment over reunification. Park was alleged
not to have completely abandoned the development of an independent nuclear
deterrent, and to have instructed the Weapons Exploitation Committee to explore that option in 1970–1971.[58] Meanwhile South Korea stalled on Nonproliferation Treaty ratification throughout the early 1970s while officials ut-
tered ambiguous statements about nuclear options. The timing—remarkably,
from the perspective of coalitional analysis—coincided with a partial return to
import-substitution, self-reliant defense, and populism during the 1971 elections. As outlined earlier in this chapter, the military-industrial complex was a
major beneficiary of the industrial deepening advanced by the bureaucrats and
military sectors that overwhelmed liberalizers in the early 1970s. The same
international context that had reinforced a more statist-nationalist deviation—
including the 1969 Guam Doctrine—bolstered advocates of a South Korean
indigenous nuclear weapons program. Under these shifting coalitional grounds,
Park sensed the pressure to tame the internationalist strategy he had forged in
the 1960s. In June 1975, at the height of the statist-nationalist interlude, Park

---

[58] Hayes (1993a); Mazarr (1995: 26). On the domestic politics of arms control in North and South
Korea, see Moon (1996).

threatened—echoing his domestic opposition—to endorse an independent nuclear deterrent if US tactical nuclear weapons were removed from South Korea, as President Carter advocated.[59]

Notwithstanding these genuflections toward a more "self-reliant" grand strategy, Park's regime avoided policies that might wholly undermine the domestic macroeconomic, regional, and international requirements of an internationalist strategy. As we have seen earlier, inflation, budget deficits, and even growing military expenditures were kept under control. In 1974 the IMF (particularly the Oil Facility), the Export-Import Bank, and other loans were crucial for balance-of-payments financing. Export-oriented firms were critically dependent on, primarily, US and Japanese investors, loans, and markets. Moreover, in an oil-dependent economy, the promise of plentiful nuclear energy from Western-supplied power plants to fuel heavy industry and intermediary sectors was at risk if nonproliferation commitments were not maintained.[60] After discovering secret nuclear South Korean activities in 1974–1975, US Secretary of State Henry Kissinger threatened a major break in bilateral economic relations—the lifeline of an internationalist strategy—unless South Korea ratified and implemented the Nonproliferation Treaty. President Ford warned in 1975 that South Korea's purchase of a reprocessing plant from France would lead to the cancellation of Export-Import Bank loans for South Korea's civilian nuclear program. The risk of antagonizing another major economic partner and guarantor of the internationalist thrust, Japan, was no less serious. The US and Japan accounted for 85 percent of all direct foreign investment in South Korea, for most of its foreign debt, and for over 60 percent of exports and imports.

Thus the domestic implications of military nuclear investments and their adverse regional and international consequences forced a more transparent approach to nuclear policy. Park, upholding the continued viability of an internationalist drive even in the midst of a statist-nationalist "correction," overruled exploration of a nuclear deterrent, ratified the Nonproliferation Treaty in April 1975, and canceled the French reprocessing plant in early 1976.[61] Despite hypothetical remarks about South Korea's ability to develop a nuclear deterrent if US tactical nuclear weapons were removed, Park now guaranteed that no such weapons program existed at the time. By 1977 he unequivocally stated that South Korea would not pursue a nuclear deterrent, although other official statements remained ambiguous, including the announcement by the minister of science and technology of intentions to build an indigenous reprocessing plant. The higher incidence of such statements between 1975 and 1978 coincided with the continued deepening and self-reliant statist-nationalist interlude strengthened by President Carter's 1977 proposals for US troop withdrawal. This interlude was exhausted by 1979, with the highest inflation since the early 1960s, declining export performance, and political turmoil unleashed by Park's assassination.

---

[59] Reiss (1988: 85–86, 93–94).

[60] On the 1973 oil crisis as a threat to South Korea's industrialization strategy, see Krueger (1993: 125).

[61] Meyer (1984: 125–27); Spector and Smith (1990: 118–37).

Chun's coup bolstered the return of EPB and neoliberal advisers to bureaucratic controls, and signaled the restoration of an internationalist strategy in all its components—domestic, regional, and global. Pointedly, no official public statements or ancillary activities (in sensitive technologies, for instance) geared to the desirability of a nuclear deterrent emerged after 1979. Chun's forceful internationalist drive was synchronized with the development of South Korea's impeccable nonproliferation credentials, including its full and effective compliance with treaty commitments.[62] For a regime taking its cues from a strong military establishment and under the ominous shadow of neighboring nuclear-capable rivals, South Korea's denuclearization makes the triumph of political-economic considerations in defining a survival strategy most remarkable. Undoubtedly, South Korea's military resources for coping with aggressive statist-nationalists in the North were not precisely a strategic equivalent of tae kwon do, a weaponless self-defense. Park had used the nuclear card to enhance South Korea's access to advanced US weapons and technology, strengthening his own military advocates of conventional deterrence. Beyond these upgraded conventional capabilities there were US commitments and tactical nuclear weapons, but the impact of "hegemonic protection" should not be exaggerated in explaining denuclearization. The uneven outcome of US pressures on—and commitments to—other states that were considering a nuclear option for decades warns against too facile a correlation between US policy and the response of would-be nuclear proliferators. More importantly, South Korea's leadership questioned the robustness of US security guarantees in the aftermath of Vietnam, the Nixon Doctrine, and normalization with Beijing.[63] In a neorealist world, South Korea's security dilemma was more alive than ever during the 1970s, just as its nuclear deterrent was being abandoned.

A coalitional perspective sheds light on this paradox, and clarifies the nature of US influence on South Korea's denuclearization. No nuclear option that would doom the internationalist strategy was acceptable to Park and his bureaucratic, military, and industrial allies. Developing a nuclear deterrent, which nowhere proved to be as cheap as its proponents had averred, had the potential of disrupting an average annual growth rate of 10 percent and unleashing domestic turmoil to the benefit of statist-nationalist challengers at home and across the border. Moreover, international responses—particularly from the US and Japan—would similarly endanger macroeconomic and political stability. The links between a commitment to an internationalized economic strategy and the renunciation of an expensive nuclear competition are thick—as with Sadat's concomitant infitah and nuclear initiatives—although more lagged in South Korea. With a conquering internationalist coalition fully in place in the 1980s, South Korea actively pursued a nuclear-weapons-free-zone despite its unquestionable capacity to overwhelm North Korea in a nuclear race. Widespread

---

[62] Hayes (1993a: 22). On Chun as the alleged architect of the effective demise of a South Korean nuclear deterrent, see Mack (1996: 21). For a clearly articulated statement of the ROK's rejection of nuclear weapons by a Korean official, see Moon (1994/1995).

[63] Reiss (1988: 80–85).

domestic support for an internationalist grand strategy, if not for its authoritarian trappings, overwhelmed the few advocates of nuclear weapons. This balance remained unchanged throughout the early 1990s, when North Korea threatened to turn Seoul into a "sea of fire," not a meek intimation to relieve the South's security predicament, which nonetheless the South's leadership could largely ignore.[64]

For Kim Il Sung's regime, nuclear weapons—or, at a minimum, ambiguity about their possession—represented the ultimate expression of national independence and technical achievement that it could brandish as evidence of the superior accomplishments and potential of North Korea's model. The viability of its grand strategy was questioned once the South's economic miracle became apparent, particularly to liberalizing elements in the North's leadership. An independent and ambiguous nuclear stand had high payoffs for soothing a restive military establishment and statist-nationalists in the party, bureaucracy, and military-industrial complex.[65] Moreover, proponents of nuclear weapons had packaged them in juche trappings as the means to prevent subordination to a foreign yoke forever, expecting to appeal not just to North Koreans but to sympathetic nationalists in the South, as well.[66] US nuclear threats during the Korean War and subsequently—notably US Secretary of Defense James Schlesinger's warning that the US would not foreclose using tactical nuclear weapons in the event of a North Korean attack—strengthened pro-nuclear forces in the North.[67] Yet liberalizers who had successfully promoted the 1984 foreign investment law, special export zones such as Rajin-Sonbong, and small-scale privatization challenged the dominance of statist-nationalists by the mid-1980s, buttressed by demonstration effects from China's opening. The timing of North Korea's Nonproliferation Treaty ratification in 1985 indicates that US and Soviet coercion alone were not enough—coercion had not yielded ratification until then—and that a nascent liberalizing camp had made North Korea more receptive to nuclear transparency.

A domestic coalitional equipoise was to project its shadow into North Korea's nuclear behavior in the subsequent decade. After ratifying the Nonproliferation Treaty, statist-nationalists prevailed in forcing North Korea's rejection of full-scope inspections by the International Atomic Energy Agency

---

[64] On Pyongyang's threat, see *FBIS-EAS* 21 March 1994: 14–24, 39–47. On the relative equanimity of South Korea's response at the popular level, see Andrew Pollack, "Nuclear Fears? Noodle Sales Say No," *New York Times* 9 May 1994: A7. On the very marginal support for a South Korean nuclear deterrent in the South, see Mazarr (1995: 63, 119), who also cites South Korea's Defense Minister Lee Hong Koo's declaration that the South would oppose sanctions on the North for its nuclear behavior, because sanctions might trigger a war in the Korean peninsula.

[65] Bracken (1992). For a well-argued case on the centrality of regime survival and on the incompleteness (at best) and incorrectness (at worst) of the external security interpretation of North Korea's behavior, see Cotton (1993). The following section on North Korea builds extensively on Mazarr (1995). See *ENSP News Release* (Monterey Institute of International Studies, 1 June 1993) for a chronology of North Korea's nuclear activities.

[66] Park (1996: 224).

[67] Mazarr (1995: 16–21); Kwak (1988: 206).

(IAEA) and of treaty commitments to sign a Safeguards Agreement. North Korea's position was suspended between a formal commitment to the Non-proliferation Treaty but an ineffective compliance with it, somewhat akin to Saddam Hussein's policy during that period. The US removal of tactical nuclear weapons from the area in September 1991 and Roh Tae Woo's expressed de-nuclearization commitments removed major excuses used by nuclear propo-nents in the North to reject international inspections.[68] Both Koreas signed the Joint Declaration for the Denuclearization of the Korean Peninsula, in 1991, stipulating verification by joint inspection teams independent of the IAEA. The South suspended 1992 Team Spirit exercises to signal its commitment to this process. In January 1992 the US inaugurated direct talks with the North, a path strongly sought by North Korean liberalizers. The North signed the safeguards agreement and admitted IAEA official inspections of its nuclear facilities for the first time.

However, lingering resistance to bilateral mutual inspections from the North's old guard provoked the South into renewing Team Spirit in 1993. Moreover, IAEA inspections throughout 1992 uncovered irregularities in plu-tonium reprocessing that triggered IAEA demands—the first ever—for special inspections of North Korea's military facilities. The military and North Korea's Atomic Energy Minister Choe U Jin rejected such inspections adamantly, and the daily *Nodong Sinmun* warned that forced inspections would unleash "the crushing calamities of war."[69] In March 1993 North Korea announced its inten-tion to withdraw from the Nonproliferation Treaty and to put its armed forces on a semi-war footing, triggering an international crisis. Like other radical stat-ist-nationalist coalitions, North Korea defied political and economic sanctions from great powers and international institutions, allowing a variety of state agencies and industries in charge of productive and distributive functions to benefit from international closure. In time, a severe economic crisis—the worst in decades—depleted this coalition's ability to protect its fiefdoms, economic and military agencies alike, leading it to articulate the position that "sanctions mean war." Signs of starvation and of domestic coalitional strife were evident by mid-1993, with the removal of Deputy Prime Minister and Chief of State Planning Kim Dal Hyon.

A new "economic policy for the period of adjustment" in 1994 to 1996 sig-naled revived liberalizing priorities in agriculture, light industry, and foreign trade.[70] In June the North suspended its withdrawal from the Nonproliferation Treaty, but haggling over the nuclear "package" intensified in late 1993 and

---

[68] Harrison (1994: 19).

[69] *FBIS-EAS* 22 February 1993: 11–13. On support for a nuclear weapon in the North Korean People's Army, and on the psychological buildup toward a war option, according to a military defector from North Korea, see Mazarr (1995: 101, 107, and 152).

[70] "Kim Chong-il's 'Pragmatist Diplomacy' Analyzed," *FBIS-EAS* 20 October 1994: 41 (trans-lated from Chungang Ilbo, Seoul). Kim Il Sung acknowledged the "grave" challenges facing the North Korean economy in a rare public admission in his 1994 New Year's address (Washington, D.C.: United States Institute of Peace *Special Report*, n.d.: 15).

early 1994. The package was clearly designed to satisfy both the risk-prone old guard and the risk-averse reformist camp. Those resisting concessions to the US or the IAEA were essentially bereft of external allies but strengthened by the failure of US, South Korean, Japanese, and multilateral promises of improved economic ties to materialize. Such failure hurt nascent liberalizers, who were willing to exploit the nuclear card to extract economic benefits that would underpin a "soft landing" and prevent the regime's total collapse.[71] President Carter's visit in June 1994 reinforced the liberalizing camp somewhat, capturing Kim Il Sung's commitment to improve relations with the US and the South and to allow resumption of IAEA inspections.

An international actor playing a nonpartisan role in domestic coalitional dynamics—nature—intervened to throw North Korea's cleavages into turmoil. Kim Il Sung died on July 8, 1994, just as the US and North Korea were converging on the nuclear package. The core question had now become whether or not Kim Jong Il was able to piece together a coherent survival coalition, a task that had essentially eluded even the older Kim in his last stretch. Kim Jong Il did push through the nuclear package, whose features revealed the imprint of his personal survival strategy: coalitional straddling. As chairman of the National Defense Committee he approved the Agreed Framework in October 1994, normalizing relations with the US, replacing the sensitive graphite-moderated reactor with a light-water reactor, guaranteeing peace and security in the Korean peninsula, and consolidating the Nonproliferation Treaty.[72] The old guard scored concessions, such as allowing spent fuel rods to remain in North Korea for five to nine years and avoiding South Korea's direct participation in negotiations. Liberalizers obtained expanded trade and investment commitments and expected the downgrading of Team Spirit exercises to deprive their domestic opponents from justification for destabilizing initiatives.[73] Access to energy resources (oil and a proliferation-resistant nuclear reactor yielding ten times the output of planned graphite systems) served both political camps well.

North Korea's unrelenting emphasis on settling with the US rather than directly with the South had mutually reinforcing advantages for both coalitions in North Korea. First, it raised the North's international profile, making it worthy of further US attention. Direct negotiations with the US also made good on the

---

[71] See interview with Kim Yong Sun, former head of the International Affairs Department of the Worker's party and the alleged architect of a breakthrough in Japanese-North Korean relations (Hayes, 1993b: 8–10 and n.d.: 7–8). Hayes links nuclear hard-liners with the coalition opposed to economic reform, and nuclear "doves"—working to undo North Korea's withdrawal from the NPT—with economic liberalizers (pp. 9–10).

[72] See "Foreign Ministry Communique on US-North Accord," *FBIS-EAS* 20 October 1994: 25 (translation from Pyongyang Korean Central Broadcasting Network).

[73] Moon (1994/1995: 104) argues that coercion and appeasement worked in favor of Pyongyang "hardliners," while luring with economic aid strengthened leaders favoring economic reform. Among the destabilizing statements from "hardliners" was that by General Choe Kwang, chief of the North Korean Army, who reiterated the Army's objective of "reunifying the fatherland with arms in the 1990s." See "Kim Il Sung and the Specter of War: North Korea's Leader Has Nothing to Lose," *World Press Review* 41, 4 (April 1994: 18–20).

pervasive rhetoric of the South as US "puppet," thus eschewing the need to recognize the South's independent statehood.[74] This strategy's affinity with Assad's policy toward Israel and the US is remarkable, and revealed a subservience to the party apparatus and the military while satisfying an emerging liberalizing camp. The North's refusal to negotiate directly with the South was no small affront, but one that the latter could afford to absorb in light of the package's expected positive long-term effects on the North. South Korea reacted to the North's unprecedented withdrawal from the Nonproliferation Treaty in very restrained fashion, suggesting a downgrading of Team Spirit, economic aid, and guarantees not to attack the North in exchange for the North's return to its treaty commitments. Kim Young Sam navigated the South's new democratic waters by ensuring a peaceful outcome to the nuclear crisis—key to the preservation of the South's miracle—while deflating nationalist opposition charges of subservience to US policy.[75] South Korea's central role in supplying two 1,000-megawatt reactors to the North—with chaebol and EPB participation—was a convenient compromise. Chaebols had remained the main instrument of the South's internationalist strategy and were to spearhead the North's transformation.

The execution of the Agreed Framework in late 1994 and 1995 bore the signature of continued coalitional tensions in North Korea. The sharp policy turns throughout the 1990s highlight the difficulty of reducing North Korea's behavior, as paranoid as it may seem, exclusively to security considerations. Such considerations remained virtually unchanged throughout 1992 and 1993, while the domestic tug-of-war in the North built up. Thus coalitional dynamics untangle the paradox of North Korea's "two-track" policy (Mazarr 1995), suggesting that a deeper look at the domestic sources of its schizophrenic behavior may hold more promise than a reaffirmation of a paranoid response to a largely unchanged security dilemma. The fact remains that despite efforts by powerful strategic allies and powerful strategic adversaries, North Korea refused to relinquish nuclear aspirations for an extended period of time. As with South Korea, domestic receptivity reveals itself as an important intervening factor between hegemonic assertion and the response of would-be nuclear powers.

The economic crisis and famine of the 1990s in North Korea—and the prospects of regime collapse—appear to have strengthened the hand of liberalizers. In September 1996 the hand of old-guard planning was evident in the intrusion of a North Korean submarine into South Korea's territorial waters, an incident that shook the confidence of South Korean investors. However, the North Ko-

---

[74] See, inter alia, "18 October US-ROK 'Air War Game' Reported," *FBIS-EAS* 20 October 1994: 27–28.

[75] See ROK Foreign Minister Han Sung-chu's formal response to the Agreed Framework in *FBIS-EAS* 31 October 1994: 57–59. See also Kim Young Sam's responses to North Korea's detention of a South Korean ship carrying rice to the North, and to North Korea's violations of the armistice in Panmunjon, in Nicholas D. Kristoff, "South Korea's President, in a Rift with North, Delays Talks," *New York Times*, 15 October 1995: 5, and David Holley, "South Korean Security Suddenly Becomes an Issue," *Los Angeles Times* 5 April 1996: A5.

rean government proceeded to extend an unprecedented formal apology to South Korea. Moreover, Trade Minister Kim Jong U acknowledged in early 1997 that North Korea is now "seeking close links with the capitalist economy," recognizing that it must change with the times and lure foreign investment.[76] That the statement was made while attending the Davos conference of the World Economic Forum—the organization gathering key international political and economic leaders of the global capitalist economy—was a powerful sign of growing liberalizing strength. The defection of Hwang Jang Yop, the very architect of juche and a former close aide to Kim Jong Il, opened an unprecedented window into internal coalitional dynamics and the old-guard's lingering strength.[77] At the same time, the appointment as premier of pioneer liberalizer Kim Dal Hyon suggested that the coalitional equipoise within North Korea could be superseded before century's end.

THE TRIAD: ECONOMIC LIBERALIZATION, DEMOCRACY, AND REGIONAL COOPERATION

First the Market and Peace, then Democracy: Korea and Taiwan

The overview of war and peace in the Korean peninsula in the last five decades highlights the essential irrelevance of democratic peace theorizing to much of this history. Conflict and cooperation evolved largely in response to coalitional dynamics and their connections with changing international structures. The emergence of cooperation—neither extensive nor intensive—can be traced to the modus vivendi achieved by competing coalitions in North and South Korea, of equally authoritarian stripes. The North has remained an authoritarian and repressive state with an uncertain future even after the South democratized. Clearly, as in the Middle East and for decades in the Southern Cone, the building blocks of the democratic peace—democracies facing each other—have been absent in the Korean peninsula. The South's progressive democratization allows a preliminary probing into interactions among an internationalist strategy, democratization, and cooperative policies.

For most of the postwar era, South Korea was ruled by coalitions operating under the centralizing power of successive presidents prone to ruthless authoritarian practices. Rhee headed a heavily repressive nominal democracy with fascist tendencies, under which he was elected by 72 percent of the vote in 1952, which declined to 55 percent in 1956. After leading a coup in 1961, Park (1964–1972) governed over another nominal democracy, under which he was reelected in 1967 by 51.4 percent of the votes against 40.9 for the main opposi-

---

[76] Quoted from *The International Herald Tribune* in the *Northeast Asia Peace and Security Network Daily Report* 4 February 1997: 2–3. Pyongyang acknowledged that its 1996 grain output could barely satisfy 50 percent of its needs (*People's Daily*, "DPRK Badly in Need of Food Help," 4 February 1997: A7, cited in *Northeast Asia Peace and Security Network Daily Report* 5 February 1997: 6).

[77] *Northeast Asia Peace and Security Network Daily Report* 14 February 1997: 1–6.

tion party. The returns of arguably fraudulent elections in 1971 did not bode well for Park's own survival, leading him to introduce martial law in 1972, in tandem with other political adjustments. Both the Yushin ("revitalizing") constitution and the Heavy and Chemical Industry Plan were designed to attract a new base of support. Chun's Fifth Republic (1980–1988) maintained a highly authoritarian system in place. The crisis year of 1980 created an opportunity for democratization, but the private sector and the middle class—fearing the unraveling of the internationalist strategy under pressure from miners, steelworkers, and students—failed to support the divided opposition at that time.[78]

South Korea's experience has been used to advance both the "authoritarian advantage" model of export-led industrialization and the theory that economic development begets democracy. Economic markets are considered necessary for democracy, because they create conditions for sustained economic growth in the long term while diffusing economic and political control over resources. South Korea's internationalist strategy was challenged repeatedly, precisely on the basis of its authoritarian form. In time, democratization became an essential imperative for saving the strategy. By 1987, with the strategy firmly rooted as the pivot of South Korea's political economy, the large middle class could transcend the dilemma between demanding democracy and undermining the strategy. Roh Tae Woo presided over a political opening while maintaining his predecessor's policies on exports, on macroeconomic stability, on restraining chaebols, and on deepening North-South economic and security cooperation. Roh shaped the new Democratic Liberal Party as his instrument to invest an internationalist strategy with democratic legitimacy.

Although the transition to democracy began in 1987, only in 1993 did South Korea become a more effective democracy, when Kim Young Sam became the first civilian democratic president since the 1950s. His proclaimed reform program aimed at improving the internationalist strategy he inherited by anchoring it in democratic institutions, in cleansed government, and in social equity. In his own words (Kim 1994): "Bold steps will be taken to internationalize and globalize all aspects of national life." The inception of democracy did not result in any profound discontinuities in South Korea's internationalist strategy or in its regional expressions (at this point South Korea's exports and imports represented over 65 percent of GDP). Kim Young Sam, who had joined the Democratic Liberal Party, maintained cooperative initiatives toward the North even at the height of a nuclear confrontation. A policy of "soft landing," enabling investments in the North and securing stability and piecemeal change in the peninsula, advanced the usual coalitional suspects in the South, notably a long list of chaebols actively seeking investments in the North's tourism, food-processing, electronics, auto, and cement industries.[79] The statist-nationalist opposition

---

[78] Haggard and Kaufman (1992: 334 and 1995: 230). On middle- and working-class support for the dominant grand strategy, see Jang Jip Choi (1993: 29–32, 44–46).

[79] The list includes Hyundai, Lotte, Jinro, Tongyang, Tongil, Daewoo, Samsung, Lucky-Goldstar, Sunkyong, Kohap, Kolon, Chillo, Tusan, and Hanwha, and other smaller and medium-sized firms seeking indirect trade with North Korea. See "Economic Projects to Invest in DRPK Reviewed,"

could now operate under a democratic framework that essentially legitimized the internationalist strategy.

South Korea's experience has been replicated in different forms but with largely similar outcomes elsewhere in East Asia, where a critical mass of internationalist coalitions produced peaceful stability on the ashes of earlier wars. Prominent among these states was Taiwan, whose postwar history shares many of the characteristics of South Korea's internationalist evolution. The early years, under Chiang Kai-shek, involved heavy state intervention and a planned economy emphasizing import-substitution. The Kuomintang (KMT) initiated a program (1958–1960) of large scale monetary, fiscal, trade, taxation, and foreign investment reform, including the monitoring of military expenses and the liquidation of state enterprises. By the early 1960s Chiang Ching-kuo had softened state intervention and embraced an export-oriented strategy, in a context in which neither agrarian nor import-substituting interests were politically strong enough to challenge.[80] Managers of state enterprises and banks as well as some party ideologues resisted reforms that would place greater economic and political power in the hands of their private entrepreneurial foes. Thus monopolistic firms remained under state control while antimonopolistic practices were enforced on the private sector. Small and medium-sized firms flourished. The extensive use of foreign direct investment helped smaller component manufacturers and prevented big monopolies like South Korea's chaebols. The KMT's openness to foreign direct investment thus preempted the rise of domestic political competitors in the form of big business, helped Taiwan break through its international isolation, and ingratiated its ruling coalition with its key benefactor, the US.

The KMT's growth strategy was anchored in price stability, an egalitarian income distribution, and decentralized (small to medium) entrepreneurship. These political principles were rooted in the KMT's interpretation of its defeat by mainland China as a result of hyperinflation, hyperinequality, and hypercorruption of business. The KMT coopted highly educated professionals and technicians fleeing the mainland (1945–1949) and native Taiwanese into the ranks of the bureaucracy. It decimated the landlord class through land reform (1949–1953) and kept private business at arms' length while creating conditions for their expansion. The inflow of experts helped build a socio-economic and political infrastructure of symbolic analysts with a natural internationalist orientation. State technocrats relied heavily in their discussions with the political leadership on the centrality of avoiding inflation to sustain the grand strategy— prices rose 2 percent between 1961 and 1970. Tight fiscal and monetary policy, high real interest rates, low money supply, and stable foreign exchange rates were core instruments of KMT policy, even during the economic crises of the 1970s. The overall rate of effective protection was 5 percent during the 1970s.

FBIS-EAS 25 October 1994: 47–48; "Hyundai 'Secretly' Meets North Officials in PRC"; "Problems in Doing Business with DPRK Noted," *FBIS-EAS* 28 October 1994: 45–46. On Kim Young Sam's grand strategy, see Kim (1994, 1995).

[80] Cheng (1990: 154–58); Cumings (1984); Gereffi (1990); Chan (1988).

Exports as a share of GDP more than doubled from 21.3 percent in 1966 to 46.7 percent in 1973. Foreign trade amounted to nearly 85 percent of Taiwan's GNP by 1985.[81]

The military initially felt threatened by the possible effects of an export-led strategy on both economic sufficiency and war preparedness, but was ultimately unable to stem the internationalist political tide. The KMT's overriding concern was economic stability, compelling a shift from rabid militarism in the early years to "an evermore absorbing interest in economic growth."[82] Facing a no less rabid adversary in the People's Republic of China, Taiwan's average military expenditures—8 percent of GNP after 1961—declined by the 1970s as its internationalist strategy took root. The US granted protection to Taiwan but was reluctant to build its military, lest it decided to challenge the mainland, which explains Taiwan's higher level of defense expenditures than South Korea's.[83] Even at those levels, Taiwan's military burden played a minor and indirect role on its GNP growth, export expansion, and improving income equality. The KMT was always reluctant to finance expensive indigenous arms industries.[84] After the initial phase of statism, militarization, and an aggressive posture toward the mainland, Taiwan pursued, like South Korea, the least confrontational policies in a highly adversarial regional context. It renounced an expensive nuclear competition and joined the nonproliferation regime effectively, despite a questionable US commitment to Taiwan following normalization with China and the abrogation of the Washington-Taipei Security Treaty.[85] Taiwan's entrepreneurs became central to the economic transformation of its archenemy—mainland China—a strategy that echoes that of South Korea's toward the North.

The last phase in Taiwan's postwar evolution was the conversion of its liberalizing strategy into a working democracy, a process that crystallized in its first free elections in December 1992, literally the day after South Korea's.

First the Market and Peace, and Then—Maybe—Democracy: ASEAN

Elsewhere in the region a slowly evolving cluster of liberalizers came to institute ASEAN, little more than a vague commitment between the ASEAN Declaration of 1967 and the first summit meeting of heads of state (Declaration of ASEAN Concord) in 1976. ASEAN initially included Thailand, Singapore, Indonesia, Malaysia, Philippines, and Brunei. It later expanded to include Vietnam and, in 1997, Myanmar, and Laos. "The concept of free enterprise . . . is the philosophical basis of ASEAN," declared Malaysia's foreign minister.[86]

---

[81] Chan and Clark (1991); Haggard (1995a: 129); Jeon (1995: 77–79); Bradford (1990: 38).

[82] Amsden (1985); Cheng (1990: 155).

[83] Cumings (1984: 26); Chan (1992b: 167); IISS (1995: 266–67); UNDP 1994: 170.

[84] On how Taiwan's export drive, fiscal conservatism, and high rate of savings relative to consumption enabled it to contain inflation despite the defense burden, see Chan (1992b).

[85] Dunn (1982: 56–57).

[86] Acharya (1992: 152).

"The most enduring lesson of history is that ambitious growing countries can expand either by grabbing territory, people and resources, or by trading with other countries. The alternative to free trade is not just poverty, it is war," proclaimed Lee Kuan Yew, the president of Singapore.[87]

Export-led strategies in Malaysia, Indonesia, and Thailand succeeded with much less emphasis on industrial policy than in South Korea and Taiwan. In Singapore the People's Action party (PAP) began implementing a high-growth strategy based on economic stability and low inflation even prior to independence in 1965. Following the forced separation from the Federation of Malaysia, the centrality of an export-led model to a city-state's political survival strategy became evident. By 1968 the shift to an export-led strategy was complete. Labor activism was repressed once PAP abandoned its socialist roots, although PAP coopted trade-union leadership, promising stability in exchange for discipline and low wages. State agencies (statutory boards) and enterprises emerged to spearhead the new strategy in the absence of private local entrepreneurs. Openness to foreign direct investment doubled the share of such investments in gross domestic investment, from 33 percent in 1966 to 68 percent in 1980. Net foreign direct investments in Indonesia grew tenfold between 1970 and 1989 and over 20 times in Malaysia and Singapore in the same period. Price stability anchored the strategy.[88] Between 1965 and 1993 the GDPs of Singapore, Indonesia, and Malaysia grew at an average annual rate of between 6 and 8 percent (higher for Singapore). The three fastest growing states had also become the most active in promoting regional stability and cooperation through ASEAN.

ASEAN military expenditures declined over time, and quite dramatically relative to the preceding statist-nationalist phase. Under Sukarno, Indonesia's foreign policy had been rather aggressive vis-à-vis its neighbors. Suharto's military coup in Indonesia—the New Order (Orde Baru)—reduced defense expenditures relative to GDP from 5 percent in 1966 to 3 percent in 1976 and down to 1.4 percent in 1994. Inflation declined from an average of 35 percent in the 1965–1980 period to about 8 percent in the 1980–1989 period. The New Order specifically proscribed competitive military allocations that could undermine the political-economic model, although it allowed military involvement in economic activities that provided it with off-budget funds, a pattern born under Sukarno. Indonesia's trade openness (imports plus exports as a percentage of GDP) nearly doubled in three years from 17.66 percent in 1965 to 33.29 percent in 1968. Suharto reversed his predecessor's regional policies, now relying on cooperative ASEAN relations to facilitate the implementation of his domestic agenda.[89] Thailand's military expenses as a percentage of GDP were halved, from 5 percent in 1985 to 2.6 percent in 1994. During that same period, Malaysia's declined from 5.6 percent to 3.9 percent, Singapore's and Brunei's from 6.7 to 4.8, and Vietnam's (a latecomer to ASEAN) from 19.4 percent to 5.7

[87] "Survey: Asia. A Billion Consumers," *Economist* (30 October 1993).
[88] Jeon (1995: 76–77).
[89] On ASEAN as a corollary of the New Order, see Anwar (1994), and Emmerson (1996: 38). Economic data from World Bank (1991: 204–5 and 1996: 208–9, 248–49).

percent. The growth in defense spending in East Asia as a whole has lagged by 50 percent behind the growth in GNP. Military expenditures in Southeast Asia were 2.8 percent of GDP in 1990–1991.[90] Inflation in Singapore and Malaysia—quite low between 1965 and 1980 at about 5 percent—declined to 1.5 percent in the 1980s.

Some ASEAN members faced armed insurgencies, notably East Timor's demands for independence from Indonesia. Regional cooperation operated with one eye on domestic challenges to the regime's grand strategy and the other on enhancing their collective appeal to foreign investors. The domestic target was—much as in Park's political logic outlined above—to deflate internal challenges by fostering economic growth, as in Indonesia's policy of *ketahanan* (resilience). The international aim was to consolidate a reputation for domestic and regional, political and economic stability to attract investments. The 1983 Basic Agreement on ASEAN Industrial Joint Ventures (AIJV) called for equity participation by at least two ASEAN partners, allowing non-ASEAN participation as well, and all with the objective of promoting joint ventures with foreign capital and technology. Business groups were behind the creation of AIJV, but until then, ASEAN economic steps were more superficial and less directly responsive to private-sector concerns.[91] The global—rather than regional—economic focus of ASEAN states is typical of an internationalist agenda aimed at universal trade liberalization. ASEAN's intraregional trade has lagged behind its initial cooperative thrust. Only twenty years after ASEAN's creation, an agreement for an ASEAN Free Trade Area was signed in 1992, emphasizing, once again, the advantages of regional integration for foreign investments. Malaysia's Mahathir Mohamad's call for a pan-Asian regional economic bloc found little response among his neighbors.

In time ASEAN cooperation deepened into security issues, and the organization established a successful record of diffusing internal disputes and managing an effective regional diplomacy.[92] Conflicts among members remained, but have been resolved in ways that uphold their common strategy. The Philippines, for instance, recalled its ambassador to Singapore in 1995 in the wake of the execution of a Philippine maid accused of murder, but the level of tension was no higher than when Australia recalled its ambassador to France in connection to the latter's nuclear tests in the Pacific. Nor did the Spratly Islands dispute involving Brunei, Malaysia, the Philippines, and Vietnam—in addition to China and Taiwan—undermine ASEAN cooperative relations. ASEAN's Regional Fo-

---

[90] *IISS* (1995: 266–67); Deger (1986); Ball (1988: 63–64). ASEAN arms imports between 1984 and 1993 remained lower than $1.5 billion in constant 1990 prices (Stockholm International Peace Research Project 1994: 510), despite exceptional GDP growth. Emmerson (1996: 62–63), Buzan and Segal (1994) and Mack and Kerr (1994: 131) oppose the notion of an arms race engulfing ASEAN states.

[91] Thambipillai (1994: 132 n17); Lim (1996: 22–23). On the weakness of populist challenges in East and Southeast Asian countries, see Haggard (1995a: 455).

[92] Shirk (1997); Richardson (1994/1995: 37).

rum, created in 1994, spearheaded an ASEAN nuclear-weapon-free-zone signed by all ten Southeast Asian states in 1995.

Myanmar, Kampuchea, Laos, and Vietnam were initially excluded from ASEAN as statist-nationalist aberrations, but their progressive liberalization opened the way to inclusion. Vietnam acceded in 1992, after its economic reform accelerated in 1989, inflation fell to 10 percent in 1992, and growth averaged 8 percent by 1991. Myanmar was accepted as an observer member—the final step before gaining full membership—in 1996. ASEAN played an important role in the global effort to stabilize Kampuchea. It also rejected external intrusion on human rights and democratic deficits in Myanmar, stressing ASEAN's abstention from intervening in domestic affairs. Democracy has never been the solvent of regional cooperation among ASEAN states, most of which remain authoritarian. Some ASEAN leaders have become the new ideologues of "authoritarian advantage"—now invested with "Asian values"—as a way of preempting their own demise, quite likely with the conversion of internationalist strategies into effective democracies.

IMPLICATIONS FOR COALITIONAL ANALYSIS AND THE DEMOCRATIC PEACE HYPOTHESIS

Coalitional dynamics have underpinned the evolving nature of North-South relations in the Korean peninsula in the last five decades, including historical shifts away from war and into a modus vivendi, contrasting policies regarding nuclear weapons, and the timing and mode of denuclearization and economic exchange. This chapter offers the following general conclusions regarding coalitional analysis and democratic peace considerations.

1. The statist-nationalist coalitions ruling North and South Korea after World War II created auspicious conditions for large-scale war. The North's revolutionary coalition under Kim Il Sung amassed the military wherewithal in 1950 and aimed at swallowing the South (and Rhee's feeble coalition), miscalculating the Cold War implications of its behavior.

2. In the early 1960s Park Chung Hee drew together a highly consensual ruling coalition behind the South's shift from import-substitution to an internationalist strategy and global access. The stronger the domestic political support for such strategy, the more persistent the South's cooperative overtures toward the North became. The tame responses of the South to aggressive provocations from the North were geared to avoid a derailment of its internationalist thrust.

3. The gradual coalitional consolidation of an internationalist strategy in the South and a statist-nationalist strategy in the North facilitated a modus vivendi between the two, leading to the very first steps in regional cooperation in the 1970s. This was a regional context of tension, mistrust, high ideological polarity, and political competition between the two strategies, but one that has avoided armed conflict since the 1950s.

4. South Korea's unilateral denuclearization provides a classic example of an internationalist coalition's emphasis on domestic and regional stability as strategic building blocks. The most ambiguous statements on its nuclear policy coincided with the heightened influence of statist-nationalist forces in the early 1970s. This interlude ended with a forceful restoration of the internationalist strategy under Chun, which signaled a transparent and full commitment to denuclearization.

5. The stronger the political foundations of an internationalist project, the weaker had become the efforts to resort to a nuclear deterrent, despite three "neorealist" incentives: first, the exacerbation of South Korea's security dilemma during the 1970s (Guam doctrine, Carter's policies), just as its nuclear deterrent was being abandoned; second, a growing capability to overwhelm the North in a nuclear race; and third, the North's threats to reduce Seoul to "a sea of fire." A coalitional perspective explains this paradox while unpackaging the nature of US influence on South Korea's denuclearization.

6. The collapse of the North's grand strategy as a result of interactive global and domestic processes, and the consequent deterioration in the old guard's ruling capability, sharpened existing coalitional cleavages. The intense competition between incipient liberalizers and guardians of the statist-nationalist model explains many of the ensuing sharp turns in North Korea's now-combative / now-cooperative policies of the 1990s, including its slide into the nuclear brink. The old modus vivendi was now obsolete.

7. Concerted hegemonic coercion by the US and Soviet Union did not succeed in forcing North Korea to abandon nuclear ambiguity prior to 1985, when it ratified the Nonproliferation Treaty, nor in the following decade, when it refused full-scope inspections. As with South Korea, domestic receptivity (connected to changes in the domestic coalitional balance) is key to understanding when hegemonic assertion yields behavioral changes among would-be nuclear powers.

8. The key domestic challenge to South Korea's ruling coalition was its authoritarian nature, and the challenge grew deeper as the internationalizing strategy grew stronger. The more authoritarianism became a central obstacle in the survival and stability of an internationalizing strategy, the more strenuous became the efforts by political entrepreneurs to shed the undemocratic baggage left by earlier liberalizers.

9. The South's internationalist strategy did not merely survive the transition to democracy but was strengthened by it, widening political support for the strategy's basic tenets by investing it with democratic institutions. The statist-nationalist opposition could now operate under a democratic framework, paradoxically endowing the internationalist strategy with greater legitimacy.

10. Personalistic authoritarian leaders played an important role in coalescing supportive coalitions for either strategy. However, internationalist strategies transcended the original leadership—as in South Korea and Taiwan—whereas statist-nationalist strategies embedded them. The death of Kim Il Sung thus undermined the survival of the original coalition, which exacerbated fears across the border that leaders in dramatic political retreat might resort to external aggression. Diversionary wars as a first resort are more common an instrument in the grand strategic kit of statist-nationalist coalitions than in the kit of their competitors, for reasons identified in Chapter Two.

11. South Korea's experience has been replicated in different forms but with largely similar outcomes elsewhere in East Asia. In Taiwan, a highly consensual ruling coalition steered an internationalist strategy that imposed extreme restraint toward mainland China, compelled Taiwan to renounce nuclear weapons, and emphasized classical "trading state" tools, including a foreign investment offensive in the mainland. The aplomb of Taiwan's response to China's militarized threats in 1996 is symptomatic of a strongly consolidated internationalist coalition.

12. Democratization exacerbated pressures for equity and, paradoxically, for Taiwan's formal independence from China. Taiwan's globalizing strategy, however, had evolved in tandem with a more egalitarian income distribution than elsewhere in the industrializing world, a feature that helped attract growing domestic political support for the strategy.[93]

13. A critical mass of internationalist coalitions in ASEAN came to create peaceful stability on the ashes of earlier wars. Despite wider security considerations in the Asia-Pacific region, ASEAN has avoided an arms race or an offensive build-up, deepened their collective internationalist agenda, and coopted remnants of statist-nationalism in the region.[94] This process unfolded with a very thin institutional foundation in place, one that fed on growing liberalization and cooperation more than it imposed either of them. With some exceptions, ASEAN continues to be about emerging—and sometimes quite vulnerable—markets, not about emerging democracies.

The experience of the East Asian states reviewed in this chapter—with internationalist strategies acting as "the compass of peace"—had worldwide demonstration effects. These effects have been marked in the Southern Cone of Latin America, less impressive in South Asia, and—as we have seen—not yet deeply rooted in the Middle East. However, the East Asian experience also highlighted the risks of an internationalist strategy—as outlined in Figure 1—including a heighted vulnerability to the global political economy. The 1997 financial crisis brought this exposure into relief but also magnified the residual vestiges of statist control of the banking system and the perils of embedding any strategy in a corrupt and nepotistic political foundation. As I point out in the concluding chapter, this proclivity—from Indonesia to Iraq—has not been the monopoly of either statist-nationalist-confessional or internationalist coalitions.

---

[93] On equitable land distribution, equitable wages and salaries distribution, and East Asian growth, see Amsden (1991). On other social indicators UNDP (1996) and World Bank (1994).

[94] On the unthreatening nature of arms acquisitions in the region, and on the restrained levels of military expenditures, see Buzan and Segal (1994) and Mack and Kerr (1994: 131).

PART THREE

Implications

CHAPTER EIGHT

Theory and Policy: An Agenda

THE EMPIRICAL CHAPTERS in Part Two cover a wide range of states, coalitional variants, and regional orders. They thus offer a rich experimental foundation both for the testing of propositions and for suggesting possible paths to refining them. I address these two tasks sequentially in this final chapter. It should be noted that predicting which coalition will prevail electorally or otherwise is beyond the main thrust of this book. Adding to the common barriers to predicting coalitional formations identified by Gourevitch (1986: 67)—the role of leadership, entrepreneurship, and circumstance—the rapidly changing institutionalization of both markets and democracy throughout most of the world makes such predictions even more precarious. As with Clausewitz's proverbial "fog of war," we are still under the fog of economic reform, of democratization, of "globalization," and of ethnic revival. Future studies of coalitional grand strategies and their regional corollaries may build on an emerging empirical foundation—in the new comparative politics of economic and political reform—in order to estimate the most critical coalitional realignments at the dawn of the new century. Although the empirical chapters explore the generic domestic and international sources of coalitional arrangements identified in Chapter Two, the book's main emphasis is twofold: first, gauging the extent to which coalitional variants behave according to their imputed grand strategic designs, given their relative domestic and regional strength, and second, asessing how different coalitional mixes throughout a region create and reproduce typical regional orders and, conversely, are affected by them.

The next section begins with an overview of the main findings in light of the hypotheses listed in Part One, and of their generalizability beyond the regions studied here. I also propose ways of adding greater conceptual resolution to prospective studies adopting coalitional approaches of the kind advanced in this book. The second section places the coalitional framework within the ecclectic family of international relations theories, suggesting conceptual convergences and divergences. The final section distills some policy directions suggested by the findings, and discusses normative considerations regarding peace, democracy, and equity.

MAIN FINDINGS, GENERALIZABILITY, AND THE TASKS AHEAD

The process of testing hypotheses embedded in a given theory is tortuous and can benefit from broadening both the empirical domain and methodological avenues. The evidence emerging from this preliminary but extensive probe certainly does not weaken the theoretical foundations of a coalitional approach but, rather, provides significant support for its further development:[1]

1. The distributional consequences of economic liberalization and the resulting coalitional landscape in individual states provide important information regarding a state's orientation to grand strategy. The general argument is not of Nostratic proportions, and does not therefore, imply that all conflict and cooperation can be traced to a single cause: coalitional grand strategies. To be sure, regional orders are not the sole result of coalitional balances and profiles, but these two provide a central lead regarding likely levels of conflict and cooperation and the forms these two might take. Regional cooperation (like war) has more than one source, suggesting that internationalist coalitions may not be necessary for at least some cooperation to come about, as was the case with Southern Cone states for decades under statist-nationalist rule. Yet the finding that internationalist coalitions—particularly strong ones—systematically beget intensive and extensive regional cooperation suggests that such coalitions tend to create sufficient conditions for the emergence of zones of stable peace.

2. The political strength of alternative coalitions vis-à-vis their domestic and regional rivals affects the degree of purity and the effective operationalization of grand strategy. Where internationalist coalitions are strongest at home and throughout a region, as in ASEAN and the Southern Cone in the early 1990s, regional cooperation appears most robust, comprehensive, least reversible, and able to overwhelm remnants of statist-nationalism (as in Myanmar and Vietnam). Internationalist coalitions with waning statist-nationalist challenges at home, as in South Korea and Taiwan, have been well positioned to deflect external aggression from statist-nationalist rivals or from neighbors affected by an unstable coalitional equipoise (like China and North Korea in the 1990s). Where internationalist coalitions face each other in a given region they can spearhead unprecedented cooperative arrangements—notably in the Middle East—even when they face significant statist-nationalist and confessional challenges domestically and regionally. Yet when such threats loom large for the political survival of feeble internationalist coalitions, they have the potential of undoing incipient cooperation and even impairing its emergence, as in the Middle East and South Asia respectively. Weak internationalist coalitions are more susceptible to demands from statist-nationalist constituencies, and therefore more prone to engage in the latter's preferred regional behavior, even if such behavior often seals the fate of their internationalist efforts.

3. Statist-nationalist (and sometimes confessional)[2] dyads and clusters have produced higher levels of military conflict—war zones—than either internationalist or mixed clusters, from the Korean War to successive Arab-Israeli and Indo-Pakistani wars, Iran-Iraq, Kampuchea and Vietnam, and Somalia and Ethiopia, among others. Statist-nationalist rulers have frequently read war opportunities too favorably, often miscalculating the resolve of extraregional actors, like Kim Il Sung in the 1950s, Leopoldo Galtieri in 1982, and Saddam Hussein in 1991. The coalitional argument expects the competitive outbidding among statist-nationalist and confessional factions

---

[1] On theory-confirming and "theory-infirming" studies, see Lijphart (1971).
[2] Statist-nationalist coalitions may or may not include a confessional component.

to heighten the slippery slope toward war, but does not assume that wars are inevitable. Statist-nationalist seas, such as the Middle East for many decades, have threatened the viability of internationalist islands (such as Jordan and Lebanon). The worldwide incidence of statist-nationalist coalitions in power is lower in the 1990s than it has ever been, but it is not insignificant. Although such low incidence is reversible, it may help explain the relative paucity of interstate wars at the end of the century, particularly relative to the preceding three decades.

4. Mixed dyads and clusters of states ruled by internationalist and statist-nationalist coalitions, respectively, are quite common in most regions. Historically, the competition between strong versions of the two ideal types appears to have precluded extensive and intensive cooperation, but also to have yielded less pressure for widespread military conflict than have statist-nationalist war zones. Mixed dyads generally eschew high values at either end of the conflict-cooperation spectrum. The avoidance of spasmic wars in these cases may well be linked to the presence of a strong internationalist coalition whose domestic program and international requirements compel moderation and regional stability. Its domestic strength shields it from the need to respond forcefully to concerted challenges of statist-nationalists at home and beyond its borders. Weaker versions of mixed dyads and clusters are more likely to experience wars, militarized disputes, and aggression.

5. A state's (or region's) ethnic and religious diversity per se is not an efficient indicator of its proneness toward conflict or cooperation. The coalitional pattern available to confessional actors at home, the relative political strength of the coalition they join, and the identity and strength of the coalitional cluster they face at the border provide a more proximate indication of a state's likely behavior. Regions ridden with ethnic and religious cleavages, such as ASEAN, may breed more cooperation under internationalist coalitions than confessionally homogeneous regions ruled by statist-nationalists, such as the Southern Cone for many decades.

6. A coalitional perspective proves its utility even for a least-likely dependent variable: nuclear behavior. Decisions regarding nuclear capabilities have more conceptual affinity, prima facie, with security dilemmas than with domestic political-economic considerations. Yet the evidence suggests that coalitional dynamics are a powerful predictor of nuclear behavior. Internationalist coalitions are more likely to shift toward cooperative nuclear policies, including denuclearization (that is, dismantling weapons programs and submitting all sensitive facilities to regional or international inspections). The stronger the internationalist coalition, as in South Korea and Taiwan, the more clear-cut the departure from nuclear ambiguity. Domestically weaker internationalist coalitions—as in India, Pakistan, and Israel in the early 1990s—are more politically constrained in curbing their nuclear programs, particularly in the presence of would-be nuclear statist-nationalist neighbors. Statist-nationalist and confessional coalitions more often shy away from cooperative nuclear commitments or violate them, while turning nuclear programs into a powerful source of myths. Of all states (beyond the original five) considering a nuclear option in the last three decades, not one ratified a nuclear-weapons-free-zone under a statist-nationalist coalition. Furthermore, only internationalist coalitions undertook effective commitments to denuclearize (Taiwan, South Korea, Egypt, South Africa, Brazil, and Argentina).

7. International and domestic institutions play critical roles in strengthening a co-alition at the expense of its rivals. In a current example, the World Bank and other international donors such as the European Union had hoped to assist the Palestinian Authority (PA) in consolidating a budding internationalist grand strategy, thus weaken-ing its nationalist-confessional opposition, an effort that yielded mixed results. At the domestic level, the birth of incipient national democratic institutions in January 1996 have invested the PA with greater legitimacy vis-à-vis its rivals—at least initially—even as they impose greater accountability.

8. Coalitional arrangements sometimes become institutionalized for the long term, yielding enormous resources to partners with rather limited support in civil society, both in democracies and nondemocracies. This was the case with the permanent al-location of certain ministries (notably Interior) to the Argentine army or to small religious parties in Israel. Institutional arrangements can thus magnify the political power of a key coalitional partner, hindering the ability to formulate a coherent grand strategy of either kind.

9. The personality and resources of political entrepreneurs are key to the logroll-ing of coalitions, both statist-nationalist and internationalist. The weakness of institu-tions other than the executive—such as legislatures, political parties, civil society groups, and the judicial system—reinforces the role of such entrepreneurs in spear-heading and implementing grand strategies, from Perón to Nasser, Park, Pinochet, and Menem. Once the grand strategy becomes politically entrenched, the centrality of the organizing entrepreneur to the strategy's survival recedes far more frequently in an internationalist context (as in South Korea) than in a statist-nationalist one (as in North Korea and Iraq). In the latter, the actual or prospective death of a leader throws the survival of the coalition and the strategy itself into question.

10. A coalitional focus offers a persuasive account of four decades of Middle East wars and a sound response to the puzzle of a cooperative breakthrough in the early 1990s. Most approaches in international relations had failed to recognize this outcome ex ante, even while the domestic coalitional interplay throughout the preceding decade suggested that the regional order was pregnant with such a breakthrough. The coali-tional perspective gains particular support here, given that the Middle East confronts it with an exceptionally hard case: economic liberalization is most tentative in this region, its political carriers are weak, the shadow of a long war-prone past is strong, an institutional structure and democratic systems that might have facilitated coopera-tion have been altogether absent—all of which add up to particularly difficult initial conditions.

11. A coalitional analysis helps capture the different texture of regional relations in the Southern Cone over five decades. Statist-nationalist populist coalitions in Argen-tina and Brazil presided over an era of guarded regional relations, limited economic exchange, and risky nuclear competition, even where initial conditions—over one hundred years free of war—would have favored greater cooperation. An entrenched statist-nationalist coalition in Argentina, the country that spearheaded this grand strat-egy in the region, including nuclearization, was the most prone to unleash military crises and mobilizations (such as the Beagle incident) and eventually a war with an extraregional actor (the Falklands / Malvinas). Interpretations of Argentine behavior

as the product of a regional power's drive for hegemony fail to explain the birth of a radically new global and regional Argentine strategy in the 1990s. Full-fledged regional cooperative strategies—effective economic integration and denuclearization—did not come about until internationalizing coalitions assumed power throughout the region in the 1990s.

12. A coalitional analysis sheds lights on the outbreak of war in the Korean peninsula, on shifts away from war, on the evolving nature of North-South relations throughout decades, on cooperative overtures, and on the reasons why each side chose alternative nuclear postures in the 1970s and 1980s, but converging ones in the 1990s. The stronger the domestic political support for an internationalizing grand strategy in the South, the more persistent the South's cooperative overtures toward the North became, geared to avoid military conflict. The gradual coalitional consolidation of an internationalist strategy in the South and a statist-nationalist strategy in the North facilitated a modus vivendi between the two, in a regional context of tension, mistrust, high ideological polarity, and political competition. The collapse of the North's grand strategy and its acute coalitional cleavages explain much of its sharp foreign policy turns in the 1990s, including its slide to the nuclear brink and back. The evolution of South Korea's grand strategy has been replicated in different forms but with largely similar outcomes in Taiwan and among ASEAN states.

13. The Cold War did not preclude the adoption of an internationalist grand strategy by different coalitions, nor does the maturing of a global political economy compel the triumph of internationalist grand strategies worldwide. The domestic competition between adversarial coalitions is not reducible to international manipulation, even if it is considerably affected by it. South Korea's behavior was clearly influenced by both the domestic and international requirements of an internationalist strategy, and its ruling coalition aligned itself with the US both for the latter's valuable contribution to internal political and economic stability and for its external protection. North Korea's behavior was guided by the unified logic of juche, which linked statist-nationalist political objectives at home with their external supportive structures. Dominant coalitions thus purposefully bring to bear certain aspects of global structures but are not uniquely defined by them. Demonstration effects—intended and unintended—do exist, and are best captured through coalitional analysis.

Our confidence in the utility of a coalitional approach is strengthened by the fact that there is no perfect correlation between the coalitional variable and other available explanatory variables, such as degree of institutionalization, the presence of democracy, or the depth of security dilemmas. Powerful internationalist coalitions—or their opponents—can be observed within highly institutionalized and poorly institutionalized contexts, within regions characterized by relatively high and low security dilemmas, within democratic, mixed, and authoritarian clusters.[3] Thus on the basis both of empirical findings and advantages over competing approaches, coalitional analysis stands on promising ground in the search for a primum mobile of regional conflict and cooperation. Given the probabilistic nature of the argument, disconfirming cases would gen-

---

[3] King, Keohane, and Verba (1994: 122, 215).

erally not threaten its viability or general analytical leverage. However, the repeated incidence of such cases would require amending, reformulating, or discarding the theoretical framework altogether. Particular consideration must be given to anomalies that emanate from "most likely" cases, where the framework should have had its easiest ride.[4] A war between relatively strong internationalist coalitions would be such an anomaly. The absence of war between a statist-nationalist confessional dyad, however, would not. These coalitions may be more risk-taking, yet their strategy is about political survival, not about waging war at any cost. Such dyads or clusters are expected to exhibit a higher incidence of militarized disputes overall (and, at times, large-scale war) and generally shallow cooperative interludes. In statist-nationalist clusters the existence of regional orders characterized by deep and sustained levels of security and economic cooperation would raise uncertainty about the coalitional perspective followed here.

Counterfactuals might help in testing the argument or hypothetical derivations from it. Had the Falklands invasion and war been unleashed by Menem, or had Pinochet responded militarily to Argentine provocations on the Beagle islands—when both of them were unleashing an unequivocally internationalizing drive—our confidence in the premises of this study would have been undermined. Although the focal dependent variable in this book is regional orders, the general argument in Chapter Two about the profile and preferences of an internationalist coalition like Menem's would render a war with an extraregional internationalist actor—Great Britain—highly unlikely. Another potentially illuminating counterfactual analysis of the Beagle dispute might explore whether or not the likelihood of war would have been higher had Chile been subjected to the same statist-nationalist coalitional outbidding that characterized Argentina in the late 1970s. This possibility, in a region where war has been an anomaly, would provide significant support for a coalitional perspective.

Our confidence regarding the empirical validity of the coalitional approach is highest at both ends of the spectrum, that is, where it is relatively easier to identify strong versions of either internationalist or statist-nationalist coalitions. In such cases, expectations regarding the probability of conflict and its scope seem to be on stronger ground. However, no pure grand strategy of either type exists in reality. On the one hand, some countries in the OECD community, East Asia, and perhaps Costa Rica approximate the ideal internationalist type. Yet, even France has a lingering statist-nationalist and military-industrial complex, which the emerging European order with its deepening internationalist agenda is progressively weakening. France recently abolished the century-old military draft unilaterally, prior to any German commitment to follow suit, as one might expect in the internationalist zone of peace par excellence. However even in the heart of Europe Helmut Kohl has declared that whether there is "war or peace in the 21st century" hinges on the introduction of the euro. On the other hand, no pure statist-nationalist coalition exists in the real world,

---

[4] Eckstein (1975: 119).

although some approach the ideal type rather faithfully, as in Iraq and North Korea. Even coalitions approximating the ideal type do not necessarily formulate and implement a coherent grand strategy at the outset. Grand strategies of either type can evolve very slowly, tentatively, and suffer retractions or major reversals, as under Eshkol in the 1960s or after Labor's defeat in Israel in 1996. The launching of a grand strategy may follow a clear coalitional transition (electoral or otherwise) or a political entrepreneur's exploitation of contextual coalitional opportunities, at home and abroad.

Far more problematic, as is often the case with most arguments in the social sciences, are instances in which the values of the independent variable concentrate in the middle. Where it is not easy to ascertain the identity or strength of a coalition, or were there is a coalitional equipoise, strategies and regional outcomes are more open-ended and difficult to predict. In such cases, however, one would expect grand strategies to be largely diluted—distant from their pure types—and unstable. A related problem in establishing unequivocally the nature and political wherewithal of coalitions is their inherently dynamic feature. Coalitions are like fireflies—now they are on and now they are off—which makes them hard to track, let alone predict their makeup. Moreover, their political strength can rise and dissipate rather quickly, following a sour foreign policy outcome or a seemingly unstoppable inflationary spiral. Further, coalitions may endorse a certain entrepreneur at elections or at the time of a coup, only to withdraw their support in their aftermath. Political entrepreneurs constantly scan the coalitional landscape to adjust either their coalition or their strategy, whichever is less costly politically. Assessing the relative costs is often no more than guesswork, as Arafat and Peres have found out. A third related problem is the difficulty in predicting thresholds of coalitional strength that enable the formulation and implementation of a given grand strategy. The PLO and Israel's Labor ventured their strategic reversal with arguably even—but not overwhelming—support. Furthermore, the objectives of a grand strategy are most often pursued piecemeal, and sometimes at the expense of internal tradeoffs among them. Internationalist coalitions in the Middle East, both in Israel and the Arab world, have sometimes yielded on confessional and military-institutional issues that weakened them in one domain (macroeconomic stability, for instance) in order to prevail in other domains (the maintenance of the peace process).

Despite these difficulties inherent in coalitional analysis, the general boundaries of most coalitions are not so elusive as to preclude a rough mapping of dominant preferences and possible logrolling tradeoffs—as in the cases of Perón, Nasser, Park, Pinochet, Menem, Rabin and Peres, or Assad, among others—across sharply different democratic and authoritarian contexts. Dominant preferences in a given coalition are a function of the relative political resources of its potential partners. Economic power is but one source of political capacity, that is, of access to decision making and organizational resources. Small and extreme confessional groups with a vocal and devoted following have proven no less resourceful in their ability to shape coalitional balances, sometimes by triggering defensive coalitions against them that would not have otherwise formed, as in the aftermath of Turkey's 1995 and India's 1996 elections. Coalition partners and supporters can use direct and indirect coercion to influence other potential partners as well as foes, ranging from terror to threats of capital flight, coups, and street violence. Coalitional strength matters a great deal, both for the sake of economic reform and for maintaining global access and regional stability and cooperation. Coalitions that may appear comparable in their substantive composition do not always yield the same strategy, because, as Ames (1987: 241) argues, "the players bargained with different histories, resources, and objectives." The tradeoffs accepted by the Chilean, South Korean, and Taiwanese military were not necessarily those demanded by their Argentine, Egyptian, or Syrian counterparts for many decades. Once again, prominent political entrepreneurs can produce coalitional exchanges that would otherwise not have come about easily.

Coalition formation by a political entrepreneur is a process always ridden with risk and uncertainty, as Sadat knew all too well before launching infitah and Camp David, and as Argentine generals frequently found out before shelving a liberalizing economic initiative. Sometimes entrepreneurs attempt to attract the support of both economic liberals and statist-nationalists—like Argentina's Galtieri and Israel's Netanyahu—only to be crushed by the tension between the two. This tension can be explained by taking into account the organic composite characterized in Chapter Two as ideal-type grand strategies. Political entrepreneurs may also selectively advance a certain aspect of an internationalist strategy—such as privatization—but not the full-fledged, coherent repertoire of domestic, regional, and global instruments sustaining such strategies. Such selectivity is often the result of the need to craft coalitions out of an unwieldy political set. Although the personal proclivities of the individual entrepreneur can affect the kind of coalition s/he puts together, constraints and contingencies force entrepreneurs into positions that may differ from their preferred policy in a given domain. Thus Galtieri might initially have favored a liberalization of the Argentine economy, but such a strategy alienated important coalitional partners, particularly within the military. Instead, he expected an assault on the Malvinas to coalesce the military itself and most other statist-nationalist constituencies, charting the course of a post-Malvinas electoral bid. Alas, this opportunity was less golden than Galtieri had estimated, in light of the British response. Reading one's domestic coalitional chances correctly is helpful, but insufficient for political survival. Reading the adversaries' coalitional profiles—beyond the tactics of the moment—is no less essential.

Political entrepreneurs confronting a domestic coalitional landscape that appears roughly balanced between internationalists and statist-nationalists face a special dilemma. Some, like Menem, surprise even their own political camp by implementing the internationalist strategy against which they campaigned, in all its domestic, regional, and global aspects. Others, like Netanyahu, hedge against breaking loose from the radical nationalist-confessional camp that brought them to power, thus undermining key aspects of an internationalist strategy. Yet others, like Kim Jong Il, are incapable of doing away with the dilemma in either of the two preceding fashions, and straddle the coalitional divide without quite consolidating a coherent coalition. Menem's post-election behavior—a strategic surprise indeed—conformed with Hirschman's (1965) expectations regarding reform-mongering and its deceptive requirements. Netanyahu assumed power after crafty—but myopic—attempts to persuade different constituencies that the economic miracle he inherited and statist-nationalist confessionalism could be easily reconciled. The complete story of Kim Jong Il's hypothesized protoreform-mongering strategies remains to be written, given the impenetrability of North Korean politics, beyond partial snapshots. Political entrepreneurs of all stripes can thus rely on "Voodoo politics" (Williamson 1994) and "bait-and-switch" strategies (Drake 1991), making promises to a constituency that they know they will have to betray as they put together a coalition that foils such promises.

The cases examined in this book are widely dispersed geographically, covering much of the industrializing world. The general argument, however, is valid beyond this domain. The interplay between internationalist and statist-nationalist coalitions and its relevance to regional orders is indeed a global feature. The Bosnian debacle of the 1990s was the outcome of the political dominance of competing statist-nationalist and confessional coalitions, led by Tudjman, Milosevic, and Izetbegovic, who fueled each other's existence, promoted myths, and reaped destruction.[5] As in other cases reviewed in this book, the phase of myth production found Bosnian Serb political entrepreneur Radovan Karadzic attracting not merely the support of General Mladic and the Serbian Orthodox Church, but also of powerful political, economic, and intellectual leaders in Banja Luka. Karadzic and Mladic used international sanctions to benefit their power base in industry, among radical confessional groups, and the military. Milosevic provided a model for statist-nationalist mobilization among the Bosnian Serbs. He presided over a coalition of 120 managers of Serbian state companies that dominated the economy, from banking to industry. He thus opposed economic (and political) reform, exacerbated ethnic tensions, and helped unleash the war in the former Yugoslavia. Milosevic succeeded in making ethnic fear the most central concern of the common Serb, thus deflating any potential support among them for a liberalizing process that would unseat him. Milosevic's main ally was uncertainty about the fate of reform and about the neighbors' intentions. The war and its aftermath helped him decimate a feeble and fragmented internationalizing opposition (including the head of the central bank).

Milosevic's coalitional structure was not very different from that of neighboring political entrepreneurs who employed similar mobilizational strategies.

---

[5] On the resistance to privatization and to dismantling their statist economies, see Jane Perlez, "Balkan Economies Stagnate in Grip of Political Leaders," *New York Times*, 20 August 1996: A1, A4. Senior members of Izetbegovic's Party of Democratic Action head major utilities and services, as do Milosevic's allies. On Milosevic's statism, see also Aleksa Djilas, "Serbs vs. Serbs in Bosnia, Belgrade," *New York Times*, 21 July 1994: A15.

Croatia's Franjo Tudjman was backed by a coalition of heads of state enterprises, protected industries, telephone, roads, railways, and other state utilities, with his daughter controlling the lucrative duty-free franchises.[6] Tudjman did not balk at relying on the mobilizational potential of Croatia's fascist brand of nationalism, straight out of the Nazi model and the Ustashe experience of World War II. By 1997 Tudjman's slow privatization still bore heavy signs of statist cronyism and protection, while his radical confessionalism continued to hinder even a partial opening to the world. Not surprisingly, Tudjman referred to his antinationalist political rival Vlado Gotovac as a "confused *internationalist* whose ideas are disconnected from reality."[7] Izetbegovic's coalition includes supporters of Bosniak nationalism and benefits from external Islamist support, moderate and radical. In sum, ruling politicians throughout the former Yugoslavia represent the statist economy, have maintained high tariffs and import-export licenses to protect it, have trapped their designs with a radical ethnic-confessional content, and have gone to war to stay in business, all of which have foiled foreign investment and stable cooperation.

The peaceful dissolution of Czechoslovakia in the early 1990s stands in sharp contrast to this war zone. The end of the Soviet empire in this case pitted an internationalist Czech coalition against a statist-nationalist and confessional coalition in Slovakia. The Czech Václav Klaus forcefully implemented a textbook case of privatization while attracting foreign capital and tourism and ensuring a peaceful political transition with an eye on European Union membership. The Slovak Vladimir Meciar bet on statist constituencies (including military enterprises and former Communist apparatchiks), as well as nationalist and confessional ones, and on fueling concerns with a presumed Hungarian buildup. Meciar failed to grasp the correspondence between the domestic, regional, and international pillars of a grand strategy: his coalition and platform were less than ideal for attracting European Community support and international investments.[8] The strong Czech internationalist coalition—reviving older historical strengths—behaved remarkably in tune with the behavior hypothesized for mixed dyads (Chapter Three). In response to Melciar's fledging statist-nationalism, the Czechs bid Slovakia farewell without a fight. The powerful presence of the European Union is expected to help rescue Slovakia from embarking on a full-fledged statist-nationalist grand strategy that would anchor it to its past.

These examples share a structural characteristic with others reviewed in this book. They are taken from a regional context undergoing the double transformation of highly statist and frequently authoritarian systems into market-ori-

[6] Tracy Wilkinson, "Prognosis Uncertain for Croatia Leader," *Los Angeles Times* 22 June 1997: A12.

[7] Chris Hedges, "Stoically, a Rival Criticizes Croatia's Leader, but Isn't Heard," *New York Times* 7 June 1997: 4. Emphasis added.

[8] John Tagliabue, "Arms Exports Bring Profits and Pain to Czechs and Especially to Slovaks," *New York Times*, 19 February 1992: 4. On Czechoslovakia's immediate and forceful efforts to inaugurate an internationalist grand strategy virtually the day after the velvet revolution, see Stanger (1995: 266–69).

ented democracies. However, the relationship between economic liberalization, political coalitions, and grand strategy operates even within the industrialized world, where market-oriented democracies have been fully in place for decades. In the United States in 1996, a statist-nationalist-confessional coalition was very much alive, sharing an astonishing affinity with many of its namesakes throughout the world. Its latest political embodiment was the product of skillful logrolling by Republican candidate Patrick Buchanan, whose combative speeches against "the institutions of the New World Order" could easily be mistaken for the political utterances of fundamentalist Shi'a Sheikh Fadlallah. Buchanan mobilized protectionist business and labor, ultranationalist and ultraconfessional constituencies, including right-wing militias and racist groups, in order to launch an assault on the UN, the World Trade Organization, regional integrative efforts such as NAFTA, internationalist coalitions in a neighboring country—Mexico—and domestic "threats" such as minorities and women, internationally oriented business, the financial community, and the Federal Reserve.[9] The Buchanan phenomenon brings into relief a defining characteristic of statist-nationalist-confessional coalitions, from India and Argentina to the Middle East: the tendency to outbid potential competitors in their own camp as vigorously as they discredit internationalist opponents. Fellow Republican candidates in the primaries were thus alleged to have "un-American" traits. The excesses of this campaign ultimately sealed its fate, but are an important reminder that no state, industrialized or otherwise, is immune to mythmaking by Goebbels-style political entrepreneurs.

IMPLICATIONS FOR INTERNATIONAL RELATIONS THEORY

The coalitional framework advanced in this book abstracts a pivotal axis or political cleavage from a far more complex reality. What it may risk in failing to capture every empirical variation, it gains in facilitating large-scale comparisons through relatively parsimonious means.[10] Internationalist and statist-nationalist coalitions seem a most promising macro-dichotomy because of their potential for subsuming the impact of economic liberalization, as well as the role of confessionalism in international conflict and their interactions with the democratic peace. The potential drawbacks of focusing on a single causal explanation—coalitional type—must be assessed against this variable *leverage*, or the ability to address most of the conceptual and empirical considerations relevant to regional orders at century's end—and dawn. To the extent that the coalitional

---

[9] On the extreme confessional component in Buchanan's campaign, including advocacy of "God's sovereignty," see transcripts of National Public Radio 21 February 1996. On Buchanan's use of pejorative language toward minorities and UN Secretary General Boutros Boutros-Ghali (whom he labeled "Boo-Boo Ghali") see the *New York Times* 22 February 1996: A16. Ironically, but only if one ignores Buchanan's penchant for defending former Nazi war criminals in his public statements, he was particularly deferential toward former UN Secretary Waldheim, a former Nazi collaborator.

[10] On the diminishing returns to parsimonious theory in the presence of a complex reality, see Snyder and Jervis (1993) and King, Keohane, and Verba (1994).

analysis offered here helps to explain alternative domestic preferences, varying foreign policy postures, different regional political, security, and economic dynamics, the role of confessional politics in regional conflict, and perhaps even the implosion of states (as in Rwanda or Somalia), the rudiments of a theory of regional orders may be in place.

Additional conceptual advantages of a coalitional framework include:

1. *Transcending old level-of-analysis categories.* The grand strategy of alternative coalitions outlined in Chapter Two links the domestic (subnational) and global domains to explain regional outcomes. Grand strategies are as much about political survival at home as they are about defining a coalition's relations with the rest of the world. The international context in which coalitions operate is built into their grand strategies, avoiding one of the common pitfalls in conceptualizing regional politics.[11] The global externalities of a dense international system are directly incorporated into how actors (entrepreneurs and coalitional partners) conceive of regional orders.

2. *Providing a unifying framework for comparing different regions.* The coalitional argument is flexible enough to allow wide variations in state-society relations and political institutionalization. Neither state autonomy nor a monolithic state is postulated; the two are both a matter of degree and subject to empirical analysis. A focus on coalitions helps avoid sterile debates between purely statist notions of an autonomous state and purely societal reductionist conceptions of states as instruments of social (particularly economic) forces. On the one hand, some coalitions are predominantly constituted by state-based actors who set the tone and pace of a grand strategy, as in Taiwan and South Korea, particularly during the early stages, or the Eshkol-Sapir period in Israel. Entrepreneurs in control of the executive play critical roles in organizing and keeping the coalition together. On the other hand, powerful societal actors can fuel a new strategy in alliance with state institutions, as with economic reform in some Arab states.[12] Societal actors may even attempt to overturn the reigning grand strategy and capture the state, as the Islamist movement in Algeria tried to do in 1991. The identification of contending coalitions thus helps transcend regional "exceptionalisms" regarding state-society relations, drawing together the common political experience of states undergoing different phases of economic liberalization and democratization.

3. *Grounding evolving regional relations in a dynamic framework.* Coalitions develop, thrive, collapse, and reconstitute, generating a changing regional context. Because coalitions are highly responsive to day-to-day politics, explanations sensitive to coalitional dynamics accommodate sudden departures from past trends in regional behavior, as well as more long-term patterns. These qualities advantage a coalitional approach relative to other structural (neorealist, interdependence, or world-systemic) and cognitive theories of interstate behavior.

4. *Explaining the roots of many civil wars.* Not all civil wars emerge out of the coalitional cleavages brought about by global economic integration. However, such cleavages are clearly central to some forms of civil war, whose incidence is expected

---

[11] Lake (1997).
[12] Migdal (1988).

to remain high under the turn-of-the-century world-time.[13] Domestic conflicts arising from the irreconcilable demands of ethnic and confessional groups—often in alignment with economic ones—may end at the borders, but may also draw in neighboring states, as in Afghanistan and Rwanda. Coalitional analysis is thus well positioned to address both internal (intercoalitional) as well as external (interstate) competition. Recent findings (Esty et al. 1997) that high levels of openness to international trade are associated with a low risk of state collapse such as ethnic wars, genocide, politicide and revolutionary wars suggest additional potential implications of the consolidation of internationalist coalitions.

5. *Avoiding reductionist interpretations of ethnic conflict.* A coalitional perspective averts the trap of either wholly economistic or wholly culturalist explanations of ethnic and confessionally based conflict. Coalitions are about the trading of most-favored positions among actors who identify their political identity either as a function of material or ideal values, or as a mix of both.[14] While averting reductionisms, coalitions offer a political tool to dissect political constructs such as grand strategies. To be sure, this book's framework is not designed to explain ethnic-confessional conflict but rather to examine the conditions under which such rivalries intersect with political and economic processes to produce domestic and regional conflict.[15]

6. *Clarifying patterns of defense expenditures.* A wide array of theories aim at explaining defense expenditures through political leadership, bureaucratic politics, the military-industrial complex, or electoral cycles. A coalitional analysis sensitive to the impact of economic liberalization helps clarify the relative weight of these different variables. The approach may also elucidate the puzzle of military juntas advancing different positions—over time and in different states—toward defense allocations and public-private mixes in the military-industrial complex. The empirical chapters highlight this variability even within a single region, as in the case of Argentina and Chile.

7. *Accommodating a wide range of methodological preferences.* A coalitional perspective yields testable propositions that can be examined along both aggregate statistical lines and more discrete modes. The latter includes studies of homogeneous or heterogeneous dyads or clusters, where coalitions evolve in nature and strength, allowing a dynamic analysis of their impact on regional orders. Studies can also concentrate on interregional comparisons or on longitudinal process-tracing of a single dyad throughout coalitional successions in each state.

8. *Eschewing exceptionalist theories of Third World behavior.*[16] Different brands of coalitional arguments have provided some of the most cogent explanations of great-power behavior and can do no less for the balance of the international system, some of which might be graduating into—or at least diluting further—the great-power cate-

---

[13] For a comprehensive overview of internal conflict and its regional dimensions, see Brown (1996).

[14] This dichotomy is often blurred in the real world. The argument that Islamic radicals aim merely at the educational and value-shaping apparatus of the state ignores their attempt to use state-derived material resources to maintain and expand their political base (Leca 1994: 56).

[15] On the causes of ethnic conflict, see Brown (1993).

[16] Exceptionalist theories come in many forms, but structural power (world-systems or neorealist) and culturalist ones are particularly prominent.

gory at the turn of the century.[17] While building on a converging, universalistic approach, the conceptualization of coalitions in this book makes allowance for the particular world-time under which coalitions find themselves defining their choices for war and peace. The empirical chapters thus identify the changing impact of Cold War effects and a fledgling global economy on coalitional formations across regions. The world-time at the end of the century sets coalitional competition against the background of a highly integrated global economy, a rapidly integrating multilateral institutional foundation in world politics, a disintegrating revival of confessional allegiances, and rising regional cooperation.

9. Finally, a coalitional analysis *alleviates the otherwise elusive task of defining regions*. Regions may have a basic geographical ontology, but coalitions can well subordinate a region's political boundaries to the requirements of their grand strategy. Coalitions can thus extend or contract their region to include potential allies (as might an isolated internationalist coalition, for instance) or to assail a Western conspiracy (as might an isolated statist-nationalist coalition). Coalitions define regions as well as different shared understandings and meanings: the purchase of a new weapon system can be regarded as underpinning the collective security of all in an internationalist context or as clear evidence of an arms race in a statist-nationalist one.

The preceding considerations and the empirical chapters in Part Two make it clear that a coalitional approach does not imply throwing the baby of available insights from international relations theory out with the bathwater. Rather, it helps articulate the conditions under which such insights seem more pertinent, and the predictions from neorealist, neoliberal, or democratic peace theory seem more likely. While relying on a coalitional perspective as the essential building blocks of emerging regional orders, it is possible to integrate some of the most important concerns and premises of different approaches to international politics. In that sense, coalitional analysis is somewhat akin to endoscopic surgery, whereby the analyst-surgeon leads his or her instrument carefully through a specific path toward the hypothesized appropriate site (the tumor, stone, or coalitional variant), but would not dare do so without knowing the general security risks and interdependent mechanisms operating on that site.

The following points of convergence and divergence between a coalitional and other approaches to international relations are worth noting.

Neorealism

The evidence from regions examined in this book suggests that a neorealist point of departure would not be useful in accounting for either the observed behavior of states or the obtaining regional outcomes, for the following main reasons.

1. At least two regions—the Middle East and the Korean peninsula—share similarly powerful security dilemmas, a structural condition that may prejudice non-neorealist explanations. In principle, therefore, these regions provide observations

---

[17] Snyder (1991); Lamborn (1991).

least likely to support a coalitional argument based on the impact of internationalization. Yet, even in these contexts where anarchy and self-help are expected to prevail, a coalitional perspective fares better than a region's polarity or the pervasiveness of security dilemmas in predicting change, conflict, and cooperation. Preliminary evidence from South Asia reinforces this claim.[18]

2. Neorealism is inherently hampered in its ability to explain cooperation, averring that cooperation is difficult to achieve and sustain because of relative-gains considerations and concern about cheating.[19] Furthermore, it is particularly unhelpful in elucidating why a region ridden with ethnic, cultural, nationalist, and territorial cleavages—such as ASEAN, and Asia-Pacific for that matter—have entered one of their most peaceful eras in this century.[20] In the Korean peninsula, a neorealist perspective cannot effectively explain shifts away from war since the 1950s, the North-South modus vivendi of the 1970s, and an incipient economic and security cooperation toward the late 1980s and early 1990s. It cannot account for different responses by the North and South to a very comparable predicament, nor for evolutionary changes in such responses. The imputed long-standing heart of the North's security dilemma—the continued presence of nearly 40,000 US troops in South Korea—remained largely unaltered while North Korea's policies evolved from highly conflictive to more cooperative, although in anything but linear fashion.

3. Neorealism fails to identify the precise structural conditions that would convert the Southern Cone from decades of nuclear competition and meager economic cooperation—virtually overnight—into a denuclearized regional emerging market. The approach is similarly unhelpful in explaining behavioral differences between comparable regional powers in that region (Argentina and Brazil), Argentina's proclivity for conflict with neighbors and extra-regional powers alike for many decades, or the dramatic reversal under Menem.

4. In South Asia, although regional politics in the 1990s have retained a shell of security dilemma considerations, slowly rising coalitions have attempted to crack it. Overall, the intermittent succession of cooperative initiatives and aggressive policies for many decades throws into question the idea of an unchanging security dilemma. The 1990s brought to power new coalitions that have not yet mustered domestic support for an internationalizing grand strategy, but have so far prevented a new all-out armed conflict in Kashmir. Conflict and cooperation in this region—including denuclearization—hang more on the coalitional balance of power than on the unclear implications of relative power.

5. Explaining cooperation in the Middle East is exceptionally difficult for neorealism, precisely because of an entrenched balance of threats, a similarly entrenched zero-sum perspective on regional politics, and the centrality of Israel's security dilemma, all of which make the region particularly inauspicious for cooperation. Thus, the progression toward cooperation in the late 1980s and early 1990s unfolded *before* neorealism could anticipate any revolutionary shifts in the regional order. Looking

[18] Solingen (1997b).
[19] Mearsheimer (1994/1995: 12).
[20] Mack and Kerr (1994).

through neorealist lenses, cooperation in the Arab-Israeli context in particular was underdetermined. The sight of Arafat and Peres virtually campaigning for each other in 1996 while leading the most zero-sum dyad of all in that region is essentially inexplicable in neorealist terms. No balance-of-power schemes can be summoned to explain this one, a relationship that fits neorealism's nightmare scenario: two political entities competing for the same territory to an extent not paralleled anywhere else in the region. Put differently, the weakest Arab adversary of all, the Palestinian Authority, was able to yield the most dramatic Israeli concessions in decades, but only under Labor. These concessions can hardly be traced to US hegemonic pressures, which were arguably the least pressing in decades. Indeed, that such pressures failed to yield desired results precisely at the height of US military and economic aid supports Walt's (1985) conclusion that the provision of such assistance is a "rather weak tool of superpower influence."

6. If neorealism exhibits so much weakness in explaining cooperation, does it fare better in explaining conflict and other favored dependent variables? The security context in the Korean peninsula indeed loaded the dice in favor of neorealism, turning it prima facie into a case least likely to support a coalitional approach as an alternative hypothesis. Yet, even the outbreak of the Korean War, which can hardly be understood without reference to the Cold War, requires extremely close attention to Kim Il Sung's grand strategy in relation to its southern political rival. The war may indeed have been overdetermined. In its aftermath, inter-Korean relations came to reflect the competitive coalitional dynamics of an internationalist South and a routinized statist-nationalist North. These coalitions brought to bear international and regional structural power considerations, but were not reducible to them. Neither were successive Middle East wars in the Arab-Israeli, inter-Arab, and Arab-Iranian arenas the product of any clear-cut, enduring, logic of relative power considerations. The only relative power that seems to have been at play systematically was the competitive outbidding of statist-nationalist coalitions against each other, at home and throughout the region.

7. A coalitional focus outperforms neorealism even in explaining nuclear behavior, where neorealism could claim its most unchallenged theoretical supremacy.[21] In a neorealist world, South Korea's security dilemma was alive and kicking more than ever during the 1970s (thanks to the Guam doctrine and Carter's policies), just as its nuclear deterrent was abandoned. Moreover, the South gave up its nuclear deterrent despite an unquestionable capability to overwhelm the North in a nuclear race, and retained its nonnuclear defense even as the North threatened to reduce Seoul to "a sea of fire." North Korea's schizoid coalitional pattern explains its nuclear stop-go responses to a rather stable security dilemma in the 1990s, and the hybrid nature of its nuclear endgame. The efforts of very powerful strategic allies and very powerful strategic adversaries have had a disparate impact on North and South, and that impact varied over time in each case. Domestic coalitional receptivity was an important intervening factor between hegemonic assertion and the response of would-be nuclear powers. The links between a commitment to a globalizing economic strategy and the

---

[21] For a preliminary application of the coalitional argument to regional nuclear outcomes, see Solingen (1994b).

renunciation of an expensive nuclear competition are rather thick not only in the Korean peninsula, but in South Asia, Latin America, and the Middle East.

Despite these difficulties and the inability to extract a single, coherent, neo-realist logic that might explain the evolution of regional orders, it would be naive to ignore contextual variations across regions regarding the depths and longevity of security dilemmas. Advancing the utility of coalitional competition as a point of departure does not preclude a systematic concern with how coalitions filter security dilemmas in the design of grand strategies. Even a rabid statist-nationalist coalition in the Southern Cone would find it far more politically prohibitive to launch a war against a neighbor in a region where the absence of war has been the norm for well over a century. Furthermore, the shadow of past security trajectories in the Middle East, the Korean peninsula, and South Asia raise barriers for internationalist coalitions, and therefore affect the speed and shape of cooperative processes and outcomes. Initial security conditions do matter—even where strong internationalist coalitions face each other—but do not tell us enough. On the one hand, the *absence* of genuine security constraints is no guarantee for regional cooperation, as decades of Southern Cone history can attest.[22] Only internationalist coalitions in the 1990s have unleashed the full cooperative potential of this region, including MERCOSUR and denuclearization. On the other hand, the constraints placed by difficult and genuine security considerations on Middle Eastern states are far heavier than for the Southern Cone, but not unsurmountable, as shown by the Oslo process. The extent to which other important regional partners share an internationalist agenda have softened the impact of such constraints, as Egypt learned since Camp David. The contrast between these two regions suggests that internationalist coalitions differ in terms of their starting points for the construction of cooperative regional orders. And the distance traveled toward the Pareto frontier matters.

Festering security dilemmas affect not only starting points but also the speed and form of the unfolding cooperation that internationalist coalitions can pursue. Distributional struggles in the context of a cooperative Middle East process clearly reflect the shadow of a zero-sum past, whereas distributional struggles among Southern Cone or ASEAN partners bear the imprint of years of variable gains from mutual interaction. External threats remain, most of the time, but coalitions differ in their proclivity to heighten or downplay their severity, according to the expected value of such manipulation for the political strategy of choice. Thus under virtually identical structural conditions, internationalist and statist-nationalist coalitions can embrace radically different grand strategies. The regional coalitional landscape—one defined by the relative dominance of internationalist or statist-nationalist coalitions—defines the severity of a security dilemma. The nature of prevailing grand political-economic strategies in the neighborhood—not geography—circumscribes a coalition's regional behavior. Coalitional balances of power at the regional level matter a great deal,

---

[22] Mares (1997).

competing with domestic coalitional balances in swaying states toward the internationalist or statist-nationalist end of the spectrum.

Coalitional competition has implications for power maximization and distribution, two key neorealist considerations. Although economic liberalization contracts the military-industrial complex, the argument that internationalist coalitions exchange security assets for economic gains seems inaccurate. As the cases of Israel, Taiwan, South Korea, and Chile suggest, the military's warfighting capability can increase significantly, even as its drain on central budgets declines. From the viewpoint of enhancing national power there is little doubt at the turn of the century that internationalists have the upper hand over statist-nationalists nearly worldwide. Regions with an aggregate preponderance of internationalist coalitions—like East Asia—have left strongly statist-nationalist and confessional regions as the Middle East, South Asia, and Africa well behind in power resources. This outcome could—but might not—be altered by the financial debacle of 1997. Moreover, strong ruling liberalizers have overwhelmed and eventually coopted their adversaries within the region, as ASEAN has done with Vietnam and Myanmar. Decades of statist-nationalism have not led India either to enhance national power or capture wealth, but to undermine both. A similar recognition seems to be at play in at least some Middle East states.

Finally, although some internationalist coalitions do not appear to have been oblivious to the lessons of history regarding potential aggression, others have misread radical statist-nationalist rivals as invariably tamable through racket payments (as Kuwait did with Iraq). Polanyi's (1944: 143) account of coalitional choices at the threshold of World War II resonates as forcefully fifty years later: "the legacy of economic liberalism barred the way to timely rearmament in the name of balanced budgets and free enterprise, which were supposed to provide the only secure foundations of economic strength in war. . . . But for the stubborn and impassioned insistence of economic liberals on their fallacies, the leaders of the race as well as the masses of free men would have been better equipped for the ordeal of the age and might perhaps even have been able to avoid it altogether."

Liberalism and Neoliberal Institutionalism

The coalitional argument advanced in this book is clearly part of a rich tradition that considers the pursuit of wealth a "calm passion" (Hirschman 1977), a self-oriented activity that tames the lust for glory. However, it departs from this tradition in a number of ways and shuns the assumption—held by liberal economic and interdependence theory—of a universally pacifying, cooperative effect of commerce.[23] The argument also privileges coalitional grand strategies as

---

[23] Classical formulations include Schumpeter (1951: 64–100), Cooper (1972), Keohane and Nye (1977), Rosecrance (1986), and Mueller (1989). For an overview, see Stein (1993). On haute finance as "the vehicle of an effeminate cosmopolitanism sapping the strength of virile nations," see

playing a far more central role than regional institutions in steering regional cooperation. At the same time, the emergence of cooperation against a tenuous institutional infrastructure does not invalidate neoliberal institutionalist arguments about the utility of institutions for advancing a cooperative agenda.[24]

1. Rather than assuming that expanded domestic welfare resulting from free trade fosters cooperative preferences, a coalitional perspective suggests that where internationalist coalitions prevail, their interests dictate compatible regional regimes. Thus, the gains from trade could be highly concentrated and not contribute to widespread societal welfare in the short term. If maintained, however, nondistributive patterns impair both the coalition's survival and its regional policies.

2. Instead of presupposing a purely economistic aggregate calculus of costs and gains from war and cooperation, a coalitional perspective examines the domestic political foundations of a coalition's regional and global policies. In doing so, it highlights the coalitions' internal political opportunities, often ignored at the expense of their external "vulnerabilities."

3. In light of the preceding two points, a coalitional perspective provides a more proximate estimation of whose relative gains matter in the formulation of preferences: those of specific coalitions. Moreover, the perspective identifies structural (regional) conditions under which relative gains play a more fundamental role, mainly in statist-nationalist clusters.

4. The analysis is not contingent on the extent of economic interdependence between / among regional interlocutors, or on bilateral / regional interdependence. The grand strategies of internationalist coalitions are particularly, although not solely, responsive to nation-to-system or internationally oriented interdependence.[25] Regional stability—not regional economic interdependence—is the main conceptual link between the regional and global dimensions of an internationalist grand strategy. Regional cooperation can thus precede, rather than result from, expanded intraregional trade and capital flows, as in Southeast Asia, the Southern Cone, GCC, and the Arab-Israeli arena.

5. The coalitional perspective does not require that states become "fully modern industrial nations" (Kaysen 1991) for the absence of war to prevail within regions, only that strong—particularly redistributive—internationalist coalitions prevail over their challengers. Indeed, coalitions may embark on a given strategy as a springboard to building a state, as in the case of the PLO-Palestinian Authority, thus superseding war and statelessness at the same time.

Polanyi (1944: 10). On international trade and the onset of war at the systemic level, see Mansfield (1994). Despite the noted differences, the coalitional argument remains largely compatible with this tradition, and particularly with "devalued utility of war" (Kaysen 1991) interpretations that are sensitive to whose costs and benefits (among domestic actors) count in opting for peace or war. At the same time, far from implying an invariable relationship between capitalism and peace, this framework suggests a varying disposition for conflict and cooperation among different capitalist segments.

[24] Baldwin (1993). For a sharp critique of the causal logic and empirical fitness of liberal institutionalism, see Mearsheimer (1994/95), and for a riposte, see Keohane and Martin (1995).

[25] On nation-to-system interdependence, see Tetreault (1980).

6. The coalitional perspective makes it clear that no linear progression toward economic liberalization or regional cooperation can be implied, and that statist-nationalist and confessional forces could be more resilient than "liberal optimists" tend to believe.[26] The possibility that economic liberalization (and democracy) may be part of cyclical "shifting involvements" and not an irrevocable process, needs to be taken into account.[27] As Krugman (1995a) points out, the centrality of free markets to economic growth was the conventional wisdom in the 1920s; the centrality of state planning and import-substitution to economic growth was taken for granted in the 1960s; and the centrality of the "Washington consensus" offers the latest wisdom on the requirements for economic growth in the 1990s, a consensus perhaps punctured by the 1997 East Asian crisis. Polanyi (1944) offers an even deeper historical understanding of what he labeled the "double movement"—self-regulating markets versus social protection—where the intolerable dislocations in society's fabric induced by the former ultimately destroy its very foundations.

7. The effects of international institutions—the main focus of neoliberal institutionalism—can hardly be understood without reference to coalitional interplays, at home and in the region. International institutions at times strengthen internationalist coalitions, at others empower their rivals. The unintended effects of international economic institutions at the end of the century can include the weakening of internationalist coalitions and of the cooperative regional orders they endorse. I return to this point in the last section.

8. At the regional level, neoliberal institutionalism assigns institutions an important role in the promotion of cooperation, stability, and peace. However, none of the regions examined here—encompassing a significant portion of the industrializing world—provides much support for this assumption. First, the emergence of cooperation in the Middle East and the Korean peninsula can be much more readily traced to coalitional developments than to any institutional infrastructure that facilitates cooperation. Such an infrastructure was altogether absent in the Korean context and superficial in the ASEAN one, whereas in the Arab Middle East its record in promoting cooperation has been rather dismal. Only a coalitional transformation in the region gave birth to compatible multilateral institutions designed to underpin a cooperative regional order. A coalitional reversal since 1996 has all but dismantled those institutions. Second, the one region with a dense institutional framework—the Southern Cone—reveals more cooperative opportunities wasted than undertaken. Institutions here neither fulfilled their original missions nor created positive "spill-over" cooperative effects; they simply "spilled around," reinventing themselves anew over decades. Only a dramatic coalitional reversal in the early 1990s infused old institutions with new life and created fresh, effective ones. Internationalist coalitions, not institutions, brought about MERCOSUR and a denuclearized Southern Cone. The absence of war in this region precedes institutional frameworks by nearly a hundred years, absolving institutions

---

[26] On "liberal optimism" and "Hobbesian pessimism," see Snyder (1991).

[27] Hirschman (1982). For different perspectives on the success and durability of economic reforms in the industrializing world, see Krugman (1995b) and Samuels (1995).

from any explanatory role in this regard as well. A coalitional perspective is thus essential in understanding why certain institutions come into being, in whose interest they operate, when they are allowed to play a significant role, and how they can lag behind—rather than lead—a cooperative praxis.

World Systems Theory

Despite its converging concern with the impact of international markets and institutions on domestic political-economic actors, the coalitional framework relies on a reading of such an impact very different from the one advanced by dependency theory and world-systems variants. The main challenges to the latter are evident in the following.

1. The global political economy does not only impose heavy constraints on "peripheral" states—which it undoubtedly does—but also provides them with opportunities. Different coalitions have different proclivities toward internationalization, depending on their expected payoffs for their domestic survival strategy from an emphasis on either constraints or opportunities. In some cases, internationalist coalitions have steered their states out of the "periphery" and into the very core of the international financial, productive, and power system.

2. Neither does integration into the global economy invariably lead to pauperization, even if it tends to deepen income disparities initially. Díaz Alejandro (1983) warned against facile inferences about the degree of openness to the international economy and domestic developmental variables such as income distribution, educational levels, political participation, or willingness to save.

3. Dependency theory and ancillary approaches have considered capitalist penetration to be an important underlying source of conflict. Yet the evidence from most regions suggests that as "peripheral" states have become more integrated into the global capitalist system since the 1960s, they have also become less involved, on average, in regional conflict. The major East Asian wars unfolded prior to the birth of among the most globally integrated states, which have largely avoided armed conflict since. A deeper cooperative relationship between Brazil and Argentina followed the most unprecedented efforts by their respective ruling coalitions to integrate both countries into the global economy. The Middle East and South Asia have resisted industrialization oriented to global markets for many decades, during which they contributed many entries to the statistical record of regional wars. Incipient internationalization has made unparalleled inroads in the direction of regional cooperation. To a significant but not invariable extent, the domestic villains of dependency theory have become the heroes of regional cooperation, whereas the heroes of import-substituting nationalism have unleashed massive wars and hindered regional economic cooperation. The drive toward regional stability with an eye on their implications for global access and investments is the missing link that dependency and world systems have perhaps overlooked. Nor is this a new phenomenon under the sun, even if different dynamics are at work at the turn of the twentieth century. In the late nineteenth century, according to

Polanyi (1944: 10), whereas national finance underwrote many colonial crimes and small wars, "the secret of the successful maintenance of general peace lay undoubtedly in the position, organization, and techniques of international finance."

4. Dependency theory identified some of the beneficiaries and victims of global penetration accurately but not others, and in either case with rather static analytical lenses. The military has been classically thrown into the "globalizing" camp, as the chief political executor of "external" designs, brutally whipping production for the global economy. Yet the historical affinity between inward-looking statism and military regimes challenges this assumption. Integration into the global economy does not compel militarism, whereas inward-looking statist-nationalism has more often than not overlapped with the expansion of the military's power. The military has chosen different paths to maintain and broaden its power, joining whatever coalitional opportunities were available. Often internal cleavages within the military revealed competing coalitional affinities with either internationalist or statist-nationalist projects. Once—and if—globalization yielded positive results, the military in power resisted killing the hen that placed golden eggs in its midst. In such cases military regimes—from South Korea to Chile—protected the internationalist strategy with the same zeal that led other military establishments—as in Syria and Iraq—to protect its rents from statist-nationalist strategies.

5. Economic liberalization has indeed unleashed pronounced shifts from militarism to monetarism, rather than the other way around, as a consequence of the essential incompatibility between successful markets and expansive military-industrial complexes at the end of the century. Macroeconomic stability and fiscal conservatism have squeezed such complexes out of the privileged political niches they had carved for themselves through statist projects in virtually every region. Menem presided over the most radical reduction of Argentina's military's industrial and institutional infrastructure in five decades. Little wonder incipient liberalizing efforts in South Asia and the Middle East have triggered the resistance of entrenched military-industrial sectors.

6. Another important political actor that dependency has failed to conceptualize properly is the private entrepreneurial sector. In consonance with its deterministic understanding of both the military and its industrial complex, and of internationally oriented private enterpreneurs, dependency theory has fueled the "authoritarian advantage" theory. Yet, the evidence suggests that integration into the global economy does not compel either a democratic or an authoritarian preference on the part of either of these two key coalitional partners.[28] I examine the specific links between economic liberalization, democratization, and regional conflict and cooperation next.

The Democratic Peace

The democratic peace hypothesis discussed in Chapter Four has become a leading contender in explaining the absence of war, and the empirical chapters examine its applicability to past and contemporary regional orders. The findings

---

[28] On how during the latter half of the nineteenth century "constitutions were foisted upon turbulent despots by business-minded bankers," see Polanyi (1944: 6).

suggest the following areas of convergence and divergence between coalitional analysis and the democratic peace hypothesis, and identify regional circumstances in which the democratic peace hypothesis plays an essentially irrelevant role.

1. Democratic peace studies have often pitted their main hypothesis—that democracies do not wage wars against each other—against other plausible alternatives, such as the potential relationship between levels or rate of development and peace.[29] Even recent studies in which trade variables have gained more serious consideration have largely focused on the impact of bilateral economic interdependence on armed conflict. Rummel (1983) drew special attention to "economic freedom" as an important complementary hypothesis, whereas Oneal and Russett (1997) have recently integrated "trade openness" into an array of other variables influencing militarized interstate disputes.[30]

2. The democratic peace research program has yet to consider more systematically a concrete theory about how economic strategies shape interstate conflict and cooperation, and how such strategies interact with democratic institutions. Put differently, the democratic peace hypothesis must be tested against a political, rather than an economistic, hypothesis, one that derives from a theory connecting a state's regional behavior to its grand strategy vis-à-vis the global political economy. As Holsti (1995: 334) argues in his large-scale study of war and peace, "democratic institutions are just part of the story, albeit an important part."

3. Statistical findings on the democratic peace have given rise to an array of hypotheses about the possible connection between democracy and peace, but not to a unified theory.[31] Instead, the coalitional perspective relies on specific assumptions about international relations, international political economy, and international security to outline a plausible relationship between grand strategies and regional orders.

4. Studies on the democratic peace have been largely circumscribed to explain the absence of war, without postulating democracy as an engine of cooperation. The coalitional perspective has a broader scope than the democratic peace hypothesis, sustaining a wider range of cooperative and conflictive behavior.

5. The democratic peace findings build not uniquely but certainly heavily on the industrialized world's "zone of peace" since 1945, where it can wield its most robust results. Although the aggregate database on regime type is global, the incidence of relevant (contiguous) democratic dyads beyond the OECD has been low.[32] Hence efforts to extrapolate democratic peace hypotheses to the industrializing world must take stock of the following considerations. First, democratic stability—not yet abun-

---

[29] Maoz and Russett (1992: 245–46); Ember, Ember, and Russett (1992: 575).

[30] Oneal, Oneal, Maoz, and Russett (1996) retain a focus on bilateral economic interdependence. Rummel (1983) provides a rather static (preindustrial / industrial) and doctrinaire (capitalist vs. socialist) classification of states unable to detect "dirigiste" states driving integration with the global economy.

[31] On the weak theoretical foundations of the democratic peace, see Owen (1994).

[32] For a critique of the presumed robustness of the democratic peace evidence, even within the prevailing empirical set, see Spiro (1994). For skepticism in extrapolating the democratic peace to the Third World, see Rothstein (1995).

dant in the industrializing world—may be a prerequisite for the operation of the democratic peace, and deserves far more attention than it has gained hitherto.[33] There are few relevant democratic dyads or clusters throughout the industrializing world with a history of stable democratic regimes, and where the concern with democratic continuity has not been pivotal. The task of explaining lags—or the required lead time for democratic institutions to breed stable cooperation—remains. Second, an even stronger concern with instability stems from the transitional character of many democratizing regimes. Many of our potential observations in the industrializing world are still traversing different phases of the journey toward democracy. As such, these transitional democracies may be subject to political pressures affecting their conduct of external affairs that are different in nature from those pressures familiar to stable democracies. The study by Mansfield and Snyder (1995) has forced greater attention to transitional effects. Third, taking into consideration the grand political-economic strategy of different coalitions steering democratization may help illuminate the conditions under which democratization can gestate war rather than peace.

6. The coalitional perspective predicts a generally positive relationship between internationalist coalitions and the propensity to cooperate regionally—particularly with similarly oriented neighbors—and a reverse relationship for statist-nationalist-confessional coalitions, regardless of whether or not they are democratic. Both democratic and nondemocratic (including democratizing) regimes have initiated and sustained statist-nationalist and internationalist strategies. Both ruling internationalist coalitions and statist-nationalist-confessional coalitions can thrive in cartelized systems, and both types can also benefit from democratization, particularly when they are in the opposition. Regime type (democracy / nondemocracy) does not seem to determine success in implementing an internationalist strategy. Both "authoritarian advantage" and "democratic efficiency" proponents find cases that support their claim. Indeed, recent findings (Przeworksi et al. 1996) suggest that the growth performance of dictatorships and democracies, on average, is indistinguishable.

7. Clearly, the democratic peace hypothesis is relevant only insofar as stable democratic dyads and clusters exist. Alas, this has been more the exception than the norm throughout the empirical cases examined in this book—quite representative of the industrializing world as a whole—rendering the democratic peace largely irrelevant until recently. As for the exception—arguably India and Pakistan since the late 1980s—they have upheld the hypothesized peace although their regional behavior more broadly (beyond the absence of war) seems shaped more by coalitional dynamics than any other consideration. Moreover, and perhaps paradoxically from a democratic peace standpoint, India and Pakistan are still considered the enduring rivals most likely to unleash a nuclear conflict at the end of the century.

8. On the basis of some preliminary analysis of the expansion of democracy in other regions, some generalizations can be suggested. In particular, the confluence of democracy and economic liberalization can make the relationship between interna-

---

[33] Doyle (1983: 213) discusses *"constitutionally secure* liberal states" (my emphasis). Maoz and Russett (1992: 245) argue that "states which can be perceived as *stable democracies* (my emphasis) are less likely to be involved in disputes with other democracies." Most and Starr (1989) argue that *democratic continuity* and the entrenchment of democratic norms played a role in the democratic peace of the postwar era.

tionalist coalitions and cooperative behavior more robust, particularly where internationalist coalitions are politically strong domestically and throughout a region. Democracy has invested internationalist grand strategies—and regional cooperation—with greater legitimacy in South Korea, Taiwan, and the Southern Cone. Weak internationalist coalitions in South Asia and the Middle East, instead, have been subjected to frequent poltical, legislative, and electoral challenges, as have been their cooperative regional postures.

9. The existence of democracy in itself has been neither necessary nor sufficient for cooperation to come about. The evidence from the Southern Cone and South Asia does not provide strong support for the view of democratic dyads as necessarily more cooperative. The relationship between regime type (democratic / nondemocratic) and conflictive or cooperative behavior in both regions has a very mixed historical record. The democratic regimes of the 1980s in the Southern Cone did not create a regional order radically different from the one they inherited from their nondemocratic predecessors. Internationalizers did. The overview of war and peace in the Korean peninsula and the Middle East in the last five decades highlights the essential irrelevance of democratic peace theorizing to much of this history, given the absence of democratic dyads. Indeed, the Middle East provides one of most dramatic reversals from conflict to cooperation in the midst of a lagging democratic impulse in the region. The absence of armed conflict in the Korean peninsula and among ASEAN countries in recent decades can be traced to anything but a meeting of democratic minds. ASEAN states have, for the most part, been concerned more with budget and balance of payment deficits than with democratic ones.

10. Democracy is not a precondition for implementing an internationalist grand strategy, at home or regionally. However, a weak ruling coalition implementing such strategy in a nondemocratic context becomes the target of a "double whammy": a concerted challenge from an alliance of statist-nationalist (and confessional) interests with prodemocracy groups, as in many a Middle East state, such as Egypt. Such challenges do not bode well for regional cooperation. Instead, strong internationalist coalitions that have managed to develop far wider support for their economic program can afford to reinvent themselves through the democratic process, as some have in East Asia. Not so with the earlier authoritarian architect-entrepreneurs, such as Chun Doo Hwan or Pinochet, whose repression is never effectively pardoned. Other such coalitions (as in China and Singapore) are still groping with the not-so-theoretical question of how long an economically internationalist context can remain undemocratic.

11. Political closure and repression, as in Iran and Iraq, can be major barriers to both liberalizing the economy and—consequently—to regional peace. Fewer and fewer democratic states are ruled by coalitions entrenched in statist-nationalist agendas at the end of the century, but this process is, as argued, potentially reversible. The more conflictive and threatening the regional environment, the easier it is for a coalition to broaden the sphere of the state—and restrict the sphere of civil society—on the grounds of national security. A conflict-prone regional environment thus strengthens statist-nationalist coalitions and antidemocratic forces at the same time.

12. In regions with lingering nuclear aspirations during recent decades, nuclear-weapons-free-zones have been most frequently advanced by internationalist coalitions, democratic or otherwise.

NORMATIVE AND PRESCRIPTIVE IMPLICATIONS

On Myopic Nationalism

The post–Cold War era has revived the concern with nationalism as a source of war. The expansion of markets and global integration have been charged with exacerbating nationalism. Experts have argued that nationalism can have a universalistic and harmonistic content, as in Avineri's (1994: 31) characterization of the Mazzini variant that sets it apart from its more aggressive and exclusivist version, the Treitschke mode. The essential political problem with nationalism lies in the ability of political entrepreneurs to transform the former variant into the latter, as in the Balkans, to cite only a recent example in a long tradition. This view is shared by students of international relations who are sensitive to nationalism's violent and destructive potential on the basis of historical and contemporary analysis.[34] External conspiratorial myths have always played a central role in the game of nationalist political mobilization, from Hitler to Juan Perón, Saddam Hussein, Hafiz al-Assad, Patrick Buchanan, Minister Farrakhan, and the Ayatollah Khomeini. Snyder (1993b: 184), while differentiating between benign nationalism and malign hypernationalism, also recognizes that the latter can masquerade as the former.

It is this slippery quality that raises deep concern with national-confessional allegiances as organizing principles of international political life. As Ghassan Salamé (1993) has argued with respect to Islamic radicalism, in practical terms moderates and militants play a political game that mutually reinforces their respective bargaining power. Moreover, presumed "moderate" nationalist and confessional leaders often embrace a defensive attitude against accusations of extreme nationalism and xenophobia, but rarely act boldly to separate themselves from extreme elements. This has been true for self-proclaimed mainstream politicians like Patrick Buchanan, with his ties to extreme racist groups, as it has been—intermittently—for President Yassir Arafat and for Likud's Benjamin's Netanyahu's temporization with fundamentalist extremists.[35] The difficult judgment call regarding the moderate versus radical distinctions in nationalist and confessional movements is identifying accurately not only who is cooptable—who is likely to shed exclusivism, xenophobia, and violence in exchange for inclusion—but also for how long and at what price.

The position that nothing can tame the rise of ultranationalism is compatible with conservative thought, most particularly with Hirschman's "futility" thesis, pointing to the presumed illusory (futile) nature of efforts at steering social

---

[34] See, inter alia, Mearsheimer (1993: 157) and Van Evera (1993 and 1994). Sociologically oriented as well as postmodern studies tend to be more "tolerant" of nationalism, but not universally so.

[35] On Patrick Buchanan's willingness to address a group of supporters that included neo-Nazi sympathizer and former Ku Klux Klan leader David Duke, see the *New York Times* 23 February 1996: A1.

change.[36] Proclaiming the futility of any efforts to stem ultranationalism—or war for that matter—has a single most likely consequence: both can be counted on to thrive if unopposed. Isolationists and critics of international institutions find comfortable shelter in the futility thesis, espousing the pauperization, marginalization, and communal strife of certain regions in the industrializing world as inevitable fate. This anticipation of impending and inevitable disaster has much in common with radical nihilist and with at least some postmodernist and cultural relativistic approaches, but is logically an extension of neoclassical economic thought as well. All overlook the fact that doing nothing often implies coming to an unwelcome rest at a point of little promise for regional or global peace. Hirschman (1991: 154) responds to this tendency with a proverb traced to Calderón de la Barca: "The worst is not always sure to happen" ("Le pire n'est pas toujours sûr"); one might add: "particularly when one works to prevent it."

Clearly, the wrong kind of intervention can be even more detrimental to global peace than nonintervention, as is the case when external forces protect the gains of nationalist aggressors.[37] Where hypernationalist coalitions enjoy widespread domestic support, international pressure should be heaviest at the earliest possible sign of such coalition's ascendancy, so that the political costs of hypernationalism are made clear and concrete at the outset. As argued throughout different chapters, it is important to explore more thoroughly the ways in which international regimes and institutions influence domestic coalitional struggles. Without an open international financial, trading, and investment system, for example, the basic requirements for pursuing an internationalist grand strategy are undermined, and with it, the domestic political platform of internationalist coalitions. Protected markets in the industrialized world do not merely threaten the grand strategy of these coalitions but can have negative security externalities at the regional level as well. Beyond market mechanisms, a dense international institutional infrastructure purposefully, but also unintendedly influences the domestic coalitional interplay. Adversarial political coalitions aim not at balancing but at overtaking their rivals, domestically and regionally, and they can rely on international and regional institutions to achieve that end. Such institutions can thus play an important role in determining the political longevity and strength of coalitions and, consequently, in shaping regional orders.

Two issues related to the supply side in the global management of regional conflict are worth considering: one has to do with willingness, the other with capabilities. On the first account, a new global order in which Western hegemony is largely unchallenged (for the foreseeable future) could lead to yet another unintended and paradoxical outcome: diminished incentives to contribute to the maintenance of such order beyond the OECD perimeter.[38] The extent to which regional conflicts will remain marginalized or create demands for intervention, and the degree to which the conditions triggering such conflicts can

---

[36] On the empirical inadequacy of approaching nationalism as an unchangeable, age-old, historical phenomenon inevitably leading to violence, see Posen (1993) and Snyder (1993c).

[37] For a discussion of positive steps in the prevention of ethnic conflict, see Brown (1993).

[38] On major powers and intervention, see Lake and Morgan (1997).

be ignored, is now a subject of intense debate in academic and policy circles. On the second account, the international ability to influence the coalitional balances and regional outcomes—through a nested global economic and political institutional network—may be higher today than ever before. This network's weight can be applied to support nascent or potential internationalist coalitions, such as the Palestinian Authority, where they are bearers of regional cooperation. International efforts could also aid moderate nationalist or confessional coalitions "traverse the valley of reform" (Przeworski 1992) toward a new social pact, domestically and regionally. European states apply this logic to renew economic exchanges with Iran and Iraq, although it is hard to remove European strategy from the ulterior considerations of domestic economic and political gain.

In the battle against nationalist mythmaking, international institutions can promote and endorse popular educational programs geared to unveil prejudice and hatred. Ultimately, however, domestic activist groups, the press, intellectuals, and educators bear the burden of this transformation, and the record here is rather discouraging. In discussing the responsibility of social scientists to unmask myths within their own states, Van Evera (1994: 32–33) reflects on the poor performance of academic communities throughout the world on that account. In the Middle East "powerful states with suborned intelligentsias and dependent middle classes have pursued great quests and messianic visions," argued Waterbury (1994: 45). Clearly, no political entrepreneur—including Hitler himself—has done it alone. "Organic intellectuals" are as frequently allied with the promotion of statist-nationalist myths as with competing internationalist ones. Notwithstanding the inherent difficulties that dedicated educational efforts often face, these should not be abandoned but intensified. Palestinian journalist Daoud Kuttab—arrested in 1997 for criticism of alleged corruption in the PA—produced a video shown on Israeli TV entitled "The Edge of Peace," dissecting Israeli and Palestinian attitudes regarding the peace negotiations.[39] Former Education Minister Shulamit Aloni introduced a new "educating for peace" curriculum in Israeli schools. That many such innovations were phased out by Netanyahu's post-1996 nationalist-fundamentalist backlash suggests that coalitional battles over minds and votes will continue to rage in the Middle East and beyond. Moreover, nationalist mythmaking is not the only threat to peaceful regional orders.

On Myopic Economic Reform

> The trading classes had no organ to sense the dangers involved in the
> exploitation of the physical strength of the worker, the destruction of family
> life, the devastation of neighborhoods, the denudation of forests, the pollution
> of rivers, the deterioration of craft standards, the disruption of folkways, and

[39] Clyde Haberman, "Fez Is a Sensation at Israel's Book Fair," *New York Times*, 3 March 1995: B1, B5.

the general degradation of existence including housing and arts, as well as the innumerable forms of private and public life that do not affect profits.

This depiction of the impact of markets aptly reflects the late twentieth century, even if it was late nineteenth-century conditions that inspired Polanyi's formulation (1944: 133). Economic liberalization that is insensitive to distributive and quality of life outcomes is no less of a threat to global peace than is hypernationalism, and operates through second-order effects: by weakening the legitimacy of the internationalist agenda, by exacerbating the appeal of statist-nationalist myths, and by endangering the viability of democratization. Political economists who advocate neoclassical medicine should be particularly familiar with "perverse" effects and counterproductive policies.[40] As natural opponents of statist-nationalist barriers and of armed conflicts that undermine the operation of markets, they may well have to accept some of the interferences they have frequently condemned. Perverse effects of economic liberalization are often the product of the willingness of political entrepreneurs to allow excessive influence of "privileged" groups poised to collect concentrated benefits from the reform process. The more concentrated the effects of privatization and international openness, and the lower the checks on speculative schemes by potential beneficiaries of both, the more illegitimately regarded the process will be. Declining legitimacy, in turn, can weaken the foundations of democratic institutions and prevent their consolidation.[41] The historical record of some of the internationalist coalitions reviewed in Part Two is deplorable in this regard, particularly where production for the global economy involved extensive pauperization, political repression, and human rights abuses.

International institutions imposing conditionality arrangements that deepen societal economic cleavages—which sometimes overlap with confessional ones—may paradoxically contribute to the demise not only of internationalist agendas but of cooperative futures as well. Harsh structural adjustments that overlook such considerations often undermine these coalitions' legitimacy and survival, and provide fertile soil for the rise of statist-nationalist challengers. To prevent such erosion of popular support, international economic regimes must encourage greater attention to domestic distributional effects. Tight conditionality arrangements have been ineffective, whereas securing a stable political environment improves the borrowers' ability to attract investments, repay debts, and stem authoritarian challenges.[42] That an internationalist agenda can proceed in tandem with equity-sensitive social policies is evident from President Ayl-

---

[40] Hirschman (1991: 27).

[41] On the danger of inequitable growth for the survival of democracy, see Bresser-Pereira, Maravalli, and Przeworski (1993) and Haggard and Kaufman (1995).

[42] Nelson (1990, 1992); Kallab and Feinberg (1989); Graham (1994); Lustig (1995). On the positive effects of income equality, education, and welfare on economic growth, see Przeworski (1992) and Fishlow (1995). On the positive impact of income equality on economic growth in democracies, see Alesina and Rodrik (1992).

win's Concertación coalition in Chile and President Cardoso's efforts in Brazil.[43] Middle East liberalizers face a special dilemma, pressed between *zakat* charity (monies from an Islamic tithe) and the market. If they allow zakat to take care of needy constituencies, they strengthen their political opposition. If they rely on market forces and merely await trickle-downs, they strengthen that opposition as well. Dedicated intervention to resolve social and educational issues are not something any would-be liberalizer can afford to weigh for long.[44] The IMF and the World Bank must thus emphasize lending for economic development, stabilization, and recovery. A 1997 IMF initiative appears to have foreshadowed a better understanding of the unwanted consequences of old-style conditionality when it extended an unprecedented offer of credit to the Argentine government contingent on evidence of "good governance," now defined as emphasizing expenditures on health and education, improving judicial practices, overhauling the tax system, and opening government ledgers, among other features.[45] Good governance so defined could double income growth, the World Bank's 1996 *World Development Report* suggests.

Paradoxically, conditionality clauses that might both alleviate transitional effects on vulnerable groups and find greater receptivity among broad segments of the population have been eschewed by the World Bank for too long. This is the case, for instance, with exacting from loan recipients a commitment to downsize military-industrial complexes. The argument that such intervention violates the principle of sovereignty is naive in light of the extent of international institutional penetration of states at the end of the century. Conditionality oriented to undermine the economic basis of the military strengthens the agenda of internationalist coalitions while enabling them to divert part of the blame. More often than not, civil society finds relief in the contraction of the military, which primarily threatens its own citizens. This is one area where internationalist coalitions can be credited with significant achievement: many have dealt a devastating blow to military-industrial complexes. In such contexts, the era of the conscript army also appears to be fading into history.[46] The dramatic retrenchment of both the military as an institution and of its ancillary industrial activities has strengthening democracy and global peace at the same time. It has also forced the definition of new missions, at home and abroad. In Argentina, for instance, domestic repression and external swaggering have been replaced

---

[43] Labán and Larraín (1995). See also Bresser-Pereira, Maravall, and Przeworski (1993). On his "ethics of conviction," see Cardoso (1995: 4–5). On employment-sensitive economic reform in Israel, see Bruno (1988: 233–37).

[44] Kuran (1995). On economic decline as leading to the rise of militant Islam, see Deeb (1992: 53).

[45] Paul Lewis, "I.M.F. Seeks Argentine Deal Linking Credit to Governing," *New York Times* 15 July 1997: C1. Michel Camdessus, IMF managing director, urged the Menem administration to "do more for the poor." In a speech to local bankers he said: "Argentina's reforms could fail if efforts are not made during this phase to reduce the gap in income distribution and to create opportunities for the disadvantaged" (Calvin Sims, "Growing Outcry in Argentina as Economy Reform Pinches," *New York Times* 1 June 1997: 3).

[46] Huntington (1995: 16).

with professionalization and peacekeeping under UN mandates. Military expenditures under Menem have been the lowest relative to health and education (51 percent) in three decades. In the absence of democracy throughout the Middle East, economic liberalization appears to be the only path to demilitarization. On the one hand, as Waterbury (1994:33) has argued, no significant protest or movement in that region—except in Israel—has ever questioned the gargantuan investments in military expenditures and preparations for war. On the other hand, even limited economic reforms have weakened the typical Middle East "mukhabarat" state, and with it, the ability of this critical partner in statist coalitions to revert to the war-making patterns of the past.

The consequences of the weakness of nascent internationalist coalitions are evident in the way in which President Yeltsin handled the Chechnya crisis in December 1994. Faced with both a floundering economic program and powerful statist-nationalist challengers, Yeltsin embraced a more aggressive posture against Chechen separatism.[47] This policy was backed by old Communists, nationalists, and sections of the military-industrial complex, all of whom opposed economic liberalization. Yeltsin's former closest advisor and bodyguard, Aleksandr A. Korzhakov, a major general and former KGB officer, described Russia's pledge to the World Bank to increase its oil output and to allow its domestic prices to conform to global prices as "absolutely impermissible," because they gave foreign interests too much influence over Russia's raw materials.[48] An ally of the military industrial complex and Yeltsin's link to nationalist and defense quarters at the time, Korzhakov strongly backed armed intervention against Chechnya. Except for Boris G. Fyodorov, Yeltsin's former finance minister and reform-minded legislator, most of the political leadership favoring liberalization—Yeltsin's erstwhile and future allies—opposed a military solution to Chechen separatist efforts.

The cooperative grand strategy of internationalist coalitions should not obscure otherwise highly negative aspects of their political performance, beyond myopic economic reform. Such coalitions have often shown callous disrespect for human rights at best, and gruesome violations at worse (as in South Korea, Chile, and Indonesia). If these coalitions do not carry the day on a range of ethical issues, neither do their statist-nationalist confessional counterparts. "Socialist" rhetoric aside, Syria's Assad spent 93 times as much on defense as on health, whereas Saudi Arabia spent 8 times as much.[49] Iraq's Saddam Hussein spent $85 billion between 1980 and 1988 on the war with Iran. As a region,

[47] On Russia's economic reforms, see Weisskopf (1995). On the August 1991 unsuccessful coup as the work of the armed forces, the military industry, and top Communist party officials, see Evangelista (1993: 177). On the alliance of heavy-industrial, military, and Russian nationalist constituencies, and its attacks on IMF conditionality, arms control agreements, and cooperative approaches to Russian neighbours, see Snyder (1993b: 190).

[48] Alessandra Stanley, "Embattled Yeltsin Finds He Is Also under Siege at Home," *New York Times*, 27 December 1994: A7; and "The Man at Yeltsin's Side: Some Russians See a Sinister Role," *New York Times*, 5 January 1995: A6.

[49] Richards and Waterbury (1990: 360). On the sacrifices of labor during the South Korean "miracle," see Ogle (1990).

East Asia performed best with respect to a UN Human Development index (HDI) combining indicators of life expectancy, educational attainment, and income worldwide—propelling its HDI values from low to high between 1960 and 1992.[50] Statist-nationalists and hybrids in Argentina and Brazil had a poor performance in poverty alleviation, a performance shared—but only initially—by their most internationalist counterpart in the region, Chile. In time Chile exhibited among the best records worldwide in its HDI in absolute terms and relative to its GNP per capita.

Beyond social neglect, both coalitional types have histories of abuse and torture. Human rights groups have recently begun documenting the existence of concentration camps in North Korea, whereas the repressive record of the South has been subject to greater scrutiny with democratization. All the Southern Cone military dictatorships—internationalist and statist-nationalist alike—share an abominable human rights and politicide record. Internationalist coalitions worldwide have been as prone to abuse and exploiting child labor as much as statist-nationalist coalitions have, with the latter also sending children to war. Corruption has been common across the internationalist and statist-nationalist coalitional divide. Chaebols received subsidies and financial assistance in strict exchange for efficiency and political financing, turning rents into a highly contingent and dynamic currency in the coalitional bargaining between private entrepreneurs and state technocrats. Rent-seeking and "kleptocracy" in import-substituting contexts had arguably a more stable, predictable pattern. The phenomenon of "extended families" deriving private benefits from the leading strategy—Saddam Hussein's Tikriti clan, Kim Il Sung's and Suharto's dynasties, and others in the Middle East and East Asia—also transcends coalitional differences. Despite corruption's ubiquity, recent efforts to measure its incidence suggest that economic reforms that strengthen legal and institutional transparency can also help detect and eradicate corruption better than in the absence of such reforms.[51] Corruption has been found to raise the cost of capital and undermine key liberalizing objectives, including economic growth, aggregate and foreign investment, and improved education. The 1997 East Asian financial debacle can be partially traced to corrupt and nepotistic practices. At the same time, economic reform itself can generate opportunities for corruption, merely converting public monopolies into private ones.

Clearly, a single-minded "all-good-things-go-together" perception of the process of economic reform—prevalent in some policy circles and academic ones as well—is wrong-headed.[52] Taking refuge in the "synergy illusion" that there is an irreversible process, steered by an invisible hand, leading to democracy, free markets, and peaceful regions may defeat all three.[53] Even the directors of the

---

[50] UNDP (1994: 95).

[51] Kaufman (1997).

[52] On the absence of a general reason why economic growth, an improving income distribution, and democratization should necessarily go hand in hand, see Hirschman (1990).

[53] On the "synergy illusion," see Hirschman (1991: 159). On conflicting predictions about the irreversibility of the third democratic wave, see Fukuyama (1992), Kennedy (1993), and Huntington

Davos Forum, a leading site of "globalization" discourse and action, recognized that "economic globalization has entered a critical phase. A mounting backlash against its effects, especially in the industrial democracies, is threatening a very disruptive impact on economic activity and social stability in many countries. The mood in these democracies is one of helplessness and anxiety, which helps explain the rise of a new brand of populist politicians. This can easily turn into revolt."[54] That stable isomorphic trends, inexorably leading toward markets, democracy, and cooperation are not inevitable is clear in the Middle East. There, an initial fit between democratization, economic liberalization, and peacemaking has not followed a linear progression, and much progress has been reversed. Democratic opponents of both peace and economic reform—in essence a democratic statist-nationalist-confessional coalition—could prevail in the absence of serious distributional efforts. Such transitional democracies are more likely to be belligerent within their region and beyond, although their actual warfighting capability will be far more limited than in the past, given their emaciated potential military partners. This Middle East problematique leads us to a final normative consideration.

On Myopic Democratic-Peace Policies

Leaders of democratic states would be misguided in interpreting the tenets of democratic peace theory as implying that no cooperation is feasible with anything less than a full democracy. Prime Minister Netanyahu (1993: 340–41) and some Indian political leaders, among others, have expressly stated their fundamental belief in this principle. Netanayhu's political camp has consistently paraded the autocratic nature of Palestinian politics to justify its own reluctance to negotiate with the PLO earlier and the Palestinian Authority later. Yet other considerations—notably a fundamental rejection of territorial compromise on the West Bank—are far more relevant to the policies of Likud and its allies. Its perennial predictions that a democratic process is not viable and that radicalism rules the Palestinian street have been overturned by the first formal national Palestinian elections in January 1996. A full-fledged democracy is indeed not the outcome of these elections, but they do mark an unprecedented turning point in the region. Moreover, the experience of democratization worldwide suggests that gradual democratization through progressive political pacts—as in Jordan and Palestine—has proven more likely to lead to stable democracies than more radical democratizing shifts. Gradual democratization is surely insufficient from a normative democratic standpoint, but could ensure against the unwanted consequences of sharp leaps that Mansfield and Snyder (1995) have

---

(1991). On pessimistic assessments of the fate of global markets and democracy as carrying within them the seeds of their own destruction, see Greider (1997) and Attali (1997), whose concerns echo Karl Polanyi's (1944: 3–4) interpretation of the unraveling of the hundred years' peace (1815–1914).

[54] Quoted in Thomas L. Friedman, "Revolt of the Wannabes," *New York Times*, 7 February 1996: A15.

identified. Finally, whereas the Oslo process had strengthened Palestinian and Israeli democratization initially, Netanyahu's coalition helped undermine both.

Scholars of the democratic peace have themselves recognized that democracy is not a necessary condition for the emergence of cooperation. The coalitional approach offered here certainly reinforces that view. Waiting for democracy may thus foil the pursuit of peace in ways that might make both more difficult to attain. Testing the theory of democratic peace must await the bloom of full democracies in the Middle East, but the peoples of the region cannot afford that pause.

REFERENCES

Abed, George T. 1994. "Developing the Palestinian Economy." *Journal of Palestine Studies* 23, 4 (Summer): 41–51.

Abrahamian, Ervand. 1993. *Khomeinism: Essays on the Islamic Republic*. Berkeley and Los Angeles: University of California Press.

Abu-Amr, Ziad. 1993. "Hamas: A Historical and Political Background." *Journal of Palestine Studies* 22, 4 (Summer): 5–19.

AbuKhalil, As'ad. 1994. "The Incoherence of Islamic Fundamentalism: Arab Islamic Thought at the End of the 20th Century." *Middle East Journal* 48, 4 (Autumn): 677–94.

ACDA (U.S. Arms Control and Disarmament Agency). 1990. *World Military Expenditures and Arms Transfers*. Washington, D.C.

Acharya, Amitav. 1992. "Regionalism and Regime Security in the Third World: Comparing the Origins of the ASEAN and the GCC." In Job, ed. (1992): 143–66.

Acuña, Carlos H. 1994. "Politics and Economics in the Argentina of the Nineties (Or, Why the Future No Longer Is What It Used to Be)." In Smith, Acuña, and Gamarra, eds. (1994b): 31–74.

Acuña, Carlos H., and William C. Smith. 1995. "The Politics of 'Military Economics' in the Southern Cone: Comparative Perspectives on Democracy and Arms Production in Argentina, Brazil, and Chile." *Political Power and Social Theory* 29: 121–57.

Adams, F. Gerard, ed. 1992. *The Macroeconomic Dimensions of Arms Reduction*. Boulder: Westview.

Adams, F. Gerard, Jere R. Behrman, and Michael Boldin. 1992. "Defense Spending and Economic Growth in the LDCs: The Cross-Section Perspective." In Adams, ed. (1992): 89–106.

Aftalion, Marcelo E. 1995. "Strange Bedfellows." *Hemisfile* 6, 4 (July–August): 8–9.

Agüero, Felipe. 1989. "Autonomy of the Military in Chile: From Democracy to Authoritarianism." In Varas, ed. (1989): 83–96.

Ahmad, Yousef A. 1991. "The Dialectics of Domestic Environment and Role Performance: The Foreign Policy of Iraq." In Korany and Dessouki, eds. (1991): 186–215.

Ahn, Byung-joon. 1994. "The Man Who Would be Kim." *Foreign Affairs* 73, 6 (November/December): 94–108.

Alesina, Alberto. 1994. "Political Models of Macroeconomic Policy and Fiscal Reforms." In Haggard and Webb, eds. (1994): 37–60.

Alesina, Alberto, and Dani Rodrik. 1992. "Distribution, Political Conflict, and Economic Growth: A Simple Theory and Some Empirical Evidence." In Alex Cukierman, Zvi Hercowitz, and Leonardo Leiderman, eds., *Political Economy, Growth, and Business Cycles*. Cambridge: MIT Press: 23–50.

Alfonsín, Raúl. 1983. *Ahora: Mi propuesta política*. Buenos Aires: Sudamericana/Planeta.

Ames, Barry. 1987. *Political Survival: Politicians and Public Policy in Latin America*. Berkeley and Los Angeles: University of California Press.

Amsden, Alice H. 1985. "The State and Taiwan's Economic Development." In Evans, Rueschemeyer, and Skocpol, eds. (1985): 78–106.

———. 1989. *Asia's Next Giant: South Korea and Late Industrialization*. New York: Oxford University Press.

Amsden, Alice H. 1991. "Diffusion of Development: The Late-Industrializing Model and Greater East Asia." *American Economic Review* 81, 2 (May): 282–86.

Amuzegar, Jahangir. 1991. *The Dynamics of the Iranian Revolution: The Pahlavi's Triumph and Tragedy.* Albany: State University of New York Press.

An, Tai Sung. 1983. *North Korea in Transition: From Dictatorship to Dynasty.* Westport, Conn.: Greenwood Press.

Anderson, Lisa. 1987. "The State in the Middle East and North Africa." *Comparative Politics* 20, 1 (October): 1–18.

Anwar, Dewi Fortuna. 1994. *Indonesia in ASEAN: Foreign Policy and Regionalism.* New York: St. Martin's.

Arafat, Yasir. 1974. *Palestine Before U.N.* Qatar: Qatar National Printing Press.

———. 1991. "We (the PLO) are Palestinians." *New Perspectives Quarterly* 8, 2 (Spring): 58.

Arian, A., I. Talmud, and T. Hermann. 1988. *National Security and Public Opinion in Israel.* Boulder: Westview.

Arian, Asher. 1989. *Politics in Israel: The Second Generation.* Chatham, N.J.: Chatham House.

Arian, Asher, and Michal Shamir, eds. 1995. *The Elections in Israel 1992.* New York: State University of New York Press.

Attali, Jacques. 1997. "The Crash of Western Civilization: The Limits of the Markets and Democracy." *Foreign Policy* 107 (Summer): 54–64.

Avineri, Shlomo. 1994. "Comments on Nationalism and Democracy." In Diamond and Plattner, eds. (1994): 28–31.

Axelrod, Robert. 1984. *The Evolution of Cooperation.* New York: Basic Books.

Ayoob, Mohammed. 1995. *The Third World Security Predicament: State Making, Regional Conflict, and the International System.* Boulder: Lynne Rienner.

Ayubi, Nazih. 1991. *Political Islam: Religion and Politics in the Arab World.* London: Routledge.

Azmeh, Aziz al-. 1994. "Populism Contra Democracy: Recent Democratic Discourse in the Arab World." In Salamé, ed. (1994): 112–29.

Baek, Jong-Chun. 1988. "North Korea's Military Strategies for Reunification: Hypotheses and Policies." In Shin, Kwak, and Olsen, eds. (1988): 159–78.

Baldwin, David A., ed. 1993. *Neoliberalism and Neorealism: The Contemporary Debate.* New York: Columbia University Press.

Baldwin, Robert E. 1988. *Trade Policy in a Changing World Economy.* Chicago: University of Chicago Press.

Ball, Desmond. 1993/94. "Arms and Influence: Military Acquisitions in the Asia-Pacific Region." *International Security* 18, 3 (Winter): 78–112.

Ball, Nicole. 1988. *Security and Economy in the Third World.* Princeton: Princeton University Press.

Banchev, Iuli. 1996. "Prerogatives of the New Foreign Economic Policy Making." In Park, ed. (1996): 189–204.

Bar-Joseph, Uri. 1982. "The Hidden Debate: The Formation of Nuclear Doctrines in the Middle East." *The Journal of Strategic Studies* 5, 2 (June): 205–27.

Barkai, Haim. 1995. *The Lessons of Israel's Great Inflation.* Westport, Conn.: Praeger.

Barkey, Henri, ed. 1992. *The Politics of Economic Reform in the Middle East.* New York: St. Martin's.

———. 1995. "Can the Middle Compete?" In Diamond and Plattner, eds. (1995): 167–81.

Barnett, Michael N. 1992. *Confronting the Costs of War—Military Power, State, and Society in Egypt and Israel*. Princeton: Princeton University Press.

Barros, Alexandre. 1978. "The Brazilian Military: Professional Socialization, Political Performance and State Building." Ph. D. dissertation, Political Science, University of Chicago.

———. 1984. "The Formulation and Implementation of Brazilian Foreign Policy: Itamaraty and the New Actors." In Muñoz and Tulchin, eds. (1984): 30–44.

———. 1990. "The Brazilian Military in the Late 1980s and Early 1990s: Is the Risk of Intervention Gone?" In Goodman, Mendelson, and Rial, eds. (1990): 177–87.

———. 1995. "The Capitalist Revolution in Latin America: When Will the People Be Happy?" *Washington Quarterly* 18, 3 (Summer): 103–13.

Barzilai, Gad. 1996. *Wars, Internal Conflicts, and Political Order: A Jewish Democracy in the Middle East*. Albany: State University of New York Press.

Bates, Robert H., and Anne O. Krueger, eds. 1993a. "Introduction" and "Generalizations Arising from the Country Studies." In Bates and Krueger, eds. (1993b): 1–26, 444–72.

———. 1993b. *Political and Economic Interactions in Economic Policy Reform: Evidence from Eight Countries*. Cambridge: Basil Blackwell.

Beblawi, H., and Giacomo Luciani. 1987. *Nation, State and Integration in the Arab World*. Vol 2: *The Rentier State*. London: Croom Helm.

Beilin, Yossi. 1992. *Israel: A Concise Political History*. New York: St. Martin's.

———. 1993. "A Vision of the Middle East." Address delivered in Tokyo, 15 December. Jerusalem: Ministry of Foreign Affairs.

Ben-Gurion, David. 1955. "Past and Future." Speech at a meeting of Merkaz-Mapai, 20 January. Tel Aviv: Merkaz Mapai.

———. 1971/1987. *Zikhronot*. Tel-Aviv: Am Oved.

Ben-Porath, Yoram ed., 1986. *The Israeli Economy: Maturing through Crises*. Cambridge: Harvard University Press.

Berglas, Eitan. 1986. "Defense and the Economy." In Ben Porath, ed. (1986): 173–91.

Betts, Richard K. 1993. "Systems of Peace as Causes of War? Collective Security, Arms Control, and the New Europe." In Snyder and Jervis, eds. (1993): 265–302.

Bhagwati, Jagdish. 1988. *Protectionism*. Cambridge: MIT Press.

———. 1993. "Regionalism and Multilateralism: An Overview." In Jaime de Melo and Arvind Panagariya, eds. *New Dimensions in Regional Integration*. New York: Cambridge University Press.

Bill, James A. and Robert Springborg. 1990. *Politics in the Middle East*. New York: HarperCollins.

Bin Talal, Hassan (Crown Prince of Jordan). 1984. *Search for Peace: The Politics of the Middle Ground in the Arab East*. London: Macmillan.

———. 1994. *A Vision for the Future*. Amman: Jordanian Businessmen Association.

Binder, Leonard. 1988. *Islamic Liberalism: A Critique of Development Ideologies*. Chicago: University of Chicago Press.

Bobrow, Davis B. 1992. "Eating Your Cake and Having It Too: The Japanese Case." In Chan and Mintz, eds. (1992): 81–98.

Bracken, Paul. 1992. "Nuclear Weapons and State Survival in North Korea," *Survival* (Autumn): 137–53.

Bradford, Colin I., Jr. 1990. "Policy Interventions and Markets: Development Strategy Typologies and Policy Options." In Gereffi and Wyman, eds. (1990): 32–54.

Brams, Steven 1976. *Paradoxes in Politics*. New York: Free Press.

Brand, Laurie A. 1988. *Palestinians in the Arab World: Institution Building and the Search for State*. New York: Columbia University Press.

Brecher, Michael. 1974. *Decisions in Israel's Foreign Policy*. London: Oxford University Press.

Bremer, Stuart A. 1992. "Dangerous Dyads: Conditions Affecting the Likelihood of Interstate War, 1816–1965." *Journal of Conflict Resolution* 36, 2: 309–41.

Bresser Pereira, Luiz C. 1978. *O colapso de uma aliança de classes: a burguesia e a crise do autoritarismo tecno-burocratico*. Sào Paulo: Editora Brasiliense.

Bresser Pereira, Luiz Carlos, José María Maravall, and Adam Przeworski. 1993. *Economic Reforms in New Democracies: A Social Democratic Approach*. New York: Cambridge University Press.

———. 1994. "Economic Reforms in New Democracies: A Social-Democratic Approach." In Smith, Acuña, and Gamarra, eds. (1994a): 181–212.

Brown, Michael E., ed. 1993. *Ethnic Conflict and International Security*. Princeton: Princeton University Press.

———. 1996. *The International Dimensions of Internal Conflict*. Cambridge: MIT Press.

Bruno, Michael. 1986. "External Shocks and Domestic Response: Macroeconomic Performance, 1965–1982." In Ben Porath, ed. (1986): 276–301.

———. 1988. "Opening Up: Liberalization with Stabilization." In Dornbusch and Helmers, eds. (1988): 223–48.

Bruno, Michael, and Boris Pleskovic, eds. 1995. *Annual World Bank Conference on Development Economics*. Washington, D.C.: World Bank.

Brynen, Rex. 1995. "The Neopatrimonial Dimension of Palestinian Politics." *Journal of Palestine Studies* 25, 1 (Autumn): 23–36.

———. 1996. "International Aid to the West Bank and Gaza: A Primer." *Journal of Palestine Studies* 25, 2 (Winter): 46–53.

Brzoska, Michael. 1992. "Military Trade, Aid, and Developing-Country Debt." In Lamb and Kallab, eds. (1992): 79–112.

Buchanan, J. M., R. D. Tollison, and G. Tullock, eds. 1980. *Toward a Theory of the Rent-Seeking Society*. College Station: Texas A & M University Press.

Budeiri, Musa K. 1995. "The Nationalist Dimension of Islamic Movements in Palestinian Politics." *Journal of Palestine Studies* 24, 3 (Spring): 89–95.

Bueno de Mesquita, Bruce, and David Lalman. 1992. *War and Reason*. New Haven: Yale University Press.

Bufman, Gil, and Leonardo Leiderman. 1995. "Israel's Stabilization: Some Important Policy Lessons." In Dornbusch and Edwards, eds. (1995): 177–222.

Buzan, Barry. 1991a. "New World Realpolitik: New Patterns of Global Security in the Twenty-First Century." *International Affairs* 67, 3 (July): 431–52.

———. 1991b. *People, States, and Fear: An Agenda for International Security Studies In the Post-Cold War Era*. Boulder: Lynne Rienner.

Buzan, Barry, and Gerald Segal. 1994. "Rethinking East Asia Security." *Survival* (Summer): 3–21.

Cable, Vincent, and David Henderson, ed. 1994. *Trade Blocs? The Future of Regional Integration*. Washinton D.C.: Brookings Institution.

Canitrot, Adolfo. 1994. "Crisis and Transformation of the Argentine State (1978–1992)." In Smith, Acuña, and Gamarra, eds. (1994b): 75–103.

Caporaso, James A. 1995. "Research Design, Falsification, and the Qualitative-Quantitative Divide." *American Political Science Review* 89, 2 (June): 457–60.

Caporaso, James A., and David P. Levine. 1992. *Theories of Political Economy.* New York: Cambridge University Press.

Carasales, Julio C. 1995. "The Argentine-Brazilian Nuclear Rapprochement." *Nonproliferation Review* (Spring/Summer): 39–48.

Cardoso, Eliana, and Ann Helwege. 1991. "Populism, Profligacy, and Redistribution." In Dornbusch and Edwards, eds. (1991): 45–70.

Cardoso, Eliana, Ricardo P. de Barros, and Andre Urani. 1995. "Inflation and Unemployment as Determinants of Inequality in Brazil: The 1980s." In Dornbusch and Edwards, eds. (1995): 151–76.

Cardoso, Fernando H. 1995. "The Ethics of Conviction." *Hemisfile* 6, 6 (November/December): 4–5.

———. 1996. "In Praise of the Art of Politics." *Journal of Democracy* 7, 3 (July): 7–19.

Cassandra. 1995. "The Impending Crisis in Egypt." *Middle East Journal* 49, 1 (Winter): 9–27.

Castro, Paulo R. de, and Marcio Ronci. 1991. "Sixty Years of Populism in Brazil." In Dornbusch and Edwards, eds. (1991): 151–73.

Cavallo, Domingo F. 1988. "Argentina." In Dornbusch and Helmers, eds. (1988): 267–84.

Cavallo, Domingo F., and Guillermo Mondino. 1995. "Argentina's Miracle? From Hyperinflation to Sustained Growth." In Bruno and Pleskovic, eds. (1995): 11–22

Chan, Stephen, and Andrew J. Williams. 1994. *Renegade States: The Evolution of Revolutionary Foreign Policy.* Manchester and New York: Manchester University Press.

Chan, Steve. 1988. "Defense Burden and Economic Growth: Unraveling the Taiwanese Enigma." *American Political Science Review* 82, 3: 913–20.

———. 1992a. "Defense, Welfare and Growth: Introduction." In Chan and Mintz, eds. (1992): 1–20.

———. 1992b. "Military Burden, Economic Growth, and Income Inequality: The Taiwan Exception." In Chan and Mintz, eds. (1992): 163–78.

Chan, Steve, and Cal Clark. 1991. *Flexibility, Foresight, and Fortuna in Taiwan's Development: Navigating between Scylla and Charybdis.* New York: Routledge.

Chan, Steve, and Alex Mintz, eds. 1992. *Defense, Welfare, and Growth.* New York: Routledge.

Chang, Ha-Joon. 1994. *The Political Economy of Industrial Policy.* New York: St. Martin's Press.

Charter of the Islamic Resistance Movement (Hamas) of Palestine. 1993. Special Document. *Journal of Palestine Studies* 22, 4 (Summer 1993): 122–34.

Chaudhry, Kiren. 1991. "On the Way to Market: Economic Liberalisation and Iraq's Invasion of Kuwait." *Middle East Report* 170: 14–23.

Cheng, Tun-jen. 1990. "Political Regimes and Development Strategies: South Korea and Taiwan." In Gereffi and Wyman, eds. (1990): 139–78.

Child, Jack. 1984. "Inter-State Conflict in Latin America in the 1980s." In Ferris and Lincoln, eds. (1984): 21–36.

———. 1990. "Geopolitical Thinking." In Goodman, Mendelson, and Rial, eds. (1990): 143–64.

Choi, Byung-Sun. 1993. "Financial Policy and Big Business in Korea: The Perils of Financial Regulation." In Haggard, Lee, and Maxfield, eds. (1993): 23–54.

Choi, Jang Jip. 1993. "Political Cleavages in South Korea." In Koo, ed. (1993): 13–50.

Chun Doo Hwan. 1984. *The 1980s: Meeting a New Challenge: Selected Speeches of President Chun Doo Hwan,* Volume 3. Seoul: Korea Textbook Co.

Chung, Kiwon. 1963. "The North Korean People's Army and the Party." In Scalapino, ed. (1963): 105–24.

Cohen, Roger. 1994. "A Cease-Fire Called Winter Settles over Bosnia." *New York Times* December 22: A6.

Coleman, Kenneth M., and Luis Quiros-Varela. 1981. "Determinants of Latin American Foreign Policies: Bureaucratic Organizations and Development Strategies. In Ferris and Lincoln, eds. (1981): 39–59.

Collier, David, ed. 1979. *The New Authoritarianism in Latin America*. Princeton: Princeton University Press.

Collor, Fernando. 1991. *Brasil: Um Projeto de Reconstruçào Nacional*. Brasilia: Secretaria de Imprensa da Presidência da República.

Cooper, Richard. 1968. *The Economics of Interdependence: Economic Policy in the Atlantic Community*. New York: Columbia University Press.

———. 1972. "Economic Interdependence and Foreign Policy in the Seventies." *World Politics* 24, 2 (January): 159–81.

———. 1994. "Korea's Balance of International Payments." In Haggard, Cooper, Collins, Kim, and Ro, eds. (1994): 261–94.

Cotton, James. 1993. "North Korea's Nuclear Ambitions." In *Asia's International Role in the Post-Cold War Era* (no editor). London: International Institute of Strategic Studies Adelphi Paper 275, Part I: 94–106.

Cox, Robert W. 1986. "Social Forces, States, and World Orders: Beyond International Relations Theory." In Robert O. Keohane, ed., *Neorealism and Its Critics*. New York: Columbia University Press: 204–54.

———. 1987. *Production, Power, and World Order: Social Forces in the Making of History*. New York: Columbia University Press.

Crystal, Jill. 1994. "Authoritarianism and Its Adversaries in the Arab World. *World Politics* 46, 2 (January): 262–89.

Cumings, Bruce. 1984. "The Origins and Development of the Northeast Asian Political Economy: Industrial Sectors, Product Cycles, and Political Consequences." *International Organization* 38, 1 (Winter): 1–40.

———. 1990. *The Origins of the Korean War*. Vol. II: *The Roaring of the Cataract 1947–1950*. Princeton: Princeton University Press.

———. 1993. "The Corporate State in North Korea." In Koo, ed. (1993): 197–230.

Dahl, Robert A. 1989. *Democracy and Its Critics*. New Haven: Yale University Press.

Deeb, Mary-Jane. 1989. "Inter Maghribi Relations since 1969: A Study of the Modalities of Unions and Mergers." *Middle East Journal* 43, 1: 20–33.

———. 1992. "Militant Islam and the Politics of Redemption." *Annals of the American Academy of Political and Social Science* 524 (November): 52–65.

Deger, Saadet. 1986. "Economic Development and Defense Expenditures." *Economic Development and Cultural Change* 35, 1: 179–96.

———. 1992. "Military Expenditure and Economic Development: Issues and Debates." In Lamb and Kallab, eds. (1992): 35–52.

De Melo, Jaime, and Arvind Panagariya, eds. 1993. *New Dimensions in Regional Integration*. New York: Cambridge University Press.

Dessouki, Ali E. Hillal. 1991. "The Primacy of Economics: The Foreign Policy of Egypt." In Korany and Dessouki, eds. (1991): 156–85.

Dessouki, Ali E. Hillal, and Karen Aboul Kheir. 1991. "The Politics of Vulnerability and Survival: The Foreign Policy of Jordan." In Korany and Dessouki, eds. (1991): 216–35.

Deutsch, Karl, et al. 1957. *Political Community and the North Atlantic Area: International Organization in the Light of Historical Experience.* Princeton: Princeton University Press.

Deyo, Frederic C., ed. 1987. *The Political Economy of the New Asian Industrialism.* Ithaca: Cornell University Press.

Di Tella, Guido, and Rudiger Dornbusch, eds. 1989. *The Political Economy of Argentina, 1946–83.* Pittsburgh: University of Pittsburgh Press.

Diamond, Larry, and Marc F. Plattner, eds. 1994. *Nationalism, Ethnic Conflict, and Democracy.* Baltimore: Johns Hopkins University Press.

———, eds. 1995. *Economic Reform and Democracy.* Baltimore: Johns Hopkins University Press.

Díaz Alejandro, Carlos F. 1970. *Essays on the Economic History of the Argentine Republic.* New Haven: Yale University Press.

———. 1983. "Open Economy, Closed Polity?" In Diana Tussie, ed., *Latin America in the World Economy: New Perspectives.* Aldershot, England: Gower: 21–54.

Dillon, G. M. 1989. *The Falklands, Politics and War.* New York: St. Martin's.

Domínguez, Jorge I. 1987. "Order and Progress in Brazil." In George C. Lodge and Ezra F. Vogel, eds., *Ideology and National Competitiveness: An Analysis of Nine Countries.* Boston: Harvard Business School Press: 241–70.

———. 1997. *Technopols: Freeing Politics and Markets in Latin America in the 1990s.* University Park: Pennsylvania State University Press.

Domke, William K. 1988. *War and the Changing Global System.* New Haven: Yale University Press.

Dornbusch, Rudiger, and Sebastian Edwards, eds. 1991. *The Macroeconomics of Populism in Latin America.* Chicago: University of Chicago Press.

———, eds. 1995. *Reform, Recovery, and Growth: Latin America and the Middle East.* Chicago: University of Chicago Press.

Dornbusch, Rudiger, and F. Leslie C. H. Helmers, eds. 1988. *The Open Economy: Tools for Policymakers in Developing Countries.* New York: Oxford University Press.

Doyle, Michael W. 1983a. "Kant, Liberal Legacies, and Foreign Affairs, Part 1." *Philosophy and Public Affairs* 12, 3: 205–35.

———. 1983b. "Kant, Liberal Legacies, and Foreign Affairs, Part 2." *Philosophy and Public Affairs* 12, 4: 323–53.

———. 1986. "Liberalism and World Politics." *American Political Science Review* 80, 1: 151–68.

Drake, Paul W. 1991. "Commment." In Dornbusch and Edwards, eds. (1991): 35–40.

Dunn, Lewis A. 1982. *Controlling the Bomb.* New Haven: Yale University Press.

Dunn, Michael C. 1994. "Algeria's Agony: The Drama So Far, The Prospects for Peace." *Middle East Policy* 3, 3: 145–56.

Eckstein, Harry. 1975. "Case Study and Theory in Political Science." In Fred Greenstein and Nelson Polsby, eds., *Handbook of Political Science 7.* Reading, Mass.: Addison-Wesley: 79–138.

Elazar, Daniel J., and Shmuel Sandler, eds. 1995. *Israel at the Polls, 1992.* London: Rowman and Littlefield.

El Sayyid, Mustapha K. 1994. "The Third Wave of Democratization in the Arab World." In Tschirgi, ed. (1994): 179–90.

Ember, C. R., M. Ember, and B. Russett. 1992. "Peace between Participatory Polities." *World Politics* 44, 4: 573–99.

Emmerson, Donald K. 1996. "Indonesia, Malaysia, Singapore: A Regional Security

Core?" In Richard J. Ellings and Sheldon W. Simon, eds., *Southeast Asian Security in the New Millennium*. Armonk, N.Y.: M.E. Sharpe.

Erro, Davide G. 1993. *Resolving the Argentine Paradox: Politics and Development, 1966–1992*. Boulder: Lynne Rienner.

Escudé, Carlos. 1987. *Patología del nacionalismo: El caso argentino*. Buenos Aires: Editorial Tesis.

Eshkol, Levi. 1967. *Be-'itsumo Shel Ma'avak*. Jerusalem: Merkaz Ha-hasbarah be-Misrad Rosh Ha-memshalah.

———. 1969. *The State Papers*. Edited, with an introduction, by Henry M. Christman. New York: Funk & Wagnalls.

Esposito, J. L. 1991. *Islam and Politics*. Syracuse: Syracuse University Press.

Esty, Daniel C., Jack A. Golstone, Ted R. Gurr, Barbara Harff, Pamela T. Surko, Alan N. Unger, and Robert Chen. 1997. "Aid and Trade: Still Crucial for Security in the Post-Cold War Era." Paper presented at the Institute on Global Conflict and Cooperation workshop on Global and Regional Governance (La Jolla, May 9–10, 1997).

Evangelista, Matthew. 1993. "Internal and External Constraints on Grand Strategy: The Soviet Case." In Rosecrance and Stein, eds. (1993): 154–78.

Evans, Peter. 1979. *Dependent Development: The Alliance of Multinational, State, and Local Capital in Brazil*. Princeton: Princeton University Press.

———. 1992. "The State as Problem and Solution: Predation, Embedded Autonomy, and Structural Change." In Haggard and Kaufman, eds. (1992): 139–81.

———. 1995. *Embedded Autonomy: States and Industrial Transformation*. Princeton: Princeton University Press.

Evans, Peter B., Harold K. Jacobson, and Robert D. Putnam, eds. 1993. *Double-Edged Diplomacy: International Bargaining and Domestic Politics*. Berkeley and Los Angeles: University of California Press.

Evans, Peter B., Dietrich Rueschemeyer, and Theda Skocpol, eds. 1985. *Bringing the State Back In*. New York: Cambridge University Press.

Evron, Yair. 1974. "Israel and the Atom: The Uses and Misuses of Ambiguity, 1957–1967." *Orbis* 17, 1: 326–43.

Fadlallah, Shaykh Muhammad Hussayn. 1995. "Islamic Unity and Political Change." Interview in *Journal of Palestine Studies* 25, 1 (Autumn): 61–75.

Fawcett, Louise, and Andrew Hurrell, eds. 1995. *Regionalism in World Politics: Regional Organization and International Order*. New York: Oxford University Press.

FBIS-EAS (Foreign Broadcast Information Service—East Asia). Selected Issues 1992–1994. Springfield, Va.: National Technical Information Service.

FBIS-NES (Foreign Broadcast Information Service—Near East and South Asia). Selected issues 1991–1996. Springfield, Va.: National Technical Information Service.

Fearon, James D. 1994. "Domestic Political Audiences and the Escalation of International Disputes." *American Political Science Review* 88, 3 (September): 577–92.

Feigenbaum, Harvey B., and Jeffry R. Henig. 1994. "The Political Underpinnings of Privatization: A Typology." *World Politics* 46, 2 (January): 185–208.

Feldman, Shai. 1982. *Israeli Nuclear Deterrence*. New York: Columbia University Press.

Ferguson, Yale. 1984. "Cooperation in Latin America: The Politics of Regional Integration." In Ferris and Lincoln, eds.: 37–56.

Fernández, Roque B. 1991. "What Have Populists Learned from Hyperinflation?" In Dornbusch and Edwards, eds.: 121–49.

Ferris, Elizabeth G., and Jennie K. Lincoln, eds. 1981. *Latin American Foreign Policies: Global and Regional Dimensions*. Boulder: Westview Press.

———. 1984. *The Dynamics of Latin American Foreign Policies: Challengers for the 1980s*. Boulder: Westview.

Filali-Ansary, Abdou. 1996. "Islam and Liberal Democracy: The Challenge of Secularization," in *Journal of Democracy* 7, 2 (April): 76–80.

Fishlow, Albert. 1989. "A Tale of Two Presidents: The Political Economy of Crisis Management." In Stepan, ed. (1989): 83–119.

———. 1992. "The State of Economics in Brazil and Latin America: Is the Past Prologue to the Future?" In Alfred Stepan, ed., *Americas: New Interpretive Essays*. New York: Oxford University Press: 57–78.

———. 1995. "Inequality, Poverty, and Growth: Where Do We Stand?" In Bruno and Pleskovic, eds. (1995): 25–39.

Flapan, Simha. 1974. "Nuclear Power in the Middle East." *New Outlook* (July): 46–54.

Fontana, Andrés M. 1987. "Political Decisionmaking by a Military Corporation: Argentina 1976–1983." Ph.D. dissertation, Political Science, University of Texas at Austin.

Foot, Rosemary. 1990. *A Substitute for Victory: The Politics of Peacemaking at the Korean Armistice Talks*. Ithaca: Cornell University Press.

Frankel, Francine R. 1978. *India's Political Economy 1947–1977: The Gradual Revolution*. Princeton: Princeton University Press.

Frederiksen, Peter C., and Robert E. Looney. 1983. "Defense Expenditures and Economic Growth in Developing Countries." *Armed Forces and Society* 9, 4 (Summer): 633–45.

Freedman, Lawrence, and Virginia Gamba-Stonehouse. 1991. *Signals of War: The Falklands Conflict of 1982*. Princeton: Princeton University Press.

Frieden, Jeffry A. 1988. "Sectoral Conflict and U.S. Foreign Economic Policy, 1914–1940." In *The State and American Foreign Economic Policy*, edited by G. John Ikenberry, David A. Lake, and Michael Mastanduno. Ithaca: Cornell University Press.

———. 1991a. "Invested Interests: The Politics of National Economic Policies in a World of Global Finance." *International Organization* 45, 4 (Autumn): 425–52.

———. 1991b. *Debt, Development, and Democracy: Modern Political Economy and Latin America*. Princeton: Princeton University Press.

———. 1995. "Capital Politics: Creditors and the International Political Economy." In Frieden and Lake, eds. (1995): 282–98.

Frieden, Jeffry A., and David A. Lake, eds. 1995. *International Political Economy: Perspectives on Global Power and Wealth*. New York: St. Martin's.

Frieden, Jeffry A., and Ronald Rogowski. 1996. In Keohane and Milner, eds. (1996): 25–47.

Fukuyama, Francis. 1992. *The End of History and the Last Man*. New York: Free Press.

Funabashi, Yoichi. 1993. "The Asianization of Asia." *Foreign Affairs* 72, 5 (November/December): 75–85.

Gamble, Andrew, and Anthony Payne, eds. 1996. *Regionalism and World Order*. New York: St. Martin's.

Garnham, David, and Mark Tessler, eds. 1995. *Democracy, War, and Peace in the Middle East*. Bloomington: Indiana University Press.

Garrett, Geoffrey, and Peter Lange. 1996. "Internationalization, Institutions, and Political Change." In Keohane and Milner, eds. (1996): 48–78.

Gasiorowski, M. J. 1986. "Economic Interdependence and International Conflict: Some Cross-National Evidence." *International Studies Quarterly* 30, 1 (March): 23–38.

Gaubatz, Kurt T. 1996. "Democratic States and Commitment in International Relations." *International Organization* 50, 1 (Winter): 109–40.

Geddes, Barbara. 1994. "Challenging the Conventional Wisdom." *Journal of Democracy* 5, 4 (October): 104–18.

Gellner, Ernest. 1983. *Nations and Nationalism*. Ithaca: Cornell University Press.

George, Alexander L., and Timothy J. McKeown. 1985. "Case Studies and Theories of Organizational Decision Making." *Advances in Information Processing in Organizations* 2: 21–58.

Gereffi, Gary. 1990. "Paths of Industrialization: An Overview." In Gereffi and Wyman, eds. (1990): 3–31.

Gereffi, Gary, and Donald L. Wyman, eds. 1990. *Manufacturing Miracles: Paths of Industrialization in Latin America and East Asia*. Princeton: Princeton University Press.

Gerges, Fawaz. 1996. "Review of W. Thom Workman's 'The Social Origins of the Iran-Iraq War.'" *International Journal of Middle East Studies* 28,1 (February): 128–30.

Gerschenkron, Alexander. 1962. *Economic Backwardness in Historical Perspective*. Cambridge: Belknap Press of Harvard University Press.

Ghabra, Shafeeq. 1994. "Democratization in a Middle Eastern State: Kuwait, 1993." *Middle East Policy* 3, 1: 102–19.

Gills, B. K. 1996. *Korea versus Korea: A Case of Contested Legitimacy*. New York: Routledge.

Gilpin, Robert. 1987. *The Political Economy of International Relations*. Princeton: Princeton University Press.

Glaser, Charles L. 1994/95. "Realists as Optimists: Cooperation as Self-Help." *International Security* 19, 3 (Winter): 50–90.

Gleditsch, Nils Petter. 1995. "Geography, Democracy, and Peace." *International Interactions* 20, 4: 297–323.

Gleysteen, William H., Jr. 1987. "Korea's Foreign Policy in the Year 2000." In Han and Myers, eds. (1987): 37–48.

Goldberg, Ellis. 1996. "Why Isn't There More Democracy in the Middle East?" *Contention* 5, 2 (Winter): 141–50.

Goldberg, Ellis, Resat Kasaba, and Joel Migdal, eds. 1993. *Rules and Rights in the Middle East: Democracy, Law, and Society*. Seattle: University of Washington Press.

Goldstone, Jack A. 1996/97. "Revolution, War, and Security." *Security Studies* 6, 2 (Winter): 127–51.

Goldwert, Marvin. 1972. *Democracy, Militarism, and Nationalism in Argentina, 1930–1966. An Interpretation*. Austin: University of Texas Press.

Goncharov, Sergei N., John W. Lewis, and Xue Litai. 1993. *Uncertain Partners: Stalin, Mao, and the Korean War*. Stanford: Stanford University Press.

Goodman, John B., and Louis W. Pauly. 1995. "The Obsolescence of Capital Controls? Economic Management in an Age of Global Markets." In Frieden and Lake, eds. (1995): 299–318.

Goodman, Louis W., Johanna S. R. Mendelson, and Juan Rial, eds. 1990. *The Military and Democracy: The Future of Civil-Military Relations in Latin America*. Lexington, Mass.: Lexington Books.

Gordon, Dennis R. 1984. "Argentina's Foreign Policies in the Post-Malvinas Era." In Ferrris and Lincoln, eds. (1984): 85–100.

Gourevitch, Peter. 1978. "The Second-Image Reversed: The International Sources of Domestic Politics." *International Organization* 32, 4 (Autumn): 881–911.

————. 1986. *Politics in Hard Times: Comparative Responses to International Economic Crises.* Ithaca: Cornell University Press.

Gowa, Joanne, and Edward D. Mansfield. 1993. "Power Politics and International Trade. *American Political Science Review* 87, 2: 408–20.

Graham, Carol. 1994. *Safety Nets, Politics, and the Poor: Transitions to Market Economies.* Washington, D.C.: Brookings Institution.

Gramsci, Antonio. 1988. *A Gramsci Reader: Selected Writings 1916–1935.* Edited by David Forgacs. London: Lawrence and Wishart.

Greider, William. 1997. *One World, Ready or Not: The Manic Logic of Global Capitalism.* New York: Simon and Schuster.

Greenberg, Joel. 1994. "Settlement Vows Fight on Peace Plan." *New York Times,* February 21: A4.

Groennings, Sven, E. W. Kelley, and Michael Leiserson, eds. 1970. *The Study of Coalitional Behavior: Theoretical Perspectives and Cases from Four Continents.* New York: Holt, Rinehart, and Winston.

Guglialmelli, Juan E. 1976. *Argentina, Brazil, y la bomba atómica.* Buenos Aires: Tierra Nueva.

Gurr, Ted. R. 1988. "War, Revolution, and the Growth of the Coercive State." *Comparative Political Studies* 21, 1 (April): 45–65.

Hadar, Leon T. 1993. "What Green Peril?" *Foreign Affairs* 27, 2 (Spring): 27–42.

Haeri, Safa. 1991. "Saudi Arabia: A Warning to the King." *Middle East International,* June 24.

Hagan, Joe D. 1993. *Political Opposition and Foreign Policy in Comparative Perspective.* Boulder: Lynne Rienner.

————. 1994. "Domestic Political Systems and War Pronneness." *Mershon International Studies Review* 38 Supplement 2 (October): 183–208.

Haggard, Stephan. 1990. *Pathways from the Periphery: The Politics of Growth in the Newly Industrializing Countries.* Ithaca: Cornell University Press.

————. 1994a. "Macroeconomic Policy through the First Oil Shock, 1970–75." In Haggard, Cooper, Collins, Kim, and Ro, eds. (1994): 23–48.

————. 1994b. "From the Heavy Industry Plan to Stabilization: Macroeconomic Policy, 1976–1980." In Haggard, Cooper, Collins, Kim, and Ro, eds. (1994): 49–74.

————. 1995a. "Inflation and Stabilization." In Frieden and Lake, eds. (1995): 447–59.

————. 1995b. *Developing Nations and the Politics of Global Integration.* Washington, D.C.: Brookings Institution.

Haggard, Stephan, and Susan Collins. 1994. "The Political Economy of Adjustment in the 1980s." In Haggard, Cooper, Collins, Kim, and Ro, eds. (1994): 75–110.

Haggard, Stephan, Richard N. Cooper, Susan Collins, Choongsoo Kim, Sung-Tae Ro. 1994. *Macroeconomic Policy and Adjustment in Korea, 1970–1990.* Cambridge: Harvard University Press.

Haggard, Stephan, Richard N. Cooper, and Chung-in Moon. 1993. "Policy Reform in Korea." In Bates and Krueger, eds. (1993b): 294–332.

Haggard, Stephan, and Robert R. Kaufman, eds. 1992. *The Politics of Economic Adjustment.* Princeton: Princeton University Press.

————. 1994. "Economic Reform and Democracy: The Challenges of Consolidation." *Journal of Democracy* 5, 4 (October): 5–16.

————. 1995. *The Political Economy of Democratic Transitions.* Princeton: Princeton University Press.

Haggard, Stephan, Chung H. Lee, and Sylvia Maxfield, eds. 1993. *The Politics of Finance in Developing Countries*. Ithaca: Cornell University Press.

Haggard, Stephan, and Sylvia Maxfield. 1996. "The Political Economy of Financial Internationalization in the Developing World." *International Organization* 50, 1 (Winter): 35–68.

Haggard, Stephan, and Chung-in Moon. 1993. "The State, Politics, and Economic Development in Postwar South Korea." In Koo, ed. (1993): 51–94.

Haggard, Stephan, and Steven B. Webb, eds. 1994. *Voting for Reform: Democracy, Political Liberalization, and Economic Adjustment*. New York: Oxford University Press.

Halevi, Nadav. 1993. "Economic Implications of Peace: The Israeli Perspective." In Stanley Fischer, Dani Rodrik, and Elias Tuma, eds., *The Economics of Middle East Peace: Views from the Region*. Cambridge: MIT Press: 87–116.

Hamilton, Alexander. 1817. *The Soundness of the Policy Protecting Domestic Manufactures*. Philadelphia: J.R.A. Skerett.

Han, Sung-Joo, and Robert J. Myers, eds. 1987. *Korea: The Year 2000*. Lanham: University Press of America.

Harik, Iliya. 1994. "Pluralism in the Arab World." *Journal of Democracy* 5, 3 (July): 43–56.

Harkabi, Yehoshafat. 1986. *Hachraot Goraliot*. Tel Aviv: Am Oved. Translated into English: *Israel's Fateful Hour*. New York: Harper and Row, 1988.

Harrison, Selig S. 1994. "The North Korean Nuclear Crisis." *Arms Control Today* 24, 9 (November): 18–20.

Hayes, Peter. 1993a. "International Missile Trade and the Two Koreas." In *Program for Nonproliferation Studies Working Paper No.1* (March). Monterey, Calif.: Monterey Institute of International Studies.

———. 1993b. "What North Korea Wants." *Bulletin of Atomic Scientists* 9 (December): 8–10.

———. n.d. "North Korea's Challenge to the Nuclear Non-proliferation Treaty." Unpublished paper.

Heikal, Mohamed Hasanayn. 1973. *The Cairo Documents; The Inside Story of Nasser and His Relationship with World Leaders, Rebels, and Statesmen*. Garden City, N.Y.: Doubleday.

———. 1975. *The Road to Ramadan*. New York: Quadrangle/New York Times Book Co.

Hewedy, Amin. 1989. *Militarization and Security in the Middle East: Its Impact on Development and Democracy*. London: Pinter.

Heydemann, Steven. 1993. "Taxation without Representation: Authoritarianism and Economic Liberalization in Syria." In Goldberg, Kasaba, and Migdal, eds. (1993): 69–101.

Hilal, Jamil. 1993. "PLO Institutions: The Challenge Ahead." *Journal of Palestine Studies* 23, 1 (Autumn): 46–60.

Hill, Stuart, and Donald Rothchild. 1993. "The Impact of Regime on the Diffusion of Political Conflict." In Midlarsky, ed. (1993): 189–208.

Hilton, Stanley E. 1985. "The Argentine Factor in Twentieth-Century Brazilian Foreign Policy Strategy." *Political Science Quarterly* 100, 1 (Spring): 27–51.

Hinnebusch, Raymond A. 1985. *Egyptian Politics under Sadat: The Post-Populist Development of an Authoritarian-Modernizing State*. New York: Cambridge University Press.

————. 1991. "Revisionist Dreams, Realist Strategies: The Foreign Policy of Syria." In Korany and Dessouki, eds. (1991): 374–409.

————. 1993. "Syria." In Niblock and Murphy, eds. (1993): 177–202.

————. 1996. "Does Syria Want Peace? Syrian Policy in the Syrian-Israeli Peace Negotiations." *Journal of Palestine Studies* 26, 1 (Autumn): 42–57.

Hirschman, Albert O. 1945. *National Power and the Structure of Foreign Trade*. Berkeley and Los Angeles: University of California Press.

————. 1958. *The Strategy of Economic Development*. New Haven: Yale University Press.

————. 1965. *Journeys toward Progress*. Garden City, N.Y.: Doubleday.

————. 1977. *The Passions and the Interests*. Princeton: Princeton University Press.

————. 1981. *Essays in Trespassing: Economics to Politics and Beyond*. New York: Cambridge University Press.

————. 1982. *Shifting Involvements: Private Interest and Public Action*. Princeton: Princeton University Press.

————. 1985. "Reflections on the Latin American Experience." In Leon N. Lindberg and Charles S. Maier, eds., *The Politics of Inflation and Economic Stagnation: Theoretical Approaches and International Case Studies*. Washington, D.C.: Brookings Institution: 53–77.

————. 1990. "The Case against 'One Thing at a Time.'" *World Development* 18, 8: 1,119–22.

————. 1991. *The Rhetoric of Reaction: Perversity, Futility, Jeopardy*. Cambridge: Belknap Press of Harvard University Press.

Hoge, James F., Jr. 1995. "Fulfilling Brazil's Promise: A Conversation with President Cardoso." *Foreign Affairs* 74, 4 (July/August): 62–75.

Holsti, Kal J. 1992. "International Theory and War in the Third World." In Job, ed. (1992): 37–62.

————. 1995. "War, Peace, and the State of the State." *International Political Science Review* 16, 4 (October): 319–40.

Hoodbhoy, Pervez. 1993. "Myth-Building: The 'Islamic' Bomb," *Bulletin of the Atomic Scientists* 5 (June): 42–49.

Hosking, Geoffrey, and George Schopflin, eds. 1997. *Myths and Nationhood*. New York: Routledge.

Hudson, Michael C. 1977. *Arab Politics*. New Haven: Yale University Press.

————. 1995. "Democracy and Foreign Policy in the Arab World." In Garnham and Tessler, eds. (1995): 195–222.

————. 1996. "Obstacles to Democratization in the Middle East." *Contention* 5, 2 (Winter): 81–106.

Hufbauer, Gary C., and Jeffrey J. Schott. 1994. *Western Hemisphere Economic Integration*. Washingon, D.C.: Institute for International Economics.

Hufbauer, Gary C., Jeffrey J. Schott, and Kimberly A. Elliott. 1990. *Economic Sanctions Reconsidered*. Washington, D.C.: Institute for International Economics.

Huntington, Samuel P. 1991. *The Third Wave: Democratization in the Late Twentieth Century*. Norman and London: University of Oklahoma Press.

————. 1995. "Reforming Civil-Military Relations." *Journal of Democracy* 6, 4 (October): 9–17.

————. 1996. *The Clash of Civilizations and the Remaking of World Order*. New York: Simon and Schuster.

Hussein I (King of Jordan). 1962. *Uneasy Lies the Head*. N.p.: Bernard Geis Associates, distributed by Random House.

―――. 1969. *Hussein of Jordan: My "War" with Israel*. As told to and with additional material by Vick Vance and Pierre Lauer. New York: William Morrow.

―――. 1994. *Selected Speeches (1988–1994)*. Amman: International Press Office, Royal Hashemite Court.

Hussein, Saddam. 1979. *Social and Foreign Affairs in Iraq*. Translated by Khalid Kishtainy. London: Croom Helm.

―――. 1992. *Saddam Hussein Speaks on the Gulf Crisis. A Collection of Documents*. Edited by Ofra Bengio. Tel Aviv: Tel Aviv University, Moshe Dayan Center for Middle Eastern and African Studies.

Ibrahim, Saad Eddin. 1994. "Arab Elites and Societies after the Gulf Crisis." In Tschirgi, ed. (1994): 77–90.

―――. 1995. "Liberalization and Democratization in the Arab World: An Overview." In Rex Brynen, Bahgat Korany, and Paul Noble, eds. *Political Liberalization and Democratization in the Arab World*. Vol. 1: *Theoretical Perspectives*. Boulder: Lynne Rienner: 29–60.

Inbar, Efraim. 1986. "Israel and Nuclear Weapons since October 1973." In Louis R. Beres, *Security or Armaggedon*. Lexington, Mass.: Lexington Books: 61–78.

International Institute for Management Development. 1997. *World Competitiveness Yearbook 1997*. Lausanne, Switzerland.

International Institute for Strategic Studies. 1992. *The Military Balance, 1992–1993*. London: Brassey's.

―――. 1995. *The Military Balance 1995/96*. London: Oxford University Press.

IRELA (Institute for European-Latin American Relations) 1997. "MERCOSUR: Prospects for an Emerging Bloc." Madrid: Dossier No. 61 (August).

Issawi, Charles. 1963. *Egypt in Revolution: An Economic Analysis*. London: Oxford University Press.

Jabber, Fuad. 1971. *Israel and Nuclear Weapons*. International Institute of Strategic Studies Monograph. London: Chatto and Windus.

Jansen, Johannes J. G. 1997. *The Dual Nature of Islamic Fundamentalism*. Ithaca: Cornell University Press.

Jeon, Jei Guk. 1995. "Exploring the Three Varieties of East Asia's State-Guided Development Model: Korea, Singapore, and Taiwan." *Studies in Comparative International Development* 30, 3 (Fall): 70–88.

Jervis, Robert. 1982. "Security Regimes." *International Organization* 36, 2: 357–78.

―――. 1986. "From Balance to Concert: A Study of International Security Cooperation." In Oye, ed. (1986): 58–79.

Job, Brian L. ed. 1992. *The Insecurity Dilemma: National Security of Third World States*. Boulder: Lynne Rienner.

―――. 1997. "Matters of Multilateralism: Implications for Regional Conflict Management." In Lake and Morgan, eds. (1997): 165–94.

Johnson, Chalmers. 1982. *MITI and the Japanese Miracle*. Stanford: Stanford University Press.

―――. 1987. "Political Institutions and Economic Performance: The Government-Business Relationship in Japan, South Korea, and Taiwan." In Deyo, ed. (1987): 136–64.

―――. 1993. "The State and Japanese Grand Strategy." In Rosecrance and Stein, eds. (1993): 201–24.

Jones, Leroy P., and Il Sakong. 1980. *Government, Business, and Entrepreneurship in Economic Development: The Korean Case.* Cambridge: Harvard University Press.

Juergensmeyer, Mark. 1993. *The New Cold War? Religious Nationalism Confronts the Secular State.* Berkeley and Los Angeles: University of California Press.

Kahler, Miles. 1984. *Decolonization in Britain and France: The Domestic Consequences of International Relations.* Princeton: Princeton University Press.

———. 1992. "External Influence, Conditionality, and the Politics of Adjustment." In Haggard and Kaufman, eds. (1992): 89–138.

Kallab, Valeriana, and Richard E. Feinberg, eds. 1989. *Fragile Coalitions: The Politics of Economic Adjustment.* New Brunswick, N.J.: Transaction.

Kanin, David B. 1989. "North Korea: Institutional and Economic Obstacles to Dynamic Succession." *Journal of Social, Political, and Economic Studies* 14, 1 (Spring): 49–77.

Kanovsky, Eliyahu. 1997. "The Middle East Economies: The Impact of Domestic and International Politics." BESA Center for Strategic Studies, Mideast Security and Policy Studies, No. 31. Tel Aviv: Bar-Ilan University.

Kant, Immanuel. 1784/1991. "Idea for a Universal History." In Hans Reiss, ed., H. B. Nisbet, trans., *Kant's Political Writings.* Cambridge: Cambridge University Press.

Karawan, Ibrahim A. 1993. "Foreign Policy Restructuring: Egypt's Disengagement from the Arab-Israeli Conflict Reconsidered." Unpublished paper. Department of Political Science, University of Utah.

Karl, Terry Lynn, and Philippe C. Schmitter. 1991. "Modes of Transition in Latin America, Southern and Eastern Europe." *International Social Science Journal* 53 (May): 269–84.

Katzenstein, Peter. 1989. "Small Nations in an Open International Economy: The Converging Balance of State and Society in Switzerland and Austria." In Evans, Rueschemeyer, and Skocpol, eds. (1989): 227–46.

———, ed. 1996. *The Culture of National Security: Norms and Identity in World Politics.* New York: Columbia University Press.

Kaufman, Daniel. 1997. "Corruption: The Facts." *Foreign Policy* 107 (Summer): 114–31.

Kaufman, Edy, Shukri B. Abed, and Robert L. Rothstein, eds. 1993. *Democracy, Peace, and the Israeli-Palestinian Conflict.* Boulder: Lynne Rienner.

Kaufman, Robert R. 1986. "Liberalization and Democratization in South America: Perspectives from the 1970s." In O'Donnell, Schmitter, and Whitehead, eds. (1986): 85–107.

———. 1989. "Domestic Determinants of Stabilization and Adjustment Choices." In *Choices in World Politics: Sovereignty and Interdependence*, edited by B. Russett, H. Starr, and R. Stoll. New York: W. H. Freeman: 261–82.

———. 1990a. "How Societies Change Developmental Models or Keep Them: Reflections on the Latin American Experience in the 1930s and the Postwar World." In Gereffi and Wyman, eds. (1990): 110–38.

———. 1990b. "Stabilization and Adjustment in Argentina, Brazil, and Mexico." In Nelson, ed. (1990): 63–112.

Kaufman, Robert R., and Barbara Stallings. 1991. "The Political Economy of Latin American Populism." In Dornbusch and Edwards, eds. (1991): 15–34.

Kaysen, Carl. 1991. "Is War Obsolete? A Review Essay." In Lynn-Jones, ed. (1991): 81–103.

Kedourie, Elie. 1992. *Politics in the Middle East.* Oxford: Oxford University Press.

Kehr, Eckart. 1977. *Economic Interest, Militarism, and Foreign Policy: Essays on Ger-*

man History. Translated by Grete Heinz. Berkeley and Los Angeles: University of California Press.

Kelley, E. W. 1970. "Theory and the Study of Coalition Behavior." In Groenings, Kelley, and Leiserson, eds. (1970): 481–88.

Kemp, Geoffrey. 1994. "Cooperative Security in the Middle East." In Janne E. Nolan, ed., *Global Engagement: Cooperation and Security in the 21st Century*. Washington, D.C.: Brookings Institution: 391–418.

Kennedy, Paul, ed. 1991. *Grand Strategies in War and Peace*. New Haven: Yale University Press.

————. 1993. *Preparing for the Twenty-First Century*. New York: Random House.

Kenworthy, Eldon. 1970. "Coalitions in the Political Development of Latin America." In Groennings, Kelley, and Leiserson, eds. (1970): 103–40.

Keohane, Robert O. 1984. *After Hegemony: Cooperation and Discourse in the World Political Economy*. Princeton: Princeton University Press.

————. 1986. "Reciprocity in International Relations." *International Organization* 40, 1 (Winter): 1–28.

Keohane, Robert O., and Lisa L. Martin. 1995. "The Promise of Institutionalist Theory," *International Security* 20, 1: 39–51.

Keohane, Robert O., and Helen V. Milner, eds. 1996. *Internationalization and Domestic Politics*. New York: Cambridge University Press.

Keohane, Robert O., and Joseph Nye, eds. 1977. *Power and Interdependence: World Politics in Transition*. Boston: Little, Brown.

Kerr, Malcolm. 1971. *The Arab Cold War 1958–1967*. Oxford: Oxford University Press.

Khalil, Samir al-. 1989. *The Republic of Fear: The Politics of Modern Iraq*. Berkeley: University of California Press.

Khazen, Jihad al-. 1995. "Interview: Editor of Al Hayat." *Middle East Policy* 3, 4 (April): 69–73.

Khouri, Riad al-. 1994. "The Political Economy of Jordan: Democratization and the Gulf Crisis." In Tschirgi, ed. (1994): 101–22.

Kim, C. I. Eugene. 1988. "North Korea's Perspective on Northeast Asian Security." In Shin, Kwak, and Olsen, eds. (1988): 133–58.

Kim Il Sung. 1975a. *On Juche in Our Revolution*. Pyongyang: Foreign Languages Publishing House.

————. 1975b. *For the Independent, Peaceful Reunification of Korea* . New York: International Publishers.

Kim, Young Sam. 1994. "Reforming while Forging Ahead." *Presidents and Prime Ministers* (March–April): 4–6.

————. 1995. *Korea's Quest for Reform and Globalization*. Selected Speeches of President Kim Young Sam. Seoul: Presidential Secretariat.

Kimmerling, Baruch, and Joel S. Migdal. 1994. *Palestinians: The Making of a People*. Cambridge: Harvard University Press.

Kindleberger, Charles P. 1951. "Group Behavior and International Trade." *Journal of Political Economy* 59 (February): 30–46.

King, Gary, Robert O. Keohane, and Sidney Verba. 1994. *Designing Social Inquiry: Scientific Inference in Qualitative Research*. Princeton: Princeton University Press.

Klieman, Aharon S., and Reuven Pedatzur. 1992. *Rearming Israel: Defense Procurement through the 1990s*. Boulder: Westview.

Koh, Byung Chul. 1984. *The Foreign Policy Systems of North and South Korea*. Berkeley and Los Angeles: University of California Press.

Kohli, Atul, ed. 1988. *India's Democracy: An Analysis of Changing State-Society Relations*. Princeton: Princeton University Press.

——. 1990. "The Politics of Economic Liberalization in India." In Suleiman and Waterbury, eds. (1990): 364–88.

Kolodziej, Edward A., and Robert E. Harkavy, eds. 1982. *Security Policies of Developing Countries*. Lexington, Mass.: Lexington Books.

Koo, Bon-hak. 1992. *Political Economy of Self-reliance: Juche and Economic Development in North Korea, 1961–1990*. Korean Unification Studies Series 14. Seoul: Research Center for Peace and Unification of Korea.

Koo, Hagen, ed. 1993. *State and Society in Contemporary Korea*. Ithaca: Cornell University Press.

Korany, Bahgat, and Ali E. Hillal Dessouki, eds. 1991. *The Foreign Policies of Arab States: The Challenge of Change*. Boulder: Westview Press.

Krasner, Stephen. 1985. *Structural Conflict*. Berkeley and Los Angeles: University of California Press.

Krueger, Anne O. 1974. "The Political Economy of the Rent-Seeking Society." *American Economic Review* 64, 3 (June): 291–303.

——. 1993. *Political Economy of Policy Reform in Developing Countries*. Cambridge: MIT Press.

——. 1995. *Trade Policies and Developing Nations*. Washington, D.C.: Brookings Institution.

Krugman, Paul. 1995a. "Cycles of Conventional Wisdom on Economic Development." *International Affairs* 71, 4 (October): 717–32.

——. 1995b. "Dutch Tulips and Emerging Markets." *Foreign Affairs* 74, 4 (July/August): 28–44.

Kuark, Yoon T. 1963. "North Korea's Industrial Development during the Post-War Period." In Scalapino, ed. (1963): 51–64.

Kupchan, Charles, and Clifford Kupchan. 1991. "Concerts, Collective Security, and the Future of Europe." *International Security* 16, 1 (Summer): 114–61.

Kuran, Timur. 1991. "Now out of Never: The Element of Surprise in the East European Revolution of 1989." *World Politics* 44, 1 (October): 7–48.

——. 1993. "Fundamentalisms and the Economy." In Martin E. Marty and R. Scott Appleby, eds. *Fundamentalisms and the State: Remaking Polities, Economies, and Militance*. Chicago: University of Chicago Press: 289–301.

——. 1997. "Islamism and Economics: Policy Implications for a Free Society." In Sohrab Behdad and Farhad Nomani, eds., *Islam and Public Policy*. Greenwich, Conn.: JAI Press: 72–102.

Kwak, Tae-Hwan. 1988. "South-North Korean Dialogue: Problems and Prospects." In Shin, Kwak, and Olsen, eds. (1988): 281–324.

Labán, Raúl, and Felipe Larraín. 1995. "Continuity, Change, and the Political Economy of Transition in Chile." In Dornbusch and Edwards, eds. (1995): 115–49.

Lake, David A. 1988. *Power, Protection, and Free Trade: International Sources of U.S. Commercial Strategy, 1887–1939*. Ithaca: Cornell University Press.

——. 1992. "Powerful Pacifists: Democratic States and War." *American Political Science Review* 86, 1: 24–37.

——. 1997. "Regional Security Complexes: A Systems Approach." In Lake and Morgan, eds. (1997): 45–67.

Lake, David, and Patrick Morgan, eds., *Regional Orders: Building Security in a New World*. University Park: Pennsylvania State University Press.

Lamb, Geoffrey, with Valeriana Kallab, eds. 1992. *Military Expenditure and Economic Development: A Symposium on Research Issues.* World Bank Discussion Paper No. 185. Washington, D.C.: World Bank.

Lamborn, Alan C. 1991. *The Price of Power.* Boston: Unwin Hyman.

Lamounier, Bolívar. 1994. "Brazil at an Impasse." *Journal of Democracy* 5, 3 (July): 72–87.

Lawrence, Robert Z. 1995. "Emerging Regional Arrangements: Building Blocks or Stumbling Blocks?" In Frieden and Lake, eds. (1995): 407–15.

Lawson, Fred H. 1994. "Domestic Transformation and Foreign Steadfastness in Contemporary Syria." *Middle East Journal* 48, 1 (Winter): 47–64.

Lebow, Richard Ned. 1989. "Miscalculation in the South Atlantic: The Origins of the Falklands War." In Robert Jervis, Richard N. Lebow, and Janice Gross Stein, *Psychology and Deterrence.* Baltimore: Johns Hopkins University Press: 89–124.

Lebow, Richard Ned, and Thomas Risse-Kappen, eds. 1995. *International Relations Theory and the End of the Cold War.* New York: Columbia University Press.

Leca, Jean. 1994. "Democratization in the Arab World: Uncertainty, Vulnerability, and Legitimacy: A Tentative Conceptualization and Some Hypotheses." In Salamé, ed. (1994): 48–83.

Lee, Chong-Sik. 1963. "Politics in North Korea: Pre-Korean War Stage." In Scalapino, ed. (1963): 3–16.

Leiserson, Michael. 1970. "Power and Ideology in Coalitional Behavior: An Experimental Study." In Groennings, Kelley, and Leiserson, eds. (1970): 323–35.

Levi, Margaret. 1988. *Of Rule and Revenue.* Berkeley and Los Angeles: University of California Press.

Levy, Jack S. 1988. "Domestic Politics and War." *Journal of Interdisciplinary History* 18, 4: 653–73.

Levy, Jack S., and Michael M. Barnett. 1992. "Alliance Formation, Domestic Political Economy, and Third World Security." *Jerusalem Journal of International Relations* 14, 4 (December): 19–40.

Levy, Jack S., and Lily I. Vakili. 1993. "Diversionary Action by Authoritarian Regimes: Argentina in the Falklands/Malvinas Case." In Midlarsky, ed. (1993): 118–46.

Liebman, Charles S. 1993. "Religion and Democracy in Israel." In Sprinzak and Diamond, eds. (1993): 273–92.

Lijphart, Arend. 1971. "Comparative Politics and the Comparative Method." *American Political Science Review* 65, 3 (September): 682–93.

Lim, Linda Y.C. 1996. "ASEAN: New Modes of Economic Cooperation." In David Wurfel and Bruce Burton, eds., *Southeast Asia in the New World Order.* New York: St. Martin's.

Linz, Juan J., and Alfred Stepan. 1996. *Problems of Democratic Transition and Consolidation: Southern Europe, South America, and Post-Communist Europe.* Baltimore: Johns Hopkins University Press.

Llaver, María del Camen. 1979. "El Problema del apovechamiento hidroeléctrico del alto Paraná." *Revista Argentina de Relaciones Internacionales* 5, 15 (September–October): 25–40.

Looney, Robert. 1989. "Internal and External Factors in Effecting Third World Military Expenditures." *Journal of Peace Research* 26, 1: 33–46.

Lustick, Ian S. 1993. *Unsettled States, Disputed Lands: Britain and Ireland, France and Algeria, Israel and the West Bank-Gaza.* Ithaca: Cornell University Press.

———. 1994. "Lessons from Ireland and Algeria." *Middle East Policy* 3, 3: 41–59.

Lustig, Nora, ed. 1995. *Coping with Austerity: Poverty and Inequality in Latin America.* Washington, D.C.: Brookings Institution.

Lynn-Jones, Sean, ed. 1993. *The Cold War and After: Prospects for Peace.* Cambridge: MIT Press.

MacIntyre, Andrew, ed. 1994. *Business and Government in Industrialising Asia.* Ithaca: Cornell University Press.

Mack, Andrew. 1996. "Proliferation in Northeast Asia." Occasional Paper No. 28 (July). Washington, D.C.: Henry L. Stimson Center.

Mack, Andrew, and Pauline Kerr. 1994. "The Evolving Security Discourse in the Asia-Pacific." *Washington Quarterly* 18, 1: 123–40.

Makovsky, David. 1996. *Making Peace with the PLO: The Rabin Government's Road to the Oslo Accord.* Boulder: Westview.

Mallon, R. D., and J. V. Sourrouille. 1975. *Economic Policymaking in a Conflict Society: The Argentine Case.* Cambridge: Harvard University Press.

Mansfield, Edward D. 1994. *Power, Trade, and War.* Princeton: Princeton University Press.

Mansfield, Edward D., and Helen V. Milner, eds. 1997. *The Political Economy of Regionalism.* New York: Columbia University Press.

Mansfield, Edward D., and Jack Snyder. 1995. "The Dangers of Democratization." *International Security* 20, 1 (Summer): 1–33.

Manzetti, Luigi. 1993. *Institutions, Parties, and Coalitions in Argentine Politics.* Pittsburgh: University of Pittsburgh Press.

Maoz, Zeev, and Nasrin Abdolali. 1989. "Regime Type and International Conflict, 1816–1976." *Journal of Conflict Resolution* 33, 1: 3–36.

Maoz, Zeev, and Bruce Russett. 1992. "Alliance, Contiguity, Wealth, and Political Stability: Is the Lack of Conflict among Democracies a Statistical Artifact?" *International Interactions* 17: 245–67.

———. 1993. "Normative and Structural Causes of Democratic Peace, 1946–1986." *American Political Science Review* 87, 3: 624–38.

Maravall, José María. 1994. "The Myth of the Authoritarian Advantage." *Journal of Democracy* 5, 4 (October): 17–31.

March, James G., and Johan P. Olsen. 1989. *Rediscovering Institutions: The Organizational Basis of Politics.* New York: Free Press.

Mares, David. 1997. "Regional Conflict Management in Latin America: Power Complemented by Diplomacy." In Lake and Morgan, eds. (1997): 195–218.

Marks, Stephen V., and John McArthur. 1993. "Empirical Analyses of the Determinants of Protection: A Survey and Some New Results." In John S. Odell and Thomas D. Willett, eds. *International Trade Policies: Gains from Exchange between Economics and Political Science.* Ann Arbor: University of Michigan Press: 105–40.

Mármora, Leopoldo. 1988. "A Integraçào Brasil-Argentina: Riscos, possibilidades, custos." *Política e Estratégia* 6, 1 (January–March): 17–35.

Marr, Phebe. 1985. *The Modern History of Iraq.* Boulder: Westview Press.

Maxfield, Sylvia. 1990. *Governing Capital: International Finance and Mexican Politics.* Ithaca: Cornell University Press.

———. 1997. *Gatekeepers of Growth: The International Political Economy of Central Banking in Developing Countries.* Princeton: Princeton University Press.

Mayer, Ann E. 1993. "The Fundamentalist Impact on Law, Politics, and Constitutions in Iran, Pakistan, and the Sudan." In Martin E. Marty and R. Scott Appleby, eds., *Fundamentalisms and the State: Remaking Polities, Economies, and Militance.* Chicago: University of Chicago Press: 110–51.

Mazarr, Michael J. 1995. *North Korea and the Bomb*. New York: St. Martin's.

McGuire, James W. 1995. "Interim Government and Democratic Consolidation: Argentina in Comparative Perspective." In Shain and Linz, eds. (1995): 179–210.

McKinnon, Ronald I. 1993. *The Order of Economic Liberalization: Financial Control in the Transition to a Market Economy*. Baltimore: Johns Hopkins University Press.

Mearsheimer, John J. 1993. "Back to the Future: Instability in Europe after the Cold War." In Lynn-Jones, ed. (1993): 141–92.

———. 1994/1995. "The False Promise of International Institutions." *International Security* 19, 3 (Winter): 5–49.

Meckstroth, T. W. 1975. "'Most Different Systems' and 'Most Similar Systems.' A Case Study on the Logic of Comparative Social Inquiry." *Comparative Political Studies* 8, 2 (July): 132–57.

Menem, Carlos S. 1993. *Conversaciones con Carlos Menem: Cómo consolidar el modelo*. Edited by Mario Baizan. Vol. 2. Buenos Aires: Fraterna.

———. 1996a. *Qué es el Mercosur?* Buenos Aires: Ciudad Argentina.

———. 1996b. "The Value of the UN for Small Countries." *New Perspectives Quarterly* (Winter): 36–37.

Meyer, Stephen M. 1984. *The Dynamics of Nuclear Proliferation*. Chicago: University of Chicago Press.

Midlarsky, Manus I., ed. 1993. *The Internationalization of Communal Strife*. New York: Routledge.

Migdal, Joel S. 1980. *Palestinian Society and Politics*. Princeton: Princeton University Press.

———. 1988. *Strong Societies and Weak States: State-Society Relations and State Capabilities in the Third World*. Princeton: Princeton University Press.

Mikheev, Vasily. 1996. "Politics and Ideology in the Post Cold War Era." In Park, ed. (1996): 88–104.

Milenky, Edward S. 1978. *Argentina's Foreign Policies*. Boulder: Westview Press.

Miller, Steven E. 1993. "The Case against a Ukrainian Nuclear Deterrent." *Foreign Affairs* 72, 3 (Summer): 67–80.

Milner, Helen. 1988a. "Trading Places: Industries for Free Trade." *World Politics* 40, 3 (April): 350–76.

———. 1988b. *Resisting Protectionism: Global Industries and the Politics of International Trade*. Princeton: Princeton University Press.

Mittelman, James H., ed. 1996. *Globalization: Critical Reflections*. Boulder: Lynne Rienner.

Moneta, Carlos J. 1984. "The Malvinas Conflict: Analyzing the Argentine Military Regime's Decision-Making Process." In Muñoz and Tulchin, eds. (1984): 119–32.

Moon, Chung-in. 1990. "Beyond Statism: Rethinking the Political Economy of Growth in South Korea." *International Studies Notes* 15, 1 (Winter): 24–27.

———. 1994. "Changing Patterns of Business-Government Relations in South Korea." In MacIntyre, ed. (1994): 142–66.

———. 1996. *Arms Control on the Korean Peninsula: International Penetrations, Regional Dynamics, and Domestic Structures*. Seoul: Yonsei University Press.

Moon, Chung-in, and In-Taek Hyun. 1992. "Muddling through Security, Growth, and Welfare: The Political Economy of Defense Spending in South Korea." In Chan and Mintz, eds. (1992): 137–62.

Moon, Young (Michael) Park. 1994/1995. "'Lure' North Korea." *Foreign Policy* 79 (Winter): 97–105.

Most, Benjamin A. 1991. *Changing Authoritarian Rule and Public Policy in Argentina, 1930–1970*. Boulder: Lynne Rienner.

Most, Benjamin A., and Harvey Starr. 1989. *Inquiry, Logic, and International Politics*. Columbia: University of South Carolina Press.

Mottahedeh, Roy P. 1995. "The Islamic Movement: The Case for Democratic Inclusion." *Contention* 4, 3 (Spring): 107–27.

Mueller, Dennis C. 1989. *Public Choice II*. New York: Cambridge University Press.

Mueller, John. 1989. *Retreat from Doomsday: The Obsolescence of Major War*. New York: Basic Books.

———. 1995. *Quiet Cataclysm: Reflections on the Recent Transformation of World Politics*. New York: HarperCollins.

Muñoz, Heraldo. 1984. "Beyond the Malvinas Crisis." *Latin American Reseach Review* 9, 1: 158–72.

Muñoz, Heraldo, and Joseph S. Tulchin, eds., 1984. *Latin American Nations in World Politics*. Boulder: Westview.

Muslih, Muhammad Y. 1988. *The Origins of Palestinian Nationalism*. New York: Columbia University Press.

———. 1995. "Arafat's Dilemma." *Current History* 94, 588 (January): 23–27.

Naim, Moises. 1995. "Latin America the Morning After." *Foreign Affairs* 74, 4 (July–August): 45–61.

Nash, Nathaniel C. 1994. "Sequel to an Old Fraud: Argentina's Powerful Nuclear Program." *New York Times*, January 18: A6.

Nasser, Gamal Abdel. 1959. *Where I Stand and Why*. Washington, D.C.: United Arab Republic, Embassy, Press Department.

———. 1962. *Gamal Abdel Nasser at the Inaugural Session of the National Congress of the Powers of the People on the Evening of 21st May, 1962*. Cairo: Information Department.

Nelson, Joan M., ed. 1989. *Fragile Coalitions: The Politics of Economic Adjustment*. New Brunswick, N.J.: Transaction.

———, ed. 1990. *Economic Crisis and Policy Choice: The Politics of Adjustment in the Third World*. Princeton: Princeton University Press.

———. 1992. "Poverty, Equity, and the Politics of Adjustment." In Haggard and Kaufman, eds. (1992): 221–69.

———. 1994. "Linkages between Politics and Economics." *Journal of Democracy* 5, 4 (October): 49–62.

Netanyahu, Benjamin. 1993. *A Place among the Nations: Israel and the World*. New York: Bantam.

Niblock, Tim. 1993. "International and Domestic Factors in the Economic Liberalization Process in Arab Countries." In Niblock and Murphy, eds. (1993): 55–87.

Niblock, Tim, and Emma Murphy, eds. 1993. *Economic and Political Liberalization in the Middle East*. London: British Academic Press.

Nimrod, Yoram. 1991. "Arms Control or Arms Race?" *New Outlook* (September/October): 15–18.

Noble, Paul C. 1991. "The Arab System: Pressures, Constraints and Opportunities." In Korany and Dessouki, eds. (1991): 49–102.

Norton, Augustus R. 1995. "The Challenge of Inclusion in the Middle East." *Current History* 94, 588 (January): 1–6.

Nye, Joseph S., Jr., ed. 1968. *International Regionalism*. Boston: Little, Brown.

O'Donnell, Guillermo. 1978. "Reflections on the Patterns of Change in the Bureaucratic-Authoritarian State." *Latin American Research Review* 13, 1: 3–38.

————. 1988. *Bureaucratic Authoritarianism.* Berkeley and Los Angeles: University of California Press.

O'Donnell, Guillermo, Philippe C. Schmitter, and Laurence Whitehead, eds. 1986. *Transitions from Authoritarian Rule: Tentative Conclusions about Uncertain Democracies.* Baltimore: Johns Hopkins University Press.

Ogle, George E. 1990. *South Korea: Dissent within the Economic Miracle.* London: Zed Books.

Olivera, Darío A. 1978. "Caso Beagle: Antecedentes." *Revista Argentina de Relaciones Internacionales* 4, 11 (May–August): 62–72.

Olmos, Mario Eduardo. 1986. *La Cooperación Argentina-Brasil.* Buenos Aires: Instituto de Publicaciones Navales.

Oneal, John R., Frances H. Oneal, Zeev Maoz, and Bruce Russett. 1996. "Liberal Peace Interdependence, Democracy, and International Conflict: 1950–1985." *Journal of Peace Research* 33, 1 (February): 11–28.

Oneal, John R., and Bruce Russett. 1997. "The Classical Liberals Were Right: Democracy, Interdependence, and Conflict, 1950–1985." *International Studies Quarterly* 41, 2 (June): 267–94.

Owen, John M. 1994. "How Liberalism Produces Democratic Peace." *International Security* 19, 2: 87–125.

Owen, Roger. 1992. *State, Power, and Politics in the Making of the Modern Middle East.* New York: Routledge.

Oye, Kenneth A. ed. 1986. *Cooperation under Anarchy.* Princeton: Princeton University Press.

————. 1992. *Economic Discrimination and Political Exchange: World Political Economy in the 1930s and 1980s.* Princeton: Princeton University Press.

Paige, Glenn D., and Dong Jun Lee. 1963. "The Post-War Politics of Communist Korea." In Scalapino, ed. (1963): 17–29.

Park Chung Hee. 1971. *To Build a Nation.* Washington, D.C.: Acropolis.

————. 1976. *Toward Peaceful Unification.* Seoul: Kwangmyong Publishing Company.

————. 1979. *Korea Reborn: A Model for Development.* Englewood Cliffs, N.J.: Prentice Hall.

Park, Han S., ed. 1996. *North Korea: Ideology, Politics, Economics.* Englewood Cliffs, N.J.: Prentice Hall.

Pasha, Mustapha Kamal, and Ahmed I. Samatar. 1996. "The Resurgence of Islam." In Mittelman, ed. (1996): 187–204.

Payne, Leigh A. 1994. *Brazilian Industrialists and Democratic Change.* Baltimore: Johns Hopkins University Press.

Peña, Félix. 1995. "New Approaches to Economic Integration in the Southern Cone." *Washington Quarterly* 18, 3 (Summer): 113–22.

Peres, Shimon. 1993. *The New Middle East.* New York: Henry Holt.

Peri, Yoram. 1983. *Between Battles and Ballots: Israeli Military in Politics.* Cambridge: Cambridge University Press.

Perlmutter, Amos, Michael Handel, and Uri Bar-Joseph. 1982. *Two Minutes over Baghdad.* London: Vallentine, Mitchell.

Perón, Juan Domingo. 1950. *Perón expone su doctrina.* Buenos Aires: Subsecretaría de Informaciones.

————. 1973. *Política y estrategia; no ataco, critico.* 2nd ed. Buenos Aires: Editorial Pleamar.

————. 1974. *La hora de los pueblos.* 4th ed. Buenos Aires: Distribuidora Baires.

Perthes, Volker. 1995. *The Political Economy of Syria under Asad.* New York: I. B. Tauris.

Pinochet Ugarte, Augusto. 1991. *Camino Recorrido: Memorias de un Soldado.* Vol. 2. Santiago: Instituto Geográfico Militar de Chile.

Pion-Berlin, David. 1985. "The Fall of Military Rule in Argentina: 1976–1983." *Journal of Interamerican Studies and World Affairs* 27 (Summer): 55–76.

————. 1995. "The Armed Forces and Politics: Gains and Snares in Recent Scholarship." *Latin American Research Review,* 30, 1: 147–62.

Pittman, Howard T. 1981. "Geopolitics and Foreign Policy in Argentina, Brazil, and Chile." In Ferris and Lincoln, eds. (1981): 165–77.

Plessner, Yakir. 1994. *The Political Economy of Israel: From Ideology to Stagnation.* Albany: State University of New York Press.

Polanyi, Karl. 1944. *The Great Transformation: The Political and Economic Origins of Our Time.* Boston: Beacon Press.

Pollack, Andrew. 1994a. "North Korea Said to Dip into Rice Reserves to Bar Unrest." *New York Times,* July 18: A3.

————. 1994b. "Nuclear Fears? Noodle Sales Say No." *New York Times,* May 9: A7.

Poneman, Daniel. 1984. "Nuclear Proliferation Prospects for Argentina," *Orbis* 27, 4 (Winter): 853–80.

Pool, David. 1993. "The Links between Economic and Political Liberalization." In Niblock and Murphy, eds. (1993): 40–52.

Porter, Bruce D. 1994. *War and the Rise of the State: The Military Foundations of Modern Politics.* New York: Free Press.

Posen, Barry R. 1984. *The Sources of Military Doctrine.* Ithaca: Cornell University Press.

————. 1993. "The Security Dilemma and Ethnic Conflict." *Survival* 35, 1 (Spring): 27–47.

Preston, Lewis T. 1991. "Strategy for the Nineties: Sustainable Development to Reduce Poverty." New York: Statement to the UN Economic and Social Council (ECOSOC), Higher Level Segment, July 7.

Przeworski, Adam. 1991. *Democracy and the Market: Political and Economic Reforms in Eastern Europe and Latin America.* Cambridge: Cambridge University Press.

————. 1992. "The Neoliberal Fallacy." *Journal of Democracy* 3, 3 (July): 45–59.

Przeworski, Adam, Mike Alvarez, José A. Cheibub, Fernando Limongi. 1996. "What Makes Democracies Endure?" *Journal of Democracy* 7, 1 (January): 39–55.

Przeworski, Adam, and Fernando Limongi. 1993. "Political Regimes and Economic Growth." *Journal of Economic Perspectives* 7, 3 (Summer): 51–69.

Przeworski, Adam, and Henry Teune. 1970/1982. *The Logic of Comparative Social Inquiry.* New York: Wiley; reprint Malabar, Fla.: Robert E. Krieger.

Putnam, Robert. 1988. "Diplomacy and Domestic Politics." *International Organization* 42, 3: 427–59.

Quandt, William B. 1994. "The Urge for Democracy." *Foreign Affairs* 73, 4: 2–7.

————. 1995. "A Deceptive Sense of Calm: A Conversation with William Quandt." *Middle East Insight* 11, 2 (January–February): 48–50.

————. 1996. "The Middle East on the Brink: Prospects for Change in the 21st Century." *Middle East Journal* 50, 1 (Winter): 9–17.

Rabin, Yitzhak. 1979. *The Rabin Memoirs.* Berkeley and Los Angeles: University of California Press.

Rabin, Yitzhak. 1994. "The Middle East: A Common Interest for Europe and Israel." *Presidents and Prime Ministers* (March–April): 19–21.

Rasler, Karen A., and William R. Thompson. 1989. *War and State Making*. Boston: Unwin Hyman.

Ray, James Lee. 1993. "Wars between Democracies: Rare or Nonexistent?" *International Interactions*, 18, 3: 251–76.

Razi, G. Hossein. 1990. "Legitimacy, Religion, and Nationalism in the Middle East." *American Political Science Review* 84, 1 (March): 69–92.

Razin, Assaf, and Efraim Sadka. 1993. *The Economy of Modern Israel: Malaise and Promise*. Chicago: University of Chicago Press.

Redick, John R. 1994. "Argentina-Brazil Nuclear Non-Proliferation Initiatives." *Programme for Promoting Nuclear Non-Proliferation* 3 (January). Southampton, United Kingdom: University of Southampton.

Reich, Robert. 1991. *The Work of Nations*. New York: Knopf.

Reiss, Mitchell. 1988. *Without the Bomb*. New York: Columbia University Press.

Remmer, Karen. 1989. *Military Rule in Latin America*. Boston: Unwin Hyman.

Rhee, Syngman. 1956. *Korea Flaming High*. Seoul: Office of Public Information.

Rich, Frank. 1995. "The Jew World Order." *New York Times*, March 9: A15.

Richards, A., and J. Waterbury. 1990. *A Political Economy of the Middle East: State, Class, and Economic Development*. Boulder: Westview.

Richardson, James L. 1994/95. "Asia-Pacific: Geopolitical Optimisim." *National Interest* 38 (Winter): 28–39.

Riker, William H., and Steven J. Brams. 1973. "The Paradox of Vote Trading." *American Political Science Review* 67 (December): 1,235–47.

Rock, David. 1993. *Authoritarian Argentina: The Nationalist Movement, Its History and Its Impact*. Berkeley and Los Angeles: University of California Press.

Rodrik, Dani. 1994. "The Rush to Free Trade in the Developing World: Why So Late? Why Now? Will It Last?" In Haggard and Webb, eds. (1994): 61–88.

———. 1997. "Sense and Nonsense in the Globalization Debate." *Foreign Policy* 107 (Summer): 19–37.

Rogowski, Ronald. 1989. *Commerce and Coalitions: How Trade Affects Domestic Political Alignments*. Princeton: Princeton University Press.

Rosecrance, Richard. 1986. *The Rise of the Trading State*. New York: Basic Books.

———. 1996. "The Rise of the Virtual State." *Foreign Affairs* 75, 4 (July/August): 45–61.

Rosecrance, Richard, and Jeffrey J. Schott. 1997. "Concerts and Regional Intervention." In Lake and Morgan, eds. (1997): 140–64.

Rosecrance, Richard, and Arthur A. Stein, eds. 1993. *The Domestic Bases of Grand Strategy*. Ithaca: Cornell University Press.

Rothstein, Robert L. 1977. *The Weak in the World of the Strong: The Developing Countries in the International System*. New York: Columbia University Press.

———. 1988. "Epitaph for a Monument to a Failed Protest? A North-South Retrospective." *International Organization* 42, 4 (Autumn): 725–50.

———. 1992. "Democracy, Conflict, and Development in the Third World." In Brad Roberts, ed., *US Foreign Policy after the Cold War*. Cambridge: MIT Press.

———. 1995. "Democracy in the Third World: Definitional Dilemmas." In Garnham and Tessler, eds. (1995): 65–81.

Rouleau, Eric. 1993. "Eric Rouleau Talks about the Peace Process and Political Islam." Interview *Journal of Palestine Studies* 22, 4 (Summer): 45–61.

Rouquié, Alain. 1978, 1982. *Poder militar y sociedad política en la Argentina: 1943–1973*. Volumes 1 and 2. Buenos Aires: Emecé.

Rowe, David M. 1993. "The Domestic Political Economy of International Economic Sanctions." Paper presented at the Annual Meeting of the American Political Science Association, Washington, D.C., September 2–5.

Roy, Olivier. 1994. *The Failure of Political Islam.* Cambridge: Harvard University Press.

Rubin, Barry. 1994. *Revolution until Victory? The Politics and History of the PLO.* Cambridge: Harvard University Press.

Rueschemeyer, Dietrich, Evelyne Huber Stephens, and John D. Stephens. 1992. *Capitalist Development and Democracy.* Chicago: University of Chicago Press.

Ruggie, John G. 1993. "Multilateralism: The Anatomy of an Institution." In J. G. Ruggie, ed., *Multilateralism Matters.* New York: Columbia University Press: 3–49.

———. 1995. "At Home Abroad, Abroad at Home: International Liberalisation and Domestic Stability in the New World Economy." *Millennium* 24, 3 (Winter): 507–26.

Rummel, Rudolph. 1983. "Libertarianism and International Violence." *Journal of Conflict Resolution* 27, 1: 27–71.

Russell, Roberto, ed. 1992. *La política exterior Argentina en el nuevo orden mundial.* Buenos Aires: Facultad Latinoamericana de Ciencias Sociales.

Russett, Bruce M. 1967. *International Regions and the International System: A Study in Political Ecology.* Chicago: Rand McNally.

———. 1993. *Grasping the Democratic Peace: Principles for a Post-Cold War World.* Princeton: Princeton University Press.

Sachs, Jeffrey. 1989. "Robbin' Hoods: How the Big Banks Spell Debt 'Relief.'" *New Republic* 200, 11 (March 13): 19–21.

Sadat, Anwar. 1978. *In Search of Identity: An Autobiography.* New York: Harper and Row.

Sadowski, Yahya M. 1993. *Scuds or Butter? The Political Economy of Arms Control in the Middle East.* Washington, D.C.: Brookings Institution.

Sahliyeh, Emile. 1990. *Religious Resurgence and Politics in the Contemporary World.* Albany: State University of New York Press.

Sakai, Takashi. 1996. "The Power Base of Kim Jong Il: Focusing on Its Formation Process." In Park, ed. (1996): 106–22.

Salamé, Ghassan. 1993. "Islam and the West," *Foreign Policy* 90 (Spring): 22–37.

———, ed. 1994. *Democracy without Democrats? The Renewal of Politics in the Muslim World.* New York: I. B. Tauris.

Samuels, Barbara C., II. 1995. "Emerging Markets Are Here to Stay." *Foreign Affairs* 74, 6 (November/December): 143–47.

Sanger, David E. 1995. "Fear, Inflation and Graft Feed Disillusion among Iranians." *New York Times,* May 30: A1, A6.

Sarney, José. 1986. "Brazil: A President's Story." *Foreign Affairs* 65, 1 (Fall): 101–17.

Sayigh, Yezid. 1992. *Arab Military Industry: Capability, Performance and Impact.* London: Brassey's.

———. 1995. "The Multilateral Middle East Peace Talks: Reorganizing for Regional Security." In Spiegel and Pervin, eds. (1995): 207–30.

Scalapino, Robert A., ed. 1963. "The Foreign Policy of North Korea." In Robert A. Scalapino, ed. *North Korea Today.* New York: Praeger: 30–50.

Scheetz, Thomas. 1992. "The Evolution of Public Sector Expenditures: Changing Political Priorities in Argentina, Chile, Paraguay, and Peru." *Journal of Peace Research* 29, 2: 175–90.

Schott, Jeffrey J., ed. 1996. *The World Trading System: Challenges Ahead.* Washington D.C.: Institute for International Economics.

Schumpeter, Joseph A. 1951. *Imperialism and Social Classes.* Translated by Heinz Norden. Oxford: Basil Blackwell.

Schweller, Randall L. 1992. "Domestic Structure and Preventive War: Are Democracies More Pacific?" *World Politics* 44, 2 (January): 235–69.

Selcher, Wayne A. 1984a. "Recent Strategic Developments in South America's Southern Cone." In Muñoz and Tulchin, eds. (1984): 101–18.

———. 1984b. "Brazil's Foreign Policy: More Actors and Expanding Agendas." In Ferris and Lincoln, eds. (1984): 101–24.

Selim, Mohamed E. 1991. "The Survival of a Nonstate Actor: The Foreign Policy of the Palestine Liberation Organization." In Korany and Dessouki, eds. (1991): 260–309.

Sha'ath, Nabil. 1996. "A State in the Making." Interview. *Palestine-Israel Journal* 3, 2: 25–34.

Shain, Yossi, and Juan J. Linz. 1995. *Between States: Interim Governments and Democratic Transitions.* New York: Cambridge University Press.

Shalev, Michael. 1992. *Labor and the Political Economy in Israel.* New York: Oxford University Press.

Sharkansky, Ira. 1993. "Israel's Political Economy." In Sprinzak and Diamond, eds. (1993): 153–70.

Shikaki, Khalil. 1994. "Current Trends in Palestinian Public Opinion." Paper presented at a Friedrich Naumann Foundation Workshop on Monitoring Change in the Israeli and Palestinian Social and Political Systems. Jerusalem, October 3–5.

———. 1996. "The Peace Process, National Reconstruction, and the Transition to Democracy in Palestine." *Journal of Palestine Studies* 25, 2 (Winter): 5–20.

Shin, Jung Hyun, Tae-Hwan Kwak, and Edward A. Olsen, eds., 1988. *Northeast Asia Security and Peace: Toward the 1990s.* Seoul: Kyung Hee University Press.

Shirk, Susan L. 1997. "Asia-Pacific Regional Security: Balance of Power or Concert of Powers? In Lake and Morgan, eds. (1997): 245–70.

Sikkink, Kathryn. 1991. *Ideas and Institutions: Developmentalism in Brazil and Argentina.* Ithaca: Cornell University Press.

Silva, Patricio. 1991. "Technocrats and Politics in Chile: From the Chicago Boys to the CIEPLAN Monks." *Journal of Latin American Studies* 23, 2 (May): 385–410.

Sims, Calvin. 1997. "Argentines See Redemption in New Alliance with U.S." *New York Times,* October 20: A6.

Sisk, Timothy D. 1992. *Islam and Democracy.* Washington, D.C.: United States Institute of Peace.

Sivan, Emmanuel. 1995. "Eavesdropping on Radical Islam." *Middle East Quarterly* 2, 1 (March): 13–24.

Siverson, R. M., and J. Emmons. 1991. "Birds of a Feather: Democratic Political Systems and Alliance Choices in the Twentieth Century." *Journal of Conflict Resolution* 35, 2: 285–306.

Skidmore, Thomas E. 1988. *The Politics of Military Rule in Brazil, 1964–85.* New York: Oxford University Press.

Smith, Anthony D. 1986. *The Ethnic Origins of Nations.* Oxford: Blackwell.

Smith, Hazel. 1994. "The Democratic People's Republic of North Korea and Its Foreign Policy in the 1990s." In Chan and Williams, eds. (1994): 96–116.

Smith, Peter H. 1991. "Crisis and Democracy in Latin America." *World Politics* 43, 4 (July): 608–34.

Smith, William C. 1991. *Authoritarianism and the Crisis of the Argentine Political Economy.* Stanford: Stanford University Press.

Smith, William C., Carlos H. Acuña, and Eduardo A. Gamarra, eds., 1994a. *Latin American Political Economy in the Age of Neoliberal Reform: Theoretical and Comparative Perspectives for the 1990s*. New Brunswick, N.J.: Transaction.

————, eds., 1994b. *Democracy, Markets, and Structural Reform in Latin America*. New Brunswick, N.J.: Transaction.

Snyder, Jack. 1989. "International Leverage on Soviet Domestic Change." *World Politics* 42, 1 (October): 1–30.

————. 1991. *Myhts of Empire: Domestic Politics and International Ambition*. Ithaca: Cornell University Press.

————. 1993a. "Averting Anarchy in the New Europe." In Lynn-Jones, ed. (1993): 104–40.

————. 1993b. "The New Nationalism: Realist Interpretations and Beyond." In Rosecrance and Stein, eds. (1993): 179–200.

————. 1993c. "Nationalism and the Crisis of the Post-Soviet State." *Survival* 35, 1 (Spring): 5–26.

Snyder, Jack, and Robert Jervis, eds. 1993. *Coping with Complexity in the International System*. Boulder: Westview.

Sofer, Sasson. 1988. *Begin: An Anatomy of Leadership*. New York: Basil Blackwell.

Sola, Lourdes. 1994. "The State, Structural Reform, and Democratization in Brazil." In Smith, Acuña, and Gamarra, eds. (1994b): 151–81.

Solingen, Etel. 1984. "Regime Type, Energy Interdependence, and Security Cooperation in the Southern Cone." Paper presented at the annual meeting of the American Political Science Association, Washington, D.C., September.

————. 1994a. "The Domestic Sources of Regional Regimes: The Evolution of Nuclear Ambiguity in the Middle East." *International Studies Quarterly* 38 (June): 305–38.

————. 1994b. "The Political Economy of Nuclear Restraint." *International Security* 19, 2 (Fall): 126–69.

————. 1995. "Multilateral Arms Control in the Middle East: The Issue of Sequences." *Peace and Change*, 20, 3 (July): 364–78.

————. 1996a. "Democracy, Economic Reform, and Regional Cooperation." *Journal of Theoretical Politics* 8, 1 (January): 79–114.

————. 1996b. *Industrial Policy, Technology, and International Bargaining: Designing Nuclear Industries in Argentina and Brazil*. Stanford: Stanford University Press.

————. 1996c. "Democratization in the Middle East: Quandaries of the Peace Process." *Journal of Democracy* 7, 3 (July): 139–53.

————. 1997a. "Economic Liberalization, Political Coalitions, and Emerging Regional Orders." In Lake and Morgan, eds. (1997): 68–100.

————. 1997b. "Domestic Coalitions and Regional Orders in South Asia." Unpublished paper, Irvine: University of California Irvine, Department of Politics and Society.

————. 1998. "Liberalizing Coalitions and Denuclearization: Lessons from the Southern Cone." In Steven Spiegel, ed., *The Dynamics of Middle East Nuclear Arms Proliferation*. University of California, Los Angeles. Center for International Relations.

Spector, Leonard S., with Jacqueline R. Smith. 1990. *Nuclear Ambitions*. Boulder: Westview Press.

Spiegel, Steven L. 1998. The Dynamics of Middle East Nuclear Arms Proliferation. University of California, Los Angeles. Center for International Relations.

Spiegel, Steven L., and David J. Pervin, eds., 1995. *Practical Peacemaking in the Middle East*. Vol. I. New York: Garland Publishing.

Spiro, David E. 1994. "The Insignificance of the Liberal Peace." *International Security* 19, 2: 50–86.

Springborg, Robert. 1989. *Mubarak's Egypt*. Boulder: Westview Press.

Sprinzak, Ehud. 1991. *The Ascendance of Israel's Radical Right*. New York: Oxford University Press.

Sprinzak, Ehud, and Larry Diamond, eds. 1993. *Israeli Democracy under Stress*. Boulder: Lynne Rienner.

Stallings, Barbara. 1992. "International Influence on Economic Policy: Debt, Stabilization, and Structural Reform." In Haggard and Kaufman, eds. (1992): 41–88.

———. 1995. *Global Change, Regional Response: The New International Context of Development*. New York: Cambridge University Press.

Stanger, Allison K. 1995. "Democratization and the International System: The Foreign Policies of Interim Governments." In Shain and Linz, eds. (1995): 255–77.

Stanley, Ruth. 1992. "Cooperation and Control: The New Approach to Nuclear Nonproliferation in Argentina and Brazil." *Arms Control* 13, 2 (September): 191–213.

Starr, Harvey. 1992. "Democracy and War: Choice, Learning and Security Communities." *Journal of Peace Research* 29, 2: 207–13.

Stein, Arthur. 1993. "Governments, International Interdependence, and International Cooperation." In Philip Tetlock, Jo L. Husbands, Robert Jervis, P. C. Stern, and Charles Tilly, eds., *Behavior, Society, and International Conflict*. New York: Oxford University Press.

Stein, Janice G. 1991. "Deterrence and Reassurance." In Philip E. Tetlock, Jo L. Husbands, Robert Jervis, Paul C. Stern, and Charles Tilly, eds., *Behavior, Society, and Nuclear War*, Vol. 2. New York: Oxford University Press: 8–72.

Stepan, Alfred. 1988. *Rethinking Military Politics: Brazil and the Southern Cone*. Princeton: Princeton University Press.

———. 1989. *Democratizing Brazil: Problems of Transition and Consolidation*. New York: Oxford University Press.

Stockholm International Peace Research Institute (SIPRI). 1994. *SIPRI Yearbook 1994*. New York: Oxford University Press.

———. 1995. *SIPRI Yearbook 1995*. New York: Oxford University Press.

———. 1996. *SIPRI Yearbook 1996*. New York: Oxford University Press.

Stopford, John M., and Susan Strange with John S. Henley. 1991. *Rival States, Rival Firms: Competition for World Market Shares*. New York: Cambridge University Press.

Strange, Susan. 1992. "States, Firms, and Diplomacy." *International Affairs* 68, 1: 1–15.

Stueck, William. 1995. *The Korean War: An International History*. Princeton: Princeton University Press.

Suleiman, Ezra N., and John Waterbury, eds. 1990. *The Political Economy of Public Sector Reform and Privatization*. Boulder: Westview.

Sullivan, John D. 1994. "Democratization and Business Interests." *Journal of Democracy* 5, 4 (October): 146–60.

Summers, Lawrence H., and Vinod Thomas. 1995. "Recent Lessons of Development." In Frieden and Lake, eds. (1995): 423–33.

Tal, Lawrence. 1995. "Dealing with Radical Islam: The Case of Jordan." *Survival* 37, 3 (Autumn): 139–56.

Taylor, Lance. 1987. "IMF Conditionality: Incomplete Theory, Policy Malpractice." In Robert J. Myers, ed. *The Political Morality of the International Monetary Fund*. New Brunswick, N.J.: Transaction: 33–46.

Tetreault, Mary A. 1980. "Measuring Interdependence." *International Organization* 34, 3 (Summer): 429–43.

Thambipillai, Pushpa. 1994. "Continuity and Change in ASEAN: The Politics of Regional Cooperation in South East Asia." In W. Andrew Axline, ed., *The Political Economy of Regional Cooperation: Comparative Case Studies*. London: Pinter: 105–35.

Thompson, William R. 1973. "The Regional Subsystem: A Conceptual Explication and a Propositional Inventory." *International Studies Quarterly* 17, 1 (March): 89–117.

Tilly, Charles. 1985. "War Making and State Making as Organized Crime." In Evans, Rueschemeyer, and Skocpol, eds. (1985): 169–91.

———. 1994. "States and Nationalism in Europe 1492–1992." *Theory and Society* 23, 6 (December): 131–46.

Tollefson, Scott D. 1996. "Nuclear Cooperation between Argentina and Brazil: A Model for Nonproliferation?" Unpublished manuscript. Department of National Security Affairs, Naval Postgraduate School.

Toukan, Abdullah. 1995. "The Middle East Peace Process, Arms Control, and Regional Security." In Spiegel and Pervin, eds. (1995): 21–42.

Trachtenberg, Marc. 1991. *History and Strategy*. Princeton: Princeton University Press.

Trebat, T. J. 1983. *Brazil's State-Owned Enterprises: A Case-Study of the State as Entrepreneur*. Cambridge: Cambridge University Press.

Trigubenko, Marina Ye. 1996. "Economic Characteristics and Prospect for Development: With Emphasis on Agriculture." In Park, ed. (1996): 142–59.

Tripp, Charles. 1995. "Regional Organizations in the Arab Middle East." In Fawcett and Hurrell, eds. (1995): 283–308.

Tschirgi, Dan, ed. 1994. *The Arab World Today*. Boulder: Lynne Rienner.

Tsebelis, George. 1995. "Decision Making in Political Systems: Veto Players in Presidentialism, Parliamentarism, Multicameralism, and Multipartyism." *British Journal of Political Science* 25, 3 (July): 289–325.

Tulchin, Joseph S. 1984. "Authoritarian Regimes and Foreign Policy: The Case of Argentina." In Muñoz and Tulchin, eds. (1984): 186–99.

UNDP (United Nations Development Programme). 1994. *Human Development Report 1994*. New York: Oxford University Press.

———. 1995. *Human Development Report 1995*. New York: Oxford University Press.

———. 1996. *Human Development Report 1996*. New York: Oxford University Press.

Vandewalle, Dirk. 1992. "Ben-Ali's New Era: Pluralism and Economic Privatization in Tunisia." In Barkey, ed. (1992): 105–28.

Van Evera, Stephen. 1993. "Primed for Peace: Europe after the Cold War." In Lynn-Jones, ed. (1993): 193–243.

———. 1994. "Hypotheses on Nationalism and War." *International Security* 18, 4 (Spring): 5–39.

Varas, Augusto. 1985. *Militarization and the International Arms Race in Latin America*. Boulder: Westview.

———. 1989. *Democracy under Siege: New Military Power in Latin America*. Westport, Conn.: Greenwood.

Vidigal, Armando A. F. 1989. "Uma nova concepçào estratégica para o Brasil. Um debate necessário." *Política e Estratégia* 7, 3: 304–24.

Viner, Jacob. 1950. *The Customs Union Issue*. New York: Carnegie Endowment for International Peace.

Viorst, Milton. 1991. "Report from Baghdad." *New Yorker* 67, 18 (June 24): 55–74.

———. 1995. "Sudan's Islamic Experiment." *Foreign Affairs* 74, 3: 45–58.

Vogel, Ezra F. 1987. "Korea in 2000: From Social Instability to Consensus?" In Han and Myers, eds. (1987): 49–64.

Voll, John O., and John L. Esposito. 1994. "Islam's Democratic Essence." *Middle East Quarterly* 1, 3 (September): 3–11.

Wade, Robert. 1992. "East Asia's Economic Success: Conflicting Perspectives, Partial Insights, Shaky Evidence." *World Politics* 44, 2 (January): 270–320.

Wallerstein, Immanuel. 1979. *The Capitalist World-Economy.* New York: Cambridge University Press.

Walt, Stephen M. 1985. "Alliance Formation and the Balance of World Power." *International Security* 9, 4 (Spring): 208–48.

———. 1987. *The Origins of Alliances.* Ithaca: Cornell University Press.

———. 1996. *Revolution and War.* Ithaca: Cornell University Press.

Waltz, Kenneth N. 1979. *Theory of International Politics.* New York: Random House.

Waterbury, John. 1983. *The Egypt of Nasser and Sadat: The Political Economy of Two Regimes.* Princeton: Princeton University Press.

———. 1992. "The Heart of the Matter? Public Enterprise and the Adjustment Process." In Haggard and Kaufman, eds. (1992): 182–220.

———. 1994. "Democracy without Democrats? The Potential for Political Liberalization in the Middle East." In Salamé, ed. (1994): 23–47.

Weber, Max. 1978. *Economy and Society: An Outline of Interpretive Sociology.* Edited by Guenther Roth and Claus Wittich. Berkeley and Los Angeles: University of California Press.

Weede, Erich. 1992. "Some Simple Calculations on Democracy and War Involvement." *Journal of Peace Research* 29, 4 (November): 377–84.

———. 1995. "Economic Policy and International Security: Rent-Seeking, Free Trade, and Democratic Peace." *European Journal of International Relations* 1, 4 (December): 519–37.

Weisskopf, Thomas E. 1995. "Russia in Transition: Perils of the Fast Track to Capitalism." In Frieden and Lake, eds. (1995): 475–90.

Wendt, Alexander, and Michael Barnett. 1993. "Dependent State Formation and Third World Militarization." *Review of International Studies* 19, 4 (October): 321–48.

West, Robert L. 1992. "Determinants of Military Expenditure in Developing Countries: Review of Academic Research." In Lamb and Kallab, eds. (1992): 19–34.

Whyman, William E. 1995. "We Can't Go on Meeting Like This: Revitalizing the G–7 Process." *Washington Quarterly* 18, 3 (Summer): 139–66.

Williamson, John, ed. 1990. *Latin American Adjustment: How Much Has Happened?* Washington, D.C.: Institute for International Economics.

———. 1994. *The Political Economy of Policy Reform.* Washington D.C.: Institute for International Economics.

Wohlforth William. 1994/95. "Realism and the End of the Cold War." *International Security* 19, 3 (Winter): 91–129.

Wolf, Charles, Jr. 1981. "Economic Success, Stability, and the 'Old' International Order." *International Security* 6, 1 (Summer): 75–92.

Workman, W. Thom. 1994. *The Social Origins of the Iran-Iraq War.* Boulder: Lynne Rienner.

World Bank. 1991. *World Development Report 1991: The Challenge of Development.* New York: Oxford University Press.

———. 1993a. *The East Asian Miracle: Economic Growth and Public Policy.* New York: Oxford University Press.

―――. 1993b. "Current Questions and Answers." Unpublished paper. Washington, D.C.: World Bank, September.

―――. 1994. *Social Indicators of Development.* Baltimore: Johns Hopkins University Press.

―――. 1996. *World Development Report 1996: From Plan to Market.* New York: Oxford University Press.

Zagorski, Paul W. 1992. *Democracy vs. National Security: Civil-Military Relations in Latin America.* Boulder: Lynne Rienner.

330

332

About the Author

ETEL SOLINGEN is Professor of Politics and Society at the
University of California, Irvine.